Software
Fault Tolerance

TRENDS IN SOFTWARE

User Interface Software
ed. Len Bass and Prasun Dewan

Configuration Management
ed. Walter Tichy

Software Fault Tolerance
ed. Michael Lyu

Software
Fault Tolerance

Edited by

Michael R Lyu
Bellcore, USA

JOHN WILEY & SONS
Chichester · New York · Brisbane · Toronto · Singapore

Other Wiley Editorial Offices

John Wiley & Sons, Inc., 605 Third Avenue,
New York, NY 10158-0012, USA

Jacaranda Wiley Ltd, 33 Park Road, Milton,
Queensland 4064, Australia

John Wiley & Sons (Canada) Ltd, 22 Worcester Road,
Rexdale, Ontario M9W 1L1, Canada

John Wiley & Sons (SEA) Pte Ltd, 37 Jalan Pemimpin #05-04,
Block B, Union Industrial Building, Singapore 2057

Library of Congress Cataloging-in-Publication Data

Software fault tolerance / edited by Michael R. Lyu
    p. cm.—(Trends in software)
    Includes bibliographical references (p.) and index.
    ISBN 0-471-95068-8
    1. Fault-tolerant computing. 2. Computer software. I. Lyu,
Michael R. II. Series
QA76.9.F38S656 1995
005.1—dc20   94-46435
                                          CIP

British Library Cataloguing in Publication Data

A catalogue record for this book is available from the British Library

ISBN 0 471 95068 8

Produced from camera-ready copy supplied by the editor
Printed and bound in Great Britain by Redwood Books, Trowbridge, Wilts.

Contents

Series Editor's Preface   ix

Preface   xi

List of Authors   xv

1 The Evolution of the Recovery Block Concept   1
B. Randell, J. Xu

1.1 Introduction   1
1.2 System Structuring   2
1.3 Recovery Blocks   4
1.4 Early Implementations and Experiments   7
1.5 Extensions and Applications of Basic Recovery Blocks   9
1.6 Recovery in Concurrent Systems   11
1.7 Linguistic Support for Software Fault Tolerance   15
1.8 Conclusions   17
Acknowledgements   18
References   18

2 The Methodology of N-Version Programming   23
A.A. Aviz̆ienis

2.1 Introduction   23
2.2 Fault-Tolerant Software Models and Techniques   26
2.3 Building N-Version Software   28
2.4 Experimental Investigations   31
2.5 A Design Paradigm for N-Version Software   33
2.6 The System Context for Fault-Tolerant Software   38
2.7 Conclusions   42
Acknowledgements   43
References   43

3 Architectural Issues in Software Fault Tolerance   47
J-C. Laprie, J. Arlat, C. Béounes, and K. Kanoun

3.1 Introduction   47
3.2 Approaches to Software Fault Tolerance   49
3.3 Analysis of Software Fault Tolerance   51
3.4 Definition and Analysis of Hardware-and-Software Fault Tolerant
Architectures   62
3.5 Conclusions   76
Acknowledgements   76
References   76

4   Exception Handling and Tolerance of Software Faults   81
F. Cristian

4.1   Introduction   81
4.2   Basic Notions   83
4.3   Exception Handling in Hierarchical Modular Programs   94
4.4   Conclusions   104
References   105

**5   Dependability Modeling for Fault-Tolerant Software
and Systems   109**
J.B. Dugan and M.R. Lyu

5.1   Introduction   109
5.2   System Descriptions   110
5.3   Modeling Assumptions and Parameter Definitions   112
5.4   System Level Modeling   114
5.5   Experimental Data Analysis   119
5.6   A Case Study in Parameter Estimation   124
5.7   Quantitative System-Level Analysis   128
5.8   Sensitivity Analysis   132
5.9   Decider Failure Probability   134
5.10 Conclusions   136
References   136

6   Analyses Using Stochastic Reward Nets   139
L.A. Tomek and K.S. Trivedi

6.1   Introduction   140
6.2   Introduction to Stochastic Reward Nets   141
6.3   Fault Tolerant Software Models   144
6.4   Dependencies in the SRN Models   152
6.5   Numerical Results   157
6.6   Conclusions   163
Acknowledgements   164
References   164

7   Checkpointing and the Modeling of Program Execution Time   167
V.F. Nicola

7.1   Introduction   167
7.2   Related Work   169
7.3   Program Execution without Checkpointing   171
7.4   Equidistant Checkpointing   173
7.5   Checkpointing in Modular Programs   176
7.6   Random Checkpointing   180
7.7   Conclusions   183
References   185

8 The Distributed Recovery Block Scheme   189
K.H. Kim

8.1 Introduction   189
8.2 Non-Negligible Fault Sources and Desirable Recovery Capabilities   190
8.3 Basic Principles of the DRB Scheme   192
8.4 Implementation Techniques   198
8.5 Experimental Validations of Real-Time Recovery   202
8.6 Issues Remaining for Future Research   205
8.7 Conclusions   207
Acknowledgements   207
References   207

9 Software Fault Tolerance by Design Diversity   211
P. Bishop

9.1 Introduction   211
9.2 N-Version Programming Research   212
9.3 Pitfalls in the Design of N-Version Experiments   220
9.4 Practical Application of N-Version Programming   222
9.5 Alternative to N-Version Programming   225
9.6 Conclusions   226
References   227

10 Software Fault Tolerance in the Application Layer   231
Y. Huang, C. Kintala

10.1 Introduction   232
10.2 Background   233
10.3 Model   235
10.4 Technologies   237
10.5 Experience   244
10.6 Conclusions   246
Acknowledgements   247
References   247

11 Software Fault Tolerance in Computer Operating Systems   249
R.K. Iyer and I. Lee

11.1 Introduction   249
11.2 Related Research   250
11.3 Measurements   251
11.4 Basic Error Characteristics   253
11.5 Evaluation of Fault Tolerance   261
11.6 Modeling and Analysis   268
11.7 Conclusions   275
Acknowledgements   276
References   276

**12 The Cost Effectiveness of Telecommunication Service
   Dependability**   **279**
   Y. Levendel

   12.1 Introduction   279
   12.2 Ten Years of Software Dependability Improvements through
        Fault Removal   283
   12.3 Recovery: A Successful But Expensive Strategy   302
   12.4 A Modern Strategy for Designing Dependable Systems   305
   12.5 Conclusions   312
   Acknowledgements   312
   References   312

13 Software Fault Insertion Testing for Fault Tolerance   **315**
   M-Y. Lai and S.Y. Wang

   13.1 Introduction   315
   13.2 Testing Fault Tolerance Using Software Fault Insertion   317
   13.3 Fault Manager   319
   13.4 Categorization of Software Faults, Errors and Failures   320
   13.5 SFIT Methodology   322
   13.6 Sample SFIT Test Plans   326
   13.7 Application and Results   329
   13.8 Conclusions   331
   Acknowledgements   332
   References   332

   Index   **335**

Series Editor's Preface

During 1990, the twentieth anniversary of *Software Practice and Experience*, two special issues (one on UNIX Tools and the other on the X Window System) were published. Each issue contained a set of refereed papers related to a single topic; the issues appeared a short time (roughly nine months) after the authors were invited to submit them. The positive experience with the special issues resulted in *Trends in Software*, a fast turn-around serial that devotes each issue to a specific topic in the software field. As with the special issues of SPE, each *Trend* will be edited by an authority in the area.

By collecting together a comprehensive set of papers on a single topic, *Trends* makes it easy for readers to find a definitive overview of a given topic. By ensuring timely publication, *Trends* guarantees readers that the information presented captures the state of the art. The collection of papers will be of practical value to software designers, researchers, practitioners and users in that field.

Papers in each *Trend* are solicited by a guest editor who is responsible for soliciting them and ensuring that the selected papers span the topic. The guest editor then subjects each paper to the rigorous peer review expected in any archival journal. As much as possible, electronic communication (e.g. electronic mail) is used as the primary means of communication between the series editor, members of the editorial board, guest editor, authors, and referees. A style document and macro package is available to reduce the turn-around time by enabling authors to submit papers in camera-ready form. During the editorial process, papers are exchanged electronically in an immediately printable format.

We aim to produce three *Trends* each year. Topics to be covered in forthcoming issues include software architecture and software processes.

The editorial board encourages readers to submit suggestions and comments. You may send them via electronic mail to bala@research.att.com or by postal mail to the address given below. Please clarify if a communication is intended for publication or not.

I would like to thank the editorial advisory board as well as the staff at John Wiley for their help in making *Trends* a reality.

Balachander Krishnamurthy
Room 2B-140
AT&T Bell Laboratories
600 Mountain Avenue
Murray Hill, NJ 07974
USA

Preface

Software permeates our modern society. The newest cameras, VCRs, and automobiles cannot be operated without software. Software is embedded in wristwatches, telephones, home appliances, and aircrafts. In airlines, software handles airplane ticket reservations, keeps track of flight numbers, airplane identifications, seat assignment, and ticketing information. Software for inventory control and automated order processing is critical to the success of manufacturing and marketing. In office buildings, software is needed to operate elevators, provide environmental control, and maintain alarm systems. Software makes automatic teller machines possible, offering us twenty-four-hour banking service. Popcorn and a *Jurassic Park* video are software-controlled — from the supermarket checkout to your microwave oven and from the animator's workstation to your home VCR.

Software is a systematic representation and processing of human knowledge. If the 20th century is the era of the explosion of information, then the forthcoming 21st century could well be defined by the explosion of computer software. Science and technology have been, and will continue to be, demanding high-performance software. We can look at virtually any industry — the automotive industry, the aircraft industry, the oil industry, the transportation industry, the telecommunications industry, the semiconductor industry, the pharmaceutical industry — all these industries will be highly, if not totally, dependent on high-performance software for their competitive edge.

The essence of software is nothing more than the logic of the human mind. As software grows more complex, the possibility for human design errors or misuse of software also grows. To date, software failures have struck virtually every kind of application arenas. Critical software failures have caused irreparable damages and enormous losses of revenues to many industries, and horror stories about software failures have frequently appeared in the headlines.

The need for highly reliable, continuously available, and extremely safe software, long understood in the scientific community, is becoming clear to the public. Traditionally, software dependability is achieved by *fault avoidance* techniques (including structured programming, software reuse, and formal methods) to prevent software faults or *fault removal* techniques (including testing, verification, and validation) to detect and delete software faults. Due to cost and complexity, another approach, *fault tolerance*, has been little used. However, highly dependable software in many applications is possible only through software fault tolerance. No matter how rigorously fault avoidance and fault removal techniques are applied, software faults remain in systems upon their delivery to the customers. Even the best quality software systems nowadays experience 0.5–1 faults per 10,000 lines of uncommented code. As the complexity of software increases, the existence of software faults during system operation also increases. Real world software can not be assured to be free of error, therefore, the capability to tolerate software faults, at least for critical applications, is evident. When the fate of a business or the life of a person depends on software, one might observe: "To err is human, to forgive, fault tolerance."

Fault tolerance is the survival attribute of computer systems which allows seamless delivery of expected service after faults have manifested themselves within a system. Issues and techniques for hardware fault tolerance are discussed in numerous book volumes. This book covers the state-of-the-art techniques and the state-of-practice approaches in software fault tolerance. The term "software fault tolerance" has two interpretations: one is "software-fault tolerance" which deals with the tolerance of software faults (namely, *design faults*), while the other is "software fault-tolerance" which discusses the control and operation of fault-tolerant mechanisms (usually hardware-oriented) through software-implemented functions. This book is titled in the former sense. In other words, software fault tolerance, in the context of this book, is concerned with all the techniques necessary to enable a system to tolerate software faults remaining in the system after its development. These software faults may or may not manifest themselves during system operations, but when they do, software fault tolerance techniques should provide the necessary mechanisms of the software system to prevent system failure from occurring.

The provision of fault tolerant mechanisms, in the *single version software* environment, involves special fault detection and recovery features on top of the fault avoidance and removal techniques. These basic fault tolerant features include program modularity, system closure, atomicity of actions, monitoring mechanisms, decision verification, and exception handling. In more advanced architectures, *design diversity* is employed where functionally equivalent yet independently developed software versions are applied in the system to provide complete tolerance to software design faults. The main techniques of this *multiple version software* approach are *recovery blocks*, *N-version programming*, and *N self-checking programming*. This volume in the John Wiley "Trends in Software" series focuses on the identification, formulation, application, modeling, and evaluation of the current software fault tolerance techniques in both single version software and multiple version software environments.

This book consists of 13 chapters in two parts. Part I (Chapters 1 – 7) surveys techniques and models in software fault tolerance, while Part II (Chapters 8 – 13) describes applications and experiments in software fault tolerance. Each chapter is written by software fault tolerance experts, including researchers and practitioners. These chapters cover the theory, design, methodology, application, modeling, evaluation, experience and assessment of software fault tolerance techniques and systems. In addition to the theoretical foundation of software fault tolerance techniques, practical applications are addressed in detail. These applications include airplane control systems, aerospace applications, nuclear reactors, telecommunications products, network systems, and other critical software applications.

Figure 1 lays out the road map for reading this book. The fundamental software fault tolerance techniques are first presented in Chapters 1 through 4. Chapter 1 discusses the recovery block concepts, Chapter 2 focuses on N-version programming methodology, and Chapter 3 describes various architectural considerations for software fault tolerance in which N self-checking programming is introduced. The most important fault tolerant scheme in the single version software environment — exception handling — is examined in Chapter 4.

Readers then can either finish reading the remainder of Part I for modeling schemes, or can go to Part II for applications of these techniques. The modeling schemes portion consists of three chapters: Chapter 5 proposes a dependable modeling technique for three fault tolerant software architectures using hardware and software parameters, while Chapter 6

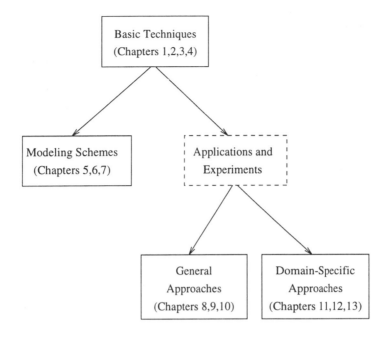

Figure 1 Guide to reading this book

applies stochastic reward nets to model the same architectures. In Chapter 7 the checkpointing schemes are surveyed, and models for program execution time constructed.

Part II concentrates on applications of software fault tolerance schemes, where readers can select general or domain-specific approaches to read. Regarding the general approaches, Chapter 8 investigates extended techniques on the recovery block scheme and their applications to real world systems. Chapter 9 studies the applications and experiments on N-version programming, and evaluates the overall results. Chapter 10 proposes a set of application-level software components to systematically detect and recover software faults. With respect to the domain-specific approaches, Chapter 11 studies software fault tolerance features in three commercial operating systems. Chapter 12 discusses the evolution of telecommunications system dependability. Finally, in Chapter 13 software fault insertion testing, a mechanism particularly useful for evaluating software fault tolerance in large telecommunications applications, is investigated.

The book is intended for practitioners and researchers who are concerned with the dependability of software systems. The topics explored in this book are the techniques and experiences regarding fault tolerance in software systems and the prevention of overall system failures. As a result, this book is intended for the following interest groups:

- engineers or managers concerned with critical applications
- software architecture designers
- software project managers
- software engineers
- software reliability and safety engineers
- system-level reliability and safety engineers

This book could also be used as a textbook or reference book for a graduate-level software engineering course or fault-tolerant computing course. As a textbook, this book is designed to be both introductory and suitable for advanced-level graduates. It is suggested that the chapters be selected in different combinations to provide courses with different orientations.

I am most indebted to the chapter authors for the completion of this project, Besides the chapter contributors who also serve as internal reviewers for other chapters, I would like to thank the following external reviewers for their thorough and constructive reviews on the chapters of this book: Tom Bowen, Jehoshua Bruck, Brian Coan, Adrian Dolinsky, George Finelli, Winfried Goerke, Jack Goldberg, Myron Hecht, Robert Horgan, Robert Horst, Mohamed Kaaniche, Nachimuthu Karunanithi, Elaine Keramidas, Taghi Khoshgoftaar, Hermann Kopetz, Yashwant Malaiya, Aditya P. Mathur, David McAllister, Isi Mitrani, Peter Neumann, James Purtilo, Francesca Saglietti, Pradip Srimani, Mark Sullivan, Robert Swarz, Ann Tai, K.C. Tai, Dali Tao, Robert Tausworthe, Pascal Traverse, Udo Voges, Mladen Vouk, and Yi-Min Wang.

I would like to thank the series editor Balachander Krishnamurthy for giving me this opportunity to edit this book.

Finally, I would like to dedicate my contribution to this book to my dearest wife, C. Felicia Lyu, for her love, understanding, and patience in supporting my work on this project. I have at times made some "faults" in devoting myself extensively to this book. Without her "tolerance," this editing job would not have been such a wonderful experience.

Michael R. Lyu
Bell Communications Research
Morristown, New Jersey
U.S.A.

List of Authors

Algirdas Avizienis
Computer Science Department
6291 Boelter Hall
University of California
Los Angeles
California 90024-1596
USA

Joanne Dugan
Dept of Electrical Engineering
University of Virginia
Thornton Hall
Charlottesville
Virginia 22903-2442
USA

Jean Arlat
LAAS-CNRS
7, avenue du Colonel Roche
31077 Toulouse
France

Yennun Huang
AT & T Bell Laboratories
600 Mountain Avenue
Murray Hill
New Jersey 07974
USA

Peter Bishop
ADELARD
Coborn House
3 Coborn Road
London
E3 2DA

Ravi Iyer
Coordinated Science Lab
University of Illinois
1308 West Main Street
Urbana
Illinois 61801-2307
USA

Flaviu Cristian
Computer Science & Engineering Dept
University of California, San Diego
La Jolla
California 92093-0114
USA

Karama Kanoun
LAAS-CNRS
7, avenue du Colonel Roche
31077 Toulouse
France

Kane H Kim
ECE Department
University of California
Irvine
California 92717
USA

Chandra Kintala
AT & T Bell Laboratories
600 Mountain Avenue
Murray Hill
New Jersey 07974
USA

Ming Lai
Bellcore
331 Newman Springs Road
Red Bank
New Jersey 07701-7030
USA

Jean-Claude Laprie
LAAS-CNRS
7, avenue du Colonel Roche
31077 Toulouse
France

Inhwan Lee
Tandem Computers Incorporated
Loc. 100-06
10555 Ridgeview Court
Cupertino
California 95014
USA

Haim Levendel
Room 4G-402
AT & T Bell Laboratories
2000 North Naperville Road
Naperville
Illinois 60566
USA

Michael R Lyu
Room 2E-358
Bellcore
445 South Street
Morristown
New Jersey 07960-6438
USA

Victor F Nicola
Tele-informatics & Open Systems Group
University of Twente
PO Box 217
7500 AE Enschede
The Netherlands

Brian Randell
Department of Computer Science
University of Newcastle
Newcastle upon Tyne
NE1 7RU

Kishor Trivedi
Dept of Electrical Engineering
1112 Hudson Hall
Box 90291
Durham
North Carolina 27708-0291
USA

Lorrie Tomek
Department of Computer Science
Duke University
Durham
North Carolina 27706

Steve Wang
Bellcore
331 Newman Springs Road
Red Bank
New Jersey 07701-7030
USA

Jie Xu
Department of Computer Science
University of Newcastle
Newcastle upon Tyne
NE1 7RU

1

The Evolution of the Recovery Block Concept

BRIAN RANDELL and JIE XU
University of Newcastle upon Tyne, England

ABSTRACT

This chapter reviews the development of the recovery block approach to software fault tolerance and subsequent work based on this approach. It starts with an account of the development and implementations of the basic recovery block scheme in the early 1970s at Newcastle, and then goes on to describe work at Newcastle and elsewhere on extensions to the basic scheme, recovery in concurrent systems, and linguistic support for recovery blocks based on the use of object-oriented programming concepts.

1.1   INTRODUCTION

A research project to investigate system reliability was initiated by the first author at the University of Newcastle upon Tyne in 1971. This was at a time when the problems of software reliability had come to the fore, for example through the discussions at the 1968 and 1969 NATO Software Engineering Conferences, concerning what at the time was termed the "software crisis". Such discussions were one of the spurs to research efforts, in a number of places, aimed at finding means of producing error-free programs. However, at Newcastle the opposite (or more accurately the complementary) problem, namely that of what to do in situations where, perhaps despite the use of the best available means of achieving error-free code, the possibility of residual design faults could not be denied, was taken as an interesting and worthwhile goal.

   A preliminary phase of the project involved a study of a representative set of large software systems, including a major banking system, and an airline reservations system. This provided interesting statistical data confirming that residual software faults were one of the most important causes of system failures and down-time. It was found that in all these systems, a sizable

Software Fault Tolerance, Edited by Lyu
© 1995 John Wiley & Sons Ltd

proportion of their code and complexity was related to provisions for (mostly hardware) fault tolerance, such as data consistency checking, and checkpointing schemes. However, these provisions, though typically rather ad hoc, were often quite effective, and indeed managed to cope with some of the software errors that were encountered in practice during system operation, even though the fault tolerance provisions had not been specifically designed to do this.

We were well aware that if we were to develop techniques aimed explicitly at tolerating software faults we would have to allow for the fact that the principal cause of residual software design faults is complexity. Therefore the use of appropriate structuring techniques would be crucial — otherwise the additional software that would be needed might well increase the system's complexity to the point of being counter-productive. Aided by what we had found in our examination of the checkpoint and restart facilities then being employed, we came to realize that although a variety of even quite disparate error detection mechanisms could usefully be employed together in a system, it was critical to have a simple, coherent and general strategy for error recovery. Moreover it was evident that such a strategy ought to be capable of coping with multiple errors, including ones that were detected during the error recovery process itself.

The first structuring technique that we developed was in fact the basic "recovery block" scheme. In what follows we use the structuring concepts that we later developed in our description of this basic scheme, and of some of the ensuing research on recovery blocks carried out at Newcastle and elsewhere, before discussing some of the latest ideas that we have been investigating on the structuring of fault-tolerant software.

1.2 SYSTEM STRUCTURING

Our interest in the problems of structuring systems so as to control their complexity, and in particular that of their fault tolerance provisions, led us to a style of system design which is based on what we term *idealized fault-tolerant components* [And81, Ran84]. Such components provide a means of system structuring which makes it easy to identify *what* parts of a system have *what* responsibilities for trying to cope with *which* sorts of fault.

We view a system as a set of components interacting under the control of a design (which is itself a component of the system) [Lee90]. Clearly, the system model is recursive in that each component can itself be considered as a system in its own right and thus may have an internal design which can identify further sub-components. Components receive requests for service and produce responses. When a component cannot satisfy a request for service, it will return an exception. An idealized fault-tolerant component should in general provide both normal and abnormal (i.e. exception) responses in the interface between interacting components, in a framework which minimizes the impact of these provisions on system complexity. Three classes of exceptional situation (i.e. in which some fault tolerance response is needed) are identified. Interface exceptions are signaled when interface checks find that an invalid service request has been made to a component. These exceptions must be treated by the part of the system which made the invalid request. Local exceptions are raised when a component detects an error that its own fault tolerance capabilities could or should deal with in the hope that the component would return to normal operations after exception handling. Lastly, a failure exception is signaled to notify the component which made the service request that, despite the

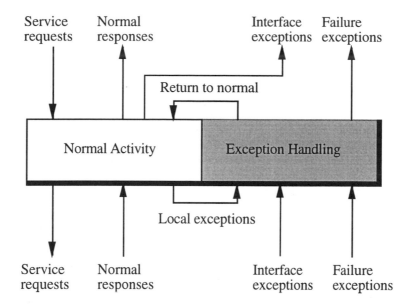

Figure 1.1   Idealized component

use of its own fault tolerance capabilities, it has been unable to provide the service requested of it (see Figure 1.1).

Our notion of an idealized component is mainly concerned with interactions of a component with its environment. It makes minimal assumptions on faults, fault masking and the fault tolerance scheme adopted, in indicating how exception-handling should be structured. Exception handling is often considered as being a limited form of software fault tolerance — for example, by detecting and recovering an error, and either ignoring the operation which generated it or by providing a pre-defined and heavily degraded response to that operation. However, such software cannot be regarded as truly fault-tolerant since some perceived departure from specification is likely to occur, although the exception handling approach can result in software which is robust in the sense that catastrophic failure can often be avoided.

In order also to achieve effective design fault tolerance, capable of completely masking the effects of many residual software errors, it is necessary to incorporate deliberate redundancy, i.e. to make use of design diversity, in such systems. The structuring scheme that we have developed [Ran93] both for describing and comparing the various existing software fault tolerance schemes, and indeed for guiding their actual implementation, is illustrated in Figure 1.2.

This shows an idealized component which consists of several sub-components, namely an adjudicator and a set of software variants (modules of differing design aimed at a common specification). The design of the component, i.e. the algorithm which is responsible for defining the interactions between the sub-components, and establishing connections between the component and the system environment, is embodied in the controller. This invokes one or more of the variants, waits as necessary for such variants to complete their execution and invokes the adjudicator to check on the results produced by the variants. As illustrated in Figure 1.2, each of these sub-components (even the adjudicator), as well as the component (controller) itself, can in principle contain its own provisions for exception handling, and indeed for full software fault tolerance, so the structuring scheme is fully recursive.

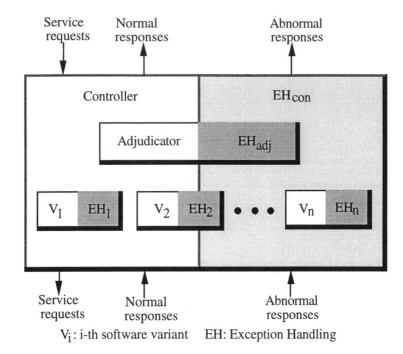

Service   Normal   Abnormal
requests   responses   responses

V_i : i-th software variant   EH: Exception Handling

Figure 1.2 Idealized component with design redundancy

Obviously, the notion of structuring systems needs to be used in such a way as to achieve an appropriate structuring of the complex asynchronous activities to which the system can give rise. in particular those related to fault tolerance. In common with other groups, we make use of so-called *atomic actions* for this purpose. The activity of a group of components constitutes an atomic action if no information flows between that group and the rest of the system for the duration of the activity [Lee90]. Atomic actions may be planned when the system is designed, or (less commonly) may be dynamically identified by exploratory techniques after the detection of an error. Planned atomic actions must be maintained by imposing constraints on communication within the system. Error recovery can be linked to the notion of an atomic action, which is said to form a restorable action if all components within the action retain the ability to perform a mutually consistent state restoration. These issues are discussed further in Section 1.6.

1.3   RECOVERY BLOCKS

In this section, we discuss recovery blocks in detail, making use of the exception handling terminology introduced above. The basic recovery block relates to sequential systems. Details of extensions for use in concurrent systems are discussed in Section 1.6. The recovery block approach attempts to prevent residual software faults from impacting on the system environment, and it is aimed at providing fault-tolerant functional components which may be nested within a sequential program. The usual syntax is as follows:

```
ensure             acceptance test
by                 primary alternate
else by            alternate 2
                       .

                       .
else by            alternate n
else error
```

Here the alternates correspond to the variants of Figure 1.2, and the acceptance test to the adjudicator, with the text above being in effect an expression of the controller. On entry to a recovery block the state of the system must be saved to permit backward error recovery, i.e. establish a checkpoint. The primary alternate is executed and then the acceptance test is evaluated to provide an adjudication on the outcome of this primary alternate. If the acceptance test is passed then the outcome is regarded as successful and the recovery block can be exited, discarding the information on the state of the system taken on entry (i.e. checkpoint). However, if the test fails or if any errors are detected by other means during the execution of the alternate, then an exception is raised and backward error recovery is invoked. This restores the state of the system to what it was on entry. After such recovery, the next alternate is executed and then the acceptance test is applied again. This sequence continues until either an acceptance test is passed or all alternates have failed the acceptance test. If all the alternates either fail the test or result in an exception (due to an internal error being detected), a failure exception will be signaled to the environment of the recovery block. Since recovery blocks can be nested, then the raising of such an exception from an inner recovery block would invoke recovery in the enclosing block. The operation of the recovery block is further illustrated in Figure 1.3.

Obviously, the linguistic structure for recovery blocks requires a suitable mechanism for providing automatic backward error recovery. Randell produced the first such "recovery cache" scheme, a description of which was included in the first paper on recovery blocks [Hor74] (although this scheme was later superseded [And76]). This paper also included a discussion of "recoverable procedures" — a rather complex mechanism that Lauer and Randell had proposed as a means of extending the recovery cache scheme to deal with programmer-defined data types. This part of the paper would undoubtedly have been much clearer if the ideas had been expressed in object-oriented terms — a point we will develop further in Section 1.7.

The overall success of the recovery block scheme rests to a great extent on the effectiveness of the error detection mechanisms used — especially (but not solely) the acceptance test. The acceptance test must be simple otherwise there will be a significant chance that it will itself contain design faults, and so fail to detect some errors, and/or falsely identify some conditions as being erroneous. Moreover, the test will introduce a run-time overhead which could be unacceptable if it is very complex. The development of simple, effective acceptance tests can thus be a difficult task, depending on the actual specification.

In fact, the acceptance test in a recovery block should be regarded as a last line of detecting errors, rather than the sole means of error detection. The expectation is that it will be buttressed by executable assertion statements within the alternates and run-time checks supported by the hardware. Generally, any such exception raised during the execution of an alternate will lead to the same recovery action as for acceptance test failure. Should the final alternate fail, for example by not passing the acceptance test, this will constitute a failure of the entire module

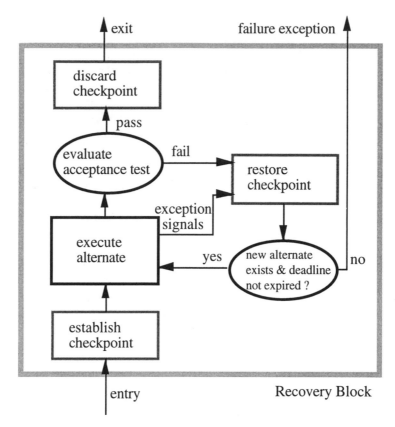

Figure 1.3   Operation of the recovery block

containing the recovery block, and will invoke recovery at the level of the surrounding recovery block, should there be one.

In other words, each alternate should itself be an ideal fault-tolerant component. An exception raised by run-time assertion statements within the alternate or by hardware error-detection mechanisms may be treated by the alternate's own fault tolerance capabilities. A failure exception is raised to notify the system (i.e. the control component in our model) if, despite the use of its own fault tolerance capabilities, the alternate has been unable to provide the service requested of it. The control component may invoke then another alternate.

In general, as described in [Mel77], forward error recovery can be further incorporated in recovery blocks to complement the underlying backward error recovery. (In fact, a forward error recovery mechanism can support the implementation of backward error recovery by transforming unexpected errors into default error conditions [Cri82].) If, for example, a real-time program communicated with its (unrecoverable) environment from within a recovery block then, if recovery were invoked, the environment would not be able to recover along with the program and the system would be left in an inconsistent state. In this case, forward recovery would help return the system to a consistent state by sending the environment a message informing it to disregard previous output from the program.

In the first paper about recovery blocks [Hor74], Horning *et al.* list four possible failure conditions for an alternate: i) failure of the acceptance test, ii) failure to terminate, detected by a timeout, iii) implicit error detection (for example divide by zero), and iv) failure exception of an inner recovery block. Although the mechanism for implementing the time-out detection measure was not discussed by the authors, the original definition of recovery blocks does cover this issue. Several implementations of watchdog timers for recovery blocks have been described [Hec76, Kim89]. Timeout can be provided as a syntactic form in the recovery block structure [Gre85]. As with the `else error` part, the `timeout` part allows the programming of a "last ditch" algorithm for the block to achieve its goal, and is really a form of forward recovery since its effects will not be undone (at least at this level).

Although each of the alternates within a recovery block endeavors to satisfy the same acceptance test there is no requirement that they all must produce the same results [Lee78]. The only constraint is that the results must be acceptable — as determined by the test. Thus, while the primary alternate should attempt to produce the desired outcome, the further alternate may only attempt to provide a degraded service. This is particularly useful in real-time systems, since there may be insufficient time available for fully-functional alternates to be executed when a fault is encountered. An extreme corresponds to a recovery block which contains a primary module and a null alternate [And83, And85]. Under these conditions, the role of the recovery block is simply to detect and recover from errors by ignoring the operation where the fault manifested itself. This is somewhat similar to forward error recovery because the manifestation of a fault will result in a loss of service to the environment. But the important difference is that forward recovery can only remove predictable errors from the system state, whereas such backward recovery can still cope with the unpredictable errors caused by residual design faults. (The only constraint is that the errors do not impact the actual recovery block mechanism.)

Most of the time, only the primary alternate of the recovery block is executed. (This keeps the run-time overhead of the recovery block to a minimum and makes good use of the system and hardware resources.) However, this could cause a problem: the alternates must not retain data locally between calls, otherwise these modules could become inconsistent with each other since not all of them are executed each time when the recovery block is invoked. The problem becomes more obvious while one attempts to design an alternate as an object. There is no guarantee that the state of the object is correctly modified unless the object is invoked each time. Distributed (parallel) execution of recovery blocks [Kim84] could solve this issue. An alternative solution is to design the alternate modules as memoryless functional components rather than as objects.

Unlike tolerance to hardware malfunctions, software fault tolerance cannot be made totally transparent to the application programmer although some operations related to its provision, such as saving and restoring the state of the system, can be made automatic and transparent. The programmer who wishes to use software fault tolerance schemes must provide software variants and adjudicators. Therefore, a set of special linguistic features or conventions is necessary for incorporating software redundancy in programs. The key point here is to attempt to keep the syntactic extension simple, natural and minimal. This will be further discussed in the Section 1.7.

1.4 EARLY IMPLEMENTATIONS AND EXPERIMENTS

The first implementation of recovery blocks involved defining and simulating a simple stack-oriented instruction set, incorporating a recovery cache [And76]. Simple test programs embodying recovery blocks could be run on this machine simulator, and subjected to deliberate faults. Test programs were run on one computer — a separate computer was used to provide data to, and to accept and check the output from, these programs. This second computer also provided facilities by means of which experimenters could make arbitrary changes to any locations in the simulated memory. Visitors to the project were typically challenged to use these facilities to try and cause a demonstration recovery block program to fail — their inability to do so was a persuasive argument for the potential of the recovery block scheme!

Another experimental system is described in [Shr78a, Shr78b] in which recovery blocks were incorporated in the language Pascal. The modification was made to the kernel and interpreter of Brinch Hansen's Pascal system to support the syntax of recovery blocks and the associated recovery caches needed for state restoration. Based on this extension and on a few experimental programs, some performance measurements for recovery blocks were reported, which generally support the belief that recovery blocks do not impose any serious runtime and recovery data space overheads. For the sample programs, the run-time overhead ranged between 1 to about 11% of T1 (execution time of a program without any recovery facilities) when no errors are detected. When a primary fails, the time taken to restore system state was up to about 30% of T1. This experiment also showed that recovery caches made a substantial saving in space, compared with complete checkpointing.

The recovery cache mechanism should ideally form an integral part of a given computer; this not being possible for the existing hardware. The next major work at Newcastle on the implementation of the basic recovery block scheme involved the design and building of a hardware recovery cache for the PDP-11 family of machines [Lee80]. This device was inserted into the bus between the CPU and memory modules without requiring hardware alterations. It intercepted writes to memory, and automatically determined whether the contents of the memory location that was about to be over-written needed to be saved beforehand. In order to minimize the overheads imposed on the host, special hardware was designed to enable concurrent operation of the recovery cache and the host system.

The controversial nature of software fault tolerance spurred extensive efforts aimed at providing evidence of the scheme's potential cost-effectiveness in real systems. (The developers of N-version programming [Avi77] were similarly motivated to undertake extensive experimental evaluations, as discussed in Section 2.4 in Chapter 2.) During 1981-84 therefore, a major project directed by Tom Anderson applied an extension of recovery blocks in the implementation of a Naval Command and Control system composed of about 8000 lines of CORAL programming, and made use of the above-mentioned hardware cache [And85]. The practical development work of the project included the design and implementation of a virtual machine which supported recovery blocks, together with extensions to the CORAL programming language to allow software fault-tolerance applications to be written in this high-level language. To maintain realism the system was constructed by experienced programmers in strict accordance with the official rules for defense-related software projects. Analysis of experimental runs of this system showed that a failure coverage of over 70% was achieved. The supplementary cost of developing the fault-tolerant software was put at 60% of the implementation cost. The system overheads were measured at 33% extra code memory, 35% extra data memory and 40% additional run time. These led to the conclusion that "by means of software fault tolerance a significant and worthwhile improvement in reliability can be achieved at acceptable cost" [And85].

Research at the Royal Military College of Science subsequently extended this experiment to the design of a demonstrator modeled on functions provided at the London Air Traffic Control

Center, and the results have reinforced confidence in the cost-effectiveness and the general applicability of the recovery block approach [Mou87].

1.5 EXTENSIONS AND APPLICATIONS OF BASIC RECOVERY BLOCKS

Many applications and varieties of recovery blocks have been explored and developed by various researchers. Some of typical experiments and extensions are considered below.

1.5.1 Distributed Execution of Recovery Blocks

H. Hecht was the first to propose the application of recovery blocks to flight control systems [Hec76, Hec86]. His work included an implementation of a watchdog timer that monitors availability of output within a specified time interval and his model also incorporates a rudimentary system to be used when all alternates of the recovery block scheme are exhausted. Since then, further researches and experiments have been conducted by Hecht and his colleagues. For example, M. Hecht *et al.* [Hec89] described a distributed fault-tolerant architecture, called the extended distributed recovery block, for nuclear reactor control and safety functions. Their architecture relies on commercially available components and thus allows for continuous and inexpensive system enhancement. The fault injection experiments during the development process demonstrate that the system could tolerate most single faults and dual faults.

K. H. Kim and his colleagues in the DREAM Laboratory have extensively explored the concept of distributed execution of recovery blocks, a combination of both distributed processing and recovery blocks, as an approach for uniform treatment of hardware and software faults [Kim84, Kim89, Kim88b, Wel83]. The details are given in Chapter 8. A useful feature of their approach is the relatively low run-time overhead it requires so that it is suitable for incorporation into real-time systems. The basic structure of the distributed recovery block is straightforward: the entire recovery block, two alternates with an acceptance test, is fully replicated on the primary and backup hardware nodes. However, the roles of the two alternate modules are not the same in the two nodes. The primary node uses the first alternate as the primary initially, whereas the backup node uses the second alternate as the initial primary. Outside of the distributed recovery block, forward recovery can be achieved in effect; but the node affected by a fault must invoke backward recovery by executing an alternate for data consistency with the other nodes. To test the execution efficiency of the approach, two experimental implementations and measurements have been conducted on distributed computer networks. The results indicate the feasibility of attaining fault tolerance in a broad range of real-time applications by means of the distributed recovery blocks.

1.5.2 Consensus Recovery Blocks

The consensus recovery block (CRB) [Sco85] is an attempt to combine the techniques used in the recovery block and N-version programming [Avi77]. It is claimed that the CRB technique reduces the importance of the acceptance test used in the recovery block and is able to handle the case where NVP would not be appropriate since there are multiple correct outputs. The CRB requires design and implementation of N variants of the algorithm which are ranked (as in the recovery block) in the order of service and reliance. On invocation, all variants are executed and their results submitted to an adjudicator, i.e. a voter (as used in N-version programming). The CRB compares pairs of results for compatibility. If two results are the same then the result is used as the output. If no pair can be found then the results of the variant with the highest ranking are submitted to an acceptance test. If this fails then the next variant is selected. This continues until all variants are exhausted or one passes the acceptance test.

[Sco87] developed reliability models for the recovery block, N-version programming and the CRB. In comparison, the CRB is shown to be superior to the other two. However, the CRB is largely based on the assumption that there are no common faults between the variants. (This of course is not the case, as was shown by such experiments as [Kni85, Sco84].) In particular, if a matching pair is found, there is no indication that the result is submitted to the acceptance test, so a correlated failure in two variants could result in an erroneous output and would cause a catastrophic failure.

1.5.3   Retry Blocks with Data Diversity

A retry block developed by Ammann and Knight [Amm87, Amm88] is a modification of the recovery block scheme that uses data diversity instead of design diversity. Data diversity is a strategy that does not change the algorithm of the system (just retry), but does change the data that the algorithm processes. It is assumed that there are certain data which will cause the algorithm to fail, and that if the data were re-expressed in a different, equivalent (or near equivalent) form the algorithm would function correctly. A retry block executes the single algorithm normally and evaluates the acceptance test. If the test passes, the retry block is complete. If the test fails, the algorithm executes again after the data has been re-expressed. The system repeats this process until it violates a deadline or produces a satisfactory output. The crucial elements in the retry scheme are the acceptance test and the data re-expression routine.

A description of some experiments with the retry block is presented by the authors. Coordinates to a radar system were altered to lie on the circumference of a small circle centered on the point, taking advantage of the fact that this application's data had limited precision. The radius of the circle and the re-expression algorithm were both changed to generate an indication of their influence. Although the overall performance of the retry block varied greatly, a large reduction in failure probability for some of the faults is observed in the study. Compared with design diversity, data diversity is relatively easy and inexpensive to implement. Although additional costs are incurred in the algorithm for data re-expression, data diversity requires only a single implementation of a specification. Of course, the retry scheme is not generally applicable and the re-expression algorithm must be tailored to the individual problem at hand and should itself be simple enough to eliminate the chance of design faults.

1.5.4   Self-Configuring Optimal Programming

SCOP (Self-configuring optimal programming) [Bon93, Xu93] is another attempt to combine some techniques used in RB and NVP in order to enhance efficiency of software fault tolerance and to eliminate some inflexibilities and rigidities. This scheme organizes the execution of software variants in phases, dynamically configuring a currently active variant set, so as to produce acceptable results with the relatively small effort and to make the efficient use of available resources. The control can be parameterized with respect to the level of fault tolerance, the amount of available resources and the desired response time. Since highly dynamic behavior can cause complexity of control and monitoring, a methodology for devising various instances of SCOP is developed by simplifying the on-line process at the price of the complex off-line design.

The gain of efficiency would be limited when the supporting system is intended for a specific application – the hardware resources saved by the SCOP scheme would be merely left idle. It is perhaps more appropriate if the application environments are complex and highly variable, such as a large distributed computing system that supports multiple competing applications.

1.5.5 Other Applications

Sullivan and Masson developed an algorithm-oriented scheme, based on the use of what they term Certification Trails [Sul90, Sul91]. The central idea of their method is to execute an algorithm so that it leaves behind a trail of data (certification trail) and, by using this data, to execute another algorithm for solving the same problem more quickly. The outputs of the two executions are compared and considered correct only if they agree. An issue with the data trail is that the first algorithm may propagate an error to the second algorithm, and this could result in an erroneous output. Nevertheless, the scheme is an interesting alternative to the recovery block scheme, despite being perhaps of somewhat limited applicability.

Delta-4 was a collaborative project carried out within the framework of the European Strategic Program for Research in Information Technology (ESPRIT) [Pow91]. Its aim was the definition and design of an open, dependable, distributed computer system architecture. The Delta-4 approach deals mainly with hardware fault tolerance, but also addresses the issue of design faults. [Bar93] describes the integration of software fault tolerance mechanisms into the existing Delta-4 architecture. The authors claimed that the incorporation of recovery blocks and dialogues (structures for supporting inter-process recovery) into the Delta-4 framework is obtained without significant overheads.

1.6 RECOVERY IN CONCURRENT SYSTEMS

Work at Newcastle on this topic dates from 1975, when we began to consider the problems of providing structuring for error recovery among sets of cooperating processes. (A few researches were also made into error recovery in the particular case of so-called competing processes where the processes communicate only for resource sharing [Shr78c, Shr79].) Having identified the dangers of what we came to term the *domino effect*, we came up with the notion of a *conversation* [Ran75] — something which we later realized was a special case of a nested atomic action.

1.6.1 Conversations

When a system of cooperating processes employs recovery blocks, each process will be continually establishing and discarding checkpoints, and may also need to restore to a previously established checkpoint. However, if recovery and communication operations are not performed in a coordinated fashion, then the rollback of a process can result in a cascade of rollbacks that could push all the processes back to their beginnings — the domino effect. This causes the loss of entire computation performed prior to the detection of the error. Figure 1.4 illustrates the domino effect with two communicating processes.

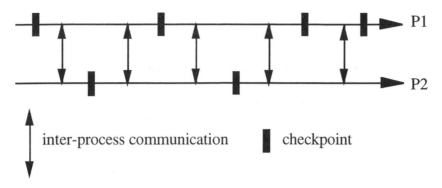

inter-process communication   ▮ checkpoint

Figure 1.4   The domino effect

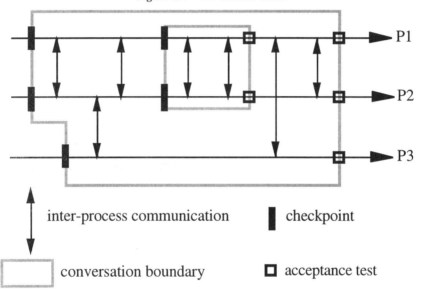

inter-process communication   ▮ checkpoint

□ conversation boundary   ☐ acceptance test

Figure 1.5   Nested conversations

The conversation scheme is in our view one of the fundamental approaches to structured design of fault-tolerant concurrent programs. It provides a means of coordinating the recovery blocks of interacting processes to avoid the domino effect. Figure 1.5 shows an example where three processes communicate within a conversation and the processes P1 and P2 communicate within a nested conversation. Communication can only take place between processes that are participating in a conversation together. The operation of a conversation is: (i) on entry to a conversation a process establishes a checkpoint; (ii) if an error is detected by any process then all the participating processes must restore their checkpoints; (iii) after restoration all processes use their next alternates; and (iv) all processes leave the conversation together. The concept of conversation facilitates failure atomicity and backward recovery in cooperating process systems in a manner analogous to that of the atomic action mechanism in object-based systems. In fact, this terminological distinction between the area of communicating process systems and that of of object-based systems is, we claim, of only surface importance [Shr93].

Considerable research has been undertaken into the subject of concurrent error recovery, including improvements on the conversation and different implementations of it. There are at least two classes of approaches to preventing the domino effect: the coordination-by-programmer approach and the coordination-by-machine approach. With the first approach, the application programmer is fully responsible for designing processes so that they establish checkpoints in a well coordinated manner [Ran75, Rus80, Kim82]. Many authors have added language constructs to facilitate the definition of restorable actions based on this approach [Rus79, And83, Gre85, Jal84, Jal86]. In contrast, the coordination-by-machine approach relies on an "intelligent" underlying processor system which automatically establishes appropriate checkpoints of interacting processes [Kim78, Bar83, Koo87, Kim90]. If restorable actions are unplanned, so that the recovery mechanism must search for a consistent set of checkpoints, such actions would be expensive and difficult to implement. However, such exploratory techniques have the advantage that no restrictions are placed on inter-process communication and that a general mechanism could be applied to many different systems [Mer78, Woo81]. To reduce synchronization delays introduced by controlled recovery, some researches have focused on the improvement of performance, such as the lookahead scheme and the pseudo-recovery block [Kim76, Kim88a, Ram88, Rus79, Shi84].

1.6.2 Extensions and Implementations of Conversations

The original description of conversations provided a structuring or design concept without any suggested syntax. [Rus79] proposed a syntax called the name-linked recovery block for the concept of conversations. Kim [Kim82] presents three different syntactic forms for conversations based on the monitor structure. The different implementations deal with the distribution of the code for the recovery blocks of individual processes. The tradeoff is either to spread the conversation among the individual processes such that all of the code of each process is in one location or have all the code for the conversation in one location.

There was no provision for linked forward error recovery in the original conversation scheme. Campbell and Randell [Cam86] proposed techniques for structuring forward error recovery measures in asynchronous systems and generalized ideas of atomic actions so as to support fault-tolerant interactions between processes. A resolution scheme is used to combine multiple exceptions into a single exception if they are raised at the same time.

Issarny extended their work to concurrent object-oriented systems by defining an exception-handling mechanism for parallel object-oriented programming [Iss93a]. This mechanism was then generalized to support both forward and backward error recovery [Iss93b]. Following the proposal in [Cam86], Jalote and Campbell described a system which contains both forward and backward error recovery within a conversation structure (also known as an FT-action). Their system was based on communicating sequential processes (CSP) [Hoa78] with one extension (the exit) statement.

Forward error recovery in an FT-action [Jal86] is achieved through linked exception handlers where each process has its own handler for each exception. When an exception is raised by a process it is propagated to all the participating processes within the FT-action. Each process then executes its own handler for that exception. Backward recovery within an FT-action is obtained by recovery blocks. Every participating process is required to have the same number of alternates. An FT-action can combine the two schemes so that forward and backward error recovery are used within the same structure. It can also cope with the issue of real-time applications through a simple timer.

Real-time applications may suffer from the possibility of *deserters* in a conversation — if a deadline is to be met then a process that fails to enter the conversation or to reach its acceptance test could cause all the processes in the conversation to miss that deadline [Kim82]. Russell and Tiedeman [Rus79] considered relaxing the requirement for all processes exiting together so as to enable some protection against deserter processes, but this could lead to the domino effect. Campbell, Horton and Belford [Cam79] proposed a deadline mechanism for dealing with timing faults. Anderson and Knight [And83] proposed *exchanges* as a simplification of conversations where the cyclic nature of real-time systems is exploited. (An exchange is a conversation in which all participating processes enter upon initiation and terminate upon exit. Error recovery is particularly easy as the recovery data is only that needed upon initiation, which should only be a small amount of frame dependent data.)

Gregory and Knight [Gre85] identified a set of problems associated with conversations. They argued that there ought to be two types of acceptance test — one for each process within a conversation to check its own goal and one for the whole structure of the conversation to check the global goal. In addition, within a conversation or other structures mentioned above the set of processes that attempt their primary alternate is the same as the set of processes which attempt all other alternates, i.e. they all roll back and try again with their further alternates. This is overly restrictive and affects independence of algorithm between alternates. In an effort to solve these problems, they developed two concepts — a *colloquy* that contains many *dialogs*.

A dialog is a way of enclosing a set of processes in an atomic action. It provides no retry method and no definition of the action to be taken upon failure. If any failure occurs, the dialog restores all checkpoints and fails, signaling the failure to the surrounding colloquy. A colloquy that contains a set of dialogs controls the execution of dialogs and decides on the recovery action to be taken if the dialog fails. The colloquy provides a means of constructing alternates using a potentially different set of processes, thereby permitting true diverse design. The dialog and colloquy allow time constraints to be specified and are accompanied by syntactic proposals that are extensions to the Ada language.

However, when attempting the integration of the syntax for the colloquy into Ada, the authors found several new and potentially serious difficulties which arise because of a conflict between the semantics of modern programming languages and the needs of concurrent backward recovery [Gre89].

1.6.3   Practical Difficulties and Possible Solutions

The practical problems mentioned in [Gre89] fall into the general categories of (i) program structure, (ii) shared objects, and (iii) process manipulation. All the problems have the potential to allow the state outside a dialog (or a conversation) to be contaminated by changes inside the dialog, i.e. *information smuggling*. For example, a major inconsistency exists between the preferred structure of concurrent programs (e.g. involving the use of service processes) and the structure for planned recovery. To avoid information smuggling, the planned backward recovery could cause the *capture effect* for service processes — in other words processes outside the (nested) dialogs cannot use the service processes until the completion of all the dialogs. Shared objects are another significant source of information smuggling, but no simple approaches solve the problem. Smuggling can occur with process manipulations (e.g. dynamic process creation) also. An initial solution to the problem merely raises several other issues. Given the complexity and subtlety of these problems, Gregory and Knight concluded that "the only workable solution might be that programming language design begin with backward error recovery as its starting point." Nevertheless, some preliminary and partial solutions can be found in [Cle93, Gre87].

The actual programming of a conversation is another major difficulty associated with the concept. Constructing an application into a sequence of conversations is not a trivial task. The application programmer has to select a boundary composed of a set of checkpoints, acceptance tests and the side walls to prevent information smuggling. This boundary should be integrated well into the structure of processes. [Tyr86] suggested a way of identifying adequate boundaries of conversations based on the specification of the application using Petri Nets. [Car91] proposed an alternative solution in which the CSP notation [Hoa78] is used to describe the application and conversation boundaries are identified through a trace evaluation, but such traces would cause an explosion of states even for simple applications. In practice, however, it is possible for some special applications to decide on the conversation placement without full trace evaluation [Tyr92].

1.7 LINGUISTIC SUPPORT FOR SOFTWARE FAULT TOLERANCE

General linguistic supports for software fault tolerance are the concern of much of our latest work. If the design of software fault-tolerant systems is to become widely used on a routine basis, one of important problems that has to be solved is how to develop and provide appropriate linguistic notations and the corresponding environments, which should effectively support the development of fault-tolerant programs without greatly complicating the program's implementation, readability, and maintenance.

1.7.1 Design Notations and Environments

[Liu92] proposed a design notation for a wide class of fault-tolerant software structures, mainly offering generality and flexibility in a modular fashion. [Bon92] showed that their BSM design description language is sufficient for expressing the typical structures of software fault tolerance, such as recovery blocks and N-version programming, without requiring semantic extensions. [Anc90] described a mechanism, called the *Recovery Metaprogram* (RMP), for the incorporation of fault tolerance functions into application programs, giving programmers a single environment that lets them use the appropriate fault tolerance scheme.

The architecture proposed in [Anc90] contains three components: the application program, the RMP and the kernel. The application programmer must define the software variants and the validation test, and indicate which portions of the application program are involved in fault tolerance. The RMP implements the controllers and the supporting mechanisms for four different schemes, inserting a number of breakpoints in the program. When a breakpoint is reached, the application program is suspended and the kernel activates the RMP which takes actions to support the fault tolerance scheme chosen. The RMP is then suspended, and the application program is reactivated until the next breakpoint is reached. The implementation of the RMP approach may incur an additional cost in the form of intensive context switches and kernel calls.

However, in contrast to the languages and environments discussed above, our major work has been greatly influenced by the now very fashionable topic of object-oriented programming. In particular, we have found it convenient to try to exploit various characteristics of C++ [Str91], a language that has been used extensively at Newcastle in connection with work on distributed systems [Shr91].

1.7.2   Implementing Software Fault Tolerance in C++

The recent extension of C++ to include generic classes and functions ("templates"), and exception handling ("catch" and "throw") makes it possible to implement both forward and backward error recovery in C++ in the form of reusable components that separate the functionality of the application from its fault tolerance [Rub93]. More generally, such facilities show prospect of providing a convenient means of achieving high levels of reuse. This would apply both to general software components implementing various fault tolerance strategies (including generalizations and combinations of recovery blocks, and N-version programs, and encompassing the use of parallelism) and to application-specific software components [Ran93]. We also provided a set of pre-defined C++ classes to support a general object-oriented framework for software fault tolerance based directly on the abstract model represented by Figure 1.2, and described in Section 1.2 [Xu94]. However, there remain certain strategies and types of structuring that cannot be implemented entirely (or at any rate elegantly) in a language like C++ even given such mechanisms as generic functions and inheritance. Instead, the programmer who wishes to employ these strategies has to obey certain conventions. For example, the application programmer who wishes to make use of our C++ classes would have to include explicit calls in each operation of an object to facilities related to the provision of state restoration.

Adherence to such conventions can be automated, by embodying them into a somewhat enhanced version of C++ and using a pre-processor to generate conventional C++ programs automatically. Although the pre-processor approach can be quite practical it does have disadvantages. In particular the language provided to application programmers becomes non-standard since programmers have in some circumstances during program development to work in terms of the program generated by the pre-processor, rather than of the one that they had written. The alternative, that of leaving it to the programmer to adhere to the conventions, is of course a fruitful source of residual program faults. But developing a new language that provides adequate syntax and runtime support to enable the implementation of various software fault tolerance could cut the work off from the mainstream of programming language developments and thus have difficulty in achieving wide acceptance.

1.7.3   Reflection and Reflective Languages

As mentioned in Section 1.3, it has to be the responsibility of the application programmers for developing software variants, acceptance tests, and even application-specific voters. Special language features and/or programming conventions therefore cannot be avoided completely. In consideration of software reliability, the key problem would become how a set of simple (thus easy to check) programming features can be developed with powerful expressibility to enable the implementation of software fault tolerance and how the supporting mechanisms can be provided in a more natural and modular manner rather than by an ad-hoc method such as system calls. Recent developments in the object-oriented language world, under the term *"reflection"* [Mae87], show considerable promise in this regard.

A reflective system can reason about, and manipulate, a representation of its own behavior. This representation is called the system's meta-level [Agh92]. Reflection improves the effectiveness of the object-level (or base-level) computation by dynamically modifying the internal organization (actually the meta-level representation) of the system so as to provide powerful expressibility. Therefore, in a reflective programming language a set of simple, well-defined language features could be used to define much more complex, dynamically changeable constructs and functionalities. In our case, it could enable the dynamic change and extension of the semantics of those programming features that support software fault tolerance concepts, whereas the application-level (or object-level) program is kept simple and elegant [Xu94]. Although C++ itself does not provide a metalevel interface, Chiba and Masuda [Chi93] describes an extension of C++ to provide a limited form of computational reflection, called Open C++, whose usefulness in expressing software fault tolerance we are now investigating.

However, quite what reflective capabilities are needed for what forms of fault tolerance, and to what extent these capabilities can be provided in more-or-less conventional programming languages, and allied to the other structuring techniques outlined in this chapter, remain to be determined. In particular, the problems of the combined provision of significant software fault tolerance and hardware fault tolerance, and of evaluating cost-effectiveness, are likely to require much further effort. When considering support for software fault tolerance in concurrent object-oriented programming, we face a greater challenge because, on the one hand, mainstream object-oriented languages such as C++ and Eiffel [Mey92] do not at present address concurrency and, on the other hand, a large number of different models for concurrent object-oriented programming have been proposed but none has yet received widespread acceptance. There exist only a few tentative proposals for treating concurrent error recovery such as the Arche language [Ben92]. However, the reflection technique seems to be a more promising approach to the structuring of concurrent object-oriented programs [Yon89].

1.8   CONCLUSIONS

Looking back on the developments that have occurred since the recovery block concept was first introduced, it is we hope fair to claim that it has proved a very useful abstraction, and starting point for much subsequent research, elsewhere as well as at Newcastle. That at Newcastle can be characterized as mainly involving over the years:

- a gradual extension of the original very basic scheme to deal with ever more complex situations, while retaining as much as possible of the essential simplicity of structuring provided by the basic scheme, and more recently (and perhaps rather belatedly)
- the investigation of appropriate linguistic support for recovery blocks and their generalizations using object-oriented structuring concepts.

Whilst we now regard recovery blocks, and N-version programming for that matter, simply as special cases of a more general scheme, there has been a somewhat surprising continued interest by others — especially those involved with statistical experiments and with mathematical modeling (for example [Arl90, Puc90, Tai93, Tom93]) — in the basic schemes. This is very flattering, but "real-world" usage of recovery block concepts (see for example [Gil83, Hau85, Gra91, Sim90, Gop91]) has always had to deal with such complexities as input-output, parallelism, hardware faults, etc. — so we would urge more concentration on the richer forms of structuring for error recovery and for design diversity which have since been developed, and which we have attempted to describe in the later sections of this chapter.

ACKNOWLEDGEMENTS

Our research at Newcastle was originally sponsored by the UK Science and Engineering Research Council and by the Ministry of Defense, but in recent years it has been supported mainly by two successive ESPRIT Basic Research projects on Predictably Dependable Computing Systems (PDCS and PDCS2). Needless to say, as will be obvious from the references we have given, the work we have attempted to summarize here has been contributed to by a large number of colleagues. It would be invidious to name just some of these, but we are very pleased to acknowledge our indebtedness to all of them.

REFERENCES

[Agh92] G. Agha, S. Frolund, R. Panwar and D. Sturman. A linguistic framework for dynamic composition of dependability protocols. In *Proc. Third International Working Conference on Dependable Computing for Critical Applications*, pages 197–207, Mondello, 1992.

[Amm87] P.E. Ammann and J.C. Knight. Data diversity: an approach to software fault tolerance. In *Proc. Seventeenth International Symposium on Fault-Tolerant Computing*, pages 122–126, Pittsburgh, 1987.

[Amm88] P.E. Ammann and J.C. Knight. Data diversity: an approach to software fault tolerance. *IEEE Transactions on Computers*, 37(4):418–425, 1988.

[Anc90] M. Ancona, G. Dodero, V. Gianuzzi, A. Clematis and E.B. Fernandez. A system architecture for fault tolerance in concurrent software. *IEEE Computer*, 23(10):23–32, 1990.

[And85] T. Anderson, P.A. Barrett, D.N. Halliwell and M.R. Moulding. Software fault tolerance: an evaluation. *IEEE Transactions on Software Engineering*, 11(12):1502–1510, 1985.

[And81] T. Anderson and P.A. Lee. *Fault Tolerance: Principles and Practice*. Prentice-Hall, 1981.

[And76] T. Anderson and R. Kerr. Recovery blocks in action: a system supporting high reliability. In *Proc. Second International Conference on Software Engineering*, pages 447–457, San Francisco, 1976.

[And83] T. Anderson and J.C. Knight. A framework for software fault tolerance in real-time systems. *IEEE Transactions on Software Engineering*, 9(3):355–364, 1983.

[Arl90] J. Arlat, K. Kanoun and J.C. Laprie. Dependability modeling and evaluation of software fault tolerant systems. *IEEE Transactions on Computers*, 39(4):504–513, 1990.

[Avi77] A. Avižienis and L. Chen. On the implementation of N-version programming for software fault-tolerance during execution. In *Proc. International Conference on Computer Software and Applications*, pages 149–155, New York, 1977.

[Bar83] G. Barigazzi and L. Strigini. Application-transparent setting of recovery points. In *Proc. Thirteenth International Symposium on Fault-Tolerant Computing*, pages 48–55, Milano, 1983.

[Bar93] P.A. Barrett and N.A. Speirs. Towards an integrated approach to fault tolerance in Delta-4. *Distributed System Engineering*, (1):59–66, 1993.

[Ben92] M. Benveniste and V. Issarny. Concurrent programming notations in the object-oriented language Arche. Research Report, 1822, Rennes, France, INRIA, 1992.

[Bon93] A. Bondavalli, F. DiGiandomenico and J. Xu. Cost-effective and flexible scheme for software fault tolerance. *Computer System Science & Engineering*, (4):234–244, 1993.

[Bon92] A. Bondavalli and L. Simoncini. Structured software fault tolerance with BSM. In *Proc. Third Workshop on Future Trends of Distributed Computing Systems*, Taipei, 1992.

[Cam79] R.H. Campbell, K.H. Horton and G.G. Belford. Simulations of a fault-tolerant deadline mechanism. In *Proc. Ninth International Symposium on Fault-Tolerant Computing*, pages 95–101, Madison, 1979.

[Cam86] R.H. Campbell and B. Randell. Error Recovery in Asynchronous Systems. *IEEE Transactions on Software Engineering*, 12(8):811–826, 1986.

[Car91] G.F. Carpenter and A.M. Tyrrell. Software fault tolerance in concurrent systems: conversation placement using CSP. *Microprocessing and Microprogramming*, (32):373–380, 1991.

[Chi93]   S. Chiba and T. Masuda. Designing an extensible distributed language with a meta-level architecture. In *Proc. Seventh European Conference on Object-Oriented Programming*, pages 482–501, 1993.

[Cle93]   A. Clematis and V. Gianuzzi. Structuring conversation in operation/procedure-oriented programming languages. *Computer Languages*, 18(3):153–168, 1993.

[Cri82]   F. Cristian. Exception handling and software fault tolerance. *IEEE Transactions on Computers*, 31(6):531–540, 1982.

[Gil83]   F.K. Giloth and K.D. Prantzen. Can the reliability of digital telecommunication switching systems be predicted and measured?. In *Proc. Thirteenth International Symposium on Fault-Tolerant Computing*, pages 392–397, Milano, 1983.

[Gop91]   G. Gopal and N.D. Griffeth. Software fault tolerance in telecommunications systems. *ACM Operating Systems Review*, 25(2):112–116, 1991.

[Gra91]   J. Gray and D.P. Siewiorek. High-availability computer systems. *IEEE Computer*, 24(9):39–48, 1991.

[Gre87]   S.T. Gregory. *Programming language facilities for backward error recovery in real-time systems*. PhD Dissertation, University of Virginia, Department of Computing Science, 1987.

[Gre85]   S.T. Gregory and J.C. Knight. A new linguistic approach to backward error recovery. In *Proc. Fifteenth International Symposium on Fault-Tolerant Computing*, pages 404–409, Michigan, 1985.

[Gre89]   S.T. Gregory and J.C. Knight. On the provision of backward error recovery in production programming languages. In *Proc. Nineteenth International Symposium on Fault-Tolerant Computing*, pages 506–511, Chicago, 1989.

[Hau85]   G. Haugk, F.M. Lax, R.D. Rover and J.R. Williams. The 5 ESS switching system: maintenance capabilities. *AT&T Technical Journal*, 64(6):1385–1416, 1985.

[Hec76]   H. Hecht. Fault-tolerant software for real-time applications. *ACM Computing Surveys*, 8(4):391–407, 1976.

[Hec86]   H. Hecht and M. Hecht. Software reliability in the system context. *IEEE Transactions on Software Engineering*, 12(1):51–58, 1986.

[Hec89]   M. Hecht, J. Agron and S. Hochhauser. A distributed fault tolerant architecture for nuclear reactor control and safety functions. In *Proc. Real-Time System Symposium*, pages 214–221, Santa Monica, 1989.

[Hoa78]   C.A.R. Hoare. Communicating sequential processes. *Communications of the ACM*, 21(8):666–677, 1978.

[Hor74]   J.J. Horning, H.C. Lauer, P.M. Melliar-Smith and B. Randell. A program structure for error detection and recovery. *Lecture Notes in Computer Science*, 16:177–193, 1974.

[Iss93a]   V. Issarny. An exception handling mechanism for parallel object-oriented programming: towards reusable, robust distributed software. *Journal of Object-Oriented Programming*, 6(6):29–40, 1993.

[Iss93b]   V. Issarny. Programming notations for expressing error recovery in a distributed object-oriented language. In *Proc. First Broadcast Open Workshop*, pages 1–19, Newcastle upon Tyne, 1993.

[Jal84]   P. Jalote and R.H. Campbell. Fault tolerance using communicating sequential processes. In *Proc. Fourteenth International Symposium on Fault-Tolerant Computing*, pages 347–352, Florida, 1984.

[Jal86]   P. Jalote and R.H. Campbell. Atomic actions for software fault tolerance using CSP. *IEEE Transactions on Software Engineering*, 12(1):59–68, 1986.

[Kim78]   K.H. Kim. An approach to programmer-transparent coordination of recovering parallel processes and its efficient implementation rules. In *Proc. International Conference on Parallel Processing*, pages 58–68, 1978.

[Kim82]   K.H. Kim. Approaches to mechanization of the conversation scheme based on monitors. *IEEE Transactions on Software Engineering*, 8(3):189–197, 1982.

[Kim84]   K.H. Kim. Distributed execution of recovery blocks: an approach to uniform treatment of hardware and software faults. In *Proc. Fourth International Conference on Distributed Computing Systems*, pages 526–532, 1984.

[Kim76]   K.H. Kim, D.L. Russell and M.J. Jenson. Language tools for fault-tolerant programming. Tech. Memo. PETP-1, USC, Electronic Sciences Laboratory, 1976.

[Kim89]   K.H. Kim and H.O. Welch. Distributed execution of recovery blocks: an approach for uniform treatment of hardware and software faults in real-time applications. *IEEE Transactions on Computers*, 38(5):626–636, 1989.

[Kim88a] K.H. Kim and S.M. Yang. An analysis of the performance impacts of lookahead execution in the conversation scheme. In *Proc. Seventh Symposium on Reliable Distributed Systems*, pages 71–81, Columbus, 1988.

[Kim88b] K.H. Kim and J.C. Yoon. Approaches to implementation of a repairable distributed recovery block scheme. In *Eighteenth International Symposium on Fault-Tolerant Computing*, pages 50–55, Tokyo, 1988.

[Kim90]   K.H. Kim and J.H. You. A highly decentralized implementation model for the programmer-transparent coordination (PTC) scheme for cooperative recovery. In *Proc. Twentieth International Symposium on Fault-Tolerant Computing*, pages 282–289, Newcastle upon Tyne, 1990.

[Kni85]   J.C. Knight, N.G. Leveson and L.D.S. Jean. A large scale experiment in N-version programming. In *Proc. Fifteenth International Symposium on Fault-Tolerant Computing*, pages 135–140, Michigan, 1985.

[Koo87]   R. Koo and S. Toueg. Checkpointing and rollback-recovery for distributed systems. *IEEE Transactions on Software Engineering*, 13(1):23–31, 1987.

[Lee78]   P.A. Lee. A reconsideration of the recovery block scheme. *Computer Journal*, 21(4):306–310, 1978.

[Lee90]   P.A. Lee and T. Anderson. *Fault Tolerance: Principles and Practice*. Springer-Verlag, second edition, 1990.

[Lee80]   P.A. Lee, N. Ghani and K. Heron. A recovery cache for the PDP-11. *IEEE Transactions on Computers*, 29(6):546–549, 1980.

[Liu92]   C. Liu. A general framework for software fault tolerance. In *Proc. IEEE Workshop on Fault-Tolerant Parallel and Distributed Systems*, Amherst, 1992.

[Mae87]   P. Maes. Concepts and experiments in computational reflection. *SIGPLAN Notices*, 22(12):147–155, 1987.

[Mel77]   P.M. Melliar-Smith and B. Randell. Software reliability: the role of programmed exception handling. *SIGPLAN Notices*, 12(3):95–100, 1977.

[Mer78]   P.M. Merlin and B. Randell. State restoration in distributed systems. In *Proc. Eighth International Symposium on Fault-Tolerant Computing*, pages 129–134, Toulouse, 1978.

[Mey92]   B. Meyer. *Eiffel: The Language*. Prentice Hall, 1992.

[Mou87]   M.R. Moulding and P. Barrett. An investigation into the application of software fault tolerance to air traffic control systems: project final report. 1049/TD.6 Version 2, RMCS, 1987.

[Pow91]   D. Powell, editor. *Delta-4: A Generic Architecture for Dependable Distributed Computing*. Springer (Berlin), 1991.

[Puc90]   G. Pucci. On the modeling and testing of recovery block structures. In *Proc. Twentieth International Symposium on Fault-Tolerant Computing*, pages 353–363, Newcastle upon Tyne, 1990.

[Ram88]   P. Ramanathan and K.G. Shin. Checkpointing and rollback recovery in a distributed system using common time base. In *Proc. Seventh Symposium on Reliable Distributed Systems*, pages 13–21, Columbus, 1988.

[Ran75]   B. Randell. System structure for software fault tolerance. *IEEE Transactions on Software Engineering*, 1(2):220–232, 1975.

[Ran84]   B. Randell. Fault tolerance and system structuring. In *Proc. Fourth Jerusalem Conference on Information Technology*, pages 182–191, Jerusalem, 1984.

[Ran93]   B. Randell and J. Xu. Object-oriented software fault tolerance: framework, reuse and design diversity. In *Proc. First Predictably Dependable Computing Systems 2 Open Workshop*, pages 165–184, Toulouse, 1993.

[Rub93]   C.M.F. Rubira-Calsavara and R.J. Stroud. Forward and backward error recovery in C++. In *Proc. First Predictably Dependable Computing Systems 2 Open Workshop*, pages 147–164, Toulouse, 1993.

[Rus80]   D.L. Russell. State restoration in systems of communicating processes. *IEEE Transactions on Software Engineering*, 6(2):183–194, 1980.

[Rus79]   D.L. Russell and M.J. Tiedeman. Multiprocess recovery using conversations. In *Proc. Nineth International Symposium on Fault-Tolerant Computing*, pages 106–109, 1979.

[Sco84]   R.K. Scott, J.W. Gault and D.F. McAllister. Investigating version dependence in fault tolerant software. In *Proc. AGARD Conference Proceedings*, 360, 1984.

[Sco85]   R.K. Scott, J.W. Gault and D.F. McAllister. The consensus recovery block. In *Proc. Total System Reliability Symposium*, pages 74–85, 1985.

[Sco87]   R.K. Scott, J.W. Gault and D.F. McAllister. Fault tolerant software reliability modeling. *IEEE Transactions on Software Engineering*, 13(5):582–592, 1987.

[Shi84]   K.G. Shin and Y. Lee. Evaluation of error recovery blocks used for cooperating processes. *IEEE Transactions on Software Engineering*, 10(6):692–700, 1984.

[Shr78a]   S.K. Shrivastava. Sequential pascal with recovery blocks. *Software — Practice and Experience*, 8:177–185, 1978.

[Shr79]   S.K. Shrivastava. Concurrent pascal with backward error recovery: language features and examples. *Software — Practice and Experience*, 9:1001–1020, 1979.

[Shr78b]   S.K. Shrivastava and A.A. Akinpelu. Fault-tolerant sequential programming using recovery blocks. In *Proc. Eighth International Symposium on Fault-Tolerant Computing*, pages 207, Toulouse, 1978.

[Shr78c]   S.K. Shrivastava and J.-P. Banatre. Reliable resource allocation between unreliable processes. *IEEE Transactions on Software Engineering*, 4(3):230–241, 1978.

[Shr91]   S.K. Shrivastava, G.N. Dixon and G.D. Parrington. An overview of the Arjuna distributed programming system. *IEEE Software*, 8(1):66–73, 1991.

[Shr93]   S.K. Shrivastava, L. V. Mancini and B. Randell. The duality of fault-tolerant system structures. *Software — Practice and Experience*, 23(7):773–798, 1993.

[Sim90]   D. Simon, C. Hourtolle, H. Biondi, J. Bernelas, P. Duverneuil, S. Gallet, P. Vielcanet, S. DeViguerie, F. Gsell and J.N. Chelotti. A software fault tolerance experiment for space applications. In *Proc. Twentieth International Symposium on Fault-Tolerant Computing*, pages 28–35, Newcastle upon Tyne, 1990.

[Str91]   Stroustrup. *The C++ Programming Language*. Addison Wesley, second edition, 1991.

[Sul90]   G.F. Sullivan and G.M. Masson. Using certification trails to achieve software fault tolerance. In *Twentieth International Symposium on Fault-Tolerant Computing*, pages 423–431, Newcastle upon Tyne, 1990.

[Sul91]   G.F. Sullivan and G.M. Masson. Certification trails for data structures. In *Proc. Twenty-First International Symposium on Fault-Tolerant Computing*, pages 240–247, Montreal, 1991.

[Tai93]   A. Tai, A. Avižienis and J. Meyer. Evaluation of fault-tolerant software: a performability modeling approach. In C.E. Landweh, B. Randell, and L. Simoncini, editors, *Dependable Computing for Critical Applications 3*, pages 113–135, 1993. Sprinter-Verlag.

[Tom93]   L.A. Tomek, J.K. Muppala and K.S. Trivedi. Modeling correlation in software recovery blocks. *IEEE Transactions on Software Engineering*, 19(11):1071–1086, 1993.

[Tyr92]   A.M. Tyrrell and G.F. Carpenter. The specification and design of atomic actions for fault tolerant concurrent software. *Microprocessing and Microprogramming*, 35:363–368, 1992.

[Tyr86]   A.M. Tyrrell and D.J. Holding. Design of reliable software in distributed systems using the conversation scheme. *IEEE Transactions on Software Engineering*, 12(9):921–928, 1986.

[Wel83]   H.O. Welch. Distributed recovery block performance in a real-time control loop. In *Proc. Real-Time Systems Symposium*, pages 268–276, Virginia, 1983.

[Woo81]   W. Wood. A decentralized recovery control protocol. In *Proc. Eleventh International Symposium on Fault-Tolerant Computing*, pages 159–164, 1981.

[Xu93]   J. Xu, A. Bondavalli and F. DiGiandomenico. Software fault tolerance: dynamic combination of dependability and efficiency. Technical Report, 442, University of Newcastle upon Tyne, Computing Science, 1993.

[Xu94]   J. Xu, B. Randell, C.M.F. Rubira-Calsavara and R.J. Stroud. Towards an object-oriented approach to software fault tolerance. In *Proc. IEEE Workshop on Fault-Tolerant Parallel and Distributed Systems*, Texas, June 1994.

[Yon89]   A. Yonezawa and T. Watanabe. An introduction to object-based reflective concurrent computation. *SIGPLAN Notices*, 24(4):50–53, 1989.

2

The Methodology of N-Version Programming

ALGIRDAS A. AVIŽIENIS

University of California, Los Angeles and Vytautas Magnus University, Kaunas, Lithuania

ABSTRACT

An N-*version software* (NVS) unit is a fault tolerant software unit that depends on a generic *decision algorithm* to determine a consensus result from the results delivered by two or more *member versions* of the NVS unit. The *process* by which the NVS versions are produced is called N-*version programming* (NVP). The major objectives of the NVP process are to maximize the *independence* of version development and to employ *design diversity* in order to minimize the probability that two or more member versions will produce similar erroneous results that coincide in time for a decision (consensus) action. This chapter describes the methodology of N-version programming. First, the concepts, goals, and basic techniques of N-version programming are introduced and two major fault-tolerant software models, N-version software and recovery blocks are reviewed. Next, the process of building N-version software is discussed in detail, including the specification, programming and execution support of NVS units. Results of five consecutive experimental investigations are summarized, and a design paradigm for NVS is presented. A discussion of several novel system analysis and design issues that are specific to the use of NVS and an assessment of the unique advantages of fault-tolerant software conclude the chapter.

2.1 INTRODUCTION

The concept of N-version programming (NVP) was first introduced in 1977 [Avi77b] as follows:

"N-*version programming* is defined as the independent generation of $N \geq 2$ functionally equivalent programs from the same initial specification. The N programs possess all the necessary attributes for concurrent execution, during which *comparison vectors* ("c-vectors") are

---

generated by the programs at certain points. The program state variables that are to be included in each c-vector and the *cross-check points* ("cc-points") at which the c-vectors are to be generated are specified along with the initial specification.

"Independent generation of programs" here means that the programming efforts are carried out by N individuals or groups that do not interact with respect to the programming process. Wherever possible, different algorithms and programming languages (or translators) are used in each effort. The *initial specification* is a formal specification in a specification language. The goal of the initial specification is to state the functional requirements completely and unambiguously, while leaving the widest possible choice of implementations to the N programming efforts. The actions to be taken at the cc-points after the exchange of c-vectors are also specified along with the initial specification. "

The following seventeen years have seen numerous investigations and some practical applications of the above stated concept, which identifies three elements of the NVP approach to software fault tolerance:

1. The *process* of initial specification and N-version programming which is intended to assure the independence and the functional equivalence of the N individual programming efforts;
2. The *product* (N-version software, or NVS) of the NVP process, which has the attributes for concurrent execution with specified cross-check points and comparison vectors for decisions;
3. The *environment* (N-version executive, or NVX) that supports the execution of the N-version software and provides decision algorithms at the specified cross-check points.

All three elements of the NVP approach are unique to the effort of independently and concurrently generating $N \geq 2$ functionally equivalent programs that are to be executed with decision-making by consensus. They are unnecessary in the case of a single program; thus the definition of NVP as an approach to software fault tolerance introduced new research topics designated as NVP, NVS, and NVX above.

This chapter presents the principles of the NVP approach to fault-tolerant software as it has evolved through a series of investigations in the 1977-1994 time period.

The justification for studying and applying NVP was stated in 1977 and has remained since then as follows [Avi77b]:

"The second major observation concerning N-version programming is that its success as a method for on-line tolerance of software faults depends on whether the residual software faults in each version of the program are *distinguishable*. Distinguishable software faults are faults that will cause a disagreement between c-vectors at the specified cc-points during the execution of the N-version set of programs that have been generated from the initial specification. Distinguishability is affected by the choice of c-vectors and cc-points, as well as by the nature of the faults themselves.

It is a fundamental conjecture of the N-version approach that the independence of programming efforts will greatly reduce the probability of identical software faults occurring in two or more versions of the program. In turn, the distinctness of faults and a reasonable choice of c-vectors and cc-points is expected to turn N-version programming into an effective method to achieve tolerance of software faults. The effectiveness of the entire N-version approach depends on the validity of this conjecture, therefore it is of critical importance that the initial specification should be free of any flaws that would bias the independent programmers toward introducing the same software faults."

It is essential to recognize that the independence of faults is an *objective* and *not* an *assumption* of the NVP approach, contrary to what was stated in [Sco84, Sco87, Kni86].

It is interesting that while the "NVP" concept did not appear in technical literature until 1977, searches through the earliest writings on the problem of errors in computing have led to two relevant observations dating back to the 1830's.

The first suggestion of multi-version computing was published in the *Edinburgh Review* of July 1834 by Dionysius Lardner, who wrote in his article "Babbage's calculating engine" as follows [Lar34]:

> *"The most certain and effectual check upon errors which arise in the process of computation, is to cause the same computations to be made by separate and independent computers; and this check is rendered still more decisive if they make their computations by different methods."*

It must be noted that the word "computer" above refers to a person who performs the computation, and not to the calculating engine. Charles Babbage himself had written in 1837 in a manuscript that was only recently published [Bab37]:

> *"When the formula to be computed is very complicated, it may be algebraically arranged for computation in two or more totally distinct ways, and two or more sets of cards may be made. If the same constants are now employed with each set, and if under these circumstances the results agree, we may then be quite secure of the accuracy of them all."*

The evolution of the software of modern computers relied on the principle of finding and eliminating software design faults either before or during the operational use of the software. Suggestions on the use of multiple versions of software for fault tolerance began appearing in the early and mid-1970's [Elm72, Gir73, Kop74, Fis75].

The effort to develop a systematic process (a *paradigm*) for the building of multiple-version software units that tolerate software faults, and function analogously to majority-voted multichannel hardware units, such as TMR, was initiated at UCLA in early 1975 as a part of research in reliable computing that was started in 1961 [Avi87b]. The process was first called "redundant programming" [Avi75], and was renamed "N-version programming" (NVP) in the course of the next two years [Avi77b].

Another major direction of evolution of fault-tolerant software has been the recovery block (RB) approach, which evolved as a result of the long-term investigation of reliable computing systems that was initiated by Brian Randell at the University of Newcastle upon Tyne in 1970 [Shr85]. In the RB technique $M \geq 2$ *alternates* and an *acceptance test* are organized in a manner similar to the dynamic redundancy (standby sparing) technique in hardware [Ran75]. RB performs run-time software, as well as hardware, error detection by applying the acceptance test to the results delivered by the first alternate. If the acceptance test is not passed, recovery is implemented by state restoration, followed by the execution of the next alternate. Recovery is considered complete when the acceptance test is passed. A concise view of the evolution of the RB concept and its place in the general context of dependable computing is presented in [Ran87]. The properties of RB software are discussed in other chapters of this book.

2.2   FAULT-TOLERANT SOFTWARE: MODELS AND TECHNIQUES

We say that a unit of software (module, CSCI, etc.) is *fault-tolerant* (abbreviated "f-t")if it can continue delivering the required service, i.e., supply the expected outputs with the expected timeliness, after *dormant* (previously undiscovered, or not removed) imperfections, called *software faults*, have become active by producing *errors* in program flow, internal state, or results generated within the software unit. When the errors disrupt (alter, halt, or delay) the service expected from the software unit, we say that it has *failed* for the duration of service disruption. A non-fault-tolerant software unit will be called a *simplex* unit.

Multiple, redundant computing channels (or "lanes") have been widely used in sets of $N = 2$, 3, or 4 to build f-t hardware systems [Avi87a]. To make a simplex software unit fault-tolerant, the corresponding solution is to add one, two, or more simplex units to form a set of $N \geq 2$ units. The redundant units are intended to compensate for, or mask a failed software unit when they are not affected by software faults that cause similar errors at cross-check points. The critical difference between multiple-channel hardware systems and f-t software units is that the simple replication of one design that is effective against random physical faults in hardware is not sufficient for software fault tolerance. Copying software will also copy the dormant software faults; therefore each simplex unit in the f-t set of N units needs to be built separately and independently of the other members of the set. This is the concept of software *design diversity* [Avi82].

Design diversity is applicable to tolerate design faults in hardware as well [Avi77a, Avi82]. Some multichannel systems with diverse hardware and software have been built; they include the flight control computers for the Boeing 737-300 [Wil83], and the Airbus [Tra88] airliners. Variations of the diversity concept have been widely employed in technology and in human affairs. Examples in technology are: a mechanical linkage backing up an electrical system to operate aircraft control surfaces, an analog system standing by for a primary digital system that guides spacecraft launch vehicles, a satellite link backing up a fiber-optic cable, etc. In human activities we have the pilot-copilot-flight engineer teams in cockpits of airliners, two- or three-surgeon teams at difficult surgery, and similar arrangements.

A set of $N \geq 2$ diverse simplex units alone is not fault-tolerant; the simplex units need an *execution environment* (EE) for f-t operation. Each simplex unit also needs fault tolerance features that allows it to serve as a *member* of the f-t software unit with support of the EE. The simplex units and the EE have to meet three requirements: (1) the EE must provide the support functions to execute the $N \geq 2$ member units in a fault-tolerant manner; (2) the specifications of the individual member units must define the fault tolerance features that they need for f-t operation supported by the EE; (3) the best effort must be made to minimize the probability of an undetected or unrecoverable failure of the f-t software unit that would be due to a single cause.

The evolution of techniques for building f-t software out of simplex units has taken two directions. The two basic models of f-t software units are *N-version software* (NVS), shown in Figure 2.1 and *recovery blocks* (RB) shown in Figure 2.2. The common property of both models is that two or more diverse units (called *versions* in NVS, and *alternates* and *acceptance tests* in RB) are employed to form a f-t software unit. The most fundamental difference is the method by which the decision is made that determines the outputs to be produced by the f-t unit. The NVS approach employs a generic *decision algorithm* that is provided by the EE and looks for a *consensus* of two or more outputs among N member versions. The RB model applies the *acceptance test* to the output of an individual alternate; this acceptance test

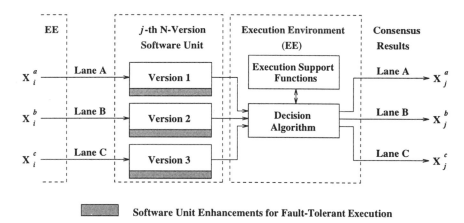

Software Unit Enhancements for Fault-Tolerant Execution

Figure 2.1   The N-version software (NVS) model with n = 3

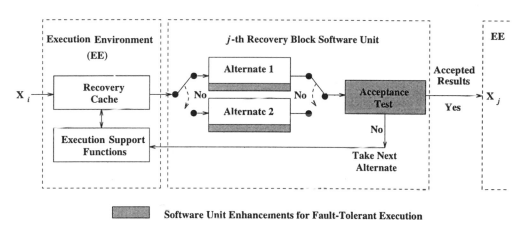

Software Unit Enhancements for Fault-Tolerant Execution

Figure 2.2   The recovery block (RB) model

must by necessity be *specific* for every distinct service, i.e., it is custom-designed for a given application, and is a member of the RB f-t software unit, but not a part of the EE.

$N = 2$ is the special case of *fail-safe* software units with two versions in NVS, and one alternate with one acceptance test in RB. They can detect disagreements between the versions, or between the alternate and the acceptance test, but cannot determine a consensus in NVS, or provide a backup alternate in RB. Either a *safe shutdown* is executed, or a *supplementary recovery process* must be invoked in case of a disagreement.

Both RB and NVS have evolved procedures for error recovery. In RB, backward recovery is achieved in a hierarchical manner through a *nesting* of RBs, supported by a *recursive cache* [Hor74], or *recovery cache* [And76] that is part of the EE. In NVS, forward recovery is done by the use of the *community error recovery* algorithm [Tso87] that is supported by the specification of *recovery points* and by the decision algorithm of the EE. Both recovery methods have limitations: in RB, errors that are not detected by an acceptance test are passed along and do not trigger recovery; in NVS, recovery will fail if a majority of versions have the same erroneous state at the recovery point.

It is evident that the RB and NVS models converge if the acceptance test is done by NVS technique, i.e., when the acceptance test is specified to be one or more independent computations of the same outputs, followed by a choice of a consensus result. It must be noted that the individual versions of NVS usually contain error detection and exception handling (similar to an acceptance test), and that the NVP decision algorithm takes the known failures of member versions into account [Kel83, Avi84]. Reinforcement of the decision algorithm by means of a preceding acceptance test (*a filter*) has been addressed in [And86], and the use of an acceptance test when the decision algorithm cannot make a decision in [Sco84, Sco87]

The remaining parts of this chapter present the various aspects of specifying, generating, and executing N-version software by the NVP method.

2.3 BUILDING N-VERSION SOFTWARE

An NVS unit is a f-t software unit that depends on a generic *decision algorithm* (part of the EE) to determine a *consensus result* from the results delivered by two or more ($N \geq 2$) *member versions* of the NVS unit. The *process* by which the NVS versions are produced is called N-*version programming*. The EE that embeds the N versions and supervises their f-t execution is called the N-*version executive*. The NVX may be implemented by means of software, hardware, or a combination of both. The major objective of the NVP process is to minimize the probability that two or more versions will produce similar erroneous results that coincide in time for a decision (consensus) action of NVX.

Building and using NVS requires three major efforts that are discussed below: (1) *to specify* the member versions of the NVS unit, including all features that are needed to embed them into the NVX; (2) *to define and execute* the NVP process in a manner that maximizes the independence of the programming efforts; (3) *to design and build* the NVX system for a very dependable and time-efficient execution of NVS units.

2.3.1   The Specification of Member Versions for NVS

The specification of the member versions, to be called "V-spec", represents the starting point of the NVP process. As such, the V-spec needs to state the functional requirements completely and unambiguously, while leaving the widest possible choice of implementations to the N programming efforts. It is the "hard core" of the NVS fault tolerance approach. Latent defects, such as inconsistencies, ambiguities, and omissions in the V-spec are likely to bias otherwise entirely independent programming or design efforts toward related design faults. The specifications for simplex software tend to contain guidance not only "what" needs to be done, but also "how" the solution ought to be approached. Such specific suggestions of "how" reduce the chances for diversity among the versions and should be systematically eliminated from the V-spec.

The V-spec may explicitly require the versions to differ in the "how" of implementation.

Diversity may be specified in the following elements of the NVP process: (1) training, experience, and location of implementing personnel; (2) application algorithms and data structures; (3) programming languages; (4) software development methods; (5) programming tools and environments; (6) testing methods and tools. The purpose of such *required diversity* is to minimize the opportunities for common causes of software faults in two or more versions (e.g., compiler bugs, ambiguous algorithm statements, etc.), and to increase the probabilities of significantly diverse approaches to version implementation. It is also possible to impose differing diversity requirements for separate software development stages, such as design, coding, testing, and even for the process of writing V-specs themselves, as discussed later.

Each V-spec must prescribe the *matching features* that are needed by the NVX to execute the member versions as an NVS unit in a fault-tolerant manner [Che78]. The V-spec defines: (1) the *functions* to be implemented, the time constraints, the inputs, and the initial state of a member version; (2) requirements for internal *error detection* and *exception handling* (if any) within the version; (3) the *diversity* requirements; (4) the *cross-check points* ("cc-points") at which the NVX decision algorithm will be applied to specified outputs of all versions; (5) the *recovery points* ("r-points") at which the NVX can execute *community error recovery* [Tso87] for a failed version; (6) the choice of the NVX *decision algorithm* and its *parameters* to be used at each cc-point and r-point; and (7) the *response* to each possible outcome of an NVX decision, including absence of consensus.

The NVX decision algorithm applies generic *consensus rules* to determine a consensus result from all valid version outputs. It has separate variants for real numbers, integers, text, etc. [Avi85b, Avi88b]. The *parameters* of this algorithm describe the allowable range of variation between numerical results, if such a range exists, as well as any other acceptable differences in the results from member versions, such as extra spaces in text output or other "cosmetic" variations.

The limiting case of required diversity is the use of two or more distinct V-specs, derived from the same set of user requirements. In early work, two cases have been practically explored: a set of three V-specs (formal algebraic OBJ, semi-formal PDL, and English) that were derived together [Kel83, Avi84], and a set of two V-specs that were derived by two independent efforts [Ram81]. These approaches provide additional means for the verification of the V-specs, and offer diverse starting points for version implementors.

In the long run, the most promising means for the writing of the V-specs are formal specification languages. When such specifications are executable, they can be automatically tested for latent defects [Kem85, Ber87], and they serve as prototypes of the versions that may be used to develop test cases and to estimate the potential for diversity. With this approach, verification is focused at the level of specification, the rest of the design and implementation process as well as its tools need not be perfect, but only as good as possible within existing resource and time constraints. The independent writing and testing by comparison of two specifications, using two formal languages, should increase the dependability of specifications beyond the present limits. Most of the dimensions of required diversity that were discussed above then can also be employed in V-spec writing. Among recently developed specification languages, promising candidates for V-specs that have been studied and used at UCLA are OBJ [Gog79] that has been further developed, the Larch family of specification languages [Gut85], PAISLey from AT&T Bell Laboratories [Zav86], and also Prolog as a specification language. A general assessment of specification languages for NVP is presented in [Avi90] and [Wu90].

2.3.2   The N-Version Programming Process: NVP

NVP has been defined from the beginning as *"the independent generation of* N $\geq$ 2 *functionally equivalent programs from the same initial specification"* [Avi77b]. "Independent generation" meant that the programming efforts were to be carried out by individuals or groups that did not interact with respect to the programming process. Wherever practical, different algorithms, programming languages, environments, and tools were to be used in each separate effort. The NVP approach was motivated by the *"fundamental conjecture that the independence of programming efforts will greatly reduce the probability of identical software faults occurring in two or more versions of the program"* [Avi77b]. The NVP process has been developed since 1975 in an effort that included five consecutive experimental investigations [Avi77b, Che78, Kel83, Kel86, Avi88a].

The application of a proven software development method, or of diverse methods for individual versions, remains the core of the NVP process. However, contemporary methods were not devised with the intent to reach the special goal of NVP, which is to minimize the probability that two or more member versions of an NVS unit will produce similar erroneous results that are coincident in time for an NVX decision at a cc-point or r-point.

NVP begins with the choice of a suitable software development process for an individual version. This process is supplemented by procedures that aim: (1) to attain the *maximum isolation* and *independence* (with respect to software faults) of the N concurrent version development efforts, and (2) to encourage the *greatest diversity* among the N versions of an NVS unit. Both procedures serve to minimize the chances of *related software faults* being introduced into two or more versions via potential *"fault leak" links*, such as casual conversations or E-mail exchanges, common flaws in training or in manuals, use of the same faulty compiler, etc.

Diversity requirements support this objective, since they provide more natural isolation against "fault leaks" between the teams of programmers. Furthermore, it is conjectured that the probability of a random, independent occurrence of faults that produce the same erroneous results in two or more versions is less when the versions are more diverse. A second conjecture is that even if related faults are introduced, the diversity of member versions may cause the erroneous results not to be similar at the NVX decision.

In addition to required diversity, two techniques have been developed to maximize the isolation and independence of version development efforts: (1) a set of mandatory rules of isolation, and (2) a rigorous communication and documentation protocol. The *rules of isolation* are intended to identify and eliminate all potential "fault leak" links between the *programming teams* (P-teams). The development of the rules is an ongoing process, and the rules are enhanced when a previously unknown "fault leak" is discovered and its cause is pinpointed. The *communication* and *documentation* (C&D) *protocol* imposes rigorous control on the manner in which all necessary information flow and documentation efforts are conducted. The main goal of the C&D protocol is to avoid opportunities for one P-team to influence another P-team in an uncontrollable and unnoticed manner. In addition, the C&D protocol documents communications in sufficient detail to allow a search for "fault leaks" if potentially related faults are discovered in two or more versions at some later time.

A *coordinating team* (C-team) is the keystone of the C&D protocol. The major functions of the C-team are: (1) to prepare the final texts of the V-specs and of the test data sets; (2) to set up the implementation of the C&D protocol; (3) to acquaint all P-teams with the NVP process, especially rules of isolation and the C&D protocol; (4) to distribute the V-specs, test data sets, and all other information needed by the P-teams; (5) to collect all P-team inquiries regarding the V-specs, the test data, and all matters of procedure; (6) to evaluate the inquiries (with help from expert consultants) and to respond promptly either to the inquiring P-team only, or to all P-teams via a broadcast; (7) to conduct formal reviews, to provide feedback when needed, and to maintain synchronization between P-teams; (8) to gather and evaluate all required documentation, and to conduct acceptance tests for every version. All communications between the C-team and the P-teams must be in standard written format only, and are stored for possible post mortems about "fault leaks". Electronic mail has proven to be the most effective medium for this purpose. Direct communications between P-teams are not allowed at all.

2.3.3 Functions of the N-Version Executive NVX

The NVX is an implementation of the set of functions that are needed to support the execution of N member versions as a f-t NVS unit. The functions are *generic*; that is, they can execute any given set of versions generated from a V-spec, as long as the V-spec specifies the proper *matching features* for the NVX. The NVX may be implemented in software, in hardware, or in a combination of both. The principal criteria of choice are very high dependability and fast operation. These objectives favor the migration of NVX functions into VLSI-implemented fault-tolerant hardware: either complete chips, or standard modules for VLSI chip designs.

The basic functions that the NVX must provide for NVS execution are: 1) the decision algorithm, or set of algorithms; 2) assurance of input consistency for all versions; 3) inter-version communication; 4) version synchronization and enforcement of timing constraints; 5) local supervision for each version; 6) the global executive and decision function for version error recovery at r-points, or other treatment of faulty versions; and 7) a user interface for observation, debugging, injection of stimuli, and data collection during N-version execution of application programs. The nature of these functions is extensively illustrated in the description of the DEDIX (DEsign DIversity eXperiment) NVX and testbed system that was developed at UCLA to support NVP research [Avi85a, Avi88b].

2.4 EXPERIMENTAL INVESTIGATIONS

At the time when the NVP approach was first formulated, neither formal theories nor past experience was available about how f-t software units should be specified, built, evaluated and supervised. Experimental, "hands-on" investigations were needed in order to gain the necessary experience and methodological insights.

The NVP research approach at UCLA was to choose some practically sized problems, to assess the applicability of N-version programming, and to generate a set of versions. The versions were executed as NVS units, and the observations were applied to refine the process and to build up the concepts of NVP. The original definition of NVP and a discussion of the first two sets of results, using 27 and 16 independently written versions, were published in 1977 and 1978, respectively [Avi77b, Che78]. The subsequent investigation employed three distinct specifications: algebraic OBJ [Gog79], structured PDL, and English, and resulted in 18 versions of an "airport scheduler" program [Kel83]. This effort was followed by five versions of a program for the NASA/Four University study [Kel86], and then by an investigation

Table 2.1   N-version programming studies at UCLA

Years	Project and Sponsor	No. of Versions	P-Team Size	Required Diversity	Programming Language
1975-76	Text Editor Software engineering class	27	1	personnel	PL/1
1977-78	PDE Solution Software engineering class	16	2	personnel & 3 algorithms	PL/1
1979-83	Airport Scheduler NSF research grant	18	1	personnel & 3 specifications	PL/1
1984-86	Sensor Redundancy Management NASA research grant	5	2	personnel	Pascal
1986-88	Automatic Aircraft Landing Research grant from Sperry Flight Systems, Phoenix, AZ	6	2	personnel & 6 languages	Pascal, Ada, Modula-2, C, Prolog, T

in which six versions of an automatic landing program for an airliner were written, using six programming languages: Pascal, C, Ada, Modula-2, Prolog, and T [Avi88a]. Table 2.1 summarizes the five NVP studies at UCLA. In parallel with the last two efforts, a distributed NVX supervisor called DEDIX (DEsign DIversity eXperimenter) was designed and programmed [Avi85a, Avi88b].

The primary goals of the five consecutive UCLA investigations were: to develop and refine the NVP process and the NVX system (DEDIX), to assess the methods for NVS specification, to investigate the types and causes of software design faults, and to design successively more focused studies. Numerical predictions of reliability gain through the use of NVS were deemphasized, because the results of any one of the NVP exercises are uniquely representative of the quality of the NVP process, the specification, and the capabilities of the programmers at that time. The extrapolation of the results is premature when the NVP process is still being refined. The NVP paradigm that is described in the next section is now considered sufficiently complete for practical application and quantitative predictions. The paradigm has been further refined by an investigation at the University of Iowa, in which 40 programmers formed 15 teams to program the automatic aircraft landing program in the C language [Lyu93].

An important criterion for NVS application is whether sufficient *potential for diversity* is evident in the version specification. Very detailed or obviously simple specifications indicate that the function is poorly suited for f-t implementation, and might be more suitable for extensive single-version V&V, or proof of correctness. The extent of diversity that can be observed between completed versions may indicate the effectiveness of NVP. A qualitative assessment of diversity through a detailed structural study of six versions has been carried out for the Six-Language NVS investigation [Avi88a]. These results have led to further research into quantitative measures of software diversity [Che90, Lyu92b].

Three pioneering practical investigations of NVS have been performed with real-time software for nuclear reactor safety control [Ram81, Bis88, Vog88b]. Significant insights into specification, the NVP process, and the nature of software faults have resulted from these efforts.

Two other early studies investigating N-version programming were conducted in which numerical results were the principal objective and an "assumption of independence" was associated with NVP [Sco84, Sco87, Kni86]. We should stress that the definition of NVP [Avi77b] has never postulated an "assumption of independence" and that NVP is a rigorous process of software development, which is examined in detail in the next section.

2.5   A DESIGN PARADIGM FOR N-VERSION SOFTWARE

The experience that had been accumulated during the preceding four investigations at UCLA [Avi77b, Che78, Kel83, Kel86] led to the rigorous definition and application of a set of guidelines, called the *NVS Design Paradigm* [Lyu88, Lyu92a] during the subsequent Six-Language NVP project [Avi88a]. The paradigm as it was further refined during this project, is summarized in *Figure 2.3* and described in this section. The purpose of the paradigm is to integrate the unique requirements of NVP with the conventional steps of software development methodology. The word "paradigm," used in the dictionary sense, means "pattern, example, model," presented here as a set of guidelines and rules with illustrations.

The objectives of the design paradigm are: (1) to reduce the possibility of oversights, mistakes, and inconsistencies in the process of software development and testing; (2) to eliminate most perceivable causes of related design faults in the independently generated versions of a program, and to identify causes of those which slip through the design process; (3) to minimize the probability that two or more versions will produce similar erroneous results that coincide in time for a decision (consensus) action of NVX.

The application of a proven software development method, or of diverse methods for individual versions, is the foundation of the NVP paradigm. The chosen method is supplemented by procedures that aim: (1) to attain suitable isolation and independence (with respect to software faults) of the N concurrent version development efforts, (2) to encourage potential diversity among the N versions of an NVS unit, and (3) to elaborate efficient error detection and recovery mechanisms. The first two procedures serve to reduce the chances of related software faults being introduced into two or more versions via potential "fault leak" links, such as casual conversations or mail exchanges, common flaws in training or in manuals, use of the same faulty compiler, etc. The last procedure serves to increase the possibilities of discovering manifested errors before they can cause an incorrect decision and consequent failure.

In Figure 2.3, the NVP paradigm is shown to be composed of two categories of activities. The first category, represented by boxes and single-line arrows at the left, contains standard software development procedures. The second category, represented by ovals and double-line arrows at the right, specifies the concurrent implementation of various fault tolerance techniques unique to N-version programming. The descriptions of the incorporated activities and guidelines are presented next.

2.5.1   System Requirement Phase : Determine Method of NVS Supervision

The NVS Execution Environment has to be determined in the system requirement phase in order to evaluate the overall system impact and to provide required support facilities. There are three aspects of this step:

(1) Choose NVS execution method and allocate resources. The overall system architecture is defined during system requirement phase, and the software configuration items are identified. The number of software versions and their interaction is determined.

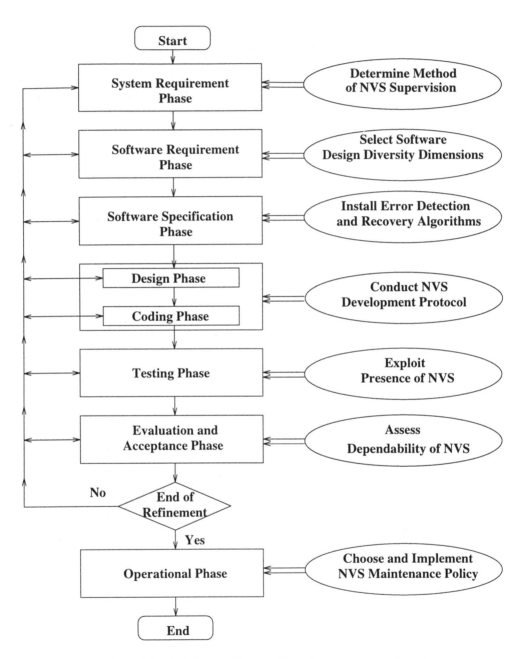

Figure 2.3   A design paradigm for N-version programming (NVP)

(2) **Develop support mechanisms and tools.** An existing NVX may be adapted, or a new one developed according to the application. The NVX may be implemented in software, in hardware, or in a combination of both. The basic functions that the NVX must provide for NVS execution are: (a) the decision algorithm, or set of algorithms; (b) assurance of input consistency for all versions; (c) interversion communications; (d) version synchronization and enforcement of timing constraints; (e) local supervision for each version; (f) the global executive and decision function for version error recovery; and (g) a user interface for observation, debugging, injection of stimuli, and data collection during N-version execution of applications programs. The nature of these functions was extensively illustrated in the descriptions of the DEDIX testbed system [Avi88b].

(3) **Select hardware architecture.** Special dedicated hardware processors may be needed for the execution of NVS systems, especially when the NVS supporting environments need to operate under stringent requirements (e.g., accurate supervision, efficient CPUs, etc.). The options of integrating NVX with hardware fault tolerance in a hybrid configuration also must be considered.

2.5.2   Software Requirement Phase : Select Software Diversity Dimensions

The major reason for specifying software diversity is to eliminate the commonalities between the separate programming efforts, as they have the potential to cause related faults among the multiple versions. Three steps of the selection process are identified.

(1) **Assess random diversity vs. required diversity.** Different dimensions of diversity could be achieved either by randomness or by requirement. The *random diversity*, such as that provided by independent personnel, causes dissimilarity because of an individual's training and thinking process. The diversity is achieved in an uncontrolled manner. The *required diversity*, on the other hand, considers different aspects of diversity, and requires them to be implemented into different program versions. The purpose of such *required diversity* is to minimize the opportunities for common causes of software faults in two or more versions (e.g., compiler bugs, ambiguous algorithm statements, etc.), and to increase the probabilities of significantly diverse approaches to version implementation.

(2) **Evaluate required design diversity.** There are four phases in which design diversity could be applied: specification, design, coding, and testing. Different implementors, different languages, different tools, different algorithms, and different software development methodologies, including phase-by-phase software engineering, prototyping, computer-aided software engineering, or even the "clean room" approach may be chosen for every phase. Since adding more diversity implies higher cost, it is necessary to evaluate cost-effectiveness of the added diversity along each dimension and phase.

(3) **Specify diversity under application constraints.** After the preceding assessments, the final combination of diversity can be determined under specific project constraints. Typical constraints are: cost, schedule, and required dependability. This decision presently involves substantial qualitative judgment, since quantitative measures for design diversity and its cost impact are not yet developed.

2.5.3 Software Specification Phase : Install Error Detection and Recovery Algorithms

The specification of the member versions, to be called "V-spec," needs to state the functional requirements completely and unambiguously, while leaving the widest possible choice of implementations to the N programming efforts. Sufficient error detection and recovery algorithms have to be selected and specified in order to detect errors that could potentially lead to system failures. Three aspects are considered below.

(1) **Specify the matching features needed by NVX.** Each V-spec must prescribe the *matching features* that are needed by the NVX to execute the member versions as an NVS unit in a fault-tolerant manner. The V-spec defines: (a) the *functions* to be implemented, the time constraints, the inputs, and the initial state of a member version; (b) requirements for internal *error detection* and *exception handling* (if any) within the version; (c) the *diversity* requirements; (d) the *cross-check points* ("cc-points") at which the NVX decision algorithm will be applied to specified outputs of all versions; (e) the *recovery points* ("r-points") at which the NVX can execute *community error recovery* for a failed version; (f) the choice of the NVX *decision algorithm* and its *parameters* to be used at each cc-point and r-point; (g) the *response* to each possible outcome of an NVX decision, including absence of consensus; and (h) the safeguards against the *Consistent Comparison problem* [Bri89].

(2) **Avoid diversity-limiting factors.** The specifications for simplex software tend to contain guidance not only "what" needs to be done, but also "how" the solution ought to be approached. Such specific suggestions of "how" reduce the chances for diversity among the versions and should be eliminated from the V-spec. Another potential diversity-limiting factor is the over-specification of cc-points and r-points. The installation of cc-points and r-points enhances error detection and recovery capability, but it imposes common constraints to the programs and may limit design diversity, The choice of the number of these points and their placement depend on the size of the software, the control flow of the application, the number of variables to be checked and recovered, and the time overhead allowed to perform these operations.

(3) **Diversify the specification.** The use of two or more distinct V-specs, derived from the same set of user requirements, can provide extensive protection against specification errors. Two examples are: a set of three V-specs (formal algebraic OBJ, semi-formal PDL, and English) that were derived together [Kel83, Avi84], and a set of two V-specs that were derived by two independent efforts [Ram81]. These approaches provide additional means for the verification of the V-specs, and offer diverse starting points for version implementors.

2.5.4 Design and Coding Phase : Conduct NVS Development Protocol

In this phase, multiple programming teams (P-teams) start to develop the NVS concurrently according to the V-spec. The main concern here is to maximize the isolation and independence of each version, and to smooth the overall software development. A coordinating team (C-team) is formed to supervise the effort. The steps are :

(1) **Impose a set of mandatory rules of isolation.** The purpose of imposing such rules on the P-teams is to assure the *independent generation* of programs, which means that programming efforts are carried out by individuals or groups that do not interact with respect to the programming process. The rules of isolation are intended to identify and avoid potential

"fault leak" links between the P-teams. The development of the rules in an ongoing process, and the rules are enhanced when a previously unknown "fault leak" is discovered and its cause pinpointed. Current isolation rules include: prohibition of any discussion of technical work between P-teams, widely separated working areas (offices, computer terminals, etc.) for each P-team, use of different host machines for software development, protection of all on-line computer files, and safe deposit of technical documents.

(2) Define a rigorous communication and documentation (C&D) protocol. The C&D protocol imposes rigorous control on all necessary information flow and documentation efforts. The goal of the C&D protocol is to avoid opportunities for one P-team to influence another P-team in an uncontrollable, and unnoticed manner. In addition, the C&D protocol documents communications in sufficient detail to allow a search for "fault leaks" if potentially related faults are discovered in two or more versions at some later time.

(3) Form a coordinating team (C-team). The C-team is the executor of the C&D protocol. The major functions of this team are: (a) to prepare the final texts of the V-specs and of the test data sets; (b) to set up the implementation of the C&D protocol; (c) to acquaint all P-teams with the NVP process, especially rules of isolation and the C&D protocol; (d) to distribute the V-specs, test data sets, and all other information needed by the P-teams; (e) to collect all P-team inquiries regarding the V-specs, the test data, and all matters of procedure; (f) to evaluate the inquiries (with help from expert consultants) and to respond promptly either to the inquiring P-team only, or to all P-teams via a broadcast; (g) to conduct formal reviews, to provide feedback when needed, and to maintain synchronization between P-teams; (h) to gather and evaluate all required documentation, and to conduct acceptance tests for every version.

2.5.5 Testing Phase : Exploit the Presence of NVS

A promising application of NVS is its use to reinforce current software verification and validation procedures during the testing phase, which is one of the hardest problems of any software development. The uses of multiple versions are:

(1) Support for verification procedures. During software verification, the NVS provides a thorough means for error detection since every discrepancy among versions needs to be resolved. Moreover, it is observed that consensus decision of the existing NVS may be more reliable than that of a "gold" model or version that is usually provided by an application expert.

(2) Opportunities for "back-to-back" testing. It is possible to execute two or three versions "back-to-back" in a testing environment. However, there is a risk that if the versions are brought together prematurely, the independence of programming efforts may be compromised and "fault leaks" might be created among the versions. If this scheme is applied in a project, it must be done by a testing team independent of the P-teams (e.g., the C-team), and the testing results should not be revealed to a P-team, if they contain information from other versions that would influence this P-team.

2.5.6 Evaluation and Acceptance Phase : Assess the Dependability of NVS

Evaluation of the software fault-tolerance attributes of an NVS system is performed by means of analytic modeling, simulation, experiments, or combinations of those techniques. The evaluation issues are:

(1) Define NVS acceptance criteria. The acceptance criteria of the NVS system depend on the validity of the conjecture that residual software faults in separate versions will cause very few, if any, similar errors at the same cc-points. These criteria depend on the applications and must be elaborated case by case.

(2) Assess evidence of diversity. Diversity requirements support the objective of independence, since they provide more natural isolation against "fault leaks" between the teams of programmers. Furthermore, it is conjectured that the probability of random, independent faults that produce the same erroneous results in two or more versions is less when the versions are more diverse. Another conjecture is that even if related faults are introduced, the diversity of member versions may cause the erroneous results not to be similar at the NVX decision. Therefore, evidence and effectiveness of diversity need to be identified and assessed [Che90, Lyu92b].

(3) Make NVS dependability predictions. For dependability prediction of NVS, there are two essential aspects: the choice of suitable software dependability models, and the definition of quantitative measures. Usually, the dependability prediction of the NVS system is compared to that of the single-version baseline system.

2.5.7   Operational Phase : Choose and Implement an NVS Maintenance Policy

The maintenance of NVS during its lifetime offers a special challenge. The two key issues are:

(1) Assure and monitor NVX functionality. The functionality of NVX should be properly assured and monitored during the operational phase. Critical parts of the NVS supervisory system NVX could themselves be protected by the NVP technique. Operational status of the NVX running NVS should be carefully monitored to assure its functionality. Any anomalies are recorded for further investigation.

(2) Follow the NVP paradigm for NVS modification. For the modification of the NVS unit, the same design paradigm is to be followed, i.e., a common specification of the modification should be implemented by independent maintenance teams. The cost of such a policy is higher, but it is hypothesized that the extra cost in maintenance phase, compared with that for single version, is relatively lower than the extra cost during the development phase. This is due to two reasons: (a) the achieved NVS reliability is higher than that of a single version, leaving fewer costly operational failures to be experienced; (b) when adding new features to the operating software, the existence of multiple program versions should make the testing and certification tasks easier and more cost-effective.

2.6   THE SYSTEM CONTEXT FOR FAULT-TOLERANT SOFTWARE

The introduction of fault-tolerant software raises some novel system analysis and design issues that are reviewed below.

2.6.1   Modeling of Fault-Tolerant Software

The benefits of fault tolerance need to be predicted by quantitative modeling of the *reliability, availability,* and *safety* of the system for specified time intervals and operating conditions.

The conditions include acceptable *service levels, timing constraints* on service delivery, and *operating environments* that include expected *fault classes* and their *rates* of occurrence. The quality of fault tolerance mechanisms is expressed in terms of *coverage* parameters for error detection, fault location, and system recovery. A different fault tolerance specification is the *minimal tolerance* requirement to tolerate one, two, or more faults from a given set, regardless where in the system they occur. The one-fault requirement in frequently stated as "no single point of failure" for given operating conditions. An analysis of the design is needed to show that this requirement is met.

The similarity of NVS and RB as f-t software units has allowed the construction of a model for the prediction of reliability and average execution time of both RB and NVS. The model employs queuing theory and a state diagram description of the possible outcomes of NVS and RB unit execution. An important question explored in this model is how the gain in reliability due to the fault tolerance mechanisms is affected when *related faults* appear in two or more versions of NVS, and when the acceptance test has less than perfect coverage (due to either incompleteness, or own faults) with respect to the faults in RB alternates. The *correlation factor* is the conditional probability of a majority of versions (in NVS) or one alternate and the acceptance test (in RB) failing in such a way that a faulty result is passed as an output of the f-t software unit. The model shows strong variation of the reliability of f-t software units as a function of the correlation factor [Grn80, Grn82].

The criticality of related faults had been recognized quite early for both RB [Hec76] and NVS [Grn80], and later in [Sco84, Eck85] which reached similar conclusions. Later studies have further explored the modeling of f-t software, including the impact of related faults on the reliability and safety of both NVS and RB [Lap84, Tso86, Lit87, Arl88]. A recent study has assessed the performability of f-t software [Tai93a, Tai93b]. Several extensive studies of the modeling and analysis of fault tolerant software are being presented in other chapters of this book and will not be reviewed here.

2.6.2   Hosting and Protection of the Execution Environment EE

The *host system* for NVS (and RB as well) interacts with the f-t software units through the EE, which communicates with the fault tolerance functions of its operating system or with fault tolerance management hardware, such as a service processor. The EE itself may be integrated with the operating system, or it may be in part, or even fully implemented in hardware. A fully developed EE for NVS is the all-software DEDIX supervisor [Avi88b], which interacts with Unix on a local network. Such a software-to-software linkage between the EE and the operating system accommodates any hardware operating under Unix, but causes delays in inter-version communication through the network. In practical NVS implementations with real-time constraints either implementing the DEDIX functions in custom hardware, or building an operating system that provides EE services along with its other functions is necessary.

The recent Newcastle RB investigation employed both the hardware recovery cache and extensions to the MASCOT operating system as the implementation of the EE [And88], while the distributed RB study employs hardware and a custom distributed operating system [Chu87]. Other examples of solutions are found in [Mak84, Lal88, Wal88].

The remaining question is the protection against design faults that may exist in the EE itself. For NVS this may be accomplished by N-fold diverse implementation of the NVX. To explore the feasibility of this approach, the prototype DEDIX environment has undergone formal specification in PAISLey [Zav86]. This specification is suitable to generate multiple diverse versions of the DEDIX software to reside on separate physical nodes of the system. It is evident that diversity in separate nodes of the NVX will cause a slowdown to the speed of the slowest version. Since the NVX provides generic, reusable support functions of limited complexity, it may be more practical to verify a single-version NVX and to move most of its functionality into custom processor hardware.

In the case of RBs, special fault tolerance attention is needed by the recovery cache and any other custom hardware. The tolerance of design faults in the EE has been addressed through the concept of multilevel structuring [Ran75]. The acceptance test, which is unique for every RB software unit, also may contain design faults. The obvious solution of 2-version or 3-version acceptance tests is costly, and verification or proof of each acceptance test appear to be the most practical solutions.

2.6.3   Multilayer Diversity

Multilayer diversity occurs when diversity is introduced at several *layers* of an N-channel computing system: application software, system software, hardware, system interfaces (e.g., diverse displays), and even specifications [Avi86]. The justification for introducing diversity in hardware, system software, and user interfaces is that tolerance should extend to design faults that may exist in those layers as well. The second argument, especially applicable to hardware, is that diversity among the channels of the hardware layer will naturally lead to greater diversity among the versions of system software and application software.

The use of diverse component technologies and diverse architectures adds more practical dimensions of hardware diversity. The diversity in component technologies is especially valuable against faults in manufacturing processes that lead to deterioration of hardware and subsequent delayed manifestation of related physical faults that could prematurely exhaust the spare supply of long-life f-t systems. The counter-argument that such diversity in hardware is superfluous may be based on the assumption that diversity in software will cause the identical host hardware channels to assume diverse states. The same hardware design fault then would not be likely to produce similar and time-coincident errors in system and application software.

Tolerance of design faults in human-machine interfaces offers an exceptional challenge. When fault avoidance is not deemed sufficient, dual or triplex diverse interfaces need to be designed and implemented independently. For example, dual or triple displays of diverse design and component technology will provide an additional safety margin against design and manufacturing faults for human operators in air traffic control, airliner cockpits, nuclear power plant control rooms, hospital intensive care facilities, etc. Redundant displays often are already employed in these and other similar applications due to the need to tolerate single physical faults in display hardware without service interruption.

The major limitations of layered diversity are the *cost* of implementing multiple independent designs and the *slowdown* of operation that is caused by the need to wait for the slowest version at every system layer at which diversity is employed. The latter is especially critical for real-time applications in which design fault tolerance is an essential safety attribute. Speed considerations strongly favor the migration of f-t EE functions into diverse VLSI circuit implementations. A few two and three version systems that employ diverse hardware and software have been designed and built. They include the flight control computers for the Boeing 737-300 [Wil83], the ATR.42, Airbus A-310, and A-320 aircraft [Tra88]. Proposed designs for the flight control computer of the planned Boeing 7J7 are the three-version GEC Avionics design [Hil88] and the four-version MAFT system [Wal88].

A different concept of *multilevel systems* with fault-tolerant interfaces was formulated by Randell for the RB approach [Ran75]. Diversity is not explicitly considered for the hardware level, but appears practical when additional hardware channels are employed, either for the acceptance test, or for parallel execution of an alternate in distributed RB [Chu87, Kim88].

2.6.4 NVS Support for System Security

Computer security and software fault tolerance have the common goal to provide reliable software for computer systems [Tur86, Dob86]. A special concern is *malicious logic,* which is defined as: "Hardware, software, or firmware that is intentionally included in a system for the purpose of causing loss or harm" [DOD85]. The loss or harm here is experienced by the user, since either incorrect service, or no service at all is delivered. Examples of malicious logic are *Trojan horses, trap doors,* and *computer viruses.* The deliberate nature of these threats leads us to classify malicious logic as *deliberate design faults* (DDFs), and to apply fault tolerance techniques to DDF detection and tolerance, such as in the case of computer virus containment by program flow monitors [Jos88a].

Three properties of NVS make it effective for tolerating DDFs: (1) the independent design, implementation, and maintenance of multiple versions makes a single DDF detectable, while the covert insertion of identical copies of DDFs into a majority of the N versions is difficult; (2) NVS enforces completeness, since several versions ensure (through consensus decision) that all specified actions are performed (i.e., omitting a required function can be a DDF); and (3) time-out mechanisms at all decision points prevent prolonged period without action (i.e., slowing down a computer system is a denial-of-service DDF). A detailed study of these issues appears in [Jos88b].

2.6.5 Modification of Operational NVS

Modification of already operational f-t software occurs for two different reasons: (1) one of the member units (version, alternate, or acceptance test) needs either the removal of a newly discovered fault, or an improvement of a poorly programmed function, while the specification remains intact; (2) all member units of a f-t software unit need to be modified to add functionality or to improve its overall performance.

In the first case, the change affects only one member and should follow the standard fault removal procedure. The testing of the modified unit should be facilitated by the existence of other members of the f-t software. Special attention is needed when a *related fault* is discovered in two or more versions or alternates, or in one alternate and the acceptance test. Here independence remains important, and the NVP process needs to be followed, using a *removal specification,* followed by isolated fault removals by separate maintenance teams.

In the second case, N independent modifications need to be done. First, the specification is modified, re-verified, and tested to assess the impact of the modification. Second, the affected f-t software units are regenerated from the specification, following the standard NVP or RB processes. The same considerations apply to modification of the alternates in RB software, but special treatment is required for modifying the unique acceptance test software unit.

2.7 CONCLUSIONS

Although at first considered to be an impractical competitor of high-quality single-version programs, fault-tolerant software has gained significant acceptance in academia and industry during the past decade. Two, three, and four version software is switching trains [Hag88], performing flight control computations on modern airliners [Wil83, Tra88], and more NVS applications are on the way [Vog88a, Wal88, Hil88]. Publications about f-t software are growing in numbers and in depth of understanding, and at least three long-term academic "hands-on" efforts are in their second decade: recovery blocks at Newcastle [Ran87, And88], distributed recovery blocks at UC Irvine [Chu87, Kim88], and N-version software at UCLA [Avi85b, Avi88a, Avi88b].

Why should we pursue these goals? Every day, humans depend on computers more and more to improve many aspects of their lives. Invariably, we find that those applications of computers that can deliver the greatest improvements in the quality of life or the highest economic benefits also can cause the greatest harm when the computer fails. Applications that offer great benefits at the risk of costly failures are: life support systems in the delivery of health care and in adverse environments; control systems for air traffic and for nuclear power plants; flight control systems for aircraft and manned spacecraft; surveillance and early warning systems for military defense; process control systems for automated factories, and so on.

The loss of service for only a few seconds or, in the worst case, service that looks reasonable but is wrong, is likely to cause injuries, loss of life, or grave economic losses in each one of these applications. As long as the computer is not sufficiently trustworthy, full benefits of the application cannot be realized, since human surveillance and decision making are superimposed, and the computers serve only in a supporting role. At this time it is abundantly clear that the trustworthiness of software is the principal prerequisite for the building of a trustworthy system. While hardware dependability also cannot be taken for granted, tolerance of physical faults is proving to be very effective in contemporary fault-tolerant systems.

At present, fault-tolerant software is the only alternative that can be expected to provide a higher level of trustworthiness and security for critical software units than test or proof techniques without fault tolerance. The ability to guarantee that any software fault, as long as it only affects only one member of an N-version unit, is going to be tolerated without service disruption may by itself be a sufficient reason to adapt fault-tolerant software as a safety assurance technique for life-critical applications.

Another attraction of fault-tolerant software is the possibility of an economic advantage over single-version software in attaining the same level of trustworthiness. The higher initial cost may be balanced by significant gains, such as faster release of trustworthy software, less investment and criticality in verification and validation, and more competition in procurement as versions can be acquired from small, but effective, enterprises in widely scattered locations.

Finally, there is a fundamental shift of emphasis in software development that takes place when N-version software is produced. In single-version software, attention is usually focused on testing and verification, i.e., the programmer-verifier relationship. In NVS, the key to success is the version specification; thus the focus shifts to the user-specifier relationship and the quality of specifications. The benefits of this shift are evident: a dime spent on specification is a dollar saved on verification.

ACKNOWLEDGMENTS

The concept and methodology of N-version programming have evolved through the author's collaboration and discussions with the members and visitors of the Dependable Computing and Fault-Tolerant Systems Laboratory at UCLA and through the efforts of the ninety-nine programmers who took part in our studies since 1975. Liming Chen had the courage to initiate the experimental investigations, John P.J. Kelly brought them to maturity, and Michael R. Lyu formulated the NVS design paradigm as it exists today. Special thanks also belong to Jean Arlat, Jia-Hong (Johnny) Chen, Per Gunninberg, Mark Joseph, Jean-Claude Laprie, Srinivas V. Makam, Werner Schuetz, Lorenzo Strigini, Pascal Traverse, Ann Tai, Kam-Sing Tso, Udo Voges, John F. Williams, and Chi-Sharn Wu for their valuable contributions. Rimas Avižienis prepared this text with care and dedication, and Yutao He put the chapter into its final form.

Financial support for fault-tolerant software research at UCLA has been provided by the following sources: National Science Foundation, Grants No. MCS-72-03633, MCS-78-18918, and MCS-81-21696; Office of Naval Research, Contract No. N0014-79-C-0866; National Aeronautics and Space Administration, Contract No. NAG1-512; Battelle Memorial Institute; Federal Aviation Administration-Advanced Computer Science Program; Sperry Commercial Flight Systems Division of Honeywell, Inc.; State of California "MICRO" Program; and CALSPAN-UB Research Center.

REFERENCES

[And76] T. Anderson and R. Kerr. Recovery blocks in action: a system supporting high reliability. In *Proc. 2nd International Conference on Software Engineering*, pages 447–457, San Francisco, CA, October 1976.

[And86] T. Anderson. A structured decision mechanism for diverse software. In *Proc. 5th Symposium on Reliability in Distributed Software and Database Systems*, pages 125–129, Los Angeles, CA, January 1986.

[And88] T. Anderson, P. A. Barrett, D. N. Halliwell, and M. R. Moulding. Tolerating software design faults in a command and control system, pages 109–128. In [Vog88a].

[Arl88] J. Arlat, K. Kanoun, and J. C. Laprie. Dependability evaluation of software fault tolerance. In *Digest of 18th FTCS*, pages 142–147, Tokyo, Japan, June 1988.

[Avi75] A. Avižienis. Fault tolerance and fault intolerance: complementary approaches to reliable computing. In *Proc. 1975 International Conference on Reliable Software*, pages 458–464, April 1975.

[Avi77a] A. Avižienis. Fault-tolerant computing — progress, problems, and prospects. In *Information Processing 77, Proc. of IFIP Congress*, pages 405–420, Toronto, Canada, August 1977.

[Avi77b] A. Avižienis and L. Chen. On the implementation of N-version programming for software fault tolerance during execution. In *Proc. IEEE COMPSAC 77*, pages 149–155, November 1977.

[Avi82] A. Avižienis. Design diversity — the challenge for the eighties. In *Digest of 12th FTCS*, pages 44–45, Santa Monica, CA, June 1982.

[Avi84] A. Avižienis and J. Kelly. Fault tolerance by design diversity: concepts and experiments. In *IEEE Computer*, 17(8):67–80, August 1984.

[Avi85a] A. Avižienis, P. Gunningberg, J. P. J. Kelly, L. Strigini, P. J. Traverse, K. S. Tso and U. Voges. The UCLA DEDIX system: a distributed testbed for multiple-version software. In *Digest of 15th FTCS*, pages 126–134, Ann Arbor, MI, June 1985.

[Avi85b] A. Avižienis. The N-version approach to fault-tolerant software. In *IEEE Transactions on Software Engineering*, SE-11(12):1491–1501, December 1985.

[Avi86] A. Avižienis and J. C. Laprie. Dependable computing: from concepts to design diversity. In *Proc. IEEE*, 74(5):629–638, May 1986.

[Avi87a]   A. Avižienis, H. Kopetz, and J. C. Laprie, editors. *The Evolution of Fault-Tolerant Computing*. Springer, Wien, New York, 1987.

[Avi87b]   A. Avižienis and D. Rennels. The evolution of fault tolerant computing at the Jet Propulsion Laboratory and at UCLA: 1955-1986, pages 141–191. In [Avi87a].

[Avi88a]   A. Avižienis, M. R. Lyu, and W. Schuetz. In search of effective diversity: a six-language study of fault-tolerant flight control software. In *Digest of 18th FTCS*, pages 15–22, Tokyo, Japan, June 1988.

[Avi88b]   A. Avižienis, M. R-T. Lyu, W. Schuetz, K-S. Tso, and U. Voges. DEDIX 87 — A supervisory system for design diversity experiments at UCLA, pages 129–168. In [Vog88a].

[Avi90]   A. Avižienis and C-S. Wu. A comparative assessment of system description methodologies and formal specification languages. *Technical Report CSD-900030, Computer Science Department, UCLA*, September 1990.

[Bab37]   C. Babbage. On the mathematical powers of the calculating engine, December 1837 (Unpublished Manuscript) Buxton MS7, Museum of the History of Science, Oxford. In B. Randell, editor. *The Origins of Digital Computers: Selected Papers*. Springer, New York, pages 17-52, 1974.

[Ber87]   E. F. Berliner and P. Zave. An experiment in technology transfer: PAISLey specification of requirements for an undersea lightwave cable system. In *Proc. 9th Int. Conference on Software Engineering*, pages 42–50, Monterey, CA, April 1987.

[Bis88]   P. G. Bishop. The PODS diversity experiment, pages 51–84. In [Vog88a].

[Bri89]   S. S. Brilliant, J. C. Knight, and N. G. Leveson. The consistent comparison problem in N-version software. In *IEEE Transactions on Software Engineering*, SE-15(11):1481–1485, November 1989.

[Che78]   L. Chen and A. Avižienis. N-version programming: a fault-tolerance approach to reliability of software operation. In *Digest of 8th FTCS*, pages 3–9, Toulouse, France, June 1978.

[Che90]   J. J. Chen. *Software Diversity and Its Implications in the N-Version Software Life Cycle*. PhD dissertation, UCLA, Computer Science Department, 1990.

[Chu87]   W. W. Chu, K. H. Kim, and W. C. McDonald. Testbed-based validation of design techniques for reliable distributed real-time systems. In *Proc. IEEE*, 75(5): 649–667, May 1987.

[DOD85]   U. S. Department of Defense. *Trusted Computer System Evaluation Criteria*. DoD Doc. 5200.28-STD. December 1985.

[Dob86]   J. E. Dobson and B. Randell. Building reliable secure computing systems out of unreliable insecure components. In *IEEE Symposium Security and Privacy*, pages 187–193, Oakland, CA, April 1986.

[Eck85]   D. E. Eckhardt and L. D. Lee. A theoretical basis for the analysis of multiversion software subject to coincident errors. In *IEEE Transactions on Software Engineering*, SE-11(12):1511–1517, December 1985.

[Elm72]   W. R. Elmendorf. Fault-tolerant programming. In *Digest of 2nd FTCS*, pages 79–83, Newton, MA, June 1972.

[Fis75]   M. A. Fischler, O. Firschein, and D. L. Drew. Distinct software: an approach to reliable computing. In *Proc. 2nd USA-Japan Computer Conference*, pages 573–579, Tokyo, Japan, August 1975.

[Gir73]   E. Girard and J. C. Rault. A programming technique for software reliability. In *Proc. 1973 IEEE Symposium on Computer Software Reliability*, pages 44–50, New York, May 1973.

[Gog79]   J. A. Goguen and J.J. Tardo. An introduction to OBJ: a language for writing and testing formal algebraic program specifications. In *Proc. Specification of Reliable Software Conference*, pages 170–189, Cambridge, MA, April 3-5 1979.

[Grn80]   A. Grnarov, J. Arlat, and A. Avižienis. On the performance of software fault tolerance strategies. In *Digest of 10th FTCS*, pages 251–253, Kyoto, Japan, October 1980.

[Grn82]   A. Grnarov, J. Arlat, and A. Avižienis. Modeling and performance evaluation of software fault-tolerance strategies. *Technical Report CSD-820608, Computer Science Department, UCLA*, June 1982.

[Gut85]   J. V. Guttag, J. J. Horning, and J. M. Wing. *Larch in Five Easy Pieces*, pages 11–21. Report No. 5. DEC Systems Research Center, Palo Alto, CA, July 24 1985.

[Hag88]   G. Hagelin. ERICSSON safety system for railway control, pages 11–21. In [Vog88a].

[Hec76]   H. Hecht. Fault-tolerant software for real-time applications. In *ACM Computing Surveys*, 8(4):391–407, December 1976.

[Hil88]   A. D. Hills and N. A. Mirza. Fault tolerant avionics. In *AIAA/IEEE 8th Digital Avionics Systems Conference*, pages 407–414, San Jose, CA, October 1988.

[Hor74]   J. J. Horning, H. C. Lauer, P. M. Melliar-Smith, and B. Randell. A program structure for error detection and recovery, E. Gelenbe and C. Kaiser, editors. *Lecture Notes in Computer Science*, 16:171–187. Springer, 1974.

[Jos88a] M. K. Joseph and A. Avižienis. A fault tolerance approach to computer viruses. In *IEEE Symposium Security and Privacy*, pages 52–58, Oakland, CA, April 1988.

[Jos88b] M. K. Joseph. *Architectural Issues in Fault-Tolerant, Secure Computing Systems*. PhD dissertation, UCLA, Computer Science Department, June 1988.

[Kel83]   J. P. J. Kelly and A. Avižienis. A specification-oriented multi-version software experiment. In *Digest of 13th FTCS*, pages 120–126, Milano, Italy, June 1983.

[Kel86]   J. Kelly, A. Avižienis, B. Ulery, B. Swain, M. Lyu, A. Tai, and K. Tso. Multi-version software development. In *Proc. IFAC Workshop SAFECOMP'86*, pages 35–41, Sarlat, France, October 1986.

[Kem85]   R. A. Kemmerer. Testing formal specifications to detect design errors. In *IEEE Transactions on Software Engineering*, SE-11(1):32–43, January 1985.

[Kim88]   K. H. Kim and J. C. Yoon. Approaches to implementation of a repairable distributed recovery block scheme. In *Digest of 18th FTCS*, pages 50–55, Tokyo, Japan, June 1988.

[Kni86]   J. C. Knight and N. G. Leveson. An experimental evaluation of the assumption of independence in multiversion programming. In *IEEE Transactions on Software Engineering*, SE-12(1):96–109, January 1986.

[Kop74]   H. Kopetz. Software redundancy in real time systems. In *Information Processing 74, Proc. of IFIP Congress*, pages 182–186, Stockholm, Sweden, August 1974.

[Lal88]   J. H. Lala and L. S. Alger. Hardware and software fault tolerance: a unified architectural approach. In *Digest of 18th FTCS*, pages 240–245, Tokyo, Japan, June 1988.

[Lap84]   J. C. Laprie. Dependability evaluation of software systems in operation. In *IEEE Transactions on Software Engineering*, SE-10(11):701–714, November 1984.

[Lar34]   D. Lardner. Babbage's calculating engine, *Edinburgh Review, July 1834*. Reprinted in P. Morrison and E. Morrison, editors, *Charles Babbage and His Calculating Engines*, page 177, Dover, New York, 1961.

[Lit87]   B. Littlewood and D. R. Miller. A conceptual model of multi-version software. In *Digest of 17th FTCS*, pages 150–155, Pittsburgh, PA, July 1987.

[Lyu88]   M. R. Lyu. *A Design Paradigm for Multi-Version Software*. PhD dissertation, UCLA, Computer Science Department, May 1988.

[Lyu92a] M. R. Lyu and A. Avižienis. Assuring design diversity in N-version software: a design paradigm for N-version programming, pages 197–218. In J. F. Meyer and R. D. Schlichting, editors, *Dependable Computing for Critical Applications 2*. Springer-Verlag, Wien, New York, 1992.

[Lyu92b] M. R. Lyu, Chen J. H., and A. Avižienis. Software diversity metrics and measurements. In *Proc. IEEE COMPSAC 1992*, pages 69–78, Chicago, Illinois, September 1992.

[Lyu93]   M. R. Lyu and Y-T. He. Improving the N-version programming process through the evolution of a design paradigm. In *IEEE Transactions Reliability*, R-42(2):179–189, June 1993.

[Mak84]   S. V. Makam and A. Avižienis. An event-synchronized system architecture for integrated hardware and software fault-tolerance. In *Proc. IEEE 4th International Conference Distributed Computing Systems*, pages 526–532, San Francisco, CA, May 1984.

[Ram81]   C. V. Ramamoorthy et al. Application of a methodology for the development and validation of reliable process control software. In *IEEE Transactions on Software Engineering*, SE-7(11):537–555, November 1981.

[Ran75]   B. Randell. System structure for software fault-tolerance. In *IEEE Transactions on Software Engineering*, SE-1(6):220–232, June 1975.

[Ran87]   B. Randell. Design fault tolerance, pages 251–270. In [Avi87a].

[Sco84]   R. K. Scott, J. W. Gault, D. F. McAllister, and J. Wiggs. Experimental validation of six fault-tolerant software reliability models. In *Digest of 14th FTCS*, pages 102–107, Orlando, FL, June 1984.

[Sco87]   R. K. Scott, J. W. Gault, and D. F. McAllister. Fault-tolerant software reliability modeling. In *IEEE Transactions on Software Engineering*, SE-13(5):582–592, May 1987.

[Shr85]   K. S. Shrivastava, editor. *Reliable Computing Systems: Collected Papers of the Newcastle Reliability Project*. Springer, Wien, New York, 1985.

[Tai93a]   A. T. Tai, A. Avižienis, and J. F. Meyer. Evaluation of Fault-Tolerant Software: A Performability Modeling Approach, pages 113–135. In C. E. Landwehr, B. Randell and L. Simoncini, editors, *Dependable Computing for Critical Applications 3*. Springer-Verlag, Wien, New York, 1993.

[Tai93b]   A. T. Tai, J. F. Meyer, and A. Avižienis. Performability enhancement of fault-tolerant software. In *IEEE Transactions Reliability*, R-42(2):227–237, June 1993.

[Tra88]   P. Traverse. AIRBUS and ATR system architecture and specification, pages 95–104. In [Vog88a].

[Tso87]   K. S. Tso and A. Avižienis. Community error recovery in N-version software: a design study with experimentation. In *Digest of 17th FTCS*, pages 127–133, Pittsburgh, PA, July 1987.

[Tso86]   K. S. Tso, A. Avižienis, and J. P. J. Kelly. Error recovery in multi-version software. In *Proc. IFAC Workshop SAFECOMP'86*, pages 35–41, Sarlat, France, October 1986.

[Tur86]   R. Turn and J. Habibi. On the interactions of security and fault tolerance. In *9th National Computer Security Conference*, pages 138–142, September 1986.

[Vog88a]   U. Voges, editor. *Software Diversity in Computerized Control Systems*. Springer, Wien, New York, 1988.

[Vog88b]   U. Voges. Use of diversity in experimental reactor safety systems, pages 29–49. In [Vog88a].

[Wal88]   C. J. Walter. MAFT: An architecture for reliable fly-by-wire flight control. In *AIAA/IEEE 8th Digital Avionics Systems Conference*, pages 415–421, San Jose, CA, October 1988.

[Wil83]   J. F. Williams, L. J. Yount, and J. B. Flannigan. Advanced autopilot flight director system computer architecture for Boeing 737-300 aircraft. In *AIAA/IEEE 5th Digital Avionics Systems Conference*, Seattle, WA, November 1983.

[Wu90]   C. S. Wu. *Formal Specification Techniques and Their Applications in N-Version Programming*. PhD dissertation, UCLA, Computer Science Department, October 1990.

[Zav86]   P. Zave and W. Schell. Salient features of an executable specification language and its environment. In *IEEE Transactions on Software Engineering*, SE-12(2):312–325, February 1986.

3

Architectural Issues in Software Fault Tolerance

JEAN-CLAUDE LAPRIE, JEAN ARLAT, CHRISTIAN BÉOUNES and KARAMA KANOUN

LAAS-CNRS, France

ABSTRACT

This chapter presents a unified overview of architectural solutions to software fault tolerance by means of design diversity, i.e., the production of two or more systems aimed at delivering the same service through separate designs and realizations. The first part synthesizes the major approaches for software-fault tolerance; in addition to the recovery blocks (discussed in Chapter 1) and N-version programming (discussed in Chapter 2) methods, a third type of approach is identified from the careful examination of current, real-life systems: N self-checking programming. Then, the three approaches to software fault tolerance are analyzed with respect to two viewpoints: dependability and cost. Finally, architectures aimed at tolerating both hardware and software faults are defined and analyzed.

3.1 INTRODUCTION

There exist two largely differing approaches to software fault tolerance, depending on the forecast aim, either preventing a task failure to lead to the system complete disruption, or ensuring service continuity. In the former case, an erroneous task will be detected as soon as possible, and will be halted to prevent error propagation; this approach is often termed as *fail-fast* [Gra86, Gra90]. The latter case requires the existence of at least another component able to fulfill the task, designed and implemented separately from the same specification; this approach thus requires the use of *design diversity*. This chapter concentrates on software fault tolerance based on design diversity.

Design-fault tolerance by means of design diversity is a concept that traces back to the very early age of informatics: see the quotations relative to Babbage's work in [Avi79, Ran87].

Closer to us, after its (re-)inception in the 70's [Elm72, Fis75, Ran75, Che78], software fault tolerance by design diversity has become a reality, as witnessed by the real-life systems and the experiments reported in [Vog88]. The currently privileged domain where design diversity is applied is the domain of safety-related systems. In such systems, an extreme attention is paid to *design faults*, where the term "design" is to be considered in a broad sense, from the system requirements to realization, during initial system production as well as in possible future modifications. Design faults are indeed a source of *common-mode* failures, which defeat fault tolerance strategies based on strict replication (thus intended to cope with physical faults), and have generally catastrophic consequences.

Pre-computer realizations of safety-related systems were classically calling for *diversified designs*, i.e., the production of two or more *variants* of a system or equipment intended to fulfill the same function through implementations based on different technologies. The aim of diversified designs is to minimize as much as possible the likelihood of occurrence of common-mode failures; a typical example is provided by a hard-wired electronic channel backed by an electro-mechanic or electro-pneumatic channel. In addition, the systems architecture was based on the *federation* of equipment implementing each one or several subfunctions of the system; one of the criteria for partitioning the system global function into subfunctions was that a failure of any equipment should be confined, and should not prevent the global function of the system to be performed, possibly in a degraded mode. When the transition was made to computer technology, the safety-related systems generally kept on the federation approach [Avi86]. Each subfunction was then implemented by a "complete" computer: hardware, executive and application software. Examples of this approach may be found in airplane flight control systems (e.g., the Boeing 757/767 [Spr80]) or nuclear plant monitoring (e.g., the SPIN system [Rem82]). A pre-requisite to confining computer failures is the auto-detection of the error(s) having led to failure. The auto-detection of errors due to design faults can be achieved through two main approaches:

- acceptance tests of the results under the form of executable assertions [And79, Mah84], which constitute a generalization and a formalization of the likelihood checks which are classical in process control;
- diversified design leading to two software variants whose results are compared; real-life examples are the Airbus A300 and A310 [Mar82, Rou86, Tra88], or the Swedish railways' interlocking system [Ste78, Hag86].

The federation approach generally leads to a very large number of processing elements, larger than what would be necessary in terms of computing power; for instance, the Boeing 757/767 flight management control system is composed of 80 distinct functional microprocessors (300 when redundancy is accounted for). Although such large numbers of processing elements are affordable due to the low cost of today's hardware, this approach suffers severe limitations, because of the subfunctions isolation, which inhibits the cooperative use of total computer resources:

- limitations to evolving towards new functionalities, due to a restricted exploitation of the software possibilities;
- limitations to the improvement of reliability and safety, due to rigid redundancy management schemes, induced by the necessity of local redundancies for the equipment.

An additional step towards a better use of the possibilities offered by computers consists in having several subfunctions implemented by software, supported by the same hardware equipment. Such an approach, which can be termed as integration, comes up against software failures, which are due to design faults only; adopting the integration approach thus requires software-fault tolerance. Moreover, a joint evolution of some safety-related systems (e.g., the flight control systems) is towards limited, if any, back-up possibilities, either manual or by non-computer technologies. This is of course an additional incitement to software fault tolerance, since a safe behavior of the system is then entirely depending on a reliable behavior of the software. Real-life examples are the NASA's space shuttle [She78, Cau81, Gar81], the Boeing 737/300 [You84], and the Airbus A320/A330/A340 [Tra88, Bri93].

This chapter elaborates on the work reported in [Lap87, Lap90, Lap94]. The remaining part of the chapter is composed of four Sections. Section 3.2 is devoted to a unified presentation of the approaches for software-fault tolerance; in addition to the recovery blocks and N-version programming methods, a third type of approach is identified from the careful examination of current, real-life systems: N self-checking programming. In Section 3.3, the three approaches to software fault tolerance are analyzed with respect to two viewpoints: dependability and cost. Section 3.4 is devoted to the definition and analysis of a set of hardware-and-software fault-tolerant architectures. Finally, Section 3.5 provides some concluding remarks.

3.2   APPROACHES TO SOFTWARE-FAULT TOLERANCE

Design diversity may be defined [Avi86] as the *production of two or more systems aimed at delivering the same service through separate designs and realizations.* The systems produced through the design diversity approach from a common service specification are termed *variants.* Besides the existence of at least two variants of a system, tolerance of design faults necessitates a *decider*, aimed at providing an — assumed as being — error-free result from the variant execution; the variant execution has to be performed from consistent initial conditions and inputs. The common specification has to address explicitly the *decision points*, i.e., a) when decisions have to be performed, and b) the data upon which decisions have to be performed, thus the data processed by the decider.

The two most well documented techniques for tolerating software design faults are the *recovery blocks* and the *N-version programming* that are described in detail in the two preceding chapters; we simply recall the main features of these techniques.

In the recovery block (RB) approach [Ran75, And81], the variants are termed alternates and the decider is an acceptance test, which is applied sequentially to the results provided by the alternates: if the results provided by the primary alternate do not satisfy the acceptance test, the secondary alternate is executed, and so on. In the N-version programming (NVP) approach [Che78, Avi85], the variants are termed versions, and the decider performs a vote on all versions' results.

The term *variant* is preferred here as a unifying term to the terms *alternate* or *version* for the following reasons:

- the term "alternate" reflects sequential execution, which is a feature specific to the recovery block approach;
- the term "version" has a widely accepted different meaning: successive versions of a system resulting from fault removal and/or functionality evolution; during the life of a diversity designed system, several versions of the variants are expected to be generated.

The RB and NVP approaches have led to a number of variations, such as the consensus recovery block [Sco87] that combines the decision procedures of NVP and RB, the $t/(n-1)$-variant programming scheme [Xu91] that uses a system-level diagnosis technique inherited from hardware diagnosis theory to isolate the faulty variant(s), or the self configuring optimistic programming technique [Bon93] that provides a trade-off between space and time redundancy needed to implement and execute the software variants.

The hardware-fault tolerant architectures equivalent to RB and to NVP are *stand-by sparing* (also termed as passive dynamic redundancy) and *N-modular redundancy* (also termed as static redundancy), respectively. The equivalent of a third approach to hardware-fault tolerance, *active dynamic redundancy* (very popular especially when based on self-checking components, as in the AT&T ESSs, Stratus systems, etc.), does not appear to have been described in the published literature as a generic technique for software-fault tolerance. However, self-checking programming has long been introduced (see, e.g., [Yau75]) where a self-checking program results from the addition of redundancy into a program to check its own dynamic behavior during execution. A self-checking software component is considered as resulting either from the association of an acceptance test to a variant, or from the association of two variants with a comparison algorithm. Fault tolerance is provided by the parallel execution of $N \geq 2$ self-checking components. At each execution of the system so constituted, a self-checking component is considered as being acting (in the sense of the delivered service, and thus of the effective delivery of the results to the controlled or monitored application); the other self-checking components are considered as — "hot" — spares. Upon failure of the acting component, service delivery is switched to a self-checking component previously considered as a spare; upon failure of a spare component, service keeps being delivered by the acting component. Error processing is thus performed through error detection and — possible — switching of the results. In what follows, we shall term such a software fault tolerance approach N *self-checking programming* (NSCP).

Our aim is not so much introducing a new software fault tolerance approach as providing a clear classification of the various approaches that may be considered. In fact, most of the real-life systems mentioned in the introduction do not actually implement either RB or NVP, but are based on self-checking software. For instance:

- the computer-controlled part of the flight control systems of the Airbus A300 and A310 and the Swedish railways' interlocking system are based on parallel execution of two variants whose results are compared, and they stop operation upon error detection;
- the flight control system of the Airbus A320 is based on two self-checking components, each of them being in turn based on parallel execution of two variants whose results are compared: tolerance to a single fault needs four variants[1].

Four additional comments on NSCP:

- when a self-checking software component is based on the association of two variants, one of the variants only may be written for the purpose of fulfilling the functions expected from the component, the other variant being an extended acceptance test; examples of such an approach are a) performing computations with a different accuracy, b) inverse function

---

[1] It is worth mentioning that the two self-checking components (each with two variants) do not exactly deliver the same service: when switching from the initially acting component to the other one, the critical functions are preserved whereas the non-critical functions are performed in a degraded mode.

when possible, or c) exploiting some intermediate results of the main variant as in the "certification-trail" approach [Sul90];

- as in N-version programming, the fact that the components are being executed in parallel[2] necessitates an input consistency mechanism;
- the acceptance tests associated to each variant or the comparison algorithms associated to a pair of variants can be the same, or specifically derived for each of them — from a common specification;
- it could be argued that NSCP is "parallel recovery block"; in our opinion, the RB concept cannot be reduced to the association of alternates together with an acceptance test: the — backward — recovery strategy is an integral part of it.

Figure 3.1 gives Petri-net execution models for the three identified strategies for software-fault tolerance. This figure is relative to the layer where diversification is performed, and thus deliberately omits some mechanisms, e.g., a) recovery points establishment in RB, b) input data consistency in NSCP and NVP, or c) replication of the decision algorithm (vote) on each of the sites supporting the versions in NVP. The most significant features of the strategies clearly appear on this figure:

- the differences in the execution schemes, i.e., sequential for RB and parallel for NSCP and NVP;
- the responsibility of each self-checking component in NSCP for the delivery or not of an acceptable result, whereas the judgment on result acceptability is cooperative in NVP.

Figure 3.2 summarizes the main characteristics of the strategies. Of particular interest, concerning the selection of a strategy for a given application, are the judgment on result acceptability, and the suspension of service delivery on error occurrence.

Figure 3.3 summarizes the main sources of overhead, from both structural and operational time viewpoints, involved in software fault tolerance, for tolerating one fault. In this table, the overheads caused by tests local to each variant such as input range checking, grossly wrong results, etc. are not mentioned: they are common to all approaches (in addition, they are — or should be — present in non fault-tolerant software systems as well).

3.3 ANALYSIS OF SOFTWARE FAULT TOLERANCE

This section is aimed at analyzing the approaches to software fault tolerance according to two viewpoints: dependability and cost.

3.3.1 Dependability Analysis

3.3.1.1 CLASSES OF FAULTS, ERRORS AND FAILURES TO BE CONSIDERED

We shall adopt here the classification and terminology of [Avi85], i.e., *independent faults* and *related faults*. Related faults result either from a fault specification — common to all the variants — or from dependencies in the separate designs and implementations. Related faults manifest under the form of *similar errors*, whereas independent faults usually cause *distinct*

---

[2] Although sequential execution of the variants in N-version programming can be theoretically considered, practical considerations of performance make this possibility as not very likely, except for experiments.

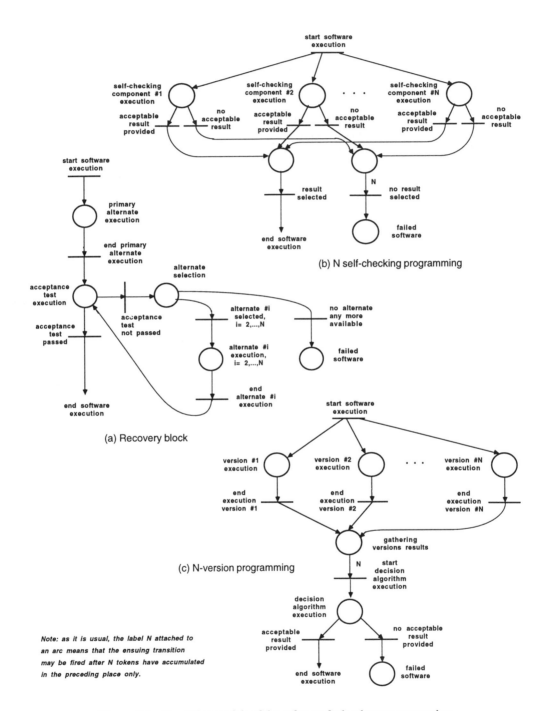

Figure 3.1 Execution models of the software-fault tolerance approaches

Method Name	Error Processing Technique		Judgement on Result Acceptability	Variant Execution Scheme	Consistency of Input Data	Suspension of Service Delivery during Error Processing	Number of Variants for Tolerance of f Sequential Faults
Recovery Blocks (RB)	Error Detection by Acceptance Test and Backward Recovery		Absolute, with respect to Specification	Sequential	Implicit, from Backward Recovery Principle	Yes, Duration Necessary for Executing One or More Variants	f+1
N Self-Checking Programming (NSCP)	Error Detection and Result Switching	Error Detection by Acceptance Test(s)	Specification	Parallel	Explicit, by Dedicated Mechanisms	Yes, Duration Necessary for Result Switching	2(f+1)
		Error Detection by Comparison	Relative, on				
N-Version Programming (NVP)	Vote		Variants Results			No	f+2

Figure 3.2 Main characteristics of the software-fault tolerance approaches

Method Name		Structural Overhead		Operational Time Overhead		
		Diversified Software Layer	Mechanisms (Layers Supporting the Diversified Software Layer)	Systematic		On Error Occurrence
				Decider	Variants Execution	
Recovery Blocks (RB)		One variant and One Acceptance Test	Recovery Cache	Acceptance Test Execution	Accesses to Recovery Cache	One Variant and Acceptance Test Execution
N Self-Checking Programming (NSCP)	Error Detection by Acceptance Tests	One variant and Two Acceptance Tests	Result Switching		Input Data Consistency and Variants Execution Synchronisation	Possible Result Switching
	Error Detection by Comparison	Three Variants	Comparators and Result Switching	Comparison Execution		
N-Version Programming (NVP)		Two Variants	Voters	Vote Execution		Usually neglectable

Figure 3.3 Overheads involved in software-fault tolerance for tolerating one fault (with respect to non fault-tolerant software)

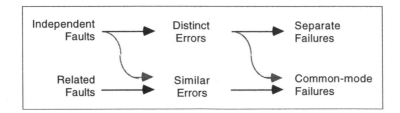

Figure 3.4   Classes of faults, errors and failures

errors, although it may happen [Avi84] that independent faults lead to similar errors. Similar errors lead to *common-mode failures*, and distinct errors usually cause *separate failures*. These definitions are illustrated by Figure 3.4.

Emphasis is put on the distinction between the different sources of failures: independent and related faults in variants and decider. In the analysis, it is assumed that only one type of fault(s), either independent or related, can be activated at each execution and produce error(s). In addition, the fault tolerance underlying mechanisms, i.e., a) recovery point establishment and restoration for the RB, and b) synchronization of the versions, cross check-points establishment and the decision mechanisms for NSCP and NVP, are not accounted for.

The failures will be classified according to two different viewpoints:

1. with respect to the type of faults whose activation has led to failure:

   - *separate failures*, which result from the activation of independent faults in the variants,
   - *common-mode failures*, which may result from the activation of either related faults or from independent faults in the decider; we shall distinguish among two types of related faults: a) related faults among the variants, and b) related faults between the variants and the decider.

2. with respect to the detection of inability to deliver acceptable results:

   - *detected failures*, when no acceptable result is identified by the decider and no output result is delivered,
   - *undetected failures*, when erroneous results are delivered.

It is assumed in the sequel that the probability of fault activation is identical for all the variants of a given architecture. This assumption is made to simplify the notation and do not alter the significance of the obtained results (the generalization to the case where the characteristics of the variants are distinguished can be easily deduced).

3.3.1.2   ANALYSIS OF RECOVERY BLOCK BEHAVIOR

Figure 3.5 presents the related- or independent-fault combinations that may affect the RB architecture made up of two alternates — a primary (P) and a secondary (S) — and of an acceptance test (AT). The table also gives the associated probabilities of fault activation and the resulting type of failures (either, detected or undetected) when the faults are not tolerated. For the sake of conciseness, when several permutations of the faulty software components correspond to an identical fault characterization, only one fault combination is shown, which is identified by symbol "◇" attached to the fault combination number, and the symbol "( )" indicates the variants included in the permutations. For example, fault combination

#	Fault Combination P	S	AT	Characterization and Probability	Failure	
$1^\diamond$	(i)	( )		Independent fault in one variant: $2\,q_{I,RB}(1 - q_{I,RB})$	—	—
2	i	i		Independent faults in the two variants: $(q_{I,RB})^2$	S	D
$3^\diamond$	(*)	(*)	i	Independent fault in the AT: $\quad q_{ID,RB}$	CM	D
4	r	r		Related fault between the two variants: $q_{2V,RB}$	CM	D
$5^\diamond$	(r)	( )	r	Related fault between the variants and the AT: $q_{RVD,RB}$	CM	U
6	r	r	r			

Faults: ☐ : no fault, [i] : independent, [*] : no fault or independent, [r] : related

$\#^\diamond$: several permutations, [( )] : variants included in the permutations

Failures: S: Separate, CM: Common-Mode; D: Detected, U: Undetected

Figure 3.5   Recovery blocks fault-failure analysis

$1^\diamond$ of Figure 3.5 covers two permutations, each having the same probability of activation: $q_{I,RB}(1 - q_{I,RB})$, where $q_{I,RB}$ denotes the probability of activation of an independent fault in one of the variants of the recovery blocks. Furthermore, fault combination $1^\diamond$ is tolerated and thus does not lead to the failure of the RB architecture.

It is assumed that related faults between the variants manifest under the form of similar errors. However, we assume that independent faults in the variants manifest under the form of distinct errors[3]. In particular, this results in the fact that the activation of two or more independent faults is either tolerated (fault combination 2) or detected (fault combinations $3^\diamond$, 4, $5^\diamond$ and 6).

Fault combination $3^\diamond$ covers all the cases when an independent fault is activated in the decider of the recovery blocks: the acceptance test; all the cases are grouped in the probability denoted by $q_{ID,RB}$. It is assumed that the AT behaves consistently with respect to each variant (no error compensation), thus when an independent fault is activated in the AT, a detected failure occurs, since undetected failures characterized by the activation of a fault in the AT are the consequences of the activation of a related fault between the variants and the decider (fault combinations $5^\diamond$ and 6).

In the case of fault combination 4, the associated probability of activation, denoted $q_{RV,RB}$, corresponds to a related fault between the two variants of the RB.

Probability $q_{RVD,RB}$ covers all the cases of activation of a related fault between the variants and the decider (fault combinations $5^\diamond$ and 6). This corresponds to the only fault combinations that lead to an undetected failure for RB.

---

[3] Although they could be traced to independent faults, faults leading to similar errors are not distinguishable at the execution level from related faults and thus they will be merged into the category of related faults.

3.3.1.3   ANALYSIS OF N SELF-CHECKING PROGRAMMING BEHAVIOR

The NSCP architecture is made up of 2 self-checking components (SCC), each of them being made up of 2 variants and a comparator C. Although all 4 variants Vi, $i = 1, \ldots, 4$, are executed simultaneously, only one SCC is *acting*, i.e., actually delivering output results, the other being used as a spare. The two probabilities of fault activation for the two comparators are assumed to be identical.

Figure 3.6 presents the related- or independent-fault combinations that may affect the NSCP architecture, their associated probabilities of activation and the resulting type of failure, if they are not tolerated. For sake of conciseness, the comparators have been omitted in the description of the fault combinations they are not involved in. The presentation of the fault combinations and the notation used for the associated probability of activation are analogous to the ones used for RB; in the sequel we focus essentially on discussing some points that are specific to the NSCP architecture.

As the comparators are assumed to be identical from the failure probability viewpoint, a) the activation of an independent fault in the comparator is fully characterized by the fault combination 6, which leads to a detected failure, and b) the only case of related fault between the variants and the comparators to be considered is identified by fault combination 12.

It is important to note that, although they correspond to the activation of a related fault between two variants, the fault combinations 7 and $9^{\diamond}$ are respectively, tolerated and detected, by the NSCP architecture. All other related-fault combinations result in undetected failures.

3.3.1.4   ANALYSIS OF N-VERSION PROGRAMMING BEHAVIOR

Figure 3.7 presents the related- or independent-fault combinations that may affect the NVP architecture.

In this case, it appears that all multiple independent fault combinations and an independent fault in the decider are detected (fault combinations $2^{\diamond}$ to 4), and that all related fault combinations lead to undetected failures (fault combinations $5^{\diamond}$ to 7).

3.3.1.5   CHARACTERIZATION OF THE PROBABILITIES OF FAILURE

Figure 3.8 gives the respective contribution of the separate/common-mode and de-tected/undetected failure viewpoints to the probability of failure of the considered software fault-tolerant architectures.

As could be expected, the table shows that, although the detected failures may correspond to both separate failures or common mode failures, the undetected failures correspond exclusively to common mode failures.

The comparison of the various failure probabilities of Figure 3.8 is difficult due to the difference in the values of the parameters characterizing each architecture. However, it is possible to make some interesting general remarks.

Although a large number of experiments have been carried out to analyze NVP, no quantitative study has been reported on the reliability associated to the decider, except for some qualitative remarks concerning a) the granularity of the decision with respect to the variables checked [Tso87], b) the magnitude of the allowed discrepancy [Kel88], and c) the investigation of the behavior of various voter schemes reported in [Lor89]. However, it has to be noted that the probabilities associated to the deciders can be significantly different. Due to

#	Fault Combination acting SCC spare SCC [V1] [V2] [C] [V3] [V4] [C]	Characterization and Probability	Failure	
$1^\diamond$	[(i)] [( )] [ ] [( )] [( )] [ ]	Independent fault in one variant: $4\ q_{I,NSCP}\ (1\text{-}q_{I,NSCP})^3$	—	—
$2^\diamond$	[(i i)] [ ] [( )] [ ]	Indep. faults in two variants belonging, either to the acting or to the spare SCCs: $2\ (q_{I,NSCP})^2\ (1 - q_{I,NSCP})^2$	—	—
$3^\diamond$	[(i)] [( )] [ ] [(i)] [( )] [ ]	Independent faults in two variants belonging to distinct SCCs: $4\ (q_{I,NSCP})^2\ (1 - q_{I,NSCP})^2$	S	D
$4^\diamond$	[(i)] [(i)] [ ] [(i)] [( )] [ ]	Ind. fault in three variants: $4\ (q_{I,NSCP})^3\ (1\text{-}q_{I,NSCP})$	S	D
5	[i] [i] [ ] [i] [i] [ ]	Independent faults in four variants: $(q_{I,NSCP})^4$	S	D
6	[*] [*] [i] [*] [*] [i]	Independent fault in the comparator: $q_{ID,NSCP}$	CM	D
7	[ ] [ ] [ ] [r] [r] [ ]	Related fault between the variants belonging to the spare SCC: $q_{2V,NSCP}$	—	—
8	[r] [r] [ ] [ ] [ ] [ ]	Related fault between the variants belonging to the acting SCC: $q_{2V,NSCP}$	CM	U
$9^\diamond$	[(r)] [( )] [ ] [(r)] [( )] [ ]	Related fault between the variants belonging to distinct SCCs: $4\ q_{2V,NSCP}$	CM	D
$10^\diamond$	[(r)] [(r)] [ ] [(r)] [( )] [ ]	Related fault between three variants: $4\ q_{3V,NSCP}$	CM	U
11	[r] [r] [ ] [r] [r] [ ]	Related fault between four variants: $q_{4V,NSCP}$	CM	U
12	[r] [r] [r] [r] [r] [r]	Related fault between the four variants and the comparator: $q_{RVD,NSCP}$	CM	U

Faults: [ ] : no fault, [i] : independent, [*] : no fault or independent, [r] : related

$\#^\diamond$: several permutations, [( )] : variants included in the permutations

Failures: S: Separate, CM: Common-Mode; D: Detected, U: Undetected

Figure 3.6 N self-checking programming fault-failure analysis

#	Fault Combination $\quad$ V1 $\quad$ V2 $\quad$ V3 $\quad$ V	Characterization and Probability	Failure	
$1^\Diamond$	(i) ( ) ( ) ☐	Independent fault in one variant: $$q_{I,NVP}(1 - q_{I,NVP})^2$$	—	—
$2^\Diamond$	(i) (i) ( ) ☐	Independent faults in two variants: $$3\,(q_{I,NVP})^2\,(1-q_{I,NVP})$$	S	D
3	i i i ☐	Independent faults in the three variants: $$(q_{I,NVP})^3$$	S	D
4	* * * i	Independent fault in the voter: $\quad q_{ID,NVP}$	CM	D
$5^\Diamond$	(i) (i) ( ) ☐	Related fault between two variants: $\quad 3\,q_{2V,NVP}$	CM	U
6	r r r ☐	Related fault between the three variants: $$q_{3V,NVP}$$	CM	U
7	r r r r	Related fault between the three variants and the voter: $\quad q_{RVD,NVP}$	CM	U

Faults: ☐ : no fault, i : independent, * : no fault or independent, r : related

$\#^\Diamond$: several permutations, ( ) : variants included in the permutations

Failures: S: Separate, CM: Common-Mode; D: Detected, U: Undetected

Figure 3.7   N-version programming fault-failure analysis

Arch. "X"	Probability of Failure: $q_{S,X} = q_{S,D,X} + q_{S,U,X}$	
	Detected Failure: $q_{S,D,X}$	Undetected Failure: $q_{S,U,X}$
RB	S: $(q_{I,RB})^2$ CM: $q_{ID,RB} + q_{2V,RB}$	CM: $q_{RVD,RB}$
NSCP	S: $4\,(q_{I,NSCP})^2[1 - q_{I,NSCP} + \dfrac{(q_{I,NSCP})}{4}]$ CM: $q_{ID,NSCP} + 4\,q_{2V,NSCP}$	CM: $q_{2V,NSCP} + 4\,q_{3V,NSCP}$ $+ q_{4V,NSCP} + q_{RVD,NSCP}$
NVP	S: $3\,(q_{I,NVP})^2\,[1 - \dfrac{2}{3}\,q_{I,NVP}]$ CM: $q_{ID,NVP}$	CM: $3\,q_{2V,NVP} + q_{3V,NVP}$ $+ q_{RVD,NVP}$

Figure 3.8   Detected/undetected failures and separate/common-mode failures

the generality and the simplicity of the functions performed by the deciders of the NSCP (comparison) and NVP (voting) architectures, it is likely that these probabilities be ranked as follows:

$$q_{ID,NSCP} \leq q_{ID,NVP} \ll q_{ID,RB} \text{ and } q_{RVD,NSCP} \leq q_{RVD,NVP} \ll q_{RVD,RB} \quad (3.1)$$

In the case of separate failures, the influence of the activation of independent faults differs significantly: for RB, the probability of separate failure is equal to the square of the probability of activation of independent faults, whereas it is almost the triple for NVP and the quadruple for NSCP[4]. This difference results from the number of variants and the type of decision used.

The fact that all related faults in NVP result in undetected failures does not mean that RB and NSCP are the only architectures that enable some related-fault combinations to be detected. Such a singularity is due to the limitation to the analysis of software redundancy for tolerating one fault[5].

Each entry of the table of Figure 3.8 summarizes the probabilities of detected/undetected failure of the software fault-tolerant architectures considered:

- $q_{S,D,X}$ = P {detected failure of the software fault-tolerant architecture X | execution},
- $q_{S,U,X}$ = P {undetected failure of the software fault-tolerant architecture X | execution},
- $q_{S,X}$ = $q_{S,D,X}$ + $q_{S,U,X}$ = P {failure of the software fault-tolerant architecture X | execution}.

Related faults between the variants has no impact on the probability of undetected failure of the RB architecture, whereas, it is the major contribution for NSCP and NVP. However, the comparison of the respective probabilities of undetected failures is not an easy task.

The results obtained agree with what has previously been reported in the literature, i.e., that the reliability of a fault-tolerant software is dominated by related faults (see e.g., [Kni86, Eck91]). This is hardly unexpected for anyone who is familiar with fault tolerance: although the underlying phenomena are different, the limit due to related faults can be compared to the usual limit in reliability for hardware-fault tolerance brought about by coverage deficiencies (either from a theoretical [Bou69, Arn73] or from a practical [Toy78] viewpoint). However, the results show that design diversity indeed brings in a significant reliability improvement as the impact of independent faults which are the major source of failure in traditional — non fault-tolerant — software, become negligible. In addition, it has been shown experimentally that some specification faults are in fact detected during the execution of multi-variant software (see e.g., [Bis86, Tra88]), thus reducing the proportion of related faults leading to failure in a multi-variant software.

3.3.2 Cost Analysis

This section is aimed at giving an estimation of the additional cost introduced by fault tolerance. Since design diversity obviously affects costs differently according to the life-cycle phases, the starting point is the cost distribution among the various activities of the life-cycle for a classical, non fault-tolerant, software. This is provided by Figure 3.9, where:

---

[4] Due to the usually low value of the $q_{I,X}$ factors, the influence of separate failures is practically limited to the consideration of the $(q_{I,X})^2$ terms.

[5] It is worth noting that increasing the number of versions would also enable some related faults to be detected by NVP (e.g., see Section 3.4.5.4).

Activities		Mnemonic	Life-Cycle Cost Breakdown [Zel 79]	Maintenance Cost Breakdown [Ram 84]			Multipliers for Critical Applications [Boe 81]	Cost Distribution	
				Corrective	Adaptive	Perfective		Development	Development and Maintenance
D e v e l o p m e n t	Requirements	R	3 %				1.3	8 %	6 %
	Specification	S	3 %			55 %	1.3	8 %	7 %
	Design	D	5 %	20 %	25 %		1.3	13 %	14 %
	Implementation	I	7 %				1.3	19 %	19 %
	V & V	V	15 %				1.8	52 %	54 %
Maintenance			67 %	100 %				100 %	100 %
			100 %						

Figure 3.9 Software cost elements for non fault-tolerant software

a) The life-cycle model that we have adopted is a simplified one [Ram84], an interesting feature of which with respect to our purpose is that all the activities relating to verification and validation (V&V) are grouped separately.

b) The three categories of maintenance are defined according to [Swa76], and cover all the operational life:

- corrective maintenance concerns fault removal; it thus involves design, implementation and testing types of activities;
- adaptive maintenance adjusts software to environmental changes; it thus involves also specification activity;
- perfective maintenance is aimed at improving the software's function; it thus actually concerns software's evolution, and as such involves activities similar to all of the activities of the development, starting from modified requirements.

c) The cost breakdown for the life-cycle [Zel79] and for maintenance [Ram84] are general, and do not address a specific class of software; however, since we are concerned with critical applications, some multiplicative factors have to be accounted for, which depend upon the considered activity [Boe81].

d) The last two columns, which have been derived from the data displayed in the other columns, give the cost distribution among the activities of the life-cycle in two cases: development only, development and maintenance.

From this table, it appears that maintenance does not affect significantly the cost *distribution* over the other activities of the life-cycle (the discrepancy is likely to be lower that the accuracy of the obtained figures); so, considering in the following one case only, say the development case as it refers to the *production* of software, is general, and covers also the whole life-cycle as we are concerned with relative costs.

To determine the cost of a fault-tolerant software, it is necessary to introduce factors a) enabling the overheads associated with the decision points and the decider(s) to be accounted for, as well as b) enabling the cost reduction in V&V induced by the commonalities among variants to be accounted for. These commonalities include actual V&V activities, such as back-to-back testing, and V&V tools, such as test harnesses. An accurate estimation of such

Number of faults tolerated	Fault Tolerance Method		N	$\left(\dfrac{C_{FT}}{C_{NFT}}\right)_{min}$	$\left(\dfrac{C_{FT}}{C_{NFT}}\right)_{max}$	$\left(\dfrac{C_{FT}}{C_{NFT}}\right)_{av}$	$\left(\dfrac{C_{FT}}{N\,C_{NFT}}\right)_{av}$
1	Recovery Blocks		2	1.33	2.17	1.75	.88
	N Self-Checking Programming	Acceptance Test					
		Comparison	4	2.24	3.77	3.01	.75
	N-Version Programming		3	1.78	2.71	2.25	.75
2	Recovery Blocks		3	1.78	2.96	2.37	.79
	N Self-Checking Programming	Acceptance Test					
		Comparison	6	3.71	5.54	4.63	.77
	N-Version Programming		4	2.24	3.77	3.01	.75

Figure 3.10   Cost of fault-tolerant software vs. non fault-tolerant software

factors is out of reach given the current state of the art; we however think that it is possible to give reasonable ranges of variations. We introduce the following factors:

- r: multiplier associated with the decision points, with $1 < r < 1.2$;
- s: multiplier associated with the decider, with $1 < s < 1.1$ for NVP and NSCP when error detection is performed through comparison, and $1 < s < 1.3$ for RB and NSCP when error detection is performed through acceptance tests; this difference is aimed at reflecting the different natures of the decider, i.e., the fact that it is specific in the case of acceptance test, whereas it is generic in the cases of comparison and of vote;
- u: proportion of the testing activities which are performed once for all variants (e.g., provision for test environments and harnesses), with $0.2 < u < 0.5$;
- v: proportion of the testing activities of each variant which take advantage of the existence of several variants (e.g., back-to-back testing), with $0.3 < v < 0.6$;
- w: cost reduction factor for the testing activities performed in common for several variants, with $0.2 < w < 0.8$.

The cost of a fault-tolerant software (C_{FT}) with respect to the cost of a non fault-tolerant software (C_{NFT}) is then given by the following expression:

$$C_{FT}/C_{NFT} = R + rsS + [Nr + (s-1)](D + I) + r\{us + (1-u)N[vw + (1-v)]\}V$$

where R,S,D,I, and V refer to the life-cycle activities of Figure 3.9, and N is the number of variants.

Figure 3.10 gives the ranges for the ratio C_{FT} / C_{NFT}, as well as the average values and the average values per variant. In this table, we do not make a distinction between RB and NSCP with error detection by acceptance test: their respective differences with respect to the cost issues are likely to be masked by our abstract cost model.

The results displayed in Figure 3.10 enable the quantification of the usual qualitative statement according to which an N variant software is less costly than N times a non fault-tolerant software. In addition, the figures that appeared previously in the literature fall within the ranges displayed in the table:

- the overhead for RB, for 2 variants, was estimated at 60% for the experiment conducted at the University of Newcastle upon Tyne [And85], that is a ratio C_{FT}/C_{NFT} equal to 1.6,
- the cost of NVP, for 3 variants, in the PODS project [Bis86] was estimated to 2.26 times the cost of a single variant program.

3.4 DEFINITION AND ANALYSIS OF HARDWARE-AND-SOFTWARE FAULT TOLERANT ARCHITECTURES

This section presents examples of architectures providing tolerance to both hardware and software faults. Emphasis will be put on: a) the dependencies among the software and hardware fault tolerance and b) the impact of the solid and soft character of the software faults, related to their persistence with respect to the computation process and their recoverability, in the definition of the architectures.

Two levels of fault tolerance requirements are successively investigated: a) architectures tolerating a single fault, and b) architectures tolerating two consecutive faults[6]. The architectures will be identified by means of a condensed expression of the form: X/i/j/..., were label X stands for the acronym of the software fault tolerance method, X ∈ RB, NSCP, NVP, i is the number of hardware faults tolerated and j is the number of software faults tolerated. Further labels will be added to this expression when necessary.

Due to the scope of this chapter, the architectures are described from a deliberately highly abstracted view. As a consequence, distinguishing features, such as a) the overhead involved by inter-component communication for synchronization, decision-making, data consistency, etc., and b) the differences in memory space necessary for each architecture, are not addressed. More specific attempts to the definition of hardware-and-software fault-tolerant architectures have already appeared in the literature, e.g., the work reported in [Kim84, Kim89] which extends the recovery block approach, or in [Lal88] which is based on N-version programming.

3.4.1 Persistence and Recoverability of Software Faults

Consideration of the persistence criterion leads to distinguish *solid* and *soft* faults. Such a distinction is usual in hardware, where solid faults are usually synonymous to permanent faults, and soft faults are usually synonymous to temporary faults, either transient or intermittent. The solidity or softness character of a fault plays an important role in fault tolerance: a component affected by a permanent fault has to be made passive after fault manifestation, whereas a component affected by a soft fault can be used in subsequent executions after error recovery has taken place.

Let us now consider software faults of *operational* programs, i.e., programs that have been thoroughly debugged, where the remaining sources of problems are likely to be more fault *conditions* rather than solid faults: limit conditions, race conditions, or strange underlying hardware conditions. Because of a slight change in the execution context, the corresponding fault conditions may not be gathered, and the software may not fail again. The notion of

---

[6] These requirements can be related respectively, to the classical Fail Op/Fail Safe and Fail Op/Fail Op/Fail Safe requirements used in the aerospace community for the hardware fault tolerance.

temporary fault may thus be extended to software, and it has been noted in practice: it has been introduced in [Elm72], has been devoted much attention in [Gra86] and is being used as a basis for increasing diversity among several variants of the same software through the concept of "data diversity" (see, e.g., [Amm87, Chr94]). A temporary software fault may then be characterized as a fault whose likelihood of manifestation recurrence upon re-execution is low enough to be neglected.

Another, important, consideration to account for is the notion of local and global variables for the components, in relation with error recovery actions (in the broad sense of the term, including the actions to be performed so that a failed variant in NSCP and in NVP may take part to future executions [Tso86]). Let us call a *diversity unit* the program comprised between two decision points. As a general rule, it can be said that recovery requires that the diversity units have to be procedures (in the sense that their activation and behavior do not depend on any internal permanent data). Stated in other terms, all the data necessary for the processing tasks of a diversity unit have to be global data. The globality of the data for a diversity unit may:

• originate directly from the nature of the application; an example is provided by the monitoring of a physical process (e.g., nuclear reactor protection [Gme79]) where tasks are initialized by acquisition of sensor data, and do not utilize data produced in previous processing steps;
• result from the system partitioning, either naturally, or from the transformation of local data into global data, at the expense in the latter case of an overhead and of a decrease in diversity (the specification of the decision points has to be made more precise); a — deliberately over-simplified — example is provided by a filtering function which would constitute a diversity unit: the past samples should be made part of the global data.

The preceding discussion applies to all the software fault tolerance methods. It is however noteworthy that some arrangements can be made to this general rule in some specific, application-dependent, cases. Examples are as follows:

• if the above-mentioned overhead cannot be afforded, or if it is estimated that transforming local data into global data is a too severe decrease in diversity, an alternative solution exists for NSCP and NVP: eliminate from further processing a failed variant;
• the application of state estimation techniques issued from the control theory (see e.g., [Cag85]).

As a summary, we shall adopt in the sequel the following definitions for soft and solid faults:

• a *soft* software fault is a fault which is temporary and recoverable,
• a *solid* software fault is a fault which is permanent or which cannot be recovered.

Finally, we implicitly considered that decision points were recovery points. In NSCP and NVP, a distinction in the decision points can be made between those which are cross-check points and those which are recovery points, the latter being possibly in a smaller number than the former [Tso86].

3.4.2   Design Decisions when Implementing Design Diversity

Among the many issues that have to be dealt with design diversity [Avi85, Avi86], two of them are especially important — and correlated — *with respect to architectural considerations*: a) the number of variants, and b) the level of fault tolerance application.

Independently from any economic consideration (see Section 3.3.2), the *number of variants* to be produced for a given software fault tolerance method is directly related to the number of faults to be tolerated (see Figure 3.2). It will be seen in this section that the soft or solid character of the software faults has a significant impact on the architecture only when dealing with the tolerance of more than one fault. It has also to be reminded that an architecture tolerating a solid fault is also able to tolerate a (theoretically) infinite sequence of soft faults — provided there is no fault coincidence phenomenon. It is noteworthy that the relation between the likelihood of such faults and the number of variants is not simple: whether increasing the number of variants will increase or decrease the number of related faults depends on several factors, some of them being antagonistic [Avi84, Kni86]. However, in NVP, an incentive to increase the number of variants is that two similar errors can outvote a good result in a three-version scheme, whereas they would be detected in a four-version scheme, thus providing an increase in safety (situations contrary to safety being defined as corresponding to an undetected error).

The *level of application of fault tolerance* encompasses two aspects: a) at what level of detail should be performed the decomposition of the system into components that will be diversified?, and b) which layers (application software, executive, hardware) have to be diversified?

The answer to the first question should at first sight result from a trade-off between two opposite considerations: on one hand, small size components enable a better mastering of the decision algorithms; on the other hand, large size components favor diversity. In addition, the decision points are "non diversity" points (and synchronization points for NSCP and NVP); as such, they have to be limited: decision points are *a priori* necessary for the interactions with environment only (sensor data acquisition, delivery of orders to actuators, interactions with operators, etc.). However, additional compromises may result from performance considerations.

Concerning the *layers where to apply diversity*, the methods mentioned can be applied to any of the software layers, either of application software, or of the executive software. They can also be applied to the hardware layer(s) [Mar82, Rou86]. The states — with respect to the computation process — of distinct variants are different. A consequence is that when the variants are executed in parallel (NSCP and NVP), thus on distinct (redundant) hardware, diversity of a given layer leads to states of the underlying layers that are different, even if they are not diversified — except of course at the decision points. A decision concerning whether layers underlying the application software have to be diversified, should include additional considerations, such as determining the influence of the portions of executive software and of hardware that are specifically designed for the considered application, and what confidence to place on experience validation for those parts which are off-the-shelf.

3.4.3   Structuring Principles for the Definition of Architectures

Structuring is a prerequisite to the mastering of complexity. This is especially true when dealing with fault tolerance [And81, Ran84, Neu86].

A usual, and useful, principle when dealing with hardware-fault tolerance is that the fault tolerance mechanisms should go along, and respect, the structuring of a system into layers [Sie82]. Especially, it is desirable that each layer be provided with fault tolerance mechanisms aimed at processing the errors produced in the considered layer, with respect a) to performance considerations in terms of time to recover from an error and b) to the damages created by error propagation. Implementation of this principle at the hardware layer when dealing with software fault tolerance requires that the redundant hardware components are in the same state with respect to the computation process in the absence of error. Such a condition can obviously be satisfied only if the variants are executed sequentially, i.e., in the RB approach.

However, the diagnosis of hardware faults may be made possible by taking advantage of the syndromes provided by the decider(s) of the considered software fault tolerance method considered.

Another useful structuring mechanism is the notion of *error confinement area* [Sie82]. This notion cannot be separated from the architectural elements considered. In relation with the scope of this chapter, the architectural elements considered will be:

- the elements providing the services necessary for an application software to be executed, i.e., hardware and the associated executive software; such elements will be termed — abusively, in the sake of conciseness — as *hardware components*;
- the *variants* of the application software.

Consideration of both hardware and software faults leads to distinguish hardware error confinement areas (HECAs) and software error confinement areas (SECAs). In our case, a HECA will cover at least one hardware component and a SECA will cover at least one software variant. It is noteworthy that, due to our definition of hardware component, a HECA corresponds to the part of the architecture that is made passive after occurrence of a solid hardware fault, and can thus be interpreted as a Line Replaceable Unit (LRU).

3.4.4 Architectures Tolerating a Single Fault

Three architectures are considered that correspond to the implementation of the three software fault-tolerance methods of Section 3.2. Figure 3.11 illustrates the configurations of the SECAs and HECAs for each case. The intersections between the SECAs and the HECAs characterize the software and hardware fault tolerance dependencies of the architectures.

3.4.4.1 THE RB/1/1 ARCHITECTURE

This architecture is obtained by the duplication of the RB composed of two variants on two hardware components. Two variants and their associated instances of the acceptance test constitute two distinct SECAs and intersect each HECA. Accordingly, each hardware component is software fault tolerant due to the RB method: the independent faults in a variant are tolerated, while the related faults between the variants are detected; however related faults between each variant and the acceptance test cannot be tolerated neither detected.

The hardware components operate in hot standby redundancy and execute at each time the same variant. This allows the design of a high coverage concurrent comparison between the results of the acceptance tests and the results provided by the hardware components to handle specifically the hardware faults. It is noteworthy that when a discrepancy between the results of the hardware components is detected during the execution of the primary alternate or of the

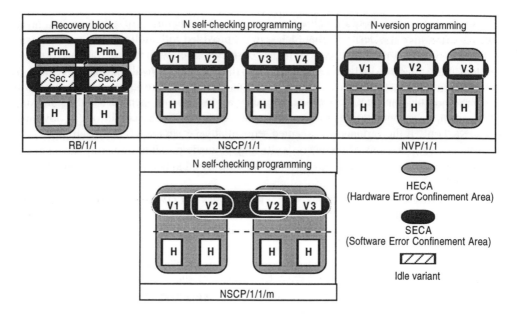

Figure 3.11   Architectures tolerating a single fault

acceptance test, it might be interesting to call for the execution of the secondary to tolerate the fault (should the fault be a soft fault). If the discrepancy would persist (what would be the case upon manifestation of a solid fault), the failed HECA could be identified by running diagnosis programs on each HECA, thus, the continuity of service would be ensured and the failed HECA made passive.

It is worth noting that after this hardware degradation, a) the architecture is still software fault tolerant, and b) the subsequent hardware faults can be detected either by means of the acceptance test or by the periodic execution of the diagnosis.

3.4.4.2   EXAMPLES OF NSCP/1/1 ARCHITECTURES

The basic architecture (NSCP/1/1 in Figure 3.11) is made up of:

- four hardware components grouped in two pairs in hot standby redundancy, each pair of hardware components forming a HECA;
- four variants grouped in two pairs; each pair constitutes a software self-checking component, error detection being carried out by comparison; each pair forms a SECA.

Each SECA is associated to a HECA. The comparison of the computational states of the hardware components cannot be directly performed due to the diversification imposed by the variants; however, the comparison between the results of each pair of variants covers also the two hardware components composing each HECA with respect to the hardware faults (including design faults); a HECA is thus also a hardware self-checking component.

In case of discrepancy between the results provided by the paired variants in one HECA, irrespective of the type of fault, the associated HECA is possibly switched out and the results are delivered by the other HECA. Should the discrepancy occurs repeatedly, characterizing thus, a solid hardware fault, then the designated HECA would be made passive. The degraded structure after this passivation still enables both software and hardware faults to be detected.

Besides the nominal tolerance of an independent software fault, the architecture ensures supplementary tolerance and detection features: a) the tolerance of two simultaneous independent faults in a SECA, b) the detection of a related fault among two variants (each pertaining to one of the two disjoint SECAs) and c) the detection of three or four simultaneous independent software faults.

The NSCP/1/1 architecture corresponds to the principle of the architecture implemented in the Airbus A320 [Rou86]. However, in some applications, the requirement of four variants would be prohibitive; it is worth noting that a modified architecture (NSCP/1/1/m) can be obtained, based on three variants only (Figure 3.11).

The major difference in error processing between the NSCP/1/1 and NCSP/1/1/m architectures can be identified when considering the activation of a software fault in V2. It is important to note that this would result in a discrepancy in both self-checking components, thus implying an associated SECA covering all the four software components and preventing any software fault tolerance. As this is the only event that can lead to such a syndrome (under the hypothesis of single independent fault), the "correct" result is immediately available as the one provided by V1 or V3, hence, the SECA associated to V2 on Figure 3.11. However, as a consequence, all the fault tolerance and detection capabilities of the NSCP/1/1 architecture termed above "supplementary" are lost.

3.4.4.3   THE NVP/1/1 ARCHITECTURE

The NVP/1/1 architecture is a direct implementation of the NVP method. It is made up of three hardware components, each running a distinct variant. The handling of the hardware faults (including design faults) and of the software faults is common and performed at the software layer by the decider of the NVP method. Besides the tolerance to an independent fault in a single variant, the architecture allows the detection of independent faults in two or three variants.

The problem of discrimination between hardware and software faults, so that the passiva tion of a hardware component occurs only upon occurrence of a solid fault, gives an example of the dependency between software and hardware fault tolerance. Due to the soft character considered for the software faults, a diagnosis of (solid) hardware fault could be easily implemented as the monitoring of a repeatedly disagreeing hardware component. After passivation of the failed hardware component, the decider has to be reconfigured as a comparator, which thus ensures a fail-safe characteristic to the architecture in case of a subsequent activation of a hardware or a software fault.

3.4.5   Architectures Tolerating Two Consecutive Faults

When dealing with the tolerance of two faults, the distinction between soft and solid software faults comes immediately into play:

- if the software faults can be considered as soft faults, then the number of variants is unchanged with respect to the architectures aimed at tolerating one fault; so these architectures will be of the type X/2/1, $X \in \{RB, NSCP, NVP\}$,

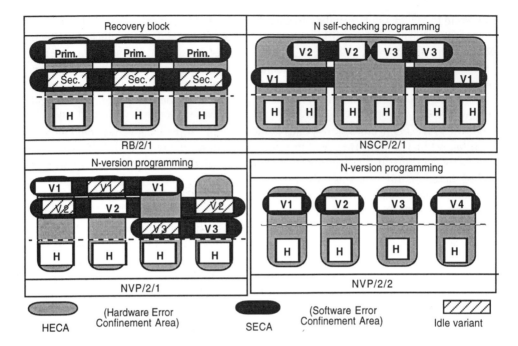

Figure 3.12   Architectures tolerating two consecutive faults

- if the software faults are to be considered as solid faults, then the number of variants must be increased in order to cope with the discarding of a failed variant from further execution; so the corresponding architectures will be of the type X/2/2.

The considered architectures for the tolerance of two faults are displayed on Figure 3.12. The first three architectures (RB/2/1, NSCP/2/1 and NVP/2/1) are characterized by the tolerance of two hardware faults and of a single software fault. The impact of the solid character of the software faults is illustrated in the case of an architecture using the NVP method; this structure (NVP/2/2) is designed to tolerate two consecutive (solid) faults in hardware or software.

3.4.5.1   THE RB/2/1 ARCHITECTURE

This architecture is made up of three hardware components arranged in TMR. Software-fault tolerance capability is unchanged with respect to RB/1/1 architecture. Upon solid hardware fault manifestation, the architecture is degraded through the passivation of the corresponding hardware component, thus resulting in an architecture analogous to the RB/1/1 architecture.

Accordingly, even if they are basically useless in the handling of the first hardware fault, local diagnosis must be incorporated in each hardware component.

3.4.5.2   THE NSCP/2/1 ARCHITECTURE

This architecture is a direct extension of the NSCP/1/1/m architecture. A supplementary duplex HECA is added that supports a software self-checking component made up of two variants. A symmetric distribution of the three SECAs among the three HECAs is thus obtained. It is noteworthy that all the variants are duplicated; this allows an instantaneous diagnosis of the hardware faults from the syndrome obtained by comparing the results delivered by all the hardware components. The architecture allows also the detection of simultaneous independent faults in two or three variants.

3.4.5.3 THE NVP/2/1 ARCHITECTURE

The NVP/2/1 architecture is derived from the NVP/1/1 architecture by addition of a hardware component without introducing another variant. To maintain the software-fault tolerance capability after passivation of one hardware component, it is necessary that at least two instances of each variant pertain to two distinct HECAs. Thus six variant instances have to be distributed among the four HECAs. A possible configuration[7] is the one shown in Figure 3.13.

Among the two distinct variants associated to each HECA, one is active and the other is idle. At a given step, three hardware components execute three distinct variants and the fourth hardware component executes a replica of one of the variants (V1 in this configuration). Besides the tolerance to an independent software fault, the architecture allows the detection of two or three simultaneous independent faults.

The tolerance of an independent fault can be obtained by a decision based on a vote in which the knowledge that two variants are identical is incorporated. The unbalanced numbers of executions of the variants can be used to improve the diagnosability with respect to the hardware faults by a double vote decision (each vote includes the results of the non duplicated variants and only one of the results of the duplicated variant); this is illustrated by considering the following cases:

- activation of a hardware fault in one of the hardware components executing the duplicated variant (V1),
- activation of a software fault in the duplicated variant,
- activation of a hardware fault in one of the hardware components executing the non duplicated variants (V2, V3) or of a software fault in one of these variants.

In the first case, the fault is, of course, easily tolerated and diagnosed as the obtained syndrome consists of a) an agreement among the three results in one vote and b) a discrepancy among the results of the second vote, hence, designating as false the result of the duplicated variant.

In the second case, the decider will identify a non-unanimity in both votes designating as false the results supplied by the duplicated variant; such a syndrome enables the duplicated variant to be diagnosed as failed and thus the "correct" result is immediately available as the one provided by the non duplicated ones.

In the last case, the tolerance is immediate, but the votes do not enable the fault to be diagnosed. Based on the assumption of non recurrent nature of the software faults, the diagnostic of hardware fault can result from the repeatedly failure of a hardware component. However, it is worth noting that another form of diagnosis is possible here that would allow to relax this assumption: upon occurrence of a localized fault (i.e., imputable to either one SECA or one HECA) the next execution step is performed after a reconfiguration of the active variants that matches the duplicated variant with the identified HECA; the decider will then have to solve one of the two cases identified above. A systematic rotation of the duplicated variants would also contribute to such a diagnosis.

---

[7] An enumeration of all the possible combinations reveals 18 solutions.

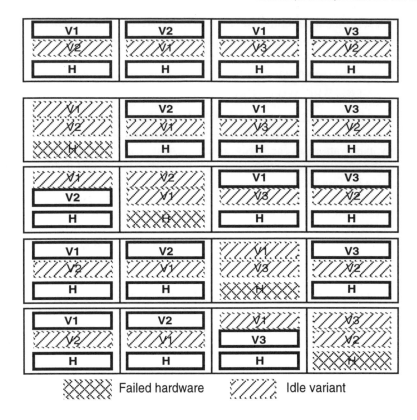

Figure 3.13   Various activations of the variants in the NVP/2/1 Architecture

After passivation of a failed hardware component, the active variants are reconfigured so that the SECAs be distributed among the remaining HECAs to form disjoint areas.

Figure 3.13 shows the distribution of active and idle variants among the three remaining HECAs after passivation of any of the HECAs of the NVP/2/1 architecture. It is noteworthy that, in each case, the reconfiguration affects only a single HECA. The decision has to be modified to a vote among the remaining variants and thus the degraded architecture is the same as the NVP/1/1 architecture.

3.4.5.4   THE NVP/2/2 ARCHITECTURE: AN EXAMPLE OF ARCHITECTURE
TOLERATING TWO SOLID SOFTWARE FAULTS

To illustrate the impact of the solid character of the software faults, on the design of architectures tolerating two faults, we consider the case of the NVP method. The definition of such an architecture requires the provision of four disjoint HECAs and SECAs, hence the NVP/2/2 architecture.

Although, this architecture appears as a direct extension of the NVP/1/1 architecture by addition of one HECA and one associated SECA, major differences exist in the processing of the errors. The fault tolerance decision is now based on the identification, among the results provided by the four variants, of a single set of agreeing results made up of two or more results. Furthermore, after the first discrepancy among the results, the hardware component (and its associated variant) designated as failed is made passive without any attempt to diagnose the fault as a hardware or software fault. The decision is then modified as a vote among the remaining versions and the degraded architecture obtained is close to the NVP/1/1 architecture. However, the same discarding action as the one described above would be carried out upon manifestation of a subsequent fault.

Besides the tolerance to two consecutive independent software faults, this architecture allows one a) to tolerate two simultaneous independent faults, b) to detect related fault among two variants and c) to detect simultaneous independent faults in three or four variants.

The Fault-Tolerant Processor-Attached Processor (FTP-AP) architecture proposed in [Lal88] may be seen as an implementation of this hardware-and-software fault-tolerant architecture. In the paper, a quad configuration of the core FTP architecture is used as a support for the management of the execution of 4 diversified applications software that are run on 4 distinct application processors.

3.4.6   Summary of the Fault Tolerance Properties of the Architectures

Figure 3.14 summarizes the main fault tolerance properties of the architectures introduced in the preceding paragraphs. Besides the generic notation identifying the software fault tolerance method and the number of hardware faults and independent software faults tolerated, the table presents for each architecture, the number of hardware components and the number of variants required. When applicable, some properties in addition to nominal fault tolerance are listed as well. Finally, the rightmost field of the table gives the fault tolerance properties of the architecture that is obtained after tolerance of a hardware fault, that is, when a HECA has been made passive.

3.4.7   Dependability Analysis of Hardware-and-Software Fault-Tolerant Architectures

The aim of this section is to show how, based on the results of Section 3.1, a dependability analysis of hardware-and-software fault-tolerant architectures can be conducted when adopting a Markov approach. Other related studies of special interest include: a) the application of a similar modeling approach to actual data derived from the experimental implementation of a real-world autopilot [Dug94], and b) the comprehensive performance and dependability (performability) analysis of fault-tolerant software carried out in [Tai93].

In what follows, three architectures are considered that enable to tolerate a single hardware or software fault, i.e., RB/1/1, NSCP/1/1 and NVP/1/1.

3.4.7.1   MODELING METHOD AND ASSUMPTIONS

To model the behavior of the architectures the following is assumed:

- only one type of fault(s) can be activated at each execution and produce error(s), either hardware or software,
- after detection and recovery of an error, the variant is not discarded and at the next step it is supplied with the new input data, i.e., faults are considered to be soft faults,
- constant failure rates are considered for the hardware components and the various sources of failure of the software-fault tolerant architectures.

Architecture	# of hardware components	# of variants	Properties in addition to nominal fault tolerance		Fault tolerance properties after a HECA has been made passive	
			Hardware faults	Software faults	Hardware	Software
RB/1/1	2	2	Low error latency	—	Detection provided by local diagnosis	Tolerance of one independent fault
NSCP/1/1	4	4	Tolerance of 2 faults in hardware components of the same SECA Detection of 3 or 4 faults in hardware components	Tolerance of 2 independent faults in the same SECA Detection of 2 related faults in disjoint SECAs Detection of 2, 3 or 4 independent faults	Detection	Detection of independent faults
NSCP/1/1/m	4	3	Tolerance of 2 faults in hardware components of the same SECA	—	Detection	Detection of independent faults
NVP1/1	3	3	Detection of 2 or 3 faults	Detection of 2 or 3 independent faults	Detection	Detection of independent faults
RB/2/1	3	2	Low error latency	—	Identical to RB/1/1	
NSCP/2/1	6	3	Detection of 3 to 6 faults in hardware components	Detection of 2 or 3 independent faults	Identical to NSCP/1/1	
NVP/2/1	4	3	Detection of 3 or 4 faults in hardware components Tolerance of combinations of single fault in hardware component and independent fault in non-duplicated variant	Detection of 2 or 3 independent faults	Identical to NVP/1/1	
NVP/2/2	4	4	Detection of 3 or 4 faults in hardware components	Detection of 2 related faults Tolerance of 2 independent faults Detection of 3 or 4 independent faults	Identical to NVP/1/1	

Figure 3.14   Synthesis of the properties of the hardware-and-software fault-tolerant architectures

Although the use of constant failure rates is quite common for hardware, the use of constant failure rates for the software-fault tolerant architectures is justified by the results presented in [Arl88], which can be summarized as follows:

- since a failed variant is not discarded but merely restarted at next execution, the state graphs of the failure behavior of the considered fault-tolerant software components are strongly connected.
- as a consequence, when constant execution rates are considered for the various activities (activation, variant(s) execution and decision(s)) of the fault-tolerant software, it is possible to define equivalent constant failure rates which are obtained as the product of the mean activation rate of the considered fault-tolerant software by the probabilities of failure.

3.4.7.2   MODELS

Architecture behavior can be modeled by the state diagrams shown on Figure 3.15-a,-b and -c for the RB/1/1, NSCP/1/1 and the NVP/1/1 architectures, respectively. For the RB/1/1 architecture, hardware and software fault tolerance mechanisms are independent: a hardware failure does not alter the software fault tolerance capabilities and vice versa. It is assumed that a near-perfect detection coverage can be achieved for hardware faults since both HECAs run simultaneously the same variant, thus, the coverage considered here for the hardware-fault tolerance mechanisms corresponds to a localization coverage due to a) the diagnosis program and b) the capacity of the acceptance test to identify hardware failures.

In the case of the NSCP/1/1 architecture, hardware and software fault tolerance techniques are not independent since the HECAs and the SECAs match. After the failure of a hardware component, the corresponding HECA (and hence, SECA) is discarded; the remaining architecture is composed of a pair of hardware components and a two-version software architecture that form a hardware- and software-fault self-checking architecture.

In the case of the NVP/1/1 architecture, again, hardware and software fault tolerance techniques are not independent: after a hardware unit has been made passive, the remaining architecture is analogous to the degraded architecture of the NSCP/1/1 architecture.

For both NSCP/1/1 and NVP/1/1 architectures, the hardware faults are tolerated at the software layer through the decision algorithm (comparison or vote); accordingly, the associated coverage will be accounted for at the software level only and thus incorporated in the probability of activation of a fault in the decider.

In the degraded architectures obtained from NSCP/1/1 and NVP/1/1 after failure of a hardware component, the software is not any more fault tolerant and thus the failure rates of the variants are of significant importance in the failure rate of the degraded configuration of the application software.

The transition rate from state i to state j is denoted T_{ij}. The expressions of the inter-state transitions of Figure 3.15 are given by Figure 3.16.

The notation is as follows:

- c is the hardware coverage factor of the RB/1/1 architecture, $\bar{c} = 1 - c$,
- $\lambda_{H,X}$ denotes the failure rate for a hardware component of the architecture X/1/1, X $\in$ {RB, NSCP, NVP},
- $\lambda_{S,D,X}$ and $\lambda_{S,U,X}$ denote respectively the detected and undetected failure rates for the fault tolerant software X, X $\in$ {RB, NSCP, NVP}; if γ denote the application software activation rate, then these failure rates can be expressed as functions of the failure probabilities

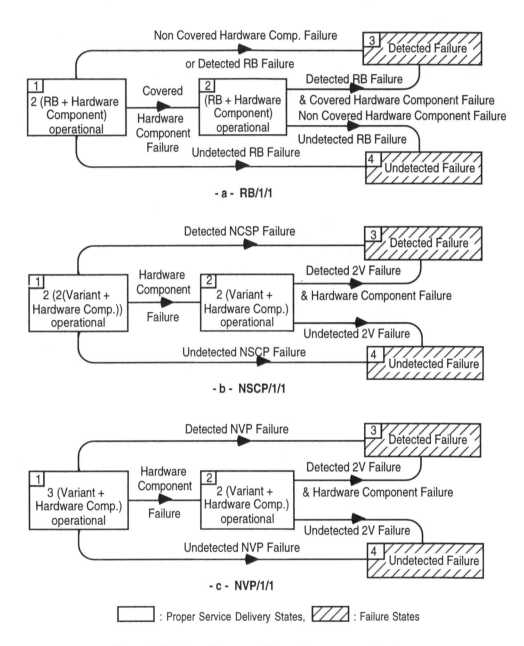

Figure 3.15   State diagrams of the architectures considered

	R B / 1 / 1	**N S C P / 1 / 1**	**N V P / 1 / 1**
T_{12}	$2\,c\,\lambda_{H,RB}$	$4\,\lambda_{H,NSCP}$	$3\,\lambda_{H,NVP}$
T_{13}	$2\,\bar{c}\,\lambda_{H,RB} + \lambda_{S,D,RB}$	$\lambda_{S,D,NSCP}$	$\lambda_{S,D,NVP}$
T_{14}	$\lambda_{S,U,RB}$	$\lambda_{S,U,NSCP}$	$\lambda_{S,U,NVP}$
T_{23}	$c\,\lambda_{H,RB} + \lambda_{S,D,RB}$	$2\,\lambda_{H,NSCP} + \lambda_{S,D,2V}$	$2\,\lambda_{H,NVP} + \lambda_{S,D,2V}$
T_{24}	$\bar{c}\,\lambda_{H,RB} + \lambda_{S,U,RB}$	$\lambda_{S,U,2V}$	$\lambda_{S,U,2V}$

Figure 3.16   Transitions and associated failure rates

given in Figure 3.8 (Section 3.3.1.5) as:

$$\lambda_{S,D,X} = [q_{S,D,X}]\gamma \text{ and } \lambda_{S,U,X} = [q_{S,U,X}]\gamma \tag{3.2}$$

- $\lambda_{S,D,2V}$ and $\lambda_{S,U,2V}$ denotes respectively the application software detected and undetected failure rates of the NSCP/1/1 and NVP/1/1 architectures, after an HECA has been
made passive; these rates are defined as:

$$\lambda_{S,D,2V} = [q_{S,D,2V}]\gamma \text{ and } \lambda_{S,U,2V} = [q_{S,U,2V}]\gamma \tag{3.3}$$

where the detected and undetected failure probabilities of the degraded 2V configuration
are defined by:

$$q_{S,D,2V} = 2q_{I,2V}(1 - \frac{q_{I,2V}}{2}) + q_{ID,2V} \text{ and } q_{S,U,2V} = q_{RVD,2V} \tag{3.4}$$

3.4.7.3   MODEL PROCESSING

Processing of the models of Figure 3.15, when accounting for the different transition rates
of Figure 3.16, enables one to derive the expressions for the time-dependent probabilities of
detected failure and undetected failure of the considered hardware-and-software fault-tolerant
architectures: $Q_{D,X}(t)$ and $Q_{U,X}(t)$, respectively, $X \in \{RB,NSCP,NVP\}$. In practice, two
types of probabilities are of interest:

- the reliability, $R_X(t) = Q_{D,X}(t) + Q_{U,X}(t)$,
- the probability of undetected failure, $Q_{U,X}(t)$.

For missions of short duration with respect to the mean times to failure, these expressions
can be simplified to the following approximate expressions:

$$R_{RB}(t) \approx 1 - (2\bar{c}\lambda_{H,RB} + \lambda_{S,RB})\,t \qquad Q_{U,RB}(t) \approx \lambda_{S,U,RB}\,t \tag{3.5}$$
$$R_{NSCP}(t) \approx 1 - \lambda_{S,NSCP}\,t \qquad Q_{U,NSCP}(t) \approx \lambda_{S,U,NSCP}\,t \tag{3.6}$$
$$R_{NVP}(t) \approx 1 - \lambda_{S,NVP}\,t \qquad Q_{U,NVP}(t) \approx \lambda_{S,U,NVP}\,t \tag{3.7}$$

These expressions show that — as could be expected — the reliability of the RB/1/1
architecture is strongly dependent on the coverage of the fault diagnosis in the hardware
components. Furthermore, it is likely that the hardware component failure rate be greater for

the RB/1/1 architecture than for the other ones, due to the extra memory needed to store the second variant; also further hardware and/or software resources would be needed to perform the comparison among the results provided by each hardware processor ensuring thus a near-perfect detection coverage and storage would be needed for the acceptance test and the diagnosis program.

The expressions also reveal an identical influence of the failure rate of the application software for the three architectures. However, this has to be tempered by the differences between the associated probabilities identified in Section 3.3.1.5.

3.5 CONCLUSIONS

In this chapter, we have a) presented in a unified way the three major approaches for tolerating software faults by design diversity, and b) defined and analyzed architectures aimed at tolerating both hardware and software faults.

In addition to recovery block and N-version programming that form the basic architectures to implement software-fault tolerance, we have introduced and analyzed the N self-checking programming scheme that corresponds to the architecture actually implemented in real-life safety-critical applications.

The careful analysis of these architectures enabled to identify their major dependability features in particular concerning their ability to cope with independent and related software fault combinations in the variants and the deciders.

The extension of the notion of error confinement areas as a structuring principle to hardware- and software-fault tolerant systems made it possible a) to carry out a systematic study of the fault tolerance features provided by the considered architectures, and b) to derive comprehensive analytical models for the evaluation of system-level dependability measures.

Finally, it is worth noting that emergence of hardware-fault tolerant commercial systems will make more sensitive the influence of design faults on the service delivered by computing systems to their users. As a foreseeable consequence, software fault tolerance is likely to spread out its currently privileged domain, i.e., safety-related systems. The approaches and results presented in this chapter are thus likely to be accordingly of a wider field of application.

ACKNOWLEDGEMENTS

This work has been partially supported by Aérospatiale and by Matra Marconi Space in the framework of the HERMES project (European Space Shuttle) and by the CEC in the framework of the ESPRIT Project "Predictably Dependable Computing Systems".

Christian Béounes passed away on April 23, 1993, after several months of painful battle against illness. Christian lives on in our memory, both for his professional and for his human qualities.

REFERENCES

[Amm87] P. E. Ammann and J. C. Knight. Data diversity: an approach to software fault tolerance. In *Proc. 17th International Symposium on Fault-Tolerant Computing (FTCS-17)*, pages 122–126, Pittsburgh, PA, July 1987. IEEE Computer Society Press.

[And79] D. M. Andrews. Using executable assertions for testing fault tolerance. In *Proc. 9th International Symposium on Fault-Tolerant Computing (FTCS-9)*, pages 102–105, Madison, WI, June 1979. IEEE Computer Society Press.

[And81] T. Anderson and P. A. Lee. *Fault Tolerance — Principles and Practice*. Prentice Hall, 1981. (See also: P.A. Lee, T. Anderson, Fault Tolerance — Principles and Practice, Dependable Computing and Fault-Tolerant Systems, volume 3, Springer-Verlag, Vienna, Austria, 1990).

[And85] T. Anderson, P. A. Barrett, D. N. Halliwell, and M. Moulding. Software fault tolerance: an evaluation. *IEEE Transactions on Software Engineering*, SE-11(12):1502–1510, 1985.

[Arl88] J. Arlat, K. Kanoun, and J.-C. Laprie. Dependability evaluation of software fault-tolerance. In *Proc. 18th International Symposium on Fault-Tolerant Computing (FTCS-18)*, pages 142–147, Tokyo, Japan, June 1988. IEEE Computer Society Press. (See also: Dependability Modeling and Evaluation of Software Fault-Tolerant Systems. *IEEE Transactions on Computers*, 39(4):504–513, 1990).

[Arn73] T. F. Arnold. The concept of coverage and its effect on the reliability model of repairable systems. *IEEE Transactions on Computers*, C-22(3):251–254, 1973.

[Avi79] A. Avižienis. Towards a discipline of reliable computing. In *Proc. EURO IFIP'79*, pages 701–705, London, UK, September 1979.

[Avi84] A. Avižienis and J. P. J. Kelly. Fault tolerance by design diversity: concepts and experiments. *IEEE Computer*, 17(8):67–80, 1984.

[Avi85] A. Avižienis. The N-version approach to fault-tolerant systems. *IEEE Transactions on Software Engineering*, SE-11(12):1491–1501, 1985.

[Avi86] A. Avižienis and J.-C. Laprie. Dependable computing: from concept to design diversity. *Proceedings of the IEEE*, 74(5):629–638, 1986.

[Bis86] P. G. Bishop, D. G. Esp, M. Barnes, P. Humphreys, G. Dahl, and J. Lahti, PODS — a project on diverse software. *IEEE Transactions on Software Engineering*, 12(9):929–940, 1986.

[Boe81] B. W. Boehm. *Software Engineering Economics*. Prentice Hall, Englewood Cliffs, NJ, 1981.

[Bon93] A. Bondavalli, F. Di Giandomenico, and J. Xu. A cost-effective and flexible scheme for software fault tolerance. *International Journal of Computer Systems Science & Engineering*, 8:234–244, 1993.

[Bou69] W. G. Bouricius, W. C. Carter, and P. R. Schneider. Reliability modeling techniques for self-repairing computer systems. In *Proc. 24th. National Conference*, pages 295–309, ACM, 1969.

[Bri93] D. Brière and P. Traverse. AIRBUS A320/A330/A340 electrical flight controls — a family of fault-tolerant systems. In *Proc. 23rd International Symposium. on Fault-Tolerant Computing (FTCS-23)*, pages 616–623, Toulouse, France, June 1993. IEEE Computer Society Press.

[Cag85] A. K. Caglayan and D. E. Eckhardt. System approach to software fault tolerance. In *Proc. 5th Computers in Aerospace Conference*, pages 361–369, Long Beach, CA, IEEE/AIAA, October 1985.

[Cau81] J.T. Caulfield. Application of redundant processing to space shuttle. In *Proc. 8th IFAC Triennal World Congress*, pages 2461–2466, Kyoto, Japan, 1981.

[Che78] L. Chen and A. Avižienis. N-version programming: a fault tolerance approach to reliability of software operation. In *Proc. 8th International Symposium on Fault-Tolerant Computing (FTCS-8)*, pages 3–9, Toulouse, France, June 1978. IEEE Computer Society Press.

[Chr94] J. Christmansson, Z. Kalbarczyk, and J. Torin. Dependable flight control system using data diversity with error recovery. *International Journal of Computer Systems Science & Engineering*, 9:98–106, April 1994.

[Dug94] J. B. Dugan and M. R. Lyu. System-level reliability and sensitivity analyses for three fault-tolerant system architectures. In *4th International Working Conference on Dependable Computing for Critical Applications*, pages 295–307, San Diego, CA, January 1994.

[Eck91] D. E. Eckhardt, A. K. Caglayan, J. C. Knight, L. D. Lee, D. F. McAllister, M. A. Vouk, and J. P. J. Kelly. An experimental evaluation of software redundancy as a strategy for improving reliability. *IEEE Transactions on Software Engineering*, 17(7):692–702, 1991.

[Elm72] W. R. Elmendorf. Fault-tolerant programming. In *Proc. 2nd International Symposium on Fault-Tolerant Computing (FTCS-2)*, pages 79–83, Newton, MA, June 1972. IEEE Computer Society Press.

[Fis75]   M. A. Fishler, P. Firshein, and D. L. Drew. Distinct software: an approach to reliable comput-
           ing. In *Proc. 2nd USA-Japan Computer Conference*, pages 573–579, Tokyo, Japan, August
           1975. IEEE Computer Society Press.

[Gar81]   J. R. Garman. The "bug" heard around the world. *ACM Sigsoft Software Engineering Notes*,
           6(5):3–10, 1981.

[Gme79]   L. Gmeiner and U. Voges. Software diversity in reactor protection systems: an experiment.
           In *Proc. International IFAC Workshop on Safety on Computer Control systems (SAFE-
           COMP'79)*, pages 89–93, Stuttgart, Germany, 1979.

[Gra86]   J. Gray, Why do computers stop and what can be done about it? In *Proc. 5th Symposium
           on Reliability in Distributed Software and Database Systems*, pages 3–12, Los Angeles, CA,
           IEEE, 1986.

[Gra90]   J. Gray. A census of Tandem system availability between 1985 and 1990. *IEEE Transactions
           on Reliability*, 39(4):409–432, 1990.

[Hag86]   G. Hagelin. ERICSSON safety system for railway control. Technical Report ENR/TB 6078,
           ERICSSON, October 1986. Also in Application of Design Diversity in Computerized Control
           Systems. In *Proceedings of the IFIP WG 10.4 Workshop on Design Diversity in Action*, Baden,
           Austria, June 1986, U. Voges, editor, volume 2 of the Series on Dependable Computing and
           Fault Tolerance, pages 11–21, Springer-Verlag, Vienna, Austria, 1988.

[Kel88]   J. P. J. Kelly, D. E. Eckhardt, M. A. Vouk, D. F. Allister, and A. K. Caglayan. A large scale
           second generation experiment in multi-version software: description and early results. In
           Proc. 18th International Symposium on Fault-Tolerant Computing (FTCS-18), pages 9–14,
           Tokyo, Japan, June 1988. IEEE Computer Society Press.

[Kim84]   K. H. Kim. Distributed execution of recovery blocks: an approach to uniform treatment of
           hardware and software faults. In *Proc. 4th International Conference on Distributed Comput-
           ing Systems*, pages 526–532, May 1984. IEEE Computer Society Press.

[Kim89]   K. H. Kim and H. O. Welch. Distributed execution of recovery blocks: an approach for uniform
           treatment of hardware and software faults in real-time applications. *IEEE Transactions on
           Computers*, C-38(5):626–636, 1989.

[Kni86]   J. C. Knight and N. G. Leveson. An empirical study of failure probabilities in multi-version
           software. In *Proc. 16th International Symposium on Fault-Tolerant Computing (FTCS-16)*,
           pages 165–170, Vienna, Austria, July 1986. IEEE Computer Society Press.

[Lal88]   J. H. Lala and L. S. Alger. Hardware and software fault tolerance: a unified architectural
           approach. In *Proc. 18th International Symposium on Fault-Tolerant Computing (FTCS-18)*,
           pages 240–245, Tokyo, Japan, June 1988. IEEE Computer Society Press.

[Lap87]   J.-C. Laprie, J. Arlat, C. Béounes, K. Kanoun, and C. Hourtolle. Hardware and software
           fault-tolerance: definition and analysis of architectural solutions. In *Proc. l7th International
           Symposium on Fault-Tolerant Computing (FTCS-17)*, pages ll6–121, Pittsburgh, PA, 1987.
           IEEE Computer Society Press.

[Lap90]   J.-C. Laprie, J. Arlat, C. Béounes, and K. Kanoun. Definition and analysis of hardware-and-
           software fault-tolerant architectures. *IEEE Computer*, 23:39–51, July 1990.

[Lap94]   J.-C. Laprie, J. Arlat, C. Béounes, and K. Kanoun. Fault tolerant computing. In *Encyclopedia
           of Software Engineering, Vol. 1 A-N*, J. Marciniak, editor, pages 482–503, J. Wiley & Sons,
           1994.

[Lor89]   P. R. Lorczak, A. K. Caglayan, and D. E. Eckhardt. A theoretical investigation of generalized
           voters for redundant systems. In *Proc. 19th International Symposium on Fault Tolerant
           Computing (FTCS-19)*, pages 444–451, Chicago, IL, June 1989. IEEE Computer Society
           Press.

[Mah84]   A. Mahmood, D. M. Andrews, and E. J. McCluskey. Executable assertions and flight software.
           In *Proc. 6th Digital Avionics Systems Conference*, pages 346–351, Baltimore, Maryland,
           AIAA/IEEE, December 1984.

[Mar82]   D. J. Martin. Dissimilar software in high integrity applications in flight controls. In *Proc.
           AGARD CP-330*, pages 36.1–36.13, September 1982.

[Neu86]   P. G. Neumann. On hierarchical design of computer systems for critical applications. *IEEE
           Transactions on Software Engineering*, SE-12(9):905–920, 1986.

[Ram84]   C. V. Ramamoorthy, A. Prakash, W.-T. Tsai, and Y. Usuda. Software engineering: problems and perspectives. *IEEE Computer*, 17(10):191–209, 1984.

[Ran75]   B. Randell. System structure for software fault tolerance. *IEEE Transactions on Software Engineering*, SE-1(2):220–232, 1975.

[Ran84]   B. Randell. Fault tolerance and system structuring. In *Proc. 4th Jerusalem Conference on Information Technology (JCIT-4)*, pages 182–191, Jerusalem, Israel, May 1984.

[Ran87]   B. Randell. Design fault tolerance. In *The Evolution of Fault-Tolerant Computing* A. Avižienis, H. Kopetz, and J.-C. Laprie, editors, volume 1 of *Dependable Computing and Fault-Tolerant Systems*, pages 251–270, Vienna, Austria: Springer-Verlag, 1987. (Also *Proc. IFIP Symposium on The Evolution of Fault-Tolerant Computing*, Baden, Austria, June 30, 1986).

[Rem82]   L. Remus. Methodology for software development of a digital integrated protection system. January 1982. (Presented at the EWICS TC-7, Brussels).

[Rou86]   J. C. Rouquet and P. Traverse. Safe and reliable computing on board Airbus and ATR aircraft. In *Proc. 5th IFAC Workshop Safety of Computer Control Systems (SAFECOMP'86)*, W. J. Quirk, editor, pages 93–97, Sarlat, France, October 1986. Pergamon Press.

[Sco87]   R. K. Scott, J. W. Gault, and D. F. McAllister. Fault-tolerant software reliability modeling. *IEEE Transactions on Software Engineering*, SE-13(5):582–592, 1987.

[She78]   C. T. Sheridan. Space shuttle software. *Datamation*, pages 128–140, 1978.

[Sie82]   D. P. Siewiorek and D. Johnson. A design methodology for high reliability systems: the Intel 432. In D. P. Siewiorek and R. S. Swarz, editors, *The Theory and Practice of Reliable System Design*, pages 621–636, 1982. Digital Press, Bedford, MA.

[Spr80]   R. E. Spradlin. Boeing 757 and 767 flight management system. In *Proc. RTCA Tech. Symposium*, pages 107–118, Washington, DC, November 1980.

[Ste78]   B. J. Sterner. Computerized interlocking system — a multidimensional structure in pursuit of safety. *IMechE Railway Engineer International*, pages 29–30, 1978.

[Sul90]   G. F. Sullivan and G. M. Masson. Using certification trails to achieve software fault tolerance. In *Proc. 20th International Symposium on Fault-Tolerant Computing (FTCS-20)*, pages 423–431, Newcastle upon Tyne, UK, June 1990. IEEE Computer Society Press.

[Swa76]   E. B. Swanson. The dimension of maintenance. In *Proc. 2nd International Conference on Software Engineering*, pages 492–497, Los Alamitos, CA, 1976. IEEE Computer Society Press.

[Tai93]   A. T. Tai, J. F. Meyer, and A. Avižienis. Performability enhancement of fault-tolerant software. *IEEE Transactions on Reliability*, 42(2):227–237, 1993.

[Toy78]   W. N. Toy. Fault-tolerant design of local ESS processors. *Proceedings of the IEEE*, 66(10):1126–1145, 1978.

[Tra88]   P. Traverse. AIRBUS and ATR system architecture and specification. In *Software Diversity in Computerized Control Systems*, U. Voges, editor, volume 2 of *Dependable Computing and Fault-Tolerant Systems*, pages 95–104, Vienna, Austria: Springer-Verlag, 1988.

[Tso86]   K. S. Tso and A. Avižienis. Error recovery in multi-version software. In *Proc. 5th IFAC Workshop Safety of Computer Control Systems (SAFECOMP'86)*, W. J. Quirk, editor, pages 35–41, Sarlat, France, October 1986. Pergamon Press.

[Tso87]   K. S. Tso and A. Avižienis. Community error recovery in N-version software: a design study with experimentation. In *Proc. 17th International Sym. on Fault-Tolerant Computing (FTCS-17)*, pages 127–133, Pittsburgh, PA, July 1987. IEEE Computer Society Press.

[Vog88]   U. Voges. Software diversity in computerized control systems. In *Dependable Computing and Fault-Tolerant Systems*, A. Avižienis, H. Kopetz, and J.-C. Laprie, editors, volume 2, Vienna, Austria: Springer-Verlag, 1988. (Also *Proc. IFIP Workshop on Design Diversity in Action, Baden, Austria*, June 28, 1986).

[Xu91]   J. Xu. The $t/(n-1)$-diagnosability and its applications to fault tolerance. In *Proc. 21st International Symposium on Fault Tolerant Computing (FTCS-21)*, pages 496–503, Montréal, Quebec, Canada, June 1991. IEEE Computer Society Press.

[Yau75]   S. S. Yau and R. C. Cheung. Design of self-checking software. In *Proc. International Conference on Reliable Software*, pages 450–457, Los Angeles, CA, April 1975. IEEE Computer Society Press.

[You84]   L. J. Yount. Architectural solutions to safety problems in digital flight-critical systems for commercial transports. In *Proc. 6th Digital Avionics Conference*, pages 28–35, Baltimore, MD, December 1984.

[Zel79]   M. Zelkowitz, A. C. Shaw, and J. D. Gannon, *Principles of Software Engineering and Design*, Prentice-Hall, Englewood Cliffs, NJ, 1979.

4

Exception Handling and Tolerance of Software Faults

FLAVIU CRISTIAN

University of California, San Diego

ABSTRACT

The first part of this chapter provides rigorous definitions for several basic concepts underlying the design of dependable programs, such as specification, program semantics, exception, program correctness, robustness, failure, fault, and error. The second part investigates what it means to handle exceptions in modular programs structured as hierarchies of data abstractions. The problems to be solved at each abstraction level, such as exception detection and propagation, consistent state recovery and masking are examined in detail. Both programmed exception handling and default exception handling (such as embodied for example in recovery blocks or database transactions) are considered. An assessment of the adequacy of backward recovery in providing tolerance of software design faults is made.

4.1 INTRODUCTION

Programs are designed to produce certain intended, or standard, state transitions in computers and their peripheral devices. Most of the time, these standard state transitions can be effectively provided to program users. However, there exist circumstances which might prevent a program from providing its specified standard service. Since such circumstances are expected to occur rarely, programmers refer to them as exceptions. Exceptions have to be handled with care, since the state of a program can be inconsistent when their occurrence is detected. A normal continuation of the program execution from an inconsistent state can lead to additional exception occurrences and ultimately to a program failure. In operational computer software

---

[1] An earlier version of this chapter was published in "Dependability of Resilient Computers", T. Anderson, Editor, BSP Professional Books, Blackwell Scientific Publications, UK, 1989, pp. 68–97

Software Fault Tolerance, Edited by Lyu
© 1995 John Wiley & Sons Ltd

systems often more than two thirds of the code is devoted to detecting and handling exceptions. Yet, since exceptions are expected to occur rarely, the exception handling code of a system is in general the least documented, tested, and understood part. Most of the design faults existing in a system seem to be located in the code that handles exceptional situations. For instance, field experience with telephone switching systems [Toy82], indicates that approximately two thirds of system failures are due to design faults in exception handling (or recovery) algorithms.

In the early stages of programming methodology development in the 60s, research has mostly focused on mastering the complexity inherent in the usual or standard program behavior. The first papers entirely devoted to exception handling began to appear only in the 70s, e.g. [Goo75, Hor74, Par72b, Wul75]. Early discussions of the issue were often marred by misunderstandings arising from the lack of precise definitions and terminology, but by the end of the 70s [Cri79a, Lis79] it became clear that all proposed exception mechanisms can be classified into two basic categories: termination mechanisms [And81, Bac79, Bes81a, Bro76, Cri79a, Cri80, Hor74, Ich79, Lis79, Mel77, Wul75] and resumption mechanisms [Goo75, Lam74, Lev77, Par72b, Yem82].

The two approaches can roughly be described as follows. With a termination mechanism, signalling the occurrence of an exception E while the body of a command C is executed leads to the (exceptional) termination of C. With a resumption mechanism, signalling an exception E leads to the temporary halt of the execution of C, the transfer of control to a handler associated with E and resumption of the execution of C with the command that follows the one that signalled E if the handler executes a resume command. If the handler does not execute such a command, control goes where the handler directs it to go. Thus, while with a termination mechanism, signalling an exception has a meaning similar to that of an exit command, with a resumption mechanism, it has a meaning similar to that of calling a procedure. For some time it was not clear which kind of mechanism will gain acceptance from programmers. Strong arguments that the termination paradigm is superior to the resumption paradigm are presented in [Cri79a, Lis79]. Roughly, these could be summarized as follows.

While with a termination mechanism, the meaning of calling a procedure of a module implementing some abstract data type depends only on the module state and the arguments of the call, with a resumption mechanism, the meaning also depends on the semantics of exception handlers outside the module, that are in general not known when the module is written. In addition, often such handlers must have knowledge of the module internals to handle the exception. Thus, while a termination mechanism mixes well with the information hiding principles underlying data abstraction, resumption does not.

With a termination mechanism, a programmer is naturally encouraged to recover a consistent state of a module in which an exception occurrence is detected before signalling it, so that further calls to module procedures find the module state consistent. With a resumption mechanism, the programmer does not know if after signalling an exception control will come back or not. If he recovers a consistent state before signalling, for example by undoing all changes made since the procedure start, this defeats the purpose of resumption, which is to save the work done so far between the procedure entry and the detection of the exception. If he does not recover a consistent state, then there is the possibility that the handler never resumes execution of the module after the signalling command, so that the module remains in the intermediate, most likely inconsistent, state that existed when the exception was detected. In the latter case, further module calls can lead to additional exceptions and failures.

The semantics of existing termination mechanisms is by far simpler to understand and master than the semantics of resumption mechanisms. Moreover, it is the experience of this author that with a termination mechanism one can program all cases that "naturally" call for resumption. To illustrate this, consider a procedure C exported by a module M that composed sequentially of two subcommands C1 and C2, which uses a resumption mechanism to signal E between C1 and C2. If the outside handler RHE resumes C2 after suitably changing the state of M so as to make continuation with C2 meaningful (i.e. ensure that the causes that have lead to the occurrence of E have disappeared), then when the execution of C2 starts all the previous work done by C1 is preserved. If C would use a termination mechanism to signal E, it would have to undo all changes made by C1 before signalling E. The handler THE associated with E would then have to first perform M state changes similar to those performed by RHE (to ensure that the causes that lead to the occurrence of E have disappeared) before invoking C again. Thus, if exception masking is possible, the only advantage of a resumption mechanism over a termination mechanism is that it saves the work done before the exception is signalled, while with a termination mechanism, that work must be undone and repeated. If exception masking is not possible, then termination is clearly advantageous, since resumption is not as inductive to recovering a consistent state for M before signalling an exception as is termination. This small advantage of resumption, namely saving the work done before an exception is signalled in case the exception can be masked, is not worth in this author's view the semantic complexities associated with resumption.

A number of recent developments confirm the view that termination mechanisms are better than resumption mechanisms. Practical feedback from users of of the Mesa programming language [Mit79] incorporating the resumption mechanism of [Lam74] indicates that the use of this type of mechanism can be quite fault-prone [Hor78, Lev85]. Interestingly enough, some of the main proponents of the resumption philosophy (B. Lampson, R. Levin, J. Mitchell, D. Parnas) have abandoned it in favor of the termination philosophy [Lev85, Mit93, Par85]. Widely used programming languages such as Ada and C++ have termination exception handling mechanisms.

The purpose of this chapter is to present a synthesis of the termination exception handling paradigm. We only deal with sequential programs. Exception handling in parallel and distributed programs is still an evolving subject where no clear consensus exists [Cam86, Cri79b, Jal84, Kim82, Lis82, Ran75, Sch89, Shr78, Woo81]. In our discussion we will only examine exceptions detected by programs running on non-faulty hardware. These include exceptions detected and signalled by hardware or by lower level services such as file services. For a text attempting to integrate software and hardware aspects of fault-tolerance, the interested reader is referred to [Cri91].

4.2   BASIC NOTIONS

The goal of this section is to provide rigorous definitions for such basic concepts as program specification, program semantics, exception, program correctness and robustness, failure, fault and error.

4.2.1   Standard Program Specifications and Semantics

When a sequential program P is invoked in some initial storage state s, the *goal* is to make the computer storage reach a final state s', such that some *intended* relationship exists between s and s'.

A storage *state* is a mapping from storage unit names to values storable in those units. Typical storage unit *types* are integer, Boolean, array, disk block, stream of characters, and so on. We denote by s an initial storage state, by s' a final state, and by S the set of all possible storage states. If $s \in S$ is a state, and n is a storage unit name (for instance an integer program variable), s(n) is the value that n has in state s. To keep notations short, the convention is followed of writing n instead of s(n), and n', instead of s'(n). This means that n is used to denote ambiguously both the name of a storage unit and the value stored in that unit. Which meaning is intended should be clear from the context.

A *standard specification* G_σ (G for goal, and "σ" for standard) of a sequential program P is a relation between initial and final storage states:

$$G_\sigma \subseteq S \times S.$$

A pair (s,s') $\in S \times S$ is in G_σ if an *intended* outcome of invoking P in the initial state s is to make P *terminate normally* in the final state s'. (Normal termination in a Pascal-like language means that control returns to the 'next' command, separated by a semicolon from P.)

For example, the standard goal of a procedure F for computing factorials

procedure F(*in out* n: Integer)

might be expressed by the relation GF_σ (Goal of Factorial procedure) defined over the set Integer of machine representable integers:

$$GF_\sigma \equiv \{(n,n') \mid n,n' \in \ Integer \ \& \ n' = n!\}.$$

(The set Integer contains all integers $i \in \mathcal{Z}$ that are not smaller than a constant min $\in \mathcal{Z}$ and that are not greater than a constant max $\in \mathcal{Z}$, min $\leq 0 \leq$ max, where $\mathcal{Z}$ denotes the infinite set of mathematical integers.) The specification GF_σ associates initial values of the parameter n with final values n', such that n'=n!, where the mathematical factorial function, denoted "!", might be defined recursively by the equation

$$n! \equiv if \ n = 0 \ then \ 1 \ else \ n \times (n-1)!.$$

In most cases encountered in practice, standard program specifications are partial. A specification G_σ is *partial* if its domain dom(G_σ) is a strict subset of the set S of all possible initial states: $dom(G_\sigma) \subset S$. The domain of a relation G_σ is the set of all initial states $s \in S$ for which there exist final states $s' \in S$ in G_σ :

$$dom(G_\sigma) \equiv \{s \in S \mid \exists s' \in \ S : (s,s') \in \ G_\sigma\}.$$

For example, GF_σ is partial. Indeed, GF_σ does not define a final value for n when its initial value is negative, because the mathematical factorial function "!" is undefined for negative integers:

$$GF_\sigma = \{(0,1),(1,1),(2,2),(3,6),(4,24),(5,120),(6,720),(7,5040),(8,40320),...\}$$

To emphasize the partial nature of a standard specification G_σ, it is customary to structure it into a standard *precondition* pre_σ that characterizes the domain of the specification

$$pre_\sigma : S \rightarrow \{true, false\}, \qquad s \in dom(G_\sigma) \equiv pre_\sigma(s) = true$$

and a standard *postcondition* $post_\sigma$ that is the characteristic predicate of G_σ

$$post_\sigma : S \times S \rightarrow \{true, false\} \qquad (s,s') \in G_\sigma \equiv post_\sigma(s,s') = true.$$

Thus, a precondition is used to indicate *when* a service can be provided, and a postcondition is used to describe *what* service will be provided.

A *program* is a syntactic object that is built according to a certain programming language *grammar*. For example, the text in Figure 4.1 (written in accordance with some Pascal-like grammar) might be taken as being a procedure that attempts to accomplish the standard goal GF_σ mentioned above:

```
procedure F(in out n: Integer);
var k,m: Integer;
  begin
    k:=0; m:=1;
    while k < n
    do k:=k+1 ;
       m:=m × k
    od;
    n:=m
  end;
```

Figure 4.1   A standard factorial program

The *standard semantics* $[P]_\sigma$ of a program P is the *actual* function from input to output states that P computes *when* it terminates normally:

$$[P]_\sigma \subseteq S \times S.$$

A pair of states (s,s') is in $[P]_\sigma$ if, when invoked in the initial state $s \in S$, the program P *terminates normally* in the final state $s' \in S$.

For example, the termination of the procedure F is normal either if n is negative (in which case the final value n' is 1) or if n is positive and n! is a machine representable integer (in which case the final value n' is n!). An overflow occurrence when trying to compute n! does not result in normal termination, as will be discussed later. On a microcomputer using signed

16-bit integer representation (where max < 8!) the standard semantics of the procedure F is the function:

$$[F]_\sigma = \{(min,1),...,(0,1),(1,1),...,(6,720),(7,5040)\}$$

That is, on such a microcomputer, F terminates normally whenever it is invoked with an argument smaller than 8.

The set of all initial states $s \in S$ for which a program P terminates normally in some final state $s' \in S$ which satisfies the standard specification G_σ is the *standard domain* SD of P (with respect to G_σ):

$$SD \equiv \{s \mid \exists s' : (s,s') \in [P]_\sigma \ \& \ (s,s') \in G_\sigma\}.$$

For example, the standard domain of the program F with respect to the specification GF_σ is the domain $\{0,1,...,7\}$ of the relation $[F]_\sigma \cap GF_\sigma$. The characteristic predicate of the standard domain can be computed as being the weakest precondition for which P terminates normally in a final state satisfying G_σ [Dij76, Cri84].

4.2.2   Exceptional Program Specification and Semantics

If a program P is invoked in an initial state which is outside the standard domain SD, the standard service G_σ specified for P *can not* be provided by P. The set of all states which are not in the standard domain is the *exceptional domain* ED of that program:

ED $\equiv$ S - SD .

For example, the exceptional domain of the factorial procedure F with respect to its standard specification GF_σ is Integer-$\{0,...,7\}$, that is, $\{min,...,-1\} \cup \{8,...,max\}$.

An invocation of a program in its exceptional domain is an *exception occurrence*. (Note that no actual detection is implied.) By the above definition, an exception occurrence is synonymous with impossibility of delivering the standard service specified for a program. If the standard domain associated with a program and specification includes the set of all possible input states, there will be no exception occurrences when that program is invoked. Unfortunately, such programs and specifications are rarely encountered in practice. Most often, the exceptional domains associated with programs and specifications are not empty.

A characteristic of an exception occurrence is that, once such an event is *detected* in a program, it is not sensible to continue with the sequential execution of the remaining operations in that program. For example, an exception occurrence (say, for an initial state $i < 0$) detected during the execution of the first operation F(i) of the program below

   F(i); F(j); m:= i+j;

reveals that the standard goal $m' = (i! + j!)$ cannot be achieved, and hence, it does not make sense to continue normal execution of the program by invoking the next operation F(j). Thus, to handle exception occurrences, it is convenient to allow for occasional (exceptional) alterations of the sequential (standard) composition rule for operation invocations.

An *exception mechanism* is a language control structure which allows a programmer to express that the standard continuation of a program is to be replaced by an exceptional continuation when an exception is detected in that program. A direct way of associating several continuations with a single program is to make that program have several *exit points*: one standard exit point, to which a standard continuation may be associated, and zero or more exceptional exit points, to which exceptional continuations may be associated.

The intention is that the program should return normally if it *can* provide its specified standard service, and should return exceptionally if it *cannot*. In this way, a program can endeavor to notify its invoker *directly* that a requested standard service is (or is not) provided by simply returning normally (or exceptionally). To let a user of a program P distinguish among different exceptional returns from P, alphanumeric *exception labels* can be used to label distinct exceptional exit points of P. The symbol σ (which cannot be confused with an exception label) will be used to denote the standard exit point of a program.

Since all examples to be given in this chapter are phrased in terms of the simple exception mechanism defined in [Cri79a, Cri84], it is appropriate at this point to briefly recall its main characteristics.

The designer of a procedure P indicates that P has an exceptional exit point "e" by declaring "e" in the header of P as follows:

procedure P *signals* e.

An invoker of P defines the exceptional continuation (if e is signalled by an invocation of P) to be some operation K by writing

P[e:K] .

To detect and handle the occurrence of e, the designer of P may explicitly insert in the body of P the following syntactic constructs:

(a)   [B:H]
(b)   O[d:H]

In the first, B is a Boolean expression (or run-time check, or executable assertion). In the second construct, O is an operation which can signal some exception d. The handler H may be a (possibly empty) sequence of operations and may terminate with a "*signal* e" exceptional sequencer. The meaning of an (a) or (b) construct inserted in the body of P may be explained informally as follows. If B evaluates to *true* or O signals d, then H is invoked. If H terminates with a "*signal* e" sequencer, then the standard continuation of the (a) or (b) construct is abandoned in favor of an exceptional continuation (*e.g.*, K) associated with the e exit point of P. In the remaining cases, *i.e.*, if B evaluates to *false* or O terminates normally or the execution of H does not terminate with a "*signal* e" sequencer, the standard continuation of the (a) or (b) construct is taken. If the designer of P did not associate the handler H with the exception d which can be signalled by O, then d would be an exit point for P too. Such an exceptional exit (not explicitly declared for P by its designer) would be taken whenever O signals d after being invoked from P.

Note that the occurrence of e can be *detected* in P either because some Boolean expression B evaluates to true, or because an operation O invoked from P signals a lower level exception d. In the latter case, the detection of e in P *coincides* with the *propagation* of the (lower level) exception d in P. The problem of systematic placement of Boolean expressions in programs so as to detect all possible exception occurrences is investigated in [Bes81a, Sta87]. The verification methods described in [Cri84] can be used to prove that all exceptions, whether detected by Boolean expression evaluations or lower level exception propagation, are correctly detected in a program.

As an example, Figure 4.2 contains a variant FE (Factorial with exceptions) of F which signals a "negative" exception whenever the input is negative.

```
procedure FE(in out n: Integer) signals negative;
var k,m: Integer;
begin
  [n<0: signal negative];
  k:=0; m:=1;
  while k < n
  do k:=k+1 ;
      m:=m × k
  od;
  n:=m
end;
```

Figure 4.2   A factorial program with exceptions

Software designers often anticipate that the exceptional domains of the programs they write may be nonempty, and decide to provide alternative *exceptional services* when the intended standard services cannot be provided. Let E be the set of exception labels that the designer of a program P *declares* for P in order to identify a set of specified exceptional services that P will deliver when the standard service G_σ cannot be provided.

As discussed above, a program P can also signal exceptions that are declared for some component operations invoked from P, but are not declared for P itself. These are the exceptions signalled by lower level operations invoked from P and for which there are no associated handlers in P. As an example, assume that the definition of the language used to write the FE procedure specifies that an integer assignment, such as m := m × k, signals the language defined exception "intovflw" when the result of evaluating the right hand side expression is an integer that is not machine representable. Although the designer of the procedure FE did not declare an "intovflw" exceptional exit point, the procedure can signal this exception whenever the execution of m := m × k results in an arithmetic overflow. In such a case, the entire procedure FE terminates at the "intovflw" exit point, which was not declared for FE. We denote by X the set of *all* (declared and undeclared) exception labels that a program P can signal.

The intended state transition that a program P should perform when an *anticipated* exception e ∈E is detected can be specified by an *exceptional specification* G_e:

$$G_e \subseteq S \times S .$$

A pair of states (s,s') is in G_e if the *intended* outcome of invoking P in the initial state s ∈ S is to make P terminate at its declared "e" exceptional exit point in the final state s' ∈ S.

Like a standard specification, an exceptional specification may be partial, and may be structured into an exceptional precondition pre_e

$$pre_e : S \rightarrow \{true, false\}, \qquad s \in dom(G_e) \equiv pre_e(s) = true$$

and an exceptional postcondition $post_e$

$$post_e : S \times S \rightarrow \{true, false\}, \qquad (s,s') \in G_e \equiv post_e(s,s') = true.$$

The exceptional preconditions pre_e, $e \in E$, divide the input space of P into several labeled exceptional sub-domains. When a program P is invoked in the e-labeled exceptional sub-domain, one says that the exception e occurs.

We illustrate the notion of an exceptional specification, by specifying that the parameter n of FE should remain unchanged when it is initially negative. This can be done either by directly giving $GF_{negative}$

$$GF_{negative} \equiv \{(n,n') \mid n,n' \in Integer \ \& \ n < 0 \ \& \ n = n'\}$$

or by giving a pair of pre- postconditions:

$$pre_{negative} \equiv n < 0, \qquad post_{negative} \equiv n = n'.$$

Although the practice of structuring specifications into pre- and postconditions is very common, to keep notations short, it will not be used further in this chapter. The definitions to be given can be translated in terms of pre- and postconditions (if desired) by using the pre- and postcondition definitions given above.

The *exceptional semantics* $[P]_e$ of a program P with respect to an exception label $e \in X$ (either declared or undeclared for P) is the function (from input to output states) that P *actually* computes between its start and its termination at the "e" exit point:

$$[P]_e \subseteq S \times S .$$

A pair of states (s,s') is in $[P]_e$ if, when invoked in the initial state $s \in S$, P *terminates* at its "e" exit point in the final state s' $\in$ S.

For example, the function computed by FE when the "negative" exception is signalled is the identity function over the set $\{min,...,-1\}$:

$$[FE]_{negative} = \{(min, min),...,(-1, -1)\}.$$

The programs F and FE also compute the functions:

$$[F]_{intovflw} = [FE]_{intovflw} = \{(8,8),(9,9),...,(max, max)\}$$

$$[FE]_\sigma = \{(0,1),(1,1),...,(6,720),(7,5040)\} .$$

4.2.3 Program Failures, Faults, and Errors

Consider a program P whose specification is structured into a standard service G_σ and zero or more exceptional services G_e, $e \in E$. The *specification* G of P is the set of all standard and exceptional specifications defined for P:

$$G \equiv \{G_x \mid x \in E \cup \{\sigma\}\},$$

where E is the set of exception labels *declared* for P, that is, the set of exceptions *anticipated* by the designer of P. By convention, the standard exit point σ is always *declared* for any program. We assume that such a specification is implementable by a deterministic program, that is we assume that:

$$\forall x, y \in (E \cup \{\sigma\}) : (x \neq y) \Rightarrow (dom(G_x) \cap dom(G_y) = \{ \}).$$

Let AI (Anticipated Inputs) denote the set of all inputs for which the behavior of P is specified:

$$AI \equiv \bigcup_{x \in E \cup \{\sigma\}} dom(G_x)$$

We denote by UI (Unanticipated Inputs) the remaining possible input states, that is, the input states for which the behavior of P was left unspecified:

$$UI \equiv S - AI.$$

A specification is *complete* if it prescribes the behavior of P for all possible input states $s \in S$:

$$S \subseteq AI .$$

For instance, the specification $GF = \{GF_\sigma, GF_{negative}\}$ is not complete, since it does not specify the result to be produced when FE is invoked with a positive argument whose factorial is not machine representable. An example of a complete specification is $CGF = \{GF_\sigma, GF_{negative}, GF_{overflow}\}$, where

$$GF_{overflow} \equiv \{(n, n') \mid n, n' \in Integer \,\&\, n! > max \,\&\, n = n'\} .$$

The *semantics* of a program P with exceptional exit points X is the set of all semantic functions $[P]_x$, $x \in X \cup \{\sigma\}$, that P computes between a start and a termination at some (declared or undeclared) exit point x:

$$[P] \equiv \{[P]_x \mid x \in X \cup \{\sigma\}\}.$$

A program P is termed totally *correct* with respect to a specification G if its actual semantics [P] is *consistent* with the intended semantics G:

$$\forall x \in E \cup \sigma : dom(G_x) \subseteq dom([P]_x) \,\&\, \forall s, s' \in dom(G_x), S : (s, s') \in [P]_x \Rightarrow (s, s') \in G_x$$

That is, P is correct if it actually terminates at some declared exit point x every time the specification G requests that it terminate at x. Moreover, any final state s' actually produced by P from an anticipated initial state $s \in dom(G_x)$, for some $x \in E \cup \{\sigma\}$, is always consistent with the stated intention G_x. Correctness does not necessarily imply that [P] and G are equal. While P must be deterministic (i.e. [P] must be a function) G might be nondeterministic (i.e. G might not be a function). Moreover, there can be states s,s' such that $(s,s') \in [P]_x$ but $s \notin dom(G_x)$. For example, P might terminate normally $((s,s') \in [P]_\sigma)$ if invoked in initial states s for which the specification does not prescribe normal termination $(s \notin dom(G_\sigma))$. Methods for proving the total correctness of programs with exceptions are discussed in [Cri84].

```
procedure RFE(in out n: Integer) signals negative, overflow;
var k,m: Integer;
begin
  [n<0: signal negative];
  k:=0; m:=1;
  while k<n
  do k:=k+1;
      m:=m × k[intovflw: signal overflow]
  od;
  n:=m
end;
```

Figure 4.3   A robust factorial program with exceptions

For example, the program FE is totally correct with respect to the specification GF, but is incorrect with respect to the complete specification CGF. An example program RFE (Robust Factorial with Exceptions) that is totally correct with respect to the complete specification CGF is given in Figure 4.3. The overflow exception declared for RFE is detected *when* the lower level machine exception intovflw is propagated into RFE.

A program that is totally correct with respect to a complete specification is *robust*, in that its behavior is predictable for *all* possible inputs. Besides other characteristics such as functionality, ease of use, and performance, robustness is one of the most important aspects of a program and its documentation. The procedure RFE is robust since its behavior is correctly predicted by the specification CGF for all possible initial values of n.

A robust program whose exceptional specifications G_e, $e \in E$, are identity relations is called *atomic* with respect to the exceptions $e \in E$. For an external observer, any invocation of such a program has an "all or nothing" effect: either the specified standard state transition is produced or an exception is signalled and the state remains unchanged. Methods for proving the correctness of data abstractions with atomic operations are discussed in [Cri82].

Remark: The adjective "atomic" is over-used in the programming community and one has to carefully distinguish among the different meanings it takes in different contexts. In a multiprocessing context, it is used to qualify the interference-free or serializable execution of parallel operations [Ber87, Bes81b]. In a context in which program interpreter crashes can occur, a command C is said to be atomic with respect to crashes if a crash occurrence during the execution of C either causes no stable state transition or causes the stable state transition specified for C [Cri85]. Clearly atomicity with respect to concurrency on one side and atomicity with respect to exceptions or crashes on the other side are fairly distinct, orthogonal concepts. Although the basic idea behind atomicity with respect to exceptions and atomicity with respect to crashes is the same, work on verifying atomicity with respect to crashes and atomicity with respect to exceptions shows that these are two fairly distinct concepts, usually implemented by distinct run-time mechanisms [Cri84, Cri85]. *End of remark.*

If a program P is not totally correct with respect to a specification G, there exist (anticipated) input states $s \in$ AI for which P's behavior *contradicts* G. The set of all input states for which the actual behavior of P contradicts the specified behavior G is the *failure domain* FD of P with respect to G:

$$FD \equiv AI - (SD \cup AED),$$

where AED denotes the set of all input states for which correct exceptional results are produced

$$AED = \bigcup_{e \in E} \{s \mid \exists s' : (s,s') \in [P]_e \ \& \ (s,s') \in G_e\} \ .$$

The characteristic predicate of the AED domain can be computed as being the disjunction of the weakest preconditions for which P terminates at declared exit points e in final states satisfying the exceptional specifications G_e [Cri84].

As an example, observe that the failure domain of the program FE with respect to the specification CGF is the set of all positive integers with non machine representable factorials. Note also that for a program P to fail for an input, the behavior of P for that input must be described by the specification G. One can talk about a *specification failure* whenever a specification fails to prescribe the program behavior for some inputs, that is, whenever UI $\neq$ { }. Specification failures are in fact as annoying as program failures.

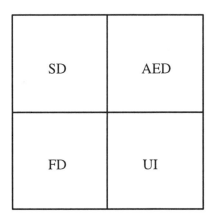

Figure 4.4   A partition over the set of all input states

The domains SD, AED, FD, and UI introduced previously define a partition over the set of all input states, in that they are pairwise disjoint and their union is the set of all possible input states S (see Figure 4.4). A goal of good software practice is to make sure that the FD and UI domains are empty. Methods for computing the domains SD, AED, FD for programs with exceptions are described in [Cri84].

A *program failure* occurs when a program is invoked in its failure domain FD. Thus, a program failure is synonymous with *divergence* between specified and actual program behavior. A failure of a sequential program P for an input $s \in$ FD can be of one the following four types:

1) P loops indefinitely: $\neg \exists x \in X \cup \{\sigma\} : s \in dom([P]_x)$
2) an exception u that was not declared for P is detected: $\exists u \in X - E : s \in dom([P]_u)$
3) P terminates normally (*i.e.*, at its standard exit point) in a final state s' which does not satisfy the standard specification of P: $\exists s' : (s,s') \in [P]_\sigma \ \& \ (s,s') \notin G_\sigma$,
4) P terminates by signalling a declared exception $e \in E$ in a final state s' which does not satisfy the exceptional specification $G_e : \exists s' : (s,s') \in [P]_e \ \& \ (s,s') \notin G_e$.

Note that the definition given to the notion of program failure does not imply that an occurrence of a program failure is actually recognized (detected) by a program user, either human or another program. Typically, failures of type (3) or (4) which result in *proper* program termination in some erroneous state (that is, termination at a declared exit point) are more difficult to detect than failures of type (1) or (2) which result in *improper* program termination. Indeed, non-termination (detected by a timeout) or termination at an undeclared exit (e.g. with a run-time "error message") are obvious indications of a faulty program for an observer external to the program (e.g. human user, other program, or operating system), while proper program termination is a behavior that an external observer expects from a correct program.

Not only are failures of type (3) and (4) more difficult to detect, but they also have a greater potential for being disruptive than those which manifest themselves by improper program termination, since they may result in further failures. Often, proper termination in some unrecognized erroneous state is followed by further program invocations from that state. These invocations can result in further unpredictable behavior, until an external human observer discovers at some later time a discrepancy between specified and actual program results. At that time, very little can be said about the consistency of the program state.

Failures of type (1) or (2) are referred to as *confined failures*, while failures of type (3) or (4) are referred to as *unconfined failures*. Corresponding to these two general failure classes, the failure domain FD can be divided into a *confined failure domain* CFD, and an *unconfined failure domain* UFD:

$$FD = CFD \cup UFD .$$

A program P which, for every input, either terminates properly in a state satisfying the specification G or suffers a confined failure will be termed *partially correct* with respect to the specification G. In other terms, a partially correct program is one that has empty UI and UFD domains. This notion of partial correctness is somewhat different from the classical notion of partial correctness [Flo67, Hoa69], where partial correctness is defined in term of a pre and postcondition. In this chapter, when we talk about partial correctness we assume a constantly true precondition and a complete specification. Our notion of partial correctness is however such a natural extension of the classical notion that we feel it does not justify the introduction of a new term for it (in [Gra93] programs that are partially correct — in the sense of having empty UI and UFD domains — are termed "fail-fast").

The interest in partially correct programs comes from the fact that such programs are *safe*, in the sense that they never output erroneous results to their users. Methods for verifying that programs with exceptions are partially correct are described in [Bac79, Bro76, Luc80]. In combination with a run-time mechanisms for detecting improper program termination and an alternate program for outputting a default "safe value" (when correct primary output is unavailable from a primary partially correct program in a timely manner), partially correct programs can be used to build *fail-safe* programs, that is, programs that either deliver a correct output in a timely manner or otherwise deliver a predefined output considered "safe" for the application at hand (like "close ATM window" when the procedure that identifies current client fails). Note also that in the literature on database transactions [Ber87, Gra93] it is standard to assume that *transactions* are implemented by partially correct programs.

The occurrence of program failures can be attributed to the *existence* of design faults. Thus, if the failure domain FD of a program P with respect to a specification G is not empty, one says that the program P has a *design fault* with respect to the specification G.

For example, any invocation of the program F (which is incorrect with respect to the complete specification CGF) with an initial value n such that n! is not machine representable results in improper termination of F. The absence of a handler associated with the intovflw language defined exception in Figure 4.1 is thus a design fault. This (confined) design fault

procedure FFE(*in out* n: Integer) *signals* negative;
var k,m: Integer;
begin
  [n<0: *signal* negative];
  k:=0; m:=1;
  while k < n
  do m:=m × k;
    k:=k+1;
  od;
  n:=m
end;

Figure 4.5 A faulty factorial program with exceptions

leads to the existence of a nonempty confined failure domain (the set of all positive integers with non-machine representable factorials) for F.

Consider now the case when the unconfined failure domain of a program P contains a state s such that, when started in s, P terminates properly at some declared exit point x in a final state s" different from the intended final state s' prescribed by the specification G_x for s. Then there exist program variables v whose state is *erroneous*, in that their value s"(v) is different from the value s'(v) prescribed by the specification G_x. The value that such a variable v possesses in s" is called an *error* (with respect to the specification G_x).

As an example of an unconfined design fault which can lead to output errors that can spread to other programs, consider the version FFE (Faulty Factorial with Exceptions) of the procedure FE, given in Figure 4.5, in which the two operations of the loop body have been transposed. The standard domain of FFE with respect to the specification CGF is {0}. Whenever FFE is invoked with an actual parameter that is strictly positive, the final value of n (0) is an error since it is different from the final value prescribed by CGF.

4.3 EXCEPTION HANDLING IN HIERARCHICAL MODULAR PROGRAMS

In this section, we investigate what it means to handle exceptions in modular programs structured as hierarchies of data abstractions. The basic problems to be solved at each abstraction level, such as exception detection, consistent state recovery, exception masking and propagation are discussed. Both programmed and default exception handling methods are considered. An assessment of the effectiveness of backward recovery based default exception handling (as embodied for example in the recovery block mechanism [Hor74]) in providing effective tolerance of residual design faults is provided.

The scope of this section is limited to discussing tolerance of program design faults, not tolerance to specification faults or lower level service failures, so we assume that specifications are correct and the lower level services on which a hierarchical modular program depends are also correctly functioning. Such lower level services might of course signal exceptions, but we assume that the standard and exceptional state transitions that these services undergo are consistent with their specification. For example if the program depends on a file service, exceptions such as "no-such directory" or "end-of-file" can be signalled, but we assume that they are detected and handled correctly at the file service level before being propagated to our hierarchical program. This topic of providing tolerance to software design faults affecting a given program is sufficiently complex to deserve consideration separate from other interesting areas like tolerance of hardware failures or lower level service failures. Our opinion is that responsibility for coping with faults specific to each interpretation level (i.e. detection and at least signalling) must fall on the designers of the level concerned. For an attempt to integrate software and hardware fault-tolerance, the interested reader is referred to [Cri91].

To keep the presentation short, we give fewer examples than in the first, more introductory, part. Detailed examples of the often tricky problems posed by exception handling in programs structured as hierarchies of abstract data types can be found in [Cri82].

4.3.1 Hierarchical Program Structure

In the 70s, it became clear that *data abstraction* is a powerful mechanism for mastering the complexity of programs [Hoa72, Lis74, Par72a, Wul76]. Researchers in programming methodology suggested that the right way to solve a programming problem was to repeatedly decompose the problem into sub-problems, where each sub-problem could be easily solved by writing an "abstract" program module in an "abstract" language which possessed all the right data types needed to make the solution to that sub-problem simple. Those data types assumed in such modules that were not available in the programming language used were called "abstract", as opposed to the built-in "concrete" types. The implementation of these abstract types then was just a new programming problem, which had to be solved recursively by writing other program modules in terms of other (possibly abstract) data types. The programming process would then continue until the problem of implementing all assumed abstract data types was solved only in terms of concrete types.

The programming methodology outlined above leads to programs which are structured into a *hierarchy of modules* [Par72a, Par74], where each module implements some instance of an abstract data type. Visually, such a hierarchy may be represented by an acyclic graph as in Figure 4.6. Modules are represented by nodes. An arrow from a node N to a node M means that N is a *user* of M, that is, the successful completion of (at least) an operation N.Q exported by N depends on the successful completion of some operation M.P exported by M. In what follows we frequently refer to the hierarchy illustrated in Figure 4.6, by using O, P, and Q as names for operations exported by the modules L, M, and N, respectively, and by using d, e, f as generic exception names for the operations O, P, and Q, respectively.

When observed from a user's point of view (*e.g.*, N), a module M is perceived as being an (abstract) *variable* declared to be of some *abstract data type*. To make use of a module M, it is only necessary to know the set of *abstract states* that may be assumed by M and the set of abstract state *transitions* that are produced when the operations exported by M are invoked. The internal structure of a module is not visible to a user. When seen from inside, a module M is a set of *state variables* and a set of *procedures*. A state variable may be either of a predefined type (*e.g.*, integer, Boolean, array) directly provided by the programming language being used, or may be of some programmer defined abstract type, in which case, it is implemented by some lower level module (*e.g.*, L).

The *internal state* of a module M is the aggregation of the abstract states of its state variables. The *abstract state* of M is the result of applying an *abstraction function* A to its internal state [Hoa72, Wul76]. In general, A is a partial function defined only over a subset $I \subseteq S$ of the set of all possible internal states of the module. (In practice, this subset is defined by using an *invariant* predicate [Hoa72, Wul76].) The internal states in I are said to be *consistent* with the

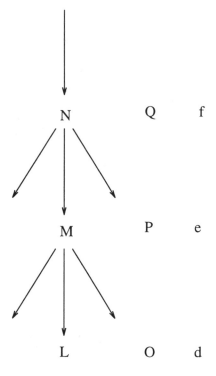

Figure 4.6   An acyclic graph representing a program hierarchy

abstraction that the module is intended to implement. During a procedure execution, a module may pass through a set of intermediate internal states i which are inconsistent (i.e. i $\notin$ I) and for which A, and hence the abstract state, are not defined.

4.3.2   Programmed Exception Handling

Every procedure P exported by a module M is designed to accomplish a specified standard service: some intended internal, and hence abstract, state transition. As discussed in the first part, P can also be required to provide zero or more exceptional services in addition to its standard service. Let

$$G \equiv \{G_x \mid x \in E \cup \{\sigma\}\}$$

denote the global specification of M.P, where E is the set of all exceptions declared for P. We require such specifications to be strong enough to exclude an inconsistent state being an intended outcome when P is invoked in a consistent state (remember that we are interested in discussing the adequacy of default exception handling in providing tolerance of program design — not specification — faults):

$$\forall x \in E \cup \{\sigma\} : \forall s \in I : \forall s' \in S : (s,s') \in G_x \Rightarrow s' \in I.$$

Usually, the standard and exceptional specifications of P are not defined by enumerating all the component pairs of each G_x, $x \in E \cup \{\sigma\}$, but by using pre and post conditions as mentioned in the first part of the chapter. We use sets and relations to specify the operations we present in our discussion instead of predicates because they provide us with a more compact representation. Of course, the entire discussion can be translated in terms of pre, postconditions, and invariants without any difficulty.

Consider now an exception e declared for a procedure P and let G_e be the specification of the state transition to be produced when e occurs. As discussed in the first part, an occurrence of e may be *detected*: (a) either by a run-time check, or (b) because a lower level exception d is propagated in P by a lower level operation O invoked from P. In the latter case the detection of e coincides with the propagation of d in P, that is, with the invocation of a handler H *of* e. Although this handler is syntactically *associated* with the lower level propagated exception d by using a (b) language construct of the form O[d:H], it is essential to understand that its semantics (the exceptional state transition it has to accomplish) is determined solely by the exceptional specification G_e. We use the phrase "handler associated with" to state a syntactic fact and the phrase "handler of" to reflect a semantic knowledge.

When an exception occurrence is detected in a module M, an intermediate *inconsistent state* outside the set I may exist. An example in [Cri82] illustrates that further invocations of a module left in such a state (by some exception occurrence not appropriately handled) can lead to unpredictable (*i.e.*, unspecified) results and to subsequent unanticipated exception occurrences. To avoid such consequences, it is necessary that measures for the recovery of a consistent state are taken by the handler H *of* e.

Let $s \in I$ be the consistent state prior to the invocation of P and $i \in S$ be the state of M when e is detected. A set of state variables of M is called a *recovery set* RS if by modifying the state that these variables have in i, a final state s' such that $(s,s') \in G_e$ can be reached. Note that according to our earlier definition of an error, the values assumed by the variables of RS in the intermediate state i are not erroneous with respect to the specification G of P, since G does not prescribe through what intermediate states P should transit between successive invocations. In general, there exist several recovery sets for an exception detection. From a performance point of view, the most interesting recovery set is the one with the fewest elements. An *inconsistency set* IS is a recovery set such that for any other recovery set RS: $| IS | \leq | RS |$, where $| \ |$ denotes set cardinality. Because of this minimality property, an IS can be regarded as being a characterization of that part of the state which is "effectively" inconsistent when the occurrence of e is detected. For nontrivial examples of inconsistency and recovery sets, the interested reader is referred to [Cri82].

If the decision is taken that module operations should be atomic with respect to exceptions, then two other kinds of recovery sets may be of interest. Let us define the *inconsistency closure* IC associated with the intermediate state i, existing when e is detected, to be the set of all state variables modified between the entry in P and the detection of e. An IC is a recovery set (for any abstraction function A and any invariant I), since by resetting all the modified variables to their initial (abstract) states, a final internal state s' identical to the initial internal state s is obtained. The second kind of recovery set is the crudest approximation one can imagine for an IS (an inconsistency closure is a better one). This approximation is obtained by taking the whole set of state variables of M (with their state in s) to form a complete *checkpoint* CP of the initial internal state s of M. Clearly, by restoring all variables of M (whether modified or not between the entry in P and the detection of e) to their state prior to the invocation of P, a final internal state s' identical to the initial state s is obtained.

procedure P *signals* e;
begin

.

.

  [DET: recover RS; *signal* e]

.

.

end;

Figure 4.7   Recovery of a consistent state before signalling an exception

After the above discussion on recovery sets, we can now describe the task of a handler H of e as being to *recover* some RS before *signalling* e. Of course, if the state i in which e is detected already satisfies the specification G_e, i.e. (s,i) $\in$ G_e, then no recovery action is necessary, that is, the IS associated with such an exception detection is empty.

If the exceptional postcondition G_e specified for the detected exception e is not the identity relation *i.e.*, P is not intended to behave atomically with respect to exceptions, then the recovery action of H is said to be *forward* [Ran78]. From an internal point of view, the recovery of an RS is "forward" if the final state of at least one variable in RS is different from its state when P was invoked. A forward recovery action is based on knowledge about the module semantics (captured by the internal invariant I, the abstraction function A, and the specification G_e) and, thus, has to be explicitly programmed by the implementer of P. However, if P is intended to have an atomic behavior, then the determination of the IC or CP recovery sets (which are independent of I, A, and G_e) can be done automatically at run-time. Checkpointing techniques have long been used for recovering consistent system states. Later, it has been proposed [Ber87, Gra93, Hor74], to leave the task of computing the inconsistency closures associated with the intermediate inconsistent states i through which a system may pass to special mechanisms, called *recovery caches* or *log managers*.

The (automatic) recovery of inconsistency closures or checkpoints is referred to as *backward recovery* [Ran78]. More generally, one can view the recovery of some RS as being "backward" if all the variables in RS recover their states prior to the invocation of P. To avoid confusion between explicitly programmed "backward" recovery and that performed by a recovery cache, a log manager, or a checkpointing mechanism, we will call the latter *automatic backward recovery*.

To conclude this discussion on the detection and recovery issues raised by the handling of an exception e in a procedure P, let us denote by "[DET:" the "[B:" or "O[d:" syntactic construct used to detect an occurrence of e. The handling of e in the procedure M.P where it is detected may be summarized as shown in Figure 4.7: a consistent state must be recovered for module M before the exception e is signalled to the user of M.P. Let us now investigate the consequences that a *propagation* of e by *M.P* may have for the invoking procedure *N.Q* (see Figure 4.6). In some cases, the propagation of a lower level exception e in a procedure Q is a consequence of invoking Q within its own exceptional domain. Such a situation was illustrated by the example of Figure 4.3 where the lower level exception intovflw is propagated in RFE whenever RFE is invoked in the exceptional subdomain n!>max. However, there exist cases in which a lower level exception may be propagated in a procedure even though that procedure was invoked within its standard domain.

As an example, suppose that module N is a file management module which exports a procedure "CREATE a file containing Z disk blocks," where Z is of type positive integer.

procedure CREATE (Z:positive-integer) *signals* ns;
begin

.

M_1.AL(Z)[do: M_2.AL(Z)[do: recover RS; *signal* ns]];

.

.

end;

Figure 4.8   Space allocation in a program

Assume that each file is completely stored either on a disk d_1 or on a disk d_2 and that M_1, M_2 are the modules which manage the free blocks left on d_1 and d_2, respectively. An initial state in which at least one disk has more than Z free blocks will be in the standard domain of CREATE and a state in which both disks have less than Z free blocks will be in its exceptional domain. Suppose that the space allocation within CREATE is programmed as shown in Figure 4.8.

If CREATE is invoked in a state in which d_1 has less than Z free blocks, then the handler associated with the "do" (Disk Overflow) exit point of the space allocation procedure M_1.AL is invoked. Now there remain two possibilities. If the initial state was in the standard domain, that is, d_2 has at least Z free blocks, then M_2.AL terminates normally and the continuation is standard (*i.e.*, the handler associated with the "do" exit point of M_2.AL , is not invoked). Otherwise, if the initial state was in the exceptional domain of CREATE, the propagation of the disk overflow exception by M_2.AL coincides with the detection of the "ns" (No Space) exception declared for CREATE. The handler *of* "ns" (the sequence "recover RS; *signal* ns") recovers a consistent state before propagating "ns" higher up in the hierarchy.

This example illustrates two points. First, the "[DET:" symbol used previously in Figure 4.7 may sometimes be a sequence of "O[d:" detection symbols (this is frequently the case when dealing with exceptions due to transient input/output faults [Cri79a]). Second, lower level exception propagations can be stopped by higher lever procedures.

If a procedure Q can provide its standard service despite the fact that a lower level exception e is propagated in Q, we say that Q *masks* the propagation of e.

4.3.3   Default Exception Handling

As mentioned in the first part, one of the main goals in program design is to achieve correctness and robustness. Despite recent advances in understanding the issues involved in the production of correct and robust programs, the design of software that is correct and robust remains a nontrivial task. In practice, instead of relying on rigorous programming and validation methods, many software designers rely upon their intuition and experience to deal with possible exception occurrences. Therefore, the identification and handling of the exceptional situations which might occur is often just as (un)reliable as human intuition.

Consider now the case of a faulty procedure P exported by a module M. Let us assume for the moment that M.P is partially correct, that is, any invocation of M.P in its (non-empty) failure domain is detected because an unanticipated exception u is propagated by a lower level operation L.O in P (in particular, u might be a time-out exception). The case when a failure of M.P remains undetected after a proper termination of M.P will be discussed later.

Now, what is a sensible reaction to such a situation? For example, what exceptional continuation should be associated with the exception u propagated from a lower level? One possible solution (adopted in ADA [Ich79]) is to continue the propagation of u in the higher level

procedure P *signals* e;
begin

.

.

.

.

end[:DH];

Figure 4.9   A default handler implicitly provided by the compiler

module N. Such free exception propagations across module boundaries may have dangerous consequences. First, according to the "information hiding principle" of modular programming [Par72a], the designer of N is not supposed to know anything about the modules L used by M. Thus, an exception label u, declared for an operation O of a lower level module L is likely to be meaningless to the designer of N and it is probable that there will be no handler explicitly associated with u in N.Q. Second, propagating u from L.O directly into N.Q violates the basic principle that after any procedure invocation from M.P control should return back in the invoking procedure M.P. Indeed, any L.O invocation which results in a propagation of u is a definitive exit from M.P (through an exit point which has not been declared for M.P!). Third, and this is perhaps the most serious consequence, if the lower level procedure L.O was invoked from M.P when M was in an intermediate inconsistent state, then the propagation of u in N.Q leaves M in that inconsistent state. Thus, there is a danger that later invocations of M will lead to unpredictable results and to additional unanticipated exception propagations.

A different approach to the problem of handling detectable failure occurrences is discussed in [Cri79a, Hor74, Lis79]. The basic idea is quite simple: associate a *default handler* DH, with any lower level (unanticipated) exception u propagated in a procedure exported by a module M. The default handler DH is implicitly provided by the compiler (Figure 4.9).

The " " before the ":" symbol stands for any exception which can be propagated in P and which has no explicitly associated handler in P. The exceptional service that such a handler attempts to provide can be identified by a language defined exception label "failure" [Cri79b, Lis79], or "error" [Hor74]. The systematic addition of default handlers to all procedures exported by modules, written in a language in which the "failure" exception is predefined, has the following consequences. For any lower level exception which may be propagated in a procedure $M.P$, there exists an exceptional continuation in M.P (either one explicitly defined or the default continuation DH). A "failure" (or "error") exit point is implicitly added to any procedure exported by a module.

Default exception handlers can be designed to solve the same problems as those mentioned previously for programmed exception handlers. These are (1) *masking*, (2) consistent state *recovery*, and (3) *signalling*. But while the programmer of an explicit handler H, specifically inserted in a specific procedure M.P, knows the intended semantics (captured by I, A, G) of M.P, and, therefore, can provide a specific masking algorithm or determine an inconsistency set to be recovered, this knowledge is not available to the programming language designer who decides on a general default exception handling strategy for *all* programs which will be written in that language.

The default exception handling strategy embodied in the CLU programming language developed at MIT [Lis79] is oriented towards solving problem (3), related to the (proper) propagation of "failure" exceptions across module boundaries, *i.e.*, each default handler is of the form DH $\equiv$ *signal* failure. In CLU, a suitable error message may be passed as a parameter to a *signal* failure sequencer to help in fixing off-line the cause of the failure detection. However, according to terminology introduced in [Mel77, Ran78], tolerance of failure detections implies at least the resolution of problems (2) and (3). Thus, one can regard the default exception handling strategy of CLU as being more oriented towards off-line debugging rather than towards the provision of on-line software-fault tolerance.

The default exception handling strategy proposed for the SESAME programming language developed at the University of Grenoble [Cri79a] was oriented towards solving the consistent state recovery (2) and propagation (3) problems. (The masking problem (1) can also be solved by using our mechanism, as will be shown later, but we have not dealt with this issue in [Cri79a].) The solution proposed to problem (2) is based on the fact that, for any exception which can be detected in a procedure M.P, there exists a recovery set, *i.e.*, the *inconsistency closure*, which can be determined at run-time without having any knowledge about the semantics of M.P. A recovery cache mechanism (more simple than that of [Hor74] because of the modular scope rules of SESAME) was designed for the automatic update of the inconsistency closures associated with all intermediate states through which a system may pass. A detailed description of this mechanism has already been published [Cri79b], so we will not repeat it here. To enable the automatic recovery of inconsistency closures, a *reset* primitive was made available in the SESAME language (as a compilation option). When invoked, *reset* recovers the "current" IC and returns normally. This primitive is mainly used in default handlers, but is also available to a programmer. (If the exceptional state transition G_e specified for some anticipated exception e is the identity relation, then by inserting a *reset* primitive in the handler of e, the programmer is relieved from the burden of explicitly identifying and restoring some recovery set.) Problem (3) is solved by requiring the propagation of "failure" exceptions to obey the same rules as the propagation of anticipated exceptions. Thus, a DH handler in SESAME is defined as DH $\equiv$ *reset*; *signal* failure.

Default handlers can be inserted only by the complier, *i.e.*, "failure" exceptions cannot be explicitly handled. Programmers can nevertheless explicitly signal "failure" exceptions. This often happens when a Boolean check for an invariant relation, which should be true if the program were correct, is actually found false at run-time. Termination of a program with a "failure" exception is *improper*. Thus, for a language which incorporates the notion of a "failure" exception, one can extend the definition of a partially correct program, given earlier, as follows:

> A program is *partially correct* if, for any possible input, it either terminates properly in a final state satisfying the program specification, or it fails to terminate properly.

It is interesting to note that the default exception handling strategy embodied in SESAME is very similar to the undo-log based strategy used to abort transaction executions that result in unanticipated exception detections or assertion violations [Ber87, Gra93]. Most database systems do not attempt to mask transaction aborts caused by exception detections to users.

The recovery block mechanism, devised at the University of Newcastle upon Tyne [Hor74], was designed to solve all the problems (1)–(3) mentioned above. Unlike the mechanisms described in [Cri79a, Lis79] which support *both* explicit and default exception handling, the recovery block mechanism is a pure default exception handling mechanism based on automatic backward recovery. To deal with a possible "failure" detection (the label "error" is used in [Hor74]) in a procedure P designed to provide some specified standard service $post_\sigma$, a programmer can define P to be the primary block P_0 of a *recovery block* possessing zero or more alternate blocks $P_1, P_2, \ldots, P_k$. and an acceptance test *at* that is supposed to check

$post_\sigma$. Assume (for simplicity) that a single alternate P_1 is provided. The syntax of a recovery block construct RB in this case is

   RB $\equiv$ *ensure at by P_0 else by P_1 else* failure.

The semantics of the recovery block can be expressed in terms of our exception handling notation as follows:

   RB $= PP_0[$: *reset*; $PP_1[$: *reset*; *signal* failure]];

where

   $PP_i \equiv$ *begin P_i*; [$\neg$ *at*: *signal* failure] *end*

If a "failure" exception is detected during the execution of the P_0 procedure (because some lower level exception is propagated in P_0 or because the acceptance test *at* evaluates to false when P_0 terminates), then the *inconsistency closure* associated with this failure detection is restored by a recovery cache device and the alternate P_1 is invoked. The aim of the alternate is to *mask* the failure detected in PP_0 by achieving the specified state transition $post_\sigma$ in a different way. Since no attempt is made at elucidating the reason why P_0 could not achieve *post*, the construction of an alternate P_1 is based on the sole assumption that, when invoked, P_1 starts in the same state as the primary P_0. If the invocation of P_1 leads to another failure detection, then the masking problem (1) cannot be successfully solved at the level of RB. Problem (2) is solved by invoking again the recovery cache to restore the inconsistency closure associated with the "failure" exception detected in PP_1. Problem (3) is dealt with by propagating a failure signal to the user of RB. The termination of an RB is standard if no failure is detected during the execution of PP_0 or if a failure detection in PP_0 can be masked by the normal termination of PP_1 in a final state in which *at* is true.

The above discussion assumes that a precise monolithic run-time check *at* equivalent to $post_\sigma$ can be programmed. In practice, postconditions usually contain logical quantifiers and other expressions not directly available in a programming language. Thus, to program a Boolean (executable) expression *at* with the same truth value as $post_\sigma$ may turn out to be at least as difficult as programming an alternate. (In [Bes81a], a methodology for splitting such monolithic acceptance checks into sets of simpler assertions without quantifiers spread among the intermediate operations which compose operations like P_0, P_1 is investigated, but pursuing such a verification-oriented approach leads naturally to a programmed, rather than default, exception handling style.) What can happen in practice is that the acceptance test *at* is an approximation of $post_\sigma$: only some, but not all, invocations of P_0, P_1 in their failure domain will be detected by *at* or by the occurrence of an unanticipated exception at run-time. In such a case, the recovery block program RB, resulting from combining the alternates P_0, P_1 with the acceptance test *at* in the manner described above, will not be partially correct, in the sense that certain invocations of RB in its failure domain will result in proper termination of the RB in an erroneous final state.

4.3.4   Exception Handling in Hierarchies of Data Abstractions

Consider a software system structured into a hierarchy of data abstractions (Figure 4.6). Let $\{C_i\}$ be the set of operations exported by data abstractions visible to system users. These data abstractions, storing information which is significant to the users, are generally implemented by high-level modules. Let us distinguish a C_i operation from other (lower level) hidden operations by calling C_i a system *command*. (If the data abstractions visible to users are stored in a data base on stable storage, what we call a command would probably corresponds to a database transaction.) A purpose of programmed and default exception handling is to ensure that system command executions preserve the internal invariant properties inherent to the data abstractions which compose the system in spite of possible exception occurrences.

Suppose that the invocation of a command C_i leads to the occurrence of an (anticipated or unanticipated) exception d when some lower level operation L.O is invoked. The operation L.O is said to be *tolerant* to the occurrence of d if d is detected and the (programmed or default) handler of d recovers a consistent state for L before propagating d to the invoking procedure M.P. If this procedure can stop the propagation of d, then M.P is said to be *mask* the occurrence of d. Otherwise, if the propagation of d coincides with the detection of a higher level exception e in M.P, M.P in its turn must be tolerant to e. In general, if an exception propagation d, e, f, . . . takes place across modules L, M, N, . . . and none of the traversed modules can perform a successful masking, then each module must be tolerant with respect to that propagation (*i.e.*, each must contain programmed or default handlers able to recover a consistent module state and continue the propagation).

Default exception handling based on automatic backward recovery can be used to tolerate or mask the unanticipated exceptions detected during the execution of system commands. After a command execution is terminated, the recovery data maintained by the recovery cache has to be discarded to allow the cache to keep track of the inconsistency closures associated with further potential exception detections during the next command execution.

4.3.5   Tolerance of Design Faults

Assume now that there is a design fault in a procedure M.P. A failure occurrence when P is invoked (in some state within its failure domain) is a *manifestation* of the design fault. Between a manifestation and a detection of the consequences of this manifestation (either by a run-time check or by a human user who observes a discrepancy between the actual and specified behavior of the system containing P), a fault is called *latent*.

A system can be called *design-fault tolerant* if its commands tolerate or mask lower level failure occurrences caused by design faults. As discussed previously default exception handling based on automatic backward recovery can be used to provide design fault tolerance, but the question is: to what extent can one depend on this technique to make tolerable the consequences of human mistakes made during the design (or debugging) of a system?

Let us call the time interval between the beginning and the termination of a command a *command execution interval* and let us call the time elapsed between a manifestation of a design fault and a detection of the consequences of this manifestation a *latency interval*. Suppose that when a command C_i is started, the internal states of the system modules are consistent, and that during the execution of C_i a design fault manifests itself. If this manifestation leads to a failure exception detection before the termination of C_i, then by invoking automatic backward recovery it is possible to restore, for all system modules invoked since the beginning of C_i, internal states which are equivalent to those which existed at the beginning of C_i. These recovered internal states are then consistent, and the danger of later additional unanticipated exception detections is avoided.

However, it is possible that the manifestation of a design fault does not cause some explicitly checked assertion to be violated, so that no failure exception is detected during the execution of the C_i command. In such a case, when C_i terminates some of the component modules of the system can be in an inconsistent state. It is then possible that a failure exception caused by the design fault which has manifested itself during the execution of C_i is detected during some later command execution C_j. The invocation of automatic backward recovery will then restore internal module states which are equivalent to those which existed at the beginning of C_j. But since these states were already inconsistent, the recovered system state will be inconsistent and the danger of further unpredictable behavior and additional unanticipated exception detections persists.

Thus, while default exception handling based on automatic backward recovery *guarantees* tolerance of design faults with latency intervals contained within command execution intervals, it is *not adequate* for coping with design faults having latency intervals which stretch over successive command executions. In other terms: in a system where the user visible commands are implemented by using recovery blocks (or database transactions), backward recovery based default exception handling guarantees proper behavior despite design faults only if the outer-most recovery blocks (or database transactions) are *partially correct*. Clearly, the use of automatic backward recovery improves the chance that crucial data will remain consistent in the presence of failure detections, since it provides tolerance for all confined design faults. Experimental studies confirm this [And85]. However, to acquire confidence that a recovery block is capable of tolerating *all* design faults that might be contained in its alternates and acceptance test is in fact as hard as proving that these alternates together with the acceptance test are partially correct.

4.4 CONCLUSIONS

This chapter gives mathematically rigorous definitions for notions basic to the design of dependable software such as specification, program semantics, exception, program correctness and robustness. It also defines with precision concepts fundamental to fault-tolerant computing, such as program failure, program design fault, and error. To define precisely these often used — but rarely defined — terms, we introduced a number of other concepts that are useful for future discussions of software-fault tolerance issues, such as standard domain, anticipated exceptional domain, failure domain, and unanticipated input domain.

The notion of an exception is defined in terms of the set of possible input states of a program and the standard specification for that program, to mean "impossibility of obtaining the specified standard service". It therefore depends on how the states of a program are defined and how the standard service of that program is specified. If the probability of invoking the program in its standard domain is in general greater than that of invoking it in its exceptional domain, this definition is consistent with the probabilistic point of view adopted in [Che86]. However, unlike in [Che86], we view exceptions purely as a specification and program *structuring tool*, and we refrain from discussing the criteria to be used when deciding on how to use exceptions to structure programs. Our definitions are general precisely because they are independent from any such criteria. Probability of successfully completing a state transition is one such criterion. This criterion might be useful when a great deal of statistical information about program inputs is available. Often, at the beginning of a design such information does not exist, and other criteria for partitioning the input domains of programs into subdomains must be adopted.

Exception occurrences can result in delivery of specified exceptional services (when anticipated) or in the delivery of unspecified results or program failures (when unanticipated). While anticipated exceptional program responses share with failures the characteristic "impossibility of obtaining the requested standard service", they also share with correct standard program responses the characteristic "the program behaves as specified". Exceptions can therefore be viewed as being a software structuring concept that helps bridge the conceptual gap which exists between behaviors as opposite as "correct standard service provided" at one extreme, and "program failure" at the other extreme.

The notions defined in Section 4.2 of this chapter are central to many programming related areas such as testing, stochastic reliability estimation, program verification, and design-fault tolerant programming. Testing attempts to hit the failure domain of a program with test data to reveal design faults. Often testing helps discover possible inputs in the unanticipated input domain of a program. Stochastic software reliability estimation methods attempt to predict the "size" of the failure domain, given the estimated sizes of the failure domains of successive program versions during a testing period. Program verification, like testing, aims at discovering program design faults, if they exist. It differs from testing in that it also attempts at proving the absence of such faults, if they do not exist. Design-fault tolerant programming techniques start from the premise that the failure domains associated with program designs are never empty, and attempt to mask component program failures by relying on the use of design diversity [Avi84, Hor74]. The intention is to construct several program versions for a single specification so that the failure domain of the resulting multi-version program is smaller than the failure domains of the individual program versions used. Empirical investigations of the likelihood of this goal being achieved for actual programs can be found in [And85, Eck91].

Section 4.3 of this chapter investigates *what is* exception handling in programs structured as hierarchies of data abstractions. The answer proposed is a simple one. At each level of abstraction, exception handling consists of: detection, attempt at masking, consistent state recovery, and propagation. Several problems posed by default exception handling in programming languages which support data abstraction (such as Ada) are. Finally, an assessment of the adequacy of automatic backward recovery based default exception handling (such as embodied in recovery blocks [Hor74] or database transactions [Ber87, Gra93]) in providing design-fault tolerance was provided: automatic backward recovery guarantees tolerance of design faults only in partially correct programs.

REFERENCES

[And81]   T. Anderson and P. A. Lee. *Fault-Tolerance: Principles and Practice*. Prentice Hall, December 1981.

[And85]   T. Anderson, P. A. Barrett, D. N. Hallivell, and M. R. Moulding. An evaluation of software fault tolerance in a practical system. In *Proc. 15th International Symposium on Fault-Tolerant Computing*, pages 140–145, Ann Arbor, Michigan, 1985.

[Avi84]   A. Avižienis and J. P. Kelly. Fault-tolerance by design diversity. *IEEE Computer*, 17(8):67–80, 1984.

[Bac79]   R. J. R. Back. Exception Handling with Multi Exit Statements. Technical report IW125, Math. Cent. Amsterdam, November 1979.

[Ber87]   P.A. Bernstein, V. Hadzilacos, and N. Goodman. *Concurrency Control and Recovery in Database Systems*, Addison-Wesley, February 1987.

[Bes81a]   E. Best and F. Cristian. Systematic detection of exception occurrences. In *Science of Computer Programming*, 1(1):115–144, 1981.

[Bes81b] E. Best and B. Randell. A formal model of atomicity in asynchronous systems. In *Acta Informatica,* 16:93–124, 1981.

[Bro76] C. Bron, M. M. Fokkinga, and A. C. M. de Haas. A Proposal for Dealing with Abnormal Termination of Programs. Memorandum Nr. 150, Department of Applied Mathematics, Twente University of Technology, Netherlands, 1976.

[Cam86] R. H. Campbell and B. Randell. Error recovery in asynchronous systems. *IEEE Transactions on Software Engineering* SE-12(8):811–826, 1986.

[Che86] D. Cheriton. Making exceptions simplify the rule and justify their handling. In *Proc. IFIP Congress 86,* pages 27–33, 1986.

[Cri79a] F. Cristian. *Le Traitement des Exceptions dans les Programmes Modulaires.* PhD Dissertation, University of Grenoble, Grenoble, France, 1979.

[Cri79b] F. Cristian. A recovery mechanism for modular software. In *Proc. 4th International Conference on Software Engineering,* Munich, Germany, 1979.

[Cri80] F. Cristian. Exception handling and software fault-tolerance. In *Proc. 10th International Symposium on Fault-Tolerant Computing,* pages 97–103, 1980, Kyoto, Japan; also in *IEEE Transactions on Computers,* C-31(6):531–540, 1982.

[Cri82] F. Cristian. Robust data types. *Acta Informatica,* 17:365–397, 1982.

[Cri84] F. Cristian. Correct and robust programs. *IEEE Transactions on Software Engineering,* SE-10(2):163–174, 1984.

[Cri85] F. Cristian. A rigorous approach to fault-tolerant programming. *IEEE Transactions on Software Engineering,* SE-11(1):23–31, 1985.

[Cri91] F. Cristian. Understanding fault-tolerant systems. *Communications of the ACM,* 34(2):56–78, February 1991.

[Dij76] E. W. Dikstra. *A Discipline of Programming,* Prentice Hall, 1976.

[Eck91] D. Eckhardt, A. Caglayan, J. Knight, L. Lee, D. McAllister, M. Vouk, and J. P. J. Kelly. An experimental evaluation of software redundancy as a strategy for improving reliability. *IEEE Transactions on Software Engineering,* 17(7):692–701, July 1991.

[Flo67] R. Floyd. Assigning meaning to programs. in *Mathematical Aspects of Computer Science.,* 19:19–31, 1967. American Mathematical Society.

[Goo75] J. Goodenough. Exception handling, issues and a proposed notation. *Communications ACM,* 18(12):683–696, 1975.

[Gra93] J. Gray and A. Reuter. *Transaction Processing: Concepts and Techniques.* Morgan Kaufmann Publishers, 1993.

[Hoa69] C. A. R. Hoare. An axiomatic approach to computer programming. *Communications ACM,* 12(10):576–580, 1969.

[Hoa72] C. A. R. Hoare. Proof of correctness of data representations. *Acta Informatica,* 1(4):271–281, 1972.

[Hor74] J. J. Horning, H. C. Lauer, P. M. Melliar-Smith, and B. Randell. A program structure for error detection and recovery. In *Lecture Notes in Computer Science,* volume 16, Springer-Verlag, New York, 1974.

[Hor78] J. J. Horning. Language features for fault-tolerance. In *Lecture Notes, Advanced Course on Computing Systems Reliability,* University of Newcastle upon Tyne, August, 1978.

[Ich79] J. Ichbiah *et al..* Rationale for the design of the ADA programming language. In *SIGPLAN Notices,* 14(6), 1979.

[Jal84] P. Jalote and R. H. Campbell. Fault-tolerance using communicating sequential processes. In Proc. *14th International Conference on Fault-Tolerant Computing,* pages 347–352, 1984.

[Kim82] K. H. Kim. Approaches to mechanization of the conversation scheme based on monitors. *IEEE Transactions on Software Engineering,* SE-8:189–197, May, 1982.

[Lam74] B. Lampson, J. Mitchell, and E. Satterthwite. On the transfer of control between contexts. In *Lecture Notes in Computer Science,* 19:181–203, 1974.

[Lev77] R. Levin. *Program Structures for Exceptional Condition Handling,* PhD Dissertation, Carnegie-Mellon University, 1977.

[Lev85] R. Levin, P. Rovner, and J. Wick. On extending Modula-2 for building large integrated systems. (B. Lampson is acknowledged as making major design contributions to this extension.) DEC Systems Research Center Technical Report number 3, January 11, 1985.

[Lis74]   B. H. Liskov and S. Zilles. Programming with abstract data types. In *Proc. ACM SIGPLAN Conference on Very High Level Languages*, SIGLAN Notices, 9(4):50–59, 1974.
[Lis79]   B. H. Liskov and A. Snyder. Exception handling in CLU. *IEEE Transactions on Software Engineering*, SE-5:546–558, 1979.
[Lis82]   B. H. Liskov. On linguistic support for distributed programs. *IEEE Transactions on Software Engineering*, SE-8:203–210, 1982.
[Luc80]   D. Luckham and W. Polak. ADA exception handling: an axiomatic approach. *ACM TOPLAS*, volume 2, 1980.
[Mel77]   M. Melliar-Smith and B. Randell. Software reliability: the role of programmed exception handling. In *Proc. ACM Conference on Lang. Design for Reliable Software*; also in *SIGPLAN Notices*, 12:95–100, 1977.
[Mit79]   J. Mitchell *et al.* Mesa Language Manual. Report CSL-79-3, Xerox PARC, Palo Alto, California, 1979.
[Mit93]   J. Mitchell. Private Communication, 1993.
[Par72a]   D. Parnas. A technique for software module specification with examples. *Communications of the ACM*, 15(5):330–336, 1972.
[Par72b]   D. Parnas. Response to Detected Errors in Well-Structured Programs. Technical report, Carnegie-Mellon University, Dept. of Computer Science, 1972.
[Par74]   D. Parnas. On a buzzword: hierarchical structure. In *Proc. IFIP Congress 1974*, North Holland Publication Company, 1974.
[Par85]   D. Parnas, Private Communication, 1985.
[Ran75]   B. Randell. System structure for software fault-tolerance. *IEEE Transactions on Software Engineering*, SE-1(2), 1975.
[Ran78]   B. Randell, P. A. Lee, and P. C. Treleaven. Reliability issues in computing systems design. *Computing Surveys*, 10(2):123–165, 1978.
[Sch89]   R. Schlichting, F. Cristian and T. Purdin. Mechanisms for failure handling in distributed programming Languages. In *Proc. 1st International Working Conference on Dependable Computing for Critical Applications*, Santa Barbara, California, 1989.
[Shr78]   S. K. Shrivastava and J. P. Banatre. Reliable resource allocation between unreliable processes. *IEEE Transactions on Software Engineering*, SE-4:230–241, May, 1978.
[Sta87]   M. E. Staknis. *A Theoretical Basis for Software Fault Tolerance*. PhD Thesis, University of Virginia, Charlottesville, CS Report RM-87-01, February 26, 1987.
[Toy82]   W. N. Toy. Fault-tolerant design of local ESS processors. In *The Theory and Practice of Reliable System Design*, D. P. Siewiorek and R. S. Swarz, Eds., Digital Press, 1982.
[Woo81]   W. G. Wood. A decentralized recovery control protocol. In *Proc. 11th International Conference on Fault-tolerant Computing*, pages 159–164, 1981.
[Wul75]   W. Wulf. Reliable hardware software architecture. In *Proc. International Conference on Reliable Software*, SIGPLAN Notices, 10(6):122–130, 1975.
[Wul76]   W. Wulf, R. London and M. Shaw. An introduction to the construction and verification of Alphard programs. *IEEE Transactions on Software Engineering*, SE-2:253–265, July 1976.
[Yem82]   S. Yemini. An axiomatic treatment of exception handling. In *Proc. 7th ACM Symposium on Principles of Programming Languages*, 1982.

5

Dependability Modeling for Fault-Tolerant Software and Systems

JOANNE BECHTA DUGAN
University of Virginia

MICHAEL R. LYU
Bell Communications Research

ABSTRACT

Three major fault-tolerant software system architectures, distributed recovery blocks, N-version programming, and N self-checking programming, are modeled by a combination of fault tree techniques and Markov processes. In these three architectures, transient and permanent hardware faults as well as unrelated and related software faults are modeled in the system-level domain. The model parameter values are determined from the analysis of data collected from a fault-tolerant avionic application. Quantitative analyses for reliability and safety factors achieved in these three fault-tolerant system architectures are presented.

5.1 INTRODUCTION

The complexity and size of current and future software systems, usually embedded in a sophisticated hardware architecture, are growing dramatically. As our requirements for and dependencies on computers and their operating software increase, the crises of computer

Software Fault Tolerance, Edited by Lyu
© 1995 John Wiley & Sons Ltd

hardware and failure failures also increase. The impact of computer failures to human life ranges from inconvenience (e.g., malfunctions of home appliances), economic loss (e.g., interceptions of banking systems) to life-threatening (e.g., failures of flight systems or nuclear reactors). As the faults in computer systems are unavoidable as the system complexity grows, computer systems used for critical applications are designed to tolerate both software and hardware faults by the configuration of multiple software versions on redundant hardware systems. Many such applications exist in the aerospace industry [Car84, You84, Hil85, Tra88], nuclear power industry [Ram81, Bis86, Vog88], and ground transportation industry [Gun88].

The system architectures incorporating both hardware and software fault tolerance are explored in three typical approaches. The distributed recovery blocks (DRB) scheme [Kim89] combines both distributed processing and recovery block (RB) [Ran75] concepts to provide a unified approach to tolerating both hardware and software faults. Architectural considerations for the support of N-version programming (NVP) [Avi85] were addressed in [Lal88], in which the FTP-AP system is described. The FTP-AP system achieves hardware and software design diversity by attaching application processors (AP) to the byzantine resilient hard core Fault Tolerant Processor (FTP). N self-checking programming (NSCP) [Lap90] uses diverse hardware and software in self-checking groups to detect hardware and software induced errors and forms the basis of the flight control system used on the Airbus A310 and A320 aircraft [Bri93].

Sophisticated techniques exist for the separate analysis of fault tolerant hardware [Gei90, Joh88] and software [Grn80, Shi84, Sco87, Cia92], but only some authors have considered their combined analysis [Lap84, Sta87, Lap92]. This chapter uses a combination of fault tree and Markov modeling as a framework for the analysis of hardware and software fault tolerant systems. The overall system model is a Markov model in which the states of the Markov chain represent the evolution of the hardware configuration as permanent faults occur and are handled. A fault tree model captures the effects of software faults and transient hardware faults on the computation process. This hierarchical approach simplifies the development, solution and understanding of the modeling process. We parameterize the values of each model by a recent fault-tolerant software project [Lyu93] to perform reliability and safety analysis of each architecture.

The chapter is organized as follows. In Section 5.2 we give a description of the three system architectures studied in this chapter. Section 5.3 provides the overall modeling assumptions and parameter definitions. In Section 5.4 we present the system level models, including reliability and safety models, of the three architectures. Experimental data analysis is presented in Section 5.5, and a case study from a fault-tolerant software project to determine the model parameter values is presented in Section 5.6. Section 5.7 describes a quantitative system-level reliability and safety analysis of the three architectures. Sensitivity analysis of model parameters is shown in Section 5.8, while the impact of decider failure probability is given in Section 5.9. Finally Section 5.10 contains some concluding remarks.

5.2   SYSTEM DESCRIPTIONS

Figure 5.1 shows the hardware and error confinement areas [Lap90] associated with the three architectures (DRB, NVP, and NSCP) being considered in this chapter. The systems are defined by the number of software variants, the number of hardware replications, and the decision algorithm. The hardware error confinement area (HECA) is the lightly shaded region,

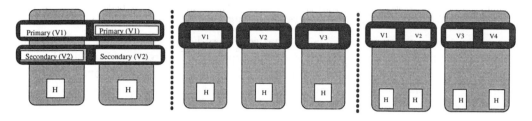

a) Distributed Recovery Block   b) N-version programming   c) N self-checking programming

Figure 5.1   Structure of a) DRB, b) NVP and c)NSCP

while the software error confinement area (SECA) is the darkly shaded region. The HECA or SECA covers the region of the system affected by faults in that component. For example, the HECA covers the software component since the software component will fail if that hardware experiences a fault. The SECA covers only the software, as no other components will be affected by a software fault.

5.2.1   DRB: Distributed Recovery Block

The recovery block approach to software fault tolerance [Ran75] is the software analogy of "standby-sparing," and utilizes two or more alternate software modules and an acceptance test. The acceptability of a computation performed by the *primary alternate* is determined by an *acceptance test*. If the results are deemed unacceptable, the state of the system is rolled back and the computation is attempted by the *secondary alternate*. The alternate software modules are designed produce the same or similar results as the primary but are deliberately designed to be as uncorrelated (orthogonal) as possible [Hec86].

There are at least two different ways to combine hardware redundancy with recovery blocks. In [Lap90], the RB/1/1 architecture duplicates the recovery block on two hardware components. In this architecture, both hardware components execute the same variant, and hardware faults are detected by a comparison of the acceptance test and computation results. The DRB (Figure 5.1a) [Kim89] executes different alternates on the different hardware components in order to improve performance when an error is detected. In the DRB system, one processor executes the primary alternate while the other executes the secondary. If an error is detected in the primary results, the results from the secondary are immediately available. The dependability analysis of both systems is identical.

5.2.2   NVP: N-Version Programming

In the NVP method [Avi85, Lyu93], N independently developed software versions are used to perform the same tasks. They are executed concurrently using identical inputs. Their outputs are collected and evaluated by a decider. If the outputs do not all match, the output produced by the majority of the versions is taken to be correct. NVP/1/1 (Figure 5.1b) [Lap90] consists of three identical hardware components, each running a distinct software version. It is a direct mapping of the NVP method onto hardware. Throughout this chapter we consider a 3-version implementation of an NVP system.

5.2.3   NSCP: N Self-Checking Programming

The NSCP architecture considered in this chapter (Figure 5.1c) is comprised of four software versions and four hardware components, each grouped in two pairs, essentially dividing the system into two halves. The hardware pairs operate in hot standby redundancy with each hardware component supporting one software version. The version pairs form self-checking software components. A self-checking software component consists of either two versions and a comparison algorithm or a version and an acceptance test. In this case, error detection is done by comparison. The four software versions are executed and the results of V1 and V2 are compared against each other, as are the results of V3 and V4. If either pair of results do not match, they are discarded and only the remaining two are used. If the results do match, the results of the two pairs are then compared. A hardware fault causes the software version running on it to produce incorrect results, as would a fault in the software version itself. This results in a discrepancy in the output of the two versions, causing that pair to be ignored.

5.3   MODELING ASSUMPTIONS AND PARAMETER DEFINITIONS

5.3.1   Assumptions

Task computation. The computation being performed is a task (or set of tasks) which is repeated periodically. A set of sensor inputs is gathered and analyzed and a set of actuations are produced. Each repetition of a task is independent. The goal of the analysis is the probability that a task will succeed in producing an acceptable output, despite the possibility of hardware or software faults. More interesting task computation processes could be considered using techniques described in [Lap92] and [Wei91]. We do not address timing or performance issues in this model. See [Tai93] for a performability analysis of fault tolerant software techniques.

Software failure probability. Software faults exist in the code, despite rigorous testing. A fault may be activated by some random input, thus producing an erroneous result. Each instantiation of a task receives a different set of inputs which are independent. Thus, a software task has a fixed probability of failure when executed, and each iteration is assumed to be statistically independent. Since we do not assign a failure rate to the software, we do not consider reliability-growth models.

Coincident software failures in different versions. If two different software versions fail on the same input, they will produce either similar or different results. In this work, we use the Arlat/Kanoun/Laprie [Arl90] model for software failures and assume that similar erroneous results are caused by *related* software faults and different erroneous results which are simultaneously activated are caused by *unrelated* (called *independent* in their terminology) software faults. There is one difference between our model and that of Arlat/Kanoun/Laprie in that our model assumes that related and unrelated software faults are statistically independent while their's assumes that related and unrelated faults are mutually exclusive. Further, this treatment of *unrelated* and *related* faults differs considerably from models for correlated failures [Eck85, Lit89, Nic90], in which unrelated and related software failures are not differentiated. Rather, software faults are considered to be statistically correlated and models for correlation are considered and proposed. A more detailed comparison of the two approaches is given in [Dug94].

Permanent hardware faults. The arrival (activation) rate of *permanent* physical faults is constant and will be denoted by λ.

Transient hardware faults. Transient hardware faults are modeled separately from permanent hardware faults. A transient hardware fault is assumed to upset the software running on the processor and produce an erroneous result which is indistinguishable from an input-activated software error. We assume that the lifetime of transient hardware faults is short when compared to the length of a task computation, and thus assign a fixed probability to the occurrence of a transient hardware fault during a single computation.

Nonmaintained systems. For the comparisons drawn from this study, we assume that the systems are unmaintained. Repairability and maintainability could certainly be included in the Markov model; we have chosen not to include them to make the comparisons clearer.

5.3.2 Parameter Definitions

The parameters used in the models are listed below.

λ: the arrival rate for a permanent hardware fault to a single processing element.

c: the coverage factor; the probability that the system can automatically recovery from a permanent hardware fault. The system fails if it is unable to automatically recover from a fault.

P_H: the probability that a transient hardware fault occurs during a single task computation.

P_V: for each version, the probability that an unrelated software fault is activated during a task computation.

P_{RV}: for each pair of versions, the probability that a related fault between the two versions is activated during a task computation.

P_{RALL}: the probability that a related fault common to all versions is activated during a single task computation.

P_D: the probability that the decider fails, either by accepting an incorrect result or by rejecting a correct result.

5.3.3 Terminology

Some of the terminology used in the system descriptions and comparisons is summarized below and defined more explicitly when first used.

DRB: distributed recovery block system
NVP: N-version programming system
NSCP: N self-checking programming system
related fault: a single fault which affects two or more software versions, causing them to produce similar incorrect results
unrelated fault: a fault which affects only a single software version, causing it to produce an incorrect result
coincident fault: the simultaneous activation of two or more different hardware and/or software faults.
by-case data: Software error detection is performed at the end of each test case, where a test case consists of approximately 5280 50 ms. time frames.
by-frame data: Software error detection is performed at the end of each time frame, where a time frame consists of approximately 50 ms. of execution.

5.4 SYSTEM LEVEL MODELING

5.4.1 Modeling Methodology

A dependability model of an integrated fault tolerant system must include at least three different factors: computation errors, system structure and coverage modeling. In this chapter we concentrate on the first two, and use coverage modeling techniques that have been developed elsewhere [Dug89].

The computation process is assumed to consist of a single software task that is executed repeatedly, such as would be found in a process control system. The software component performing the task is designed to be fault tolerant. A single task iteration consists of a task execution on a particular set of input values read from sensors. The output is the desired actuation to control the external system. During a single task iteration, several types of events can interfere with the computation. The particular set of inputs could activate a software fault in one or more of the software versions and/or the decider. Also, a hardware transient fault could upset the computation but not cause permanent hardware damage. The combinations of software faults and hardware transients that can cause an erroneous output for a single computation is modeled with a fault tree. The solution of the fault tree yields the probability that a single task iteration produces an erroneous output. We note that in the more general case where more than one task is performed, the analyses of each task can be combined accordingly.

The longer-term system behavior is affected by permanent faults and component repair which require system reconfiguration to a different mode of operation. The system structure is modeled by a Markov chain, where the Markov states and transitions model the long term behavior of the system as hardware and software components are reconfigured in and out of the system. Each state in the Markov chain represents a particular configuration of hardware and software components and thus a different level of redundancy. The fault and error recovery process is captured in the coverage parameter used in the Markov chain [Dug89].

The short-term behavior of the computation process and the long-term behavior of the system structure are combined as follows. For each state in the Markov chain, there is a different combination of hardware transients and software faults that can cause a computation error, and thus a different probability that an unacceptable result is produced.

The fault tree model solution produces, for each state i in the Markov model, the probability q_i that an output error occurs during a single task computation while the state is in state i. The Markov model solution produces $P_i(t)$, the probability that the system is in state i at time t. The overall model combines these two measures to produce $Q(t)$, the probability that an unacceptable result is produced at time t.

$$Q(t) = \sum_{i=1}^{n} q_i P_i(t)$$

We assume that the system is unable to produce an acceptable result while in the failure state, thus $q_{fail} = 1$.

The models of the three systems being analyzed (DRB, NVP and NSCP; see Figure 5.1) consist of two fault trees and one Markov model. Since each of the systems can tolerate one permanent hardware fault, there are two operational states in the Markov chain. The initial state in each of the Markov chains represents the full operational structure, and an intermediate state represents the system structure after successful automatic reconfiguration to handle a single permanent hardware fault. The reconfiguration state provides a degraded level of fault tolerance, as some failed hardware component has been discarded. There is a single failure state which is reached when the second hard physical fault is activated or when a coverage failure occurs. The full analytical solution of the models appears in [Dug95].

5.4.2 Reliability Models

The three-part reliability model of DRB is shown in Figure 5.2. The Markov model details the system structure. In the initial state the recovery block structure is executed on redundant hardware. In the reconfigured state, after the the activation of a permanent hardware fault, a single copy of the RB is executed. The first fault tree details the causes of unacceptable results while in the initial configuration. A single task computation will produce unacceptable results if the software module fails (both primary and secondary fail on the same input) or if both hardware components experience transient faults, or if the decider fails. The second fault tree details the combination of events which cause an unacceptable result in the reconfigured state, where a single recovery block module executes on the remaining processor. The key difference between the two fault trees is the reduction in hardware redundancy.

Figure 5.3 shows the reliability model of NVP. With three software versions running on three separate processors, several different failure scenarios must be considered, including coincident unrelated faults as well as related software faults, coincident hardware transients and combinations of hardware and software faults. For the Markov model, we assume that the system is reconfigured to simplex mode after the first permanent hardware fault. In this reconfigured state, an unreliable result is caused by either a hardware transient or a software fault activation, as shown in the second fault tree of Figure 5.3.

The reliability model of the NSCP system is shown in Figure 5.4. The Markov model shows that the system discards both a failed processor and its mate after the first permanent hardware fault occurs. When in the initial state, a two unrelated errors (one in each half of the system) are necessary to cause a mismatch. However, a single related software fault in two versions results in an unacceptable result. If a related error crosses the SECA boundary, then both halves will fail the comparison test. If an unrelated error affects both versions in the same half, then each half will pass the comparison test, but the higher level comparison (between the results from the two halves) will cause a mismatch.

5.4.3 Safety Models

The safety models for the three systems are similar to the reliability models, in that they consist of a Markov model and two associated fault trees. The major difference between a reliability and safety analysis is in the definition of failure. In the reliability models, any unacceptable result (whether or not it is detected) is considered a failure. In a safety model, a detected error is assumed to be handled by the system in a fail-safe manner, so an unsafe result only occurs if an unacceptable result is not detected.

In the Markov part of the safety models, two failure states are defined. The fail-safe state is reached when the second covered permanent hardware fault is activated. The fail-unsafe state is reached when any uncovered hardware fault occurs. The system is considered safe when in the absorbing fail-safe state. This illustrates a key difference between a reliability analysis and a safety analysis. A system which is shut-down safely (and thus is not operational) is inherently safe, although it is certainly not reliable.

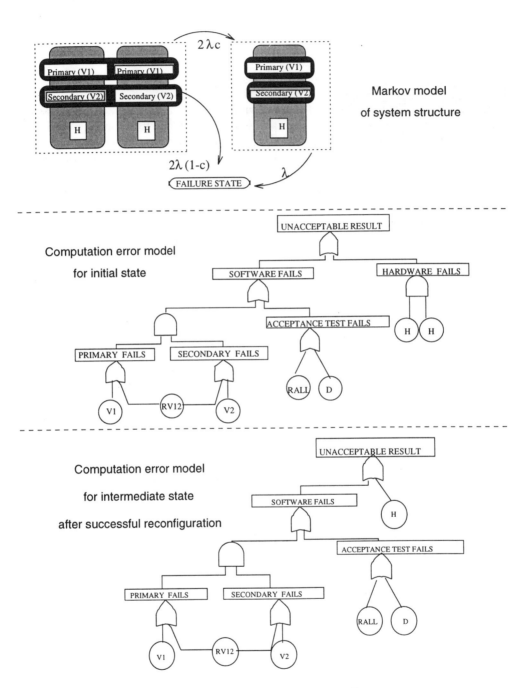

Figure 5.2   Reliability model of DRB

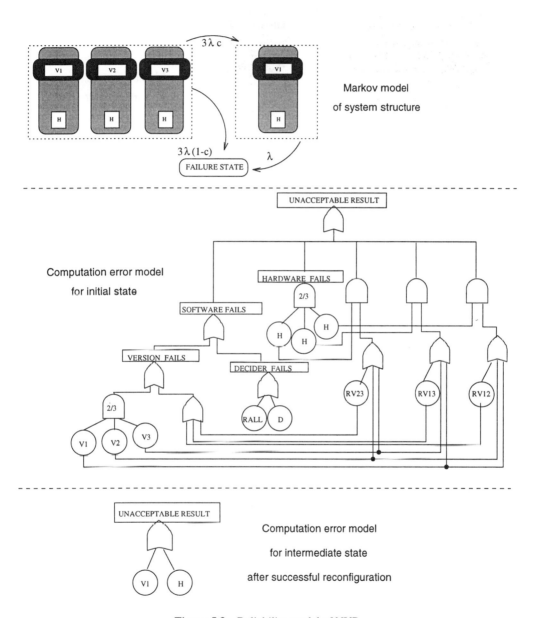

Figure 5.3 Reliability model of NVP

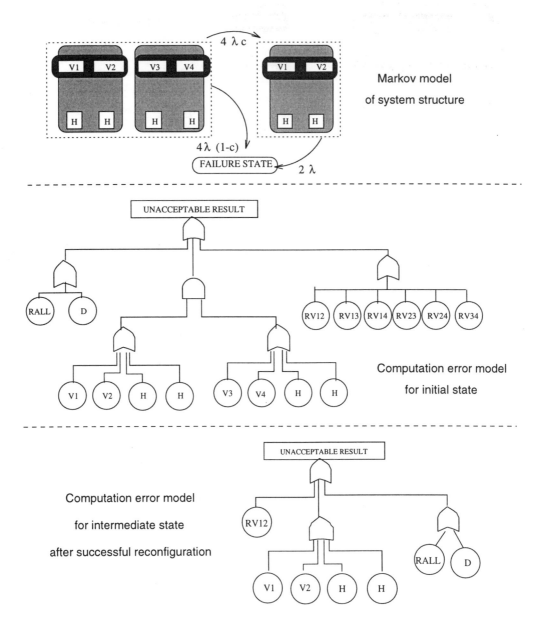

Figure 5.4   Reliability model of NSCP

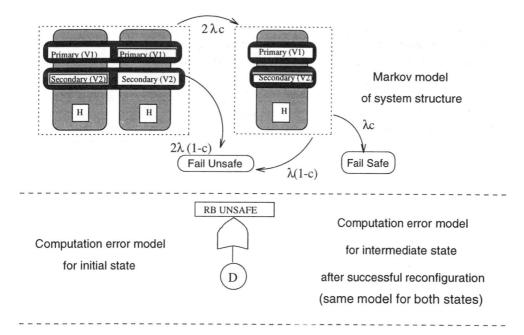

Figure 5.5   Safety model of DRB

The safety model of DRB, shown in Figure 5.5, shows that an acceptance test failure is the only software cause of an unsafe result. As long as the acceptance test does not accept an incorrect result, then a safe output is assumed to be produced. The hardware redundancy does not increase the safety of the system, as the system is vulnerable to the acceptance test in both states. An interesting result of a safety analysis is that the hardware redundancy can actually decrease the safety of the system, since the system is perfectly safe when in the fail-safe state, and the hardware redundancy delays absorption into this state [Vai93].

The NVP safety model (Figure 5.6) shows that the safety of the NVP system is vulnerable to related faults as well as decider faults. In the Markov model, we assume that the reconfigured state uses two versions (rather than one, as was assumed for the reliability model) so as to increase the opportunity for comparisons between alternatives and thus increase error detectability.

The NSCP safety model (Figure 5.7) shows the same vulnerability of the NSCP system to related faults. When the system is fully operational, all 2-way related faults will be detected by the self-checking arrangements, leaving the system vulnerable only to a decider faults, and a fault affecting all versions similarly. After reconfiguration, a related fault affecting both remaining versions could also produce an undetected error.

5.5   EXPERIMENTAL DATA ANALYSIS

A quantitative comparison of the three fault tolerant systems described in the previous section requires an estimation of reasonable values for the model parameters. The estimation of failure probabilities for hardware components has been considered for a number of years, and reasonable estimates exist for generic components (such as a processor). However, the

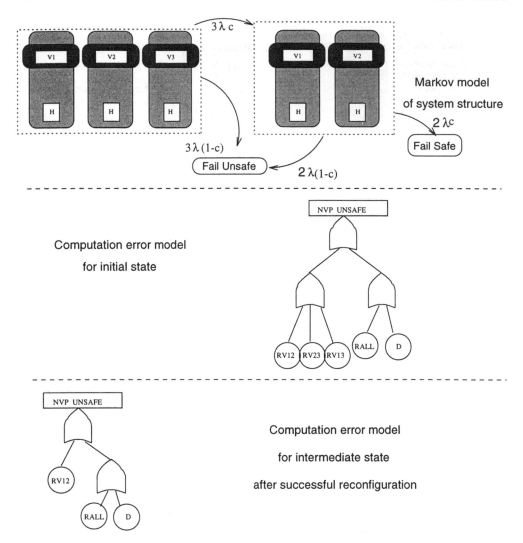

Figure 5.6   Safety model of NVP

estimation of software version failure probability is less accessible, and the estimation of the probability of related faults is more difficult still. In this section we will describe a methodology for estimating model parameter values from experimental data followed by a case study using a set of experimental data.

Several experiments in multi-version programming have been performed in the past decade. Among other measures, most experiments provide some estimate of the number of times different versions fail coincidentally. For example, the NASA-LaRC study involving 20 programs from 4 universities [Eck91] provides a table listing how many instances of coincident failures were detected. The Knight-Leveson study of 28 versions [Kni86] provides an estimated probability of coincident failures. The Lyu-He study [Lyu93] considered three and five version configurations formed from 12 different versions. These sets of experimental data can be used to estimated the probabilities for the basic events in a model of a fault tolerant software system.

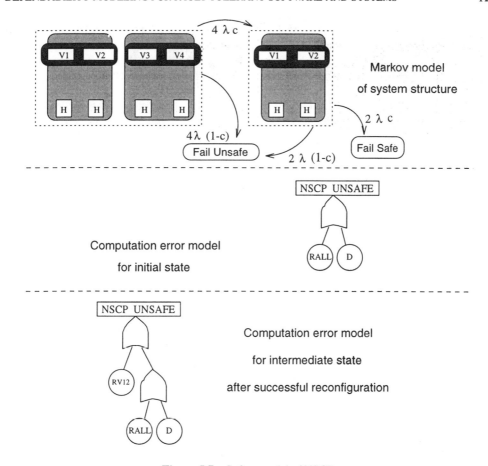

Figure 5.7   Safety model of NSCP

Coincident failures in different versions can arise from two distinct causes. First, two (or more) versions may both experience unrelated faults that are activated by the same input. If two programs fail independently, there is always a finite probability that they will fail coincidentally, else the programs would not be independent. A coincident failure does not necessarily imply that a related fault has been activated. Second, the input may activate a fault that is related between the two versions. In order to estimate the probabilities of unrelated and related faults, we will determine the (theoretical) probability of failure by unrelated faults. To the extent that the observed frequency of coincident faults exceeds this value, we will attribute the excess to related faults.

The experimental data is necessarily coarse. As it is infeasible to exhaustively test a single version, it is more difficult to exhaustively observe every possible instance of coincident failures in multiple versions. The experimental data provides an estimate of the probabilities of coincident failures, rather than the exact value. Considering the coarseness of the experimental data, we will limit ourselves to the estimation of three parameter values: P_V, the probability of an unrelated fault in a version; P_{RV}, the probability of a related fault between two versions; and P_{RALL}, the probability of a related fault in all versions. To attempt to estimate more, for example the probability of a related fault that affects exactly three versions or exactly four versions, seems unreasonable. Notice that we will assume that the versions are all statistically identical, and do not try to attempt to estimate different probabilities of failure for each individual version, or each individual case of two simultaneous versions.

The first parameter that we estimate is P_V, the probability that a single version fails. The estimate for P_V comes from considering F_0 (the observed frequency of no failures) and F_1 (the observed frequency of exactly one failure). When considering N different versions processing the same input, the probability that there are no failures is set equal to the observed frequency of no failures.

$$F_0 = (1 - P_V)^N (1 - P_{RV})^{\binom{N}{2}}(1 - P_{RALL}) \qquad (5.1)$$

Then, considering the case where only a single failure occurs, we observe that a single failure can occur in any of the N programs, and implies that a related fault does not occur (else more than one version would be affected). This is then set equal to the observed frequency of a single failure of the N versions.

$$F_1 = N(1 - P_V)^{(N-1)} P_V (1 - P_{RV})^{\binom{N}{2}}(1 - P_{RALL}) \qquad (5.2)$$

Dividing equation 5.1 by equation 5.2 yields an estimate for P_V.

$$P_V = \frac{F_1}{NF_0 + F_1} \qquad (5.3)$$

Estimating the probability of a related fault between two versions, P_{RV}, is more involved, but follows the same basic procedure. First, consider the case where exactly two versions are observed to fail coincidentally. This event can be caused by one of three events:

- the simultaneous activation of two unrelated faults, or
- the activation of a related fault between two versions or
- both (the activation of two unrelated and a related fault between the two versions).

The probabilities of each of these events will be determined separately. The probability that unrelated faults are simultaneously activated in two versions (and no related faults are activated) is

$$\binom{N}{2} P_V^2 (1 - P_V)^{(N-2)}(1 - P_{RV})^{\binom{N}{2}}(1 - P_{RALL}) \qquad (5.4)$$

The probability that a single related fault (and no unrelated fault) is activated is given by

$$\binom{N}{2}(1 - P_V)^N P_{RV}(1 - P_{RV})^{(\binom{N}{2}-1)}(1 - P_{RALL}) \qquad (5.5)$$

Finally, the probability that both an unrelated fault and two related faults are simultaneously activated is give by

$$\binom{N}{2} P_V^2 P_{RV}(1 - P_V)^{(N-2)}(1 - P_{RV})^{(\binom{N}{2}-1)}(1 - P_{RALL}) \qquad (5.6)$$

Because the three events are disjoint, we can sum their probabilities, and set the sum equal to

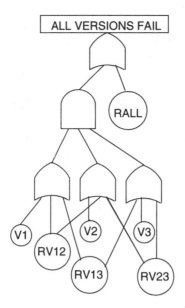

Figure 5.8 Fault tree model used to estimate P_{RALL} for a 3-version system

F_2, the observed frequency of two coincident errors.

$$F_2 = \binom{N}{2}(P_V^2 + P_{RV} - P_V^2 P_{RV})(1 - P_V)^{(N-2)}(1 - P_{RV})^{(\binom{N}{2}-1)}(1 - P_{RALL}) \quad (5.7)$$

Dividing equation 5.7 by 5.2 and performing some algebraic manipulations yields an estimate for P_{RV} which depends on the experimental data and the previously derived estimate for P_V.

$$P_{RV} = \frac{2F_2 P_V(1 - P_V) - (N - 1)F_1 P_V^2}{2F_2 P_V(1 - P_V) + (N - 1)F_1(1 - P_V^2)} \quad (5.8)$$

The estimate for P_{RALL} is more involved, as there are many ways in which all versions can fail. There may be a related fault between all versions that is activated by the input, or all versions might simultaneously fail from a combination of unrelated and related faults. Consider the case where there are three versions. In addition to the possibility of a single fault affecting all three versions, all three versions could experience a simultaneous activation of unrelated faults, or one of three combinations of an unrelated and related fault affecting different versions may be activated. The fault tree in Figure 5.8 illustrates the combinations of events which can cause all three versions to fail coincidentally. A simple (but inelegant) methodology for estimating P_{RALL} could use the previously determined estimates for P_V and P_{RV} and repeated guessing for P_{RALL} in the solution of the fault tree in Figure 5.8, until the fault tree solution for the probability of simultaneous errors approximates the observed frequency of all versions failing simultaneously.

The fault tree model for three versions can easily be generalized to the case where there are N versions. The top event of the fault tree is an *OR* gate with two inputs, an *AND* gate showing all versions failing, and a basic event, representing a related fault that affects all versions simultaneously. The *AND* gate has N inputs, one for each version. Each of the N inputs to the *AND* gate is itself an *OR* gate with N inputs, all basic events. Each *OR* gate has one input representing an unrelated fault in the version, and N − 1 inputs representing related faults with each other possible version.

5.6   A CASE STUDY IN PARAMETER ESTIMATION

In this section we analyze experimental data from a recent multiversion programming experiment to determine parameter values for our models of fault-tolerant software systems. The data is derived from an experimental implementation of a real-world automatic (i.e., computerized) airplane landing system, or so-called "autopilot." The software systems of this project were developed and programmed by 15 programming teams at the University of Iowa and the Rockwell/Collins Avionics Division. A total of 40 students (33 from ECE and CS departments at the University of Iowa, 7 from the Rockwell International) participated in this project to independently design, code, and test the computerized airplane landing system, as described in the Lyu-He study [Lyu93].

5.6.1   System Description

The software project in the Lyu-He study was scheduled and conducted in six phases: (1) Initial design phase for four weeks; (2) Detailed design phase for two weeks; (3) Coding phase for three weeks; (4) Unit testing phase for one week; (5) Integration testing phase for two weeks; (6) Acceptance testing phase for two weeks. It is noted that the acceptance testing was a two-step formal testing procedure. In the first step (AT1), each program was run in a test harness of four nominal flight simulation profiles. For the second step (AT2), one extra simulation profile, representing an extremely difficult flight situation, was imposed. By the end of the acceptance testing phase, 12 of the 15 programs passed the acceptance test successfully and were engaged in operational testing for further evaluations. The average size of these programs were 1564 lines of uncommented code, or 2558 lines when comments were included. The average fault density of the program versions which passed AT1 was 0.48 faults per thousand lines of uncommented code. The fault density for the final versions was 0.05 faults per thousand lines of uncommented code.

5.6.1.1   THE NVP OPERATIONAL ENVIRONMENT

The operational environment for the application was conceived as airplane/autopilot interacting in a simulated environment, as shown in Figure 5.9. Three channels of diverse software independently computed a surface command to guide a simulated aircraft along its flight path. To ensure that significant command errors could be detected, random wind turbulences of different levels were superimposed in order to represent difficult flight conditions. The individual commands were recorded and compared for discrepancies that could indicate the presence of faults.

This configuration of a 3-channel flight simulation system consisted of three lanes of control law computation, three command monitors, a servo control, an Airplane model, and a turbulence generator. The lane computations and the command monitors would be the accepted software versions generated by the programming teams. Each lane of independent computation monitored the other two lanes. However, no single lane could make the decision

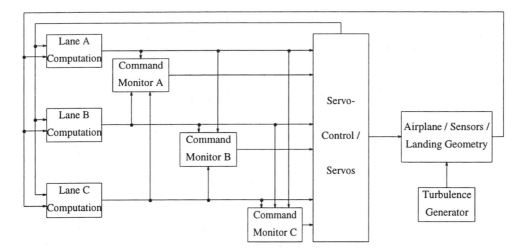

Figure 5.9 3-channel flight simulation configuration

as to whether another lane was faulty. A separate servo control logic function was required to make that decision. The aircraft mathematical model provided the dynamic response of current medium size, commercial transports in the approach/landing flight phase. The three control signals from the autopilot computation lanes were inputs to three elevator servos. The servos were force-summed at their outputs, so that the mid-value of the three inputs became the final elevator command. The Landing Geometry and Turbulence Generator were models associated with the Airplane simulator.

In summary, one run of flight simulation was characterized by the following five initial values regarding the landing position of an airplane: (1) initial altitude (about 1500 feet); (2) initial distance (about 52800 feet); (3) initial nose up relative to velocity (range from 0 to 10 degrees); (4) initial pitch attitude (range from -15 to 15 degrees); and (5) vertical velocity for the wind turbulence (0 to 10 ft/sec). One simulation consisted of about 5280 iterations of lane command computations (50 milliseconds each) for a total landing time of approximately 264 seconds.

5.6.1.2 OPERATIONAL ERROR DISTRIBUTION

During the operational phase, 1000 flight simulations, or over five million program executions, were conducted. For a conservative estimation of software failures in the NVP system, we took the program versions which passed the AT1 for study. The reason behind this was that had the Acceptance Test not included an extreme situation of AT2, more faults would have remained in the program versions. We were interested in seeing how the remaining faults would be manifested during the operational testing, and how they would or would not be tolerated in various NVP configurations.

Table 5.1 shows the software failures encountered in each single version. We examine two levels of granularity in defining software execution errors and coincident errors: "by-case" or "by-frame." The first level was defined based on test cases (1000 in total). If a version failed at any time in a test case, it was considered failed for the whole case. If two or more versions failed in the same test case (no matter at the same time or not), they were said to have coincident errors for that test case. The second level of granularity was defined based

Table 5.1   Error characteristics for individual versions

Version Id	Number of failures	Prob. by-case	Prob. by-frame
β	510	0.51	0.000096574
γ	0	0.0	0.0
ϵ	0	0.0	0.0
ζ	0	0.0	0.0
η	1	0.001	0.000000189
θ	360	0.36	0.000068169
κ	0	0.0	0.0
λ	730	0.73	0.000138233
μ	140	0.14	0.000026510
ν	0	0.0	0.0
ξ	0	0.0	0.0
o	0	0.0	0.0
Average	145.1	0.1451	0.000027472

Table 5.2   Error characteristics for two-version configurations

Category	BY-CASE		BY-FRAME	
	Number of cases	Frequency	Number of cases	Frequency
F_0 - no errors	53150	0.8053	348522546	0.99994786
F_1 - single error	11160	0.1691	18128	0.00005201
F_2 - two coincident	1690	0.0256	46	0.00000013
Total	66000	1.0000	348540720	1.000000

on execution time frames (5,280,920 in total). Errors were counted only at the time frame upon which they manifested themselves, and coincident errors were defined to be the multiple program versions failing at the same time frame in the same test case (with or without the same variables and values).

In Table 5.1 we can see that the average failure probability for single version is 0.145 measured by-case, or 0.000027 measured by-frame.

5.6.2   Data Analysis and Parameter Estimation

The 12 programs accepted in the Lyu-He experiment were configured in pairs, whose outputs were compared for each test case. Table 5.2 shows the number of times that 0, 1, and 2 errors were observed in the 2-version configurations. The data from Table 5.2 yields an estimate of $P_V = 0.095$ for the probability of activation of an unrelated fault in a 2-version configuration, and an estimate of $P_{RV} = 0.0167$ for the probability of a related fault for the by-case data. The by-frame data in Table 5.2 produces $P_V = 0.000026$ and $P_{RV} = 1.3 \times 10^{-7}$ as estimates.

Next, the 12 versions were configured in sets of three programs. Table 5.3 shows the number of times that 0, 1, 2, and 3 errors were observed in the 3-version configurations. The data from Table 5.3 yields an estimate of $P_V = 0.0958$ for the probability of activation of an independent fault in a 3-version configuration. Table 5.4 compares the probability of activation of 1, 2 and 3 faults as predicted by a model assuming independence between versions, with the observed values. The observed frequency of two simultaneous errors is lower than predicted by the

Table 5.3 Error characteristics for three-version configurations

Category	BY-CASE		BY-FRAME	
	Number of cases	Frequency	Number of cases	Frequency
F_0 - no errors	163370	0.7426	1161707015	0.99991790
F_1 - single error	51930	0.2360	94835	0.00008163
F_2 - two coincident	4440	0.0202	550	0.00000047
F_4 - three coincident	260	0.0012	0	0.0
Total	220000	1.0000	1161802400	1.000000

Table 5.4 Comparison of independent model with observed data for 3 versions (by-case)

No. errors activated	Independent model	Observed frequency
0	0.7393	0.7426
1	0.2350	0.2360
2	0.0249	0.0202
3	0.0009	0.0012

independent model, while the observed frequency of three simultaneous errors is higher than predicted. For this set of data we will assume therefore that $P_{RV} = 0$ and will instead derive an estimate for P_{RALL}.

Using the assumption that $P_{RV} = 0$, the probability that three simultaneous errors are activated is given by

$$F_3 = P_V{}^3 + P_{RALL} - P_V{}^3 P_{RALL},\qquad (5.9)$$

yielding an estimate of $P_{RALL} = 0.0003$ for the by-case data.

The by-frame data in Table 5.3 produces $P_V = 0.000027$ as an estimate. For this by-frame data, when the failure probabilities which are predicted by the independent model are compared to the actual data (Table 5.5), the observed frequency of two errors is two orders of magnitude higher than the predicted probability. There were no cases for which all three programs produced erroneous results. Thus, we will estimate $P_{RALL} = 0$ and derive an estimate for $P_{RV} = 1.57 \times 10^{-7}$.

The same 12 programs which passed the acceptance testing phase of the software development process were analyzed in combinations of four programs, the results are shown in Table 5.6. The by-case data from Table 5.6 yields an estimate of $P_V = 0.106$ for the probability of activation of an unrelated fault in a 4-version configuration. Table 5.7 compares the probability of activation of 1, 2, 3 and 4 faults as predicted by a model assuming independence between versions, with the observed values. The observed frequency of two simultaneous errors is lower than predicted by the independent model, while the observed frequency of three simultaneous errors is higher than predicted. For this set of data we will assume that

Table 5.5 Comparison of independent model with observed data for 3 versions (by-frame)

No. errors activated	Independent model	Observed frequency
0	0.999919	0.999918
1	0.000081	0.0000816
2	2×10^{-9}	5×10^{-7}
3	2×10^{-14}	0.0

Table 5.6   Error characteristics for four-version configurations

Category	BY-CASE		BY-FRAME	
	Number of cases	Frequency	Number of cases	Frequency
F_0 - no errors	322010	0.65052	2613781410	0.9998951
F_1 - single error	152900	0.30889	2719200	0.001040
F_2 - two coincident	16350	0.03303	2070	0.00000079
F_3 - three coincident	3700	0.00747	0	0.0
F_4 - four coincident	40	0.00008	0	0.0
Total	495000	1.0000	2614055400	1.000000

Table 5.7   Comparison of independent model with observed data for 4 versions (by-case)

No. errors activated	Independent model	Observed frequency
0	0.63878	0.65052
1	0.30296	0.30889
2	0.05388	0.03303
3	0.00426	0.00747
4	0.00013	0.00008

$P_{RV} = 0$. The observed frequency of four simultaneous failures is also lower than predicted by the independent model, so we will also assume that $P_{RALL} = 0$. The by-frame data in Table 5.6 produces $P_V = 0.000026$ and $P_{RALL} = 1.3 \times 10^{-7}$ as estimates.

Table 5.8 summarizes the parameters estimated from the Lyu-He data. The parameter values for the three systems were applied to the fault tree models shown in Figure 5.10, using both the by-case and by-frame data. The predicted failure probability using the derived parameters in the fault tree models agrees quite well with the observed data, as listed in Table 5.8. The observed failure frequence for the 4-version configuration is difficult to estimate because of the possibility of a 2-2 split vote. The data for the occurrences of such a split are not available. Thus the observed failure frequency in Table 5.8 is a lower bound (it is the sum of the observed cases of 3 or 4 coincident failures). If the data on a 2-2 split were available, then the probability of a 2-2 split would be added to the observed frequency values listed in Table 5.8. For the by-frame data, for example, if 5% of the 2 coincident failures produced similar wrong results, then the model and the observed data would agree quite well.

The parameters are derived from a single experimental implementation and so may not be generally applicable. Similar analysis of other experimental data will help to establish a set of reasonable parameters that can be used in models that are developed during the design phase of a fault tolerant system.

5.7   QUANTITATIVE SYSTEM-LEVEL ANALYSIS

This section contains a quantitative analysis of the system-level reliability and safety models for the DRB, NVP and NSCP systems. The software parameter values used in this study are those derived from the Lyu-He data, with the exception of values for decider failure. For the DRB system models, the parameter values from the 2-version configurations are used; for the

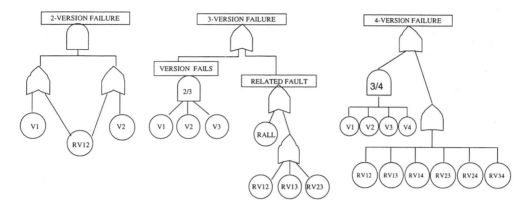

Figure 5.10 Fault tree models for 2, 3 and 4 version systems

Table 5.8 Summary of parameter values derived from Lyu-He data

2-version model	3-version model	4-version model
BY-CASE DATA		
$P_V = 0.095$	$P_V = 0.0958$	$P_V = 0.106$
$P_{RV} = 0.0167$	$P_{RV} = 0$	$P_{RV} = 0$
	$P_{RALL} = 0.0003$	$P_{RALL} = 0$
Predicted failure probability (from the model)		
0.0265	0.0262	0.0044
Observed failure probability (from the data)		
0.0256	0.0214	0.0076
BY-FRAME DATA		
$P_V = 0.000026$	$P_V = 0.000027$	$P_V = 0.000026$
$P_{RV} = 1.3 \times 10^{-7}$	$P_{RV} = 1.57 \times 10^{-7}$	$P_{RV} = 1.3 \times 10^{-7}$
	$P_{RALL} = 0$	$P_{RALL} = 0$
Predicted failure probability (from the model)		
1.31×10^{-7}	4.73×10^{-7}	7.8×10^{-7}
Observed failure probability (from the data)		
1.32×10^{-7}	4.73×10^{-7}	0

NVP system models, we use the parameters derived from the 3-version configurations, while the NSCP model uses the parameters derived from the 4-version configurations.

Since no decider failures were observed during the experimental implementation, it is difficult to estimate this probability. The decider used for the recovery block system is an acceptance test, and for this application is likely to be significantly more complex than the comparator used for the NVP and NSCP systems. For the sake of comparison, for the by-case data we will assume that the comparator used in the NVP and NSCP systems has a failure probability of only 0.0001 and that the acceptance test used for the DRB system has a failure probability of 0.001 . For the by-frame data, the decider is considered to be extremely reliable, with a failure probability of 10^{-7} for all three systems. If the decider were any less reliable, then its failure probability would dominate the system analysis, and the results would be far less interesting.

Typical permanent failure rates for processors range in the 10^{-5} per hour range, with transients perhaps an order of magnitude larger. Thus we will use $\lambda_p = 10^{-5}$ per hour for the Markov model.

In the by-case scenario, a typical test case contained 5280 time frames, each time frame being 50 ms., so a typical computation executed for 264 seconds. Assuming that hardware transients occur at a rate $\lambda_t = (10^{-4}/3600)$ per second, we see that the probability that a hardware transient occurs during a typical test case is

$$1 - e^{-\lambda_t \times 264 \text{ seconds}} = 7.333 \times 10^{-6} \tag{5.10}$$

We conservatively assume that a hardware transient that occurs anywhere during the execution of a task disrupts the entire computation running on the host.

For the by-frame data, the probability that a transient occurs during a time frame is

$$1 - e^{-\lambda_t \times 0.05 \text{ seconds}} = 1.4 \times 10^{-9} \tag{5.11}$$

If we further assume that the lifetime of a transient fault is one second, then a transient can affect as many as 20 time frames. We thus take the probability of a transient to be 20 times the value calculated in equation 5.11, or 2.8×10^{-8}.

Finally, for both the by-case and by-frame scenarios, we assume a fairly typical value for the coverage parameter in the Markov model, $c = 0.999$.

5.7.1 Analysis Results

Figure 5.11 compares the predicted reliability of the three systems. Under both the by-case and by-frame scenarios, the recovery block system is most able to produce a correct result, followed by NVP. NSCP is the least reliable of the three. Of course, these comparisons are dependent on the experimental data used and assumptions made. More experimental data and analysis are needed to enable a more conclusive comparison.

Figure 5.12 gives a closer look at the comparisons between the NVP and DRB systems during the first 200 hours. The by-case data shows a crossover point where NVP is initially more reliable but is later less reliable than DRB. Using the by-frame data, there is no crossover point, but the estimates are so small that the differences may not be statistically significant.

Figure 5.13 compares the predicted safety of the three systems. Under the by-case scenario, NSCP is the most likely to produce a safe result, and DRB is an order of magnitude less safe

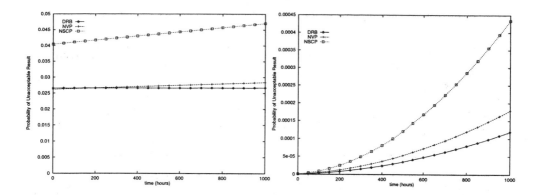

Figure 5.11   Predicted reliability, by-case data (left) and by-frame data (right)

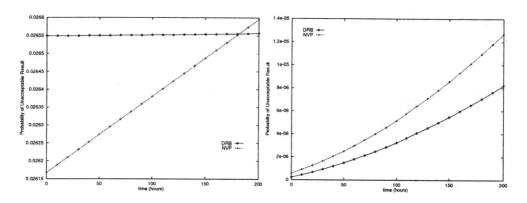

Figure 5.12   Predicted reliability, by-case data (left) and by-frame data (right)

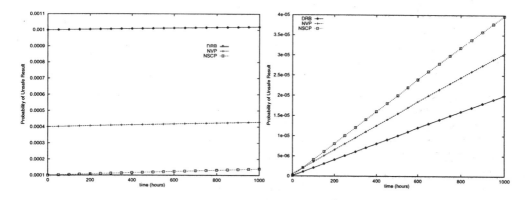

Figure 5.13   Predicted safety, by-case data (left) and by-frame data (right)

Table 5.9   Sensitivity to parameter change for DRB reliability model

	BY-CASE Data		BY-FRAME Data	
Parameter	Result	Percent Change	Result	Percent Change
Nominal	0.0265		2.31×10^{-7}	
$P_V + 10\%$	0.0284	7%	2.31×10^{-7}	no change
$P_{RV} + 10\%$	0.0282	6.2%	2.44×10^{-7}	5.6%
$P_D + 10\%$	0.0266	1.9%	2.41×10^{-7}	4.3%

Table 5.10   Sensitivity to parameter change for NVP reliability model

	BY-CASE Data		BY-FRAME Data	
Parameter	Result	Percent Change	Result	Percent Change
Nominal	0.02617		5.73×10^{-7}	
$P_V + 10\%$	0.03137	19.9%	5.74×10^{-7}	0.2%
$P_{RV} + 10\%$			6.20×10^{-7}	8.2%
$P_{RALL} + 10\%$	0.0262	0.1%		
$P_D + 10\%$	0.02618	0.04%	5.83×10^{-7}	1.7%

than NVP or NSCP. This difference is caused by the difference in assumed failure probability associated with the decider. Interestingly, the opposite ordering results from the by-frame data. Using the by-frame data to parameterize the models, DRB is predicted to be the safest, while NSCP is the least safe. The reversal of ordering between the by-case and by-frame parameterizations is caused by the relationship between the probabilities of related failure and decider failure. The by-case data parameter values resulted in related fault probabilities that were generally lower than the decider failure probabilities, while the by-frame data resulted in related fault probabilities that were relatively high. In the safety models, since there were fewer events that lead to an unsafe result, this relationship between related faults and decider faults becomes significant.

5.8   SENSITIVITY ANALYSIS

5.8.1   Sensitivity of Reliability Model

To see which parameters are the strongest determinant of the system reliability, we increased each of the non-zero failure probabilities in turn by 10 percent and observed the effect on the predicted unreliability. The sensitivity of the predictions to a ten-percent change in input parameters for the DRB model is shown in Table 5.9. It can be seen that the DRB model is most sensitive to a change in the probability of an unrelated fault for the by-case data, and to a change in the probability of a related fault for the by-frame data.

Table 5.10 shows, the change in the predicted unreliability (at t = 0) when each of the non-zero NVP nominal parameters is increased. For the by-case data, a ten percent increase in the probability of an unrelated software fault results in a twenty percent increase in the probability of an unacceptable result. A ten-percent increase in the probability of a related or decider fault activation has an almost negligible effect on the unreliability. For the by-frame data, the proability of a related fault has the largest impact on the probability of an unacceptable result. This is similar to the DRB model.

Table 5.11 Sensitivity to parameter change for NSCP reliability model

	BY-CASE Data		BY-FRAME Data	
Parameter	Result	Percent Change	Result	Percent Change
Nominal	0.04041		8.83×10^{-7}	
$P_V + 10\%$	0.04833	19.6%	8.83×10^{-7}	
$P_{RV} + 10\%$			9.61×10^{-7}	8.8%
$P_D + 10\%$	0.04042	0.02%	8.93×10^{-7}	2.1%

Table 5.12 Sensitivity to parameter change for NVP safety model

	BY-CASE Data		BY-FRAME Data	
Parameter	Result	Percent Change	Result	Percent Change
Nominal	4×10^{-4}		5.71×10^{-7}	
$P_{RV} + 10\%$			6.18×10^{-7}	8.2%
$P_{RALL} + 10\%$	4.3×10^{-4}	7.5%		
$P_D + 10\%$	4.1×10^{-4}	2.5%	5.81×10^{-7}	1.7%

The sensitivity of the NSCP model to the nominal parameters is shown in Table 5.11. The fault tree models and the sensitivity analysis show that NSCP is vulnerable to related faults, whether they involve versions in the same error confinement area or not.

5.8.2 Sensitivity of Safety Model

The sensitivity analysis for the DRB safety model is simple, as the only software fault contributing to an unsafe result is a decider failure. A ten-percent increase in the decider failure probability leads to a ten percent increase in the probability of an unsafe result.

Table 5.12 shows the sensitivity of the safety prediction to a ten-percent change in the non-zero parameter values. For the by-case data, the prediction is sensitive to a change in either the decider failure probability or the probability of a related fault affecting all versions. For the by-frame data, the prediction is much more sensitive to a change in the probability of a two-way related fault than to a change in the decider failure probability.

Table 5.13 shows the sensitivity of the safety analysis to a change in a parameter value. A change in the decider failure probability directly affects the system safety prediction for the by-case parameter values.

Table 5.13 Sensitivity to parameter change for NSCP safety model

	BY-CASE Data		BY-FRAME Data	
Parameter	Result	Percent Change	Result	Percent Change
Nominal	1×10^{-4}		1×10^{-7}	
$P_{RV} + 10\%$			1×10^{-7}	no change
$P_D + 10\%$	1.1×10^{-4}	10%	1.1×10^{-7}	10%

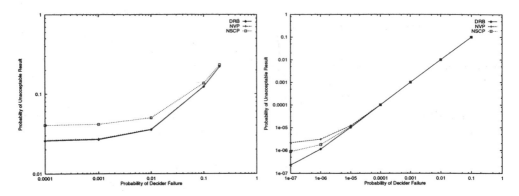

Figure 5.14   Effect of equal decider failure probabilities on reliability analysis, by-case data (left) and by-frame data (right)

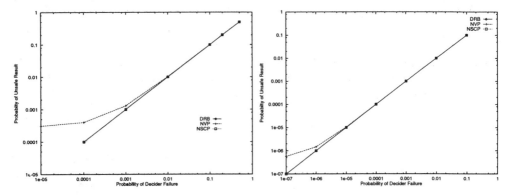

Figure 5.15   Effect of equal decider failure probabilities on safety analysis, by-case data (left) and by-frame data (right)

5.9   DECIDER FAILURE PROBABILITY

The probability of a decider failure may be an important input parameter to the comparative analysis of software fault tolerant systems. In this section we vary the decider failure probability to assess its importance. Figures 5.14 and 5.15 show the unreliability and unsafety of the three systems as the probability of decider failure is varied. For these analyses, we set the probability of failure for the decider to the same value for all three models, and show the probability of an unacceptable or unsafe result at time $t = 0$.

For the parameters derived from the by-case experimental data, if all three systems have the same probability of decider failure, it seems that DRB and NVP are nearly equally reliable, and that DRB and NSCP are nearly equally safe. In fact, the safety analysis plots for DRB and NSCP appear collinear. Under the by-frame parameterization, the probability of related faults at first dominates the decider failure probability and provides the same relative ranking for NSCP, NVP and DRB, from least to most reliable and safe.

It is not reasonable for this application to assume equally reliable deciders for both DRB and NVP or NSCP. The decider for the DRB system is an acceptance test, while that for the NVP is a simple voter and NSCP a simple comparator. For this application, it seems likely that

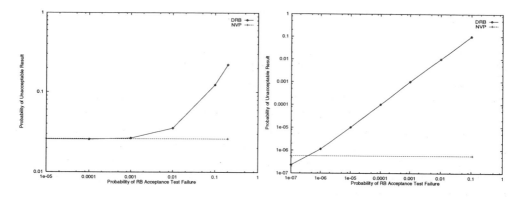

Figure 5.16 Effect on reliability of varying acceptance test failure probability for DRB, (while holding that of NVP constant), by-case data(left) and by-frame data (right)

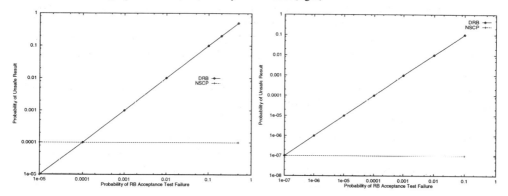

Figure 5.17 Effect on safety of varying acceptance test failure probability for DRB, (while holding that of NVP constant), by-case data(left) and by-frame data (right)

an acceptance test will be more complicated than a majority voter. The increased complexity is likely to lead to a decrease in reliability, with a corresponding impact on the reliability and safety of the system. In fact, reliability of DRB will collapse if the acceptance test in DRB is as complex and unreliable as its primary or secondary software versions. For example, if the probability of failure in acceptance test (P_D) is close to P_V, which is 0.095 by-case or 0.0004 by-frame, then Figure 5.14 indicates that DRB will initially perform the worst comparing with NVP and NSCP.

Figure 5.16 shows how the reliability comparison between DRB and NVP is affected by a variation in the probability of failure for the acceptance test. Figure 5.17 shows how the safety comparison between DRB and NSCP is affected by a variation in the probability of failure for the acceptance test. The parameters for the NVP and NSCP analysis were held constant, and the parameters (other than the probability of acceptance test failure) for the DRB model were also held constant. Figures 5.16 and 5.17 show that the acceptance test for a recovery block system must be very reliable for it to be comparable in reliability to a similar NVP system, or comparable in safety to an NSCP system.

5.10   CONCLUSIONS

This chapter proposed a system-level modeling approach to study the reliability and safety behavior of three types of fault-tolerant architectures: DRB, NVP and NSCP. Using a recent fault-tolerant software project data, we parameterized the models and displayed the probabilities of unacceptable results and unsafe results from each of the three architectures.

We used two types of data to parameterize the models. The "by-case" data could detect error only at the end of a test case, each representing a complete simulation profile of five thousand program iterations, while the "by-frame" data performed error detection and recovery at the end of each iteration. A drastic improvement of safety and reliability were observed in the second situation where a finer and more frequent error detection mechanism was assumed by the decider for each architecture.

In comparing reliability analysis of the three different architectures, DRB performed better than NVP which in turn was better than NSCP. DRB also enjoyed the feature of relative insensitivity to time in its reliability function. This comparison, however, had to be conditioned by the probability of decider failures. In the safety analysis NSCP became the best in the by-case parameters, followed by NVP and then DRB. In the by-frame data the order was reversed again. As explained in the text, this phenomenon was due to the relative probabilities of related faults and decider failure.

We also performed a sensitivity analysis over the three models. It was noted from the by-case data that varying the probability of an unrelated software fault had the major impact to the system reliability, while from the by-frame data, varying the probability of a related fault had the largest impact. This could be due to the fact that the by-frame data compares results in a finer granularity level, and was thus more sensitive to related faults among program versions.

In the decider failure analysis, the impact of decider was clearly seen. It was noted that related faults were the dominant cause of failure when the decider failure probability was low, then the decider failure probability dominated as it increased. Moreover, if the acceptance test in DRB was as unreliable as its application versions, DRB lost its advantage to NVP and NSCP.

Finally, we believe more data points are necessary for at least two purposes. First, the modeling methodology must be validated by considering other experimental data and models for related or correlated faults. Second, the current parameters were derived from a single experimental implementation and so may not be generally applicable. Similar analysis of other experimental data will help to establish a set of reasonable parameters that can be used in a broader comparison of these and other fault-tolerant architectures.

REFERENCES

[Arl90]   Jean Arlat, Karama Kanoun, and Jean-Claude Laprie. Dependability modeling and evaluation of software fault-tolerant systems. *IEEE Transactions on Computers*, 39(4):504–513, April 1990.

[Avi85]   Algirdas Avižienis. The N-version approach to fault-tolerant software. *IEEE Transactions on Software Engineering*, SE-11(12):1491–1501, December 1985.

[Bis86]   P.G. Bishop, D.G. Esp, M. Barnes, P. Humphreys, G. Dahl, and J. Lahti. PODS - a project of diverse software. *IEEE Transactions on Software Engineering*, SE-12(9):929–940, September 1986.

[Bri93]   D. Briere and P. Traverse. Airbus A320/A330/A340 electrical flight controls: a family of fault-tolerant systems. In *Proc. of the 23rd Symposium on Fault Tolerant Computing*, pages

616–623, 1993.

[Car84] G.D. Carlow. Architecture of the space shuttle primary avionics software system. *Communications of the ACM*, 27(9):926–936, September 1984.

[Cia92] Gianfranco Ciardo, Jogesh Muppala, and Kishor Trivedi. Analyzing concurrent and fault-tolerant software using stochastic reward nets. *Journal of Parallel and Distributed Computing*, 15:255–269, 1992.

[Dug94] Joanne Bechta Dugan. Experimental analysis of models for correlation in multiversion software. In *Proc. of the International Symposium on Software Reliability Engineering*, 1994.

[Dug95] Joanne Bechta Dugan. Software reliability analysis using fault trees. In Michael R. Lyu, editor, *McGraw-Hill Software Reliability Engineering Handbook*. McGraw-Hill, New York, NY, 1995.

[Dug89] Joanne Bechta Dugan and K. S. Trivedi. Coverage modeling for dependability analysis of fault-tolerant systems. *IEEE Transactions on Computers*, 38(6):775–787, 1989.

[Eck91] Dave E. Eckhardt, Alper K. Caglayan, John C. Knight, Larry D. Lee, David F. McAllister, Mladen A. Vouk, and John P.J. Kelly. An experimental evaluation of software redundancy as a strategy for improving reliability. *IEEE Transactions on Software Engineering*, 17(7), July 1991.

[Eck85] Dave E. Eckhardt and Larry D. Lee. Theoretical basis for the analysis of multiversion software subject to coincident errors. *IEEE Transactions on Software Engineering*, 11(12):1511–1517, December 1985.

[Gei90] Robert Geist and Kishor Trivedi. Reliability estimation of fault-tolerant systems: tools and techniques. *IEEE Computer*, pages 52–61, July 1990.

[Grn80] A. Grnarov, J. Arlat, and A. Avižienis. On the performance of software fault tolerance strategies. In *Digest of 10th FTCS*, pages 251–253, Kyoto, Japan, October 1980.

[Gun88] Gunnar Hagelin. ERICSSON safety system for railway control. In U. Voges, editor, *Software Diversity in Computerized Control Systems*, pages 11–21. Springer-Verlag, 1988.

[Hec86] Herbert Hecht and Myron Hecht. Fault-tolerant software. In D.K.Pradhan, editor, *Fault-Tolerant Computing: Theory and Techniques*, 2:658–696. Prentice-Hall, 1986.

[Hil85] A. D. Hills. Digital fly-by-wire experience. In *Proc. AGARD Lecture Series*, (143), October 1985.

[Joh88] Allen M. Johnson and Miroslaw Malek. Survey of software tools for evaluating reliability availability, and serviceability. *ACM Computing Surveys*, 20(4):227–269, December 1988.

[Kim89] K.H. Kim and Howard O. Welch. Distributed execution of recovery blocks: an approach for uniform treatment of hardware and software faults in real-time applications. *IEEE Transactions on Computers*, 38(5):626–636, May 1989.

[Kni86] John C. Knight and Nancy G. Leveson. An experimental evaluation of the assumption of independence in multiversion programming. *IEEE Transactions on Software Engineering*, SE-12(1):96–109, January 1986.

[Lal88] Jaynarayan H. Lala and Linda S. Alger. Hardware and software fault tolerance: a unified architectural approach. In *Proc. IEEE International Symposium on Fault-Tolerant Computing, FTCS-18*, pages 240–245, June 1988.

[Lap84] Jean-Claude Laprie. Dependability evaluation of software systems in operation. *IEEE Transactions on Software Engineering*, SE-10(6):701–714, November 1984.

[Lap90] Jean-Claude Laprie, Jean Arlat, Christian Béounes, and Karama Kanoun. Definition and Analysis of Hardware- and Software- Fault-Tolerant Architectures. *IEEE Computer*, pages 39–51, July 1990.

[Lap92] Jean-Claude Laprie and Karama Kanoun. X-ware reliability and availability modeling. *IEEE Transactions on Software Engineering*, pages 130–147, February, 1992.

[Lit89] Bev Littlewood and Douglas R. Miller. Theoretical basis for the analysis of multiversion software subject to coincident errors. *IEEE Transactions on Software Engineering*, 15(12):1596–1614, December 1989.

[Lyu93] Michael R Lyu and Yu-Tao He. Improving the N-version programming process through the evolution of a design paradigm. *IEEE Transactions on Reliability*, 42(2):179–189, June 1993.

[Nic90] Victor F. Nicola and Ambuj Goyal. Modeling of correlated failures and community error recovery in multiversion software. *IEEE Transactions on Software Engineering*, 16(3), March 1990.

[Ram81]   C. V. Ramamoorthy, Y. Mok, F. Bastani, G. Chin, , and K. Suzuki. Application of a method-
          ology for the development and validation of reliable process control software. *IEEE Trans-
          actions on Software Engineering*, SE-7(6):537–555, November 1981.

[Ran75]   Brian Randell. System structure for software fault tolerance. *IEEE Transactions on Software
          Engineering*, SE-1(2):220–232, June 1975.

[Sco87]   R. Keith Scott, James W. Gault, and David F. McAllister. Fault-tolerant software reliability
          modeling. *IEEE Transactions on Software Engineering*, SE-13(5):582–592, May 1987.

[Shi84]   Kang G. Shin and Yann-Hang Lee. Evaluation of error recovery blocks used for cooperating
          processes. *IEEE Transactions on Software Engineering*, SE-10(6):692–700, November 1984.

[Sta87]   George. E. Stark. Dependability evaluation of integrated hardware/software systems. *IEEE
          Transactions on Reliability*, pages 440–444, October 1987.

[Tai93]   Ann T. Tai, John F. Meyer, and Algirdas Avizienis. Performability enhancement of fault-
          tolerant software. *IEEE Transactions on Reliability*, pages 227–237, June 1993.

[Tra88]   Pascal Traverse. Airbus and ATR system architecture and specification. In U. Voges, editor,
          Software Diversity in Computerized Control Systems, pages 95–104. Springer-Verlag, June
          1988.

[Vai93]   Nitin H. Vaidya and Dhiraj K. Pradhan. Fault-tolerant design strategies for high reliability
          and safety. *IEEE Transactions on Computers*, 42(10), October 1993.

[Vog88]   Udo Voges. Use of diversity in experimental reactor safety systems. In U. Voges, editor,
          Software Diversity in Computerized Control Systems, pages 29–49. Springer-Verlag, 1988.

[Wei91]   Liubao Wei. *A Model Based Study of Workload Influence on Computing System Dependability*.
          PhD thesis, University of Michigan, 1991.

[You84]   L. J. Yount. Architectural solutions to safety problems of digital flight-critical systems for
          commercial transports. In *Proc. AIAA/IEEE Digital Avionics Systems Conference*, pages 1–8,
          December 1984.

6

Analyses Using Stochastic Reward Nets

LORRIE A. TOMEK
IBM Corporation, Research Triangle Park, North Carolina

KISHOR S. TRIVEDI
Duke University

ABSTRACT

In this chapter, we examine the power of stochastic reward nets (SRNs), a variant of stochastic Petri nets, to model fault tolerant software systems. The three types of software fault tolerance we examine are: N-version programming, recovery blocks, and N self-checking programming. SRNs allow each fault tolerance technique to be specified in a concise manner. Complex dependencies, such as common-mode versus separate failures and detected versus undetected failures, associated with these systems are incorporated into each SRN model without undue complication. Underlying an SRN is a Markov reward model. Each SRN is automatically converted into a Markov reward model from which steady-state, transient, cumulative transient, and sensitivity measures are easily obtained. We study several measures, including reliability, safety, and performance measures, which are of interest in the evaluation of fault tolerant software techniques. We parameterize our model to account for common-mode failures between variants using distributions from experimental data, and then provide numerical results using the stochastic Petri net package (SPNP) [Cia89].

Software Fault Tolerance, Edited by Lyu
© 1995 John Wiley & Sons Ltd

6.1 INTRODUCTION

In this chapter, we explore the capability to model various software fault tolerance techniques using a generalization of stochastic Petri nets (SPNs) called *stochastic reward nets (SRNs)*. SRNs, like stochastic Petri nets, allow a particular system to be expressed concisely during the design phase. Tools have been developed to automatically convert the net into its underlying (equivalent) Markov model [Cia89, Chi85, Cou91]. Although the underlying Markov model can be very large, efficient solution techniques have been developed to obtain steady-state, transient, cumulative, and sensitivity measures. Stochastic Petri nets (SPNs) have been used successfully to represent systems under design in order to study their performance [Ibe90], safety [Tom94], reliability [Tom91], and availability [Ibe89]. We demonstrate that SRNs are well-suited to the task of modeling fault tolerant software systems.

The software fault tolerance strategies we will consider are N-version programming, recovery blocks, and N self-checking programming. These techniques require the development of two or more software modules which are termed *variants*. The variants are executed sequentially in the case of recovery blocks, and in parallel in the case of N-version programming and N self-checking programming. Each strategy employs a different *decision mechanism* to diagnose variant output as correct or incorrect. In *N-version programming (NVP)*, the results of all variants are collected and a voter determines the system output [Avi85]. In *recovery blocks (RB)*, the result of each sequentially executed variant is processed by an acceptance test; this acceptance test either accepts the variant's result or the next variant is executed (until all variants have been executed) [Ran75, And81]. In *N self-checking programming (NSCP)*, there are two possible decision mechanisms [Lap90]. The first possibility is that each variant has its own acceptance test. The second possibility is that each pair of variants is compared using a comparison algorithm associated with the pair of variants. The system's output is given by the active variant (or variant pair) that diagnoses its own output as correct. The active status cycles between the variants (or variant pairs), so that if at least one variant (or variant pair) diagnoses its output to be correct, the system does produce an output. In each of the above possibilities, the acceptance test associated with each variant or the comparison algorithm associated with a pair of variants can be identical or can be independently derived.

Associated with these techniques are several dependencies that are important to the accurate study of fault tolerant software systems. Dependencies in fault tolerant systems are generally classified according to the source of the failure. Laprie [Lap90] differentiates failures by the following two important classifications:

First, with respect to the type of failures:

1. *Separate failures* result from independent faults.
2. *Common mode failures* result from related faults or from independent faults with similar errors.

Second, with respect to error detection:

1. *Detected failures* occur when no unacceptable output is delivered.
2. *Undetected failures* occur when incorrect output is delivered.

In the SRN models, we consider both separate and common-mode failures by careful definition of system parameters. The distinction between detected and undetected failures is accounted for by the structure of the SRN model. There are many sources of common mode failures. One source is design faults that occur during the specification and/or implementation phase where the initial specification, design, or code is use in the development of more than one variant. Another source of common mode failure is that a single input is shared by all variants within the execution of the fault tolerant software block. If all inputs are equally difficult, then the variant failure probabilities are independent. If some inputs are more difficult than others (as has been shown in measurements of experimental systems), then the variant failure probabilities are dependent random variables.

SRNs are well suited to express each software fault tolerance technique and account for these complexities. In addition, since SRNs are equal in modeling power to Markov reward models (MRMs), the wide range of measures available for MRMs can be easily obtained for SRNs. Using SRNs, we are able to numerically study safety, reliability, and performance of each software fault tolerance technique.

The chapter is organized as follows. In Section 6.2, we describe SRNs including the measures that can be readily obtained for SRNs. In Section 6.3, we describe three fault tolerant software techniques which we model using SRNs. The techniques considered are N-version programming, recovery blocks, and N self-checking programming. Section 6.4 discusses issues defined by software fault tolerant systems including detected versus undetected failures and common-mode versus separate failures. The SRN models of each software fault tolerant technique are then revisited to explore how these issues are incorporated into the model. In Section 6.5, we study numerical results for performance, reliability, and safety measures. The numerical study incorporates parameters measured in the multi-version software experiment of Lyu and He [Lyu93]. Section 6.6 summarizes the chapter.

6.2   INTRODUCTION TO STOCHASTIC REWARD NETS

Stochastic reward nets (SRNs) are a generalization of generalized stochastic Petri nets (GSPNs), which in turn are a generalization of stochastic Petri nets (SPNs). We first describe SPNs, then GSPNs, and then SRNs.

6.2.1   Stochastic Petri Nets (SPNs)

A Petri net (PN) is a bipartite directed graph with two disjoint sets called *places* and *transitions* [Pet81]. Directed arcs in the graph connect places to transitions (called *input arcs*) and transitions to places (called *output arcs*). Places may contain an integer number of entities called *tokens*. The state or condition of the system is associated with the presence or absence of tokens in various places in the net. The condition of the net may enable some transitions to fire. This *firing of a transition* is the removal of tokens from one or more places in the net and/or the arrival of tokens in one or more places in the net. The tokens are removed from places connected to the transition by an input arc; the tokens arrive in places connected to the transition by an output arc. A *marked Petri net* is obtained by associating tokens with places. The *marking* of a PN is the distribution of tokens in the places of the PN. A marking is represented by a vector $M = (\#(P_1), \#(P_2), \cdots, \#(P_n))$ where $\#(P_i)$ is the number of tokens in place i and n is the number of places in the net.

In a graphical representation of a PN, places are represented by circles, transitions are represented by bars and the tokens are represented by dots or integers in the circles (places). The *input places* of a transition are the set of places which connect to that transition through input arcs. Similarly, *output places* of a transition are those places to which output arcs are drawn from that transition.

A transition is considered *enabled* to fire in the current marking if each of its input places contains the number of tokens assigned to the input arc (called the *arc multiplicity*). The firing of a transition is an atomic action in which the designated number of tokens are removed from each input place of that transition and one or more tokens (as specified by the output arc multiplicity) are added to each output place of that transition, possibly resulting in a new marking of the PN.

If exponentially distributed *firing times* correspond with the transitions, the result is a *stochastic Petri net* [Flo91, Mol82, Nat80]. Allowing transitions to have either zero firing times (immediate transitions) or exponentially distributed firing times (timed transitions) gives rise to the *generalized stochastic Petri net (GSPN)* [Ajm84]. The transitions with exponentially distributed firing time are drawn as unfilled rectangles; immediate transitions are drawn as lines.

6.2.2   Generalized Stochastic Petri Nets (GSPNs)

Other extensions to SPNs in the development of GSPNs include the inhibitor arc. An *inhibitor arc* is an arc from a place to a transition that inhibits the firing of the transition when a token is present in the input place.

Each distinct marking of the PN constitutes a separate state of the PN. A marking is reachable from another marking if there exists a sequence of transition firings occur starting from the original marking that results in the new marking. The *reachability set (graph)* of a PN is the set (graph) of markings that are reachable from the other markings.

In any marking of the PN, a number of transitions may be simultaneously enabled. The tie between simultaneously enabled transitions can be broken by specifying priorities, by specifying probabilities, or by a race. *Priorities* are non-negative integers that permit a partial ordering of transitions. Whenever a transition with a priority δ is enabled, all transitions with priorities less than δ are inhibited from firing. If *probabilities* are assigned to the transitions, they are interpreted as weights of each transition. With some probability, any of the enabled transitions may be the first to fire; any enabled transition with positive probability may fire next. Immediate transitions which can be simultaneously enabled must have either priorities or probabilities assigned to avoid ambiguity in the net. For timed transitions, the decision as to which transition fires next can be decided by a *race*; the transition with the minimal delay prior to firing will fire next.

The markings of a GSPN are classified into two types: tangible and vanishing. A marking is *tangible* if the only transitions enabled (if any are enabled) are timed transitions. A marking is *vanishing* if one or more immediate transitions are enabled in the marking.

Ajmone Marsan et al [Ajm84] showed that a GSPN is equivalent in power to a continuous time Markov chain (CTMC). All CTMCs can be converted to an equivalent GSPN model; any GSPN model can be converted to an equivalent CTMC. The same techniques used for steady state, transient, cumulative, and sensitivity measures of a CTMC can be used to solve for the same measures of a GSPN (once the GSPN is converted to a CTMC.)

6.2.3   Stochastic Reward Nets (SRNs)

Stochastic reward nets (SRNs) are a superset of GSPNs [Cia89, Cia92]. SRNs substantially increase the modeling power of the GSPN by adding guard functions, marking dependent arc multiplicities, general transition priorities, and reward rates at the net level.

A *guard function* is a Boolean function associated with a transition [Cia89, Cia92]. Whenever the transition satisfies all the input and inhibitor conditions in a marking M, the guard is evaluated. The transition is considered enabled only if the guard function evaluates to true.

Marking dependent arc multiplicities allow either the number of tokens required for the transition to be enabled, or the number of tokens removed from the input place, or the number of tokens placed in an output place to be a function of the current marking of the PN. Such arcs are called *variable cardinality arcs*.

6.2.4   Measures

Stochastic Reward Nets (SRNs) provide the same modeling capability as Markov reward models (MRMs). A *Markov reward model* is a Markov chain with reward rates (real numbers) assigned to each state [How71]. A state of an SRN is actually a marking (labeled $(\#(P_1),\#(P_2),...,\#(P_n))$ if there are n places in the net). We label the set of all possible markings that can be reached in the net as Ω. These markings are subdivided into tangible markings Ω_T and vanishing markings Ω_V. For each tangible marking i in Ω_T, a reward rate r_i is assigned. This reward is determined by examining the overall measures to be obtained. In Section 6.5, we examine the reward definitions needed to generate reliability, safety, and performance measures.

Several measures are obtained using Markov reward models. These include the expected reward rate both in steady state and at a given time, the expected accumulated reward until either absorption or a given time, and the distribution of accumulated reward either until absorption or a given time.

The *expected reward rate in steady state* can be computed using the steady state probability of being in each marking i for all $i \in \Omega_T$. For steady state distribution π_i, the expected reward rate is given by

$$E[\mathcal{R}] = \sum_{i \in \Omega_T} r_i \pi_i$$

The *expected reward rate at time t* can be computed by using the transient probability of being in each marking $i \in \Omega_T$, labeled $p_i(t)$. The expected reward rate at time t is then given by

$$E[\mathcal{R}(t)] = \sum_{i \in \Omega_T} r_i p_i(t)$$

The *distribution of reward rate at time t* $P\{\mathcal{R}(t) \leq x\}$ is given by

$$P\{\mathcal{R}(t) \leq x\} = \sum_{r_i \leq x, i \in \Omega_T} p_i(t)$$

The *accumulated reward* in $(0,t]$, $Y(t)$, is defined as $Y(t) = \int_0^t \mathcal{R}(u)\,du$. The *expected accumulated reward in (0,t]* can be computed as

$$E[Y(t)] = E[\int_0^t \mathcal{R}(u)\,du] = \int_0^t E[\mathcal{R}(u)]\,du = \sum_{i\in\Omega_T} r_i \int_0^t p_i(u)\,du$$

The *expected accumulated reward until absorption*, labeled $E[Y(\infty)]$, can be computed as

$$E[Y(\infty)] = \sum_{i\in\Omega_T} r_i \int_0^\infty p_i(u)\,du$$

The *distribution of accumulated reward* is a measure of considerable interest. The distribution of accumulated reward until absorption is defined as $\mathcal{Y}(x) = P\{Y(\infty) \leq x\}$. This distribution was first studied by Beaudry [Bea78] for an underlying CTMC model with strictly positive reward rates, and was extended by Ciardo et al. [Cia90] to allow an underlying semi-Markov model with non-negative reward rates.

Sensitivities (derivatives) of the above measures with respect to one or more model parameters can also be obtained [Cia92].

6.3   FAULT TOLERANT SOFTWARE MODELS

Next, we develop SRN models for recovery blocks, N-version programming blocks, and N self-checking programming blocks. In this section, we focus on the basic model. We revisit each model in Section 6.4 to discuss issues such as detected versus undetected failures and common-mode versus separate failures.

6.3.1   Recovery Blocks

A recovery block (RB) consists of two or more variants and a single acceptance test (AT). The variants are ordered with the first variant called the *primary* and the others called *alternates*. The primary and the alternate variants are independently developed, based on different algorithms and implemented by different programmers. For each input to the recovery block, the primary is executed first and its output is evaluated using the AT. If the AT fails to accept the output, a rollback recovery is attempted; this process is repeated for each alternate variant in succession until either (1) a variant produces an output that is accepted by the AT, (2) the rollback recovery fails, or (3) all variants execute without satisfying the AT. In the last case, the RB is said to have failed on this input dataset. The pseudocode for a RB with N variants (a primary and $N - 1$ alternates) is shown below.

```
ensure acceptance test
    by primary variant (#1)
    else by alternate variant (#2)
    else by alternate variant (#3)
      ...
    else by alternate variant (#N)
else error
```

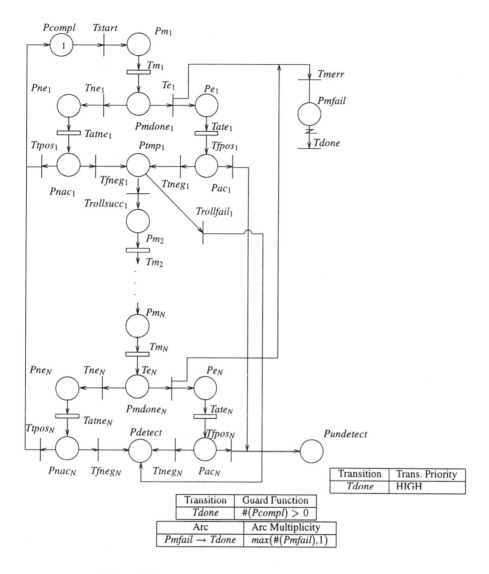

Figure 6.1   SRN model of a software recovery block (RB)

The parameters required for a recovery block model are difficult to obtain. Following the categories of Pucci [Puc90, Puc92], events in the recovery blocks are classified into the following four types of events.

1. Variant i produces correct output which the AT accepts.
2. Variant i produces correct output which the AT rejects.
3. Variant i produces incorrect output which the AT rejects.
4. Variant i produces incorrect output which the AT accepts.

In addition, we will consider both successful and unsuccessful rollback recovery attempts following a negative AT diagnosis.

The SRN model of a recovery block is shown in Figure 6.1. The net is nearly self-explanatory. Place $Pcompl$ is the starting point of the RB. The firing of transition $Tstart$, which places a token in place Pm_1, indicates that the recovery block has begun executing the next (or first in this case) dataset. A token in place Pm_1 indicates that the primary variant in the recovery block has begun execution on the current dataset. The firing of transition Tm_1 corresponds to the completion of the execution of the primary variant. Transitions Tne_1 and Te_1 correspond to the events that the output produced by the variant are correct and incorrect respectively. Transition Tne_1 moves the token from place $Pmdone_1$ to place Pne_1 indicating that the variant produced a correct output. Transition Te_1 moves the token from place $Pmdone_1$ to both places Pe_1 and $Pmfail$. A token in place Pe_1 indicates that the first variant produced an incorrect output. Place $Pmfail$ counts the number of variants producing an incorrect result on the current dataset; this is needed to represent common-mode failures. Transition $Tatne_1$ represents the execution of the AT after the variant produces a correct output. The immediate transitions $Ttpos_1$ and $Tfneg_1$, which correspond to a correct positive diagnosis by the AT and a false negative diagnosis by the AT respectively, are then enabled. Transition $Tate_1$ represents the execution of the AT after the variant produces an incorrect output. The immediate transitions $Ttneg_1$ and $Tfpos_1$, which correspond to correct negative diagnosis by the AT and a false positive diagnosis by the AT respectively, are then enabled. A false positive AT diagnosis causes the token to be moved to place $Pundetect$ indicating an undetected block failure. A true positive AT diagnosis causes the token to be moved to place $Pcompl$ indicating the block has completed execution on the current dataset. The block then begins operation on the next dataset.

If an error is discovered, represented by the firing of either $Tfneg_1$ and $Ttneg_1$, the system initiates a rollback recovery action. Transition $Trollsucc_1$ represents a successful rollback. Transition $Trollfail_1$ represents an unsuccessful rollback resulting in an RB failure. The output arc from $Trollsucc_1$ leads to Pm_2, the starting place of the first alternate variant, while the output arc from $Trollfail_1$ leads to $Pdetect$ which represents a detected RB failure. The alternate variants are similarly modeled by the other places and transitions indexed from 2 to N. The structure of the last variant is slightly different, since the failure of the last variant automatically results in a detected system failure. Thus, the output arcs from transitions $Tfneg_N$ and $Ttneg_N$ lead to place $Pdetect$.

When the recovery block completes (the token is returned to place Pm_1) then transition $Tdone$ fires and all tokens are removed from place $Pmfail$ for the next execution of the recovery block.

6.3.2 N-Version Programming

In N-version programming (NVP), all variants operate on the same input in parallel. The results of all variants are collected and a voter determines the system output [Avi85]. The reliability of this mechanism is dependent upon individual variant results. If more than half of the variants produce results that are within the required error tolerance, the prevailing result is declared correct. If half or less than half of the variants produce the same result, the result is declared incorrect. In this case, no output would be released by the block.

In Figure 6.2, an SRN model of an N-version programming system is shown. Initially, a single token is in place $Pcompl$. The software block begins operating on the next input immediately with the firing of transition $Tstart$. This transition places one token in each of the places Pm_1, Pm_2, ..., Pm_N, representing the fact that each variant begins operation on

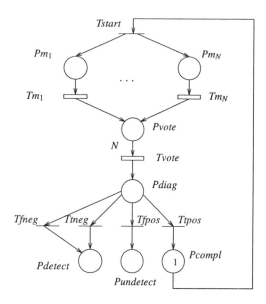

Figure 6.2   SRN model of N-version programming

the provided input. Transitions Tm_i for $i \in 1,2,...,N$ represents the completion of execution of variant i. When all variants have completed, place $Pvote$ will contain N tokens, enabling transition $Tvote$. Transition $Tvote$ represents the execution of the voting mechanism. When voting is complete, a single token is moved to place $Pdiag$ where the voting result is diagnosed. If less than half of the variants produced correct output, then the voting result can be either a true negative, represented by the firing of transition $Ttneg$, or a false positive, represented by the firing of transition $Tfpos$. If at least half of the variants produced correct output, then the voting result can be either a true positive, represented by the firing of transition $Ttpos$, or a false negative, represented by the firing of transition $Tfneg$. If the voting result is negative, either transition $Ttneg$ or transition $Tfneg$ fire, moving the token to place $Pdetect$. This represents a detected error. If the voting result is a false positive, transition $Tfpos$ fires, moving the token to place $Pundetect$, indicating an undetected error. If the voting result is a true positive, transition $Ttpos$ fires, moving the token to place $Pcompl$, indicating the software block as successfully completed execution on the current dataset. Once the token is returned to place $Pcompl$, the N-version programming block begins operating on the next input.

6.3.3   N Self-Checking Programming

In *N self-checking programming (NSCP)*, all variants operate in parallel on the same input. There are two possible decision mechanisms [Lap90] using this technique. The first possibility is that each variant has its own acceptance test. The second possibility is that each pair of variants is compared using a comparison algorithm associated with the pair. In each of the above possibilities, the acceptance test associated with each variant or comparison algorithm associated with a pair of variants can be identical or independently derived. One variant is always considered to be the active variant. If the active variant produces an output that is

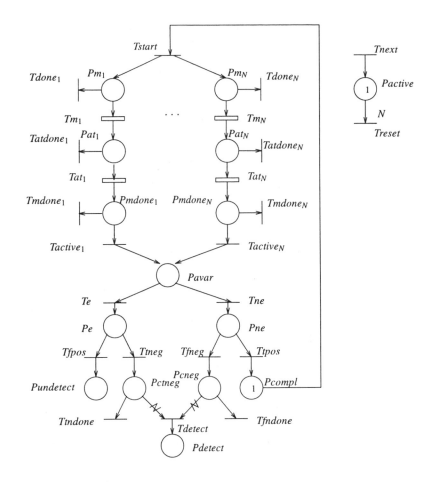

Figure 6.3   SRN model of N self-checking programming using an acceptance test for error diagnosis

diagnosed as correct, then that output is the block output. If the active variant diagnoses its output to be incorrect, then the status of active variant is passed to one of the alternate variants.

6.3.3.1   NSCP WITH ACCEPTANCE TEST

First, we study the case where each variant diagnoses the correctness or incorrectness of its output using an acceptance test as shown in Figure 6.3. The transition priorities, guard functions, and arc multiplicities associated with this model are given in Figure 6.4. Initially, there is a single token in both places $Pcompl$ and $Pactive$. The software block begins operating on the next input immediately with the firing of transition $Tstart$. This transition places one token in each of places Pm_1, Pm_2, ..., Pm_N, representing the fact that each variant begins operation on the provided input. Transitions Tm_i for $i \in 1,2,...,N$ represents the execution of each variant i. As each variant completes execution, a token is placed in Pat_i (for variant i). The self-checking procedure (acceptance test execution) is modeled by transition Tat_i. When the acceptance test completes, the token is moved from place Pat_i to place $Pmdone_i$ (for variant i). Place $Pactive$ contains the number of tokens representing the number of the

Transition	Trans. Priority
Tnext	LOW
Treset	HIGH
Tstart	LOW
Tactive$_i$, for $i \in [1,N]$	HIGH
Tdetect	HIGH
Tdone$_i$, for $i \in [1,N]$	HIGH
Tatdone$_i$, for $i \in [1,N]$	HIGH
Tmdone$_i$, for $i \in [1,N]$	HIGH
Ttndone	HIGH
Tfndone	HIGH

Transition	Guard Function
Tnext	$\#(Pm_i) + \#(Pat_i) + \#(Pmdone_i) + \#(Pavar) + \#(Pe) + \#(Pne) + \#(Pdetect) + \#(Pundetect) + \#(Pcompl) == 0$ where $i = \#(Pactive)$
Treset	$\#(Pactive) > N$
Tactive$_i$, for $i \in [1,N]$	$\#(Pactive) == i$
Tdetect	$\#(Pctneg) + \#(Pcfneg) == N$
Tdone$_i$, for $i \in [1,N]$	$\#(Pcompl) + \#(Pdetect) + \#(Pundetect) > 0$
Tatdone$_i$, for $i \in [1,N]$	$\#(Pcompl) + \#(Pdetect) + \#(Pundetect) > 0$
Tmdone$_i$, for $i \in [1,N]$	$\#(Pcompl) + \#(Pdetect) + \#(Pundetect) > 0$
Tfndone	$\#(Pcompl) + \#(Pdetect) + \#(Pundetect) > 0$
Ttndone	$\#(Pcompl) + \#(Pdetect) + \#(Pundetect) > 0$

Arc	Arc Multiplicity
$Pctneg \rightarrow Tdetect$	$\#(Pctneg)$
$Pcfneg \rightarrow Tdetect$	$\#(Pcfneg)$
$Pctneg \rightarrow Ttndone$	$max(\#(Pctneg),1)$
$Pcfneg \rightarrow Tfndone$	$max(\#(Pcfneg),1)$

Figure 6.4 Function definitions for SRN model of N self-checking programming using an acceptance test for error diagnosis

active variant (a number between 1 and N). When the active variant completes its acceptance test, then a token is in place $Pmdone_i$ enabling transition $Tactive_i$, where i is the number of tokens in place $Pactive$. The firing of transition $Tactive_i$ moves the token to place $Pavar$. This enables transitions Tc, representing the fact that the active variant has produced incorrect output, and transition Tne, representing the fact that the variant has produced correct output. If the variant produced incorrect output, the firing of transition Te moves the token to place Pe. The diagnosis of incorrect output can be either a false positive diagnoses or a true negative diagnosis represented by transitions $Tfpos$ and $Ttneg$ respectively. If a false positive diagnosis occurs, the token is moved to place $Pundetect$, representing an undetected error. If a true negative diagnosis is detected, the token is moved to place $Pctneg$. Place $Pctneg$ counts the number of incorrect variant outputs which are diagnosed as true negative. The tokens remain in place $Pctneg$ until either all variants are diagnosed as incorrect or the block completes execution without detecting a failure.

If the variant produced incorrect output, transition Tne fires moving the token from place $Pavar$ to place Pne. The diagnosis of correct output can be either a false negative or a true positive represented by transitions $Tfneg$ and $Ttpos$. Transition $Tfneg$ moves the token from place Pne to place $Pcfpos$. Place $Pcfpos$ counts the number of correct variant outputs which are diagnosed as false negative. The tokens remain in place $Pcfpos$ until either all variants are diagnosed as incorrect or the active variant pair diagnoses its output to be correct. If the sum of the number of tokens in place $Pctneg$ and $Pcfpos$ is equal to N, all variants have been

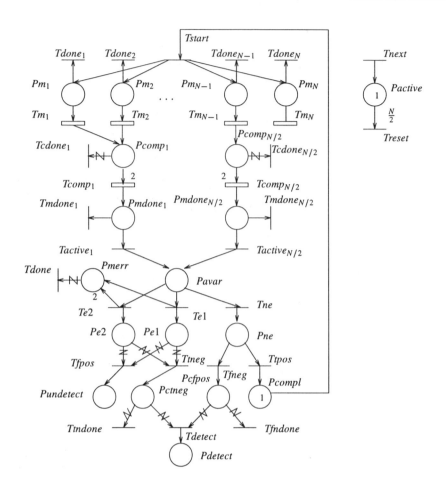

Figure 6.5   SRN model of N self-checking programming using a comparison test for error diagnosis

diagnosed as incorrect. This enables transition $Tdetect$, which removes all tokens from places $Pctneg$ and $Pcfpos$ and places a single token in place $Pdetect$; this represents a detected failure. If the diagnosis of the correct output is a true positive, transition $Ttpos$ fires, moving the token from place Pne to place $Pcompl$.

A token in place $Pcompl$ satisfies the guard function for transitions $Tdone_i$, $Tatdone_i$, and $Tmdone_i$ for $i \in [1,N]$ and transitions $Ttndone$ and $Tfndone$. All tokens in these places are removed from the net, effectively resetting the net to its initial state. After this reset, the N self-checking programming block begins execution of the next input.

6.3.3.2   NSCP WITH COMPARISON ALGORITHM

Now, we study the case where the outputs of pairs of variants are diagnosed by a comparison algorithm as shown in Figure 6.5. The transition priority, guard, and arc multiplicity functions are given in Figure 6.6. This model is very similar to the previously discussed NSCP with acceptance test model. Initially, there is a single token in both places $Pcompl$ and $Pactive$.

Transition	Trans. Priority
Tnext	LOW
Treset	HIGH
Tstart	LOW
Tactive$_i$, for $i \in [1,N/2]$	HIGH
Tdetect	HIGH
Tdone$_i$, for $i \in [1,N]$	HIGH
Tcdone$_i$, for $i \in [1,N/2]$	HIGH
Tmdone$_i$, for $i \in [1,N/2]$	HIGH
Ttndone	HIGH
Tfndone	HIGH
Tedone	HIGH

Transition	Guard Function
Tnext	$\#(Pm_{i\times2}) + \#(Pcomp_i) + \#(Pmdone_i) + \#(Pavar) + \#(Pe) +$ $\#(Pne) + \#(Pdetect) + \#(Pundetect) + \#(Pcompl) == 0$ where $i = \#(Pactive)$
Treset	$\#(Pactive) > N/2$
Tactive$_i$, for $i \in [1,N/2]$	$\#(Pactive) == i$
Tfpos	$\#(Pe1) + \#(Pe2) > 0$
Ttneg	$\#(Pe1) + \#(Pe2) > 0$
Tdetect	$\#(Pctneg) + \#(Pcfneg) == N/2$
Tdone$_i$, for $i \in [1,N]$	$\#(Pcompl) + \#(Pdetect) + \#(Pundetect) > 0$
Tcdone$_i$, for $i \in [1,N/2]$	$\#(Pcompl) + \#(Pdetect) + \#(Pundetect) > 0$
Tmdone$_i$, for $i \in [1,N/2]$	$\#(Pcompl) + \#(Pdetect) + \#(Pundetect) > 0$
Ttndone	$\#(Pcompl) + \#(Pdetect) + \#(Pundetect) > 0$
Tfndone	$\#(Pcompl) + \#(Pdetect) + \#(Pundetect) > 0$
Tedone	$\#(Pcompl) + \#(Pdetect) + \#(Pundetect) > 0$

Arc	Arc Multiplicity
Pctneg $\rightarrow$ *Tdetect*	$\#(Pctneg)$
Pcfneg $\rightarrow$ *Tdetect*	$\#(Pcfneg)$
Pctneg $\rightarrow$ *Ttndone*	$max(\#(Pctneg),1)$
Pcfneg $\rightarrow$ *Tfndone*	$max(\#(Pcfneg),1)$
Pcomp$_i$ $\rightarrow$ *Tcdone$_i$*, for $i \in [1,N/2]$	$max(\#(Pcomp_i),1)$
Pei $\rightarrow$ *Tfpos*, for $i = 1,2$	$\#(Pe_i)$
Pei $\rightarrow$ *Ttneg*, for $i = 1,2$	$\#(Pe_i)$

Figure 6.6 Function definitions for SRN model of N self-checking programming using a comparison test for error diagnosis

The software block begins operating on the next input immediately with the firing of transition *Tstart*. This transition places one token in each of places Pm_1, Pm_2, ..., Pm_N, representing the fact that each variant begins operation on the provided input. Transitions Tm_i for $i \in 1,2,...,N$ represents the execution of each variant i. As each variant completes execution, a token is placed in $Tcomp_{\lceil i/2 \rceil}$ (for variant i). The self-checking procedure (comparison algorithm execution) is modeled by transition $Tcomp_i$. This transition is enabled only when both variants in a pair have completed execution (when two tokens are in place $Pcomp_i$). When the comparison test completes, the token is moved from place $Pcomp_i$ to place $Pmdone_i$ (for variant pair i). Place $Pactive$ contains the number of tokens representing the number of the active variant pair (a number between 1 and $N/2$). When the active variant pair completes its comparison algorithm, a token is in place $Pmdone_i$, enabling transition $Tactive_i$, where i is the number of tokens in place $Pactive$. The firing of transition $Tactive_i$ moves the token to place $Pavar$. This enables transitions $Te1$, $Te2$, and Tne. The firing of transition $Te1$ means one of the two variants produced an incorrect output and therefore the comparison test result should be negative. The firing of transition $Te2$ means both of the two variants produced an incorrect output and therefore the comparison test result should be negative. The firing of transition Tne means neither of the two variants produced an incorrect output and therefore the comparison test result should be positive. The firing of transition $Te1$ moves a token to place $Pe1$ and to place $Pmerr$. The firing of transition $Te2$ moves a token to place $Pe2$ and two tokens to place $Pmerr$. The number of tokens in place $Pmerr$ represents the number of variants that produced an incorrect output on the current dataset. A token in place $Pe1$, indicating one of the variant pair produced an incorrect output. A token in place $Pe2$ indicates that both of the variants in the pair produced an incorrect output. A token in either $Pe1$ or $Pe2$ enables transitions $Tfpos$ and $Ttneg$, which indicate a false positive diagnoses and a true negative diagnoses respectively. A false positive diagnoses causes the token to move to place $Pundetect$, indicating an undetected error. If a true negative diagnosis is detected, the token is moved to place $Pctneg$. Place $Pctneg$ counts the number of incorrect variant pair outputs which are diagnosed as true negative. The tokens remain in place $Pctneg$ until either all variants pairs are diagnosed as incorrect or the active variant pair diagnoses its output to be correct.

If both variants in the pair produced incorrect output, transition Tne fires, moving the token from place $Pavar$ to place Pne. The diagnosis of correct output can be either a false negative or a true positive represented by transitions $Tfneg$ and $Ttpos$. Transition $Tfneg$ moves the token from place Pne to place $Pcfneg$. Place $Pcfneg$ counts the number of correct variant pair outputs diagnosed as false negative. The tokens remain in place $Pcfneg$ until either all variants are diagnosed as incorrect or the active variant diagnoses its output as correct. If the sum of the number of tokens in place $Pctneg$ and $Pcfpos$ is equal to $N/2$, all variant pairs have been diagnosed as incorrect. This enables transition $Tdetect$, which removes all tokens from places $Pctneg$ and $Pcfpos$ and places a single token in place $Pdetect$; this represents a detected failure. If the diagnosis of the correct output is a true positive, transition $Ttpos$ fires, moving the token from place Pne to place $Pcompl$.

A token in place $Pcompl$ satisfies the guard function for transitions $Tdone_i$ for $i \in [1,N]$, transitions $Tcdone_i$ and $Tmdone_i$ for $i \in [1,N/2]$, and transitions $Ttndone$, $Tfndone$, and $Tedone$. All tokens in these places are removed from the net, effectively resetting the net to its initial state. After this reset, the N self-checking programming block begins execution of the next input.

6.4   DEPENDENCIES IN THE SRN MODELS

Dependencies in fault tolerant systems are generally classified according to the source of the failure. Laprie [Lap90] classified failures in fault tolerant software systems using two criteria. First, failures are classified as either *separate* or *common-mode*. Sources of common-mode failures include *design faults* from shared specification or implementation, *similar errors* from independent faults, and the inherent difficulty of *shared input*. Next, failures can either be *detected* or *undetected*. It is most important in the development of a model to account for these dependencies. In our SRN models, these dependencies are accounted for by the structure of the model, and by judicious definition of the immediate transition probabilities.

6.4.1   Detected versus Undetected Failures

First, consider the distinction between detected and undetected failures. In the previous section, we developed the SRN model of each software fault tolerance technique which included places $Pdetect$, for detected failures, and $Pundetect$, for undetected failures. Defining separate places for detected and undetected failures, rather a single place (to indicate any type of failure), allows numerical study of several additional measures of interest.

Safety measures include both steady state and transient measures. A steady state measure of interest is the probability the system will eventually fail due to an unsafe failure. An unsafe failure is indicated by the existence of a token in place $Pundetect$. A transient measure of interest is $S(t)$, the safety distribution, defined to be the probability the system does not enter an unsafe state by time t.

Reliability measures can be obtained by considering block failure as the existence of a token in either place $Pdetect$ or $Pundetect$. Mean time to failure is a cumulative measure of the expected time until a token arrives in either place $Pdetect$ or $Pundetect$. The transient reliability function, $R(t)$, is the probability that there are no tokens in either place $Pdetect$ or $Pundetect$ at time t.

6.4.2   Common-Mode versus Separate Failures

Next, consider the distinction between separate and common-mode failures. Separate failures result from independent faults with distinct errors. Common-mode failures result from related faults or independent faults subject to similar errors. Measurements have shown that software variants do not exhibit separate failures. Measurements provide a probability mass function $p_N(\cdot)$ where $p_N(i)$ is the probability that i of the N variants produce incorrect output. If all variant failures are separate, then $p_N(\cdot)$ is a binomial probability mass function.

Common-mode variant failures can be easily accounted for in the SRN model by carefully structuring the model to retain tokens in places which provide needed information; state dependent transition probabilities can then be defined to use this information. The state information needed to model common-mode variant failures includes n_{vdone}, the number of variants in the program block which have completed execution, and n_{fail}, the number of the variants which have completed and produced incorrect results.

In addition, to simplify the probability functions needed in the SRN models, we include in the state information $n_{totfail}$, the number of variants out of N producing incorrect output. This variable is computed using probability mass function $p_N(\cdot)$ each time a new dataset begins processing.

Using the assumption that variants are stochastically identical, we can compute several probabilities of interest in fault tolerant software systems. The probability a variant produces incorrect output is given by

$$prob(\text{variant failure}) = \frac{n_{totfail} - n_{fail}}{N - n_{vdone}}$$

The probability that less than $N/2$ variants produce incorrect output is given by

$$prob(\text{no. variants fail} < N/2) = 1_{n_{totfail} < N/2}$$

where 1_x is an indicator function which evaluates to 1 if x is true and 0 otherwise. If we

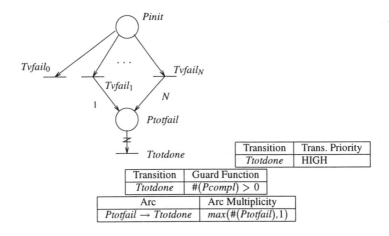

Figure 6.7 Subnet added to SRN models for common-mode failures

consider a pair of variants, we can compute the probabilities that one, both, or neither of the pair of variants fail. The probability both variants produce correct output is

$$prob(\text{neither variant fails}) = \left(1.0 - \frac{n_{totfail} - n_{fail}}{N - n_{vdone}}\right) \times \left(1.0 - \frac{n_{totfail} - n_{fail}}{N - (n_{vdone} + 1)}\right)$$

The probability both variants produce incorrect output is

$$prob(\text{both variants fail}) = \frac{n_{totfail} - n_{fail}}{N - n_{vdone}} \times \frac{n_{totfail} - (n_{fail} + 1)}{N - (n_{vdone} + 1)}$$

The probability that one of the two variants produce incorrect output and the other produces correct output is

$$prob(\text{one of two variants fail}) = 1.0 - (prob(\text{neither variant fails})$$

$$+ prob(\text{both variants fail}))$$

6.4.3   SRN Models with Common-Mode and Separate Failures

Figure 6.7 shows a subnet that is added to each previously described SRN model to simplify the incorporation of common-mode failures. A token arrives in transition $Pinit$ as a result of the firing of transition $Tstart$. Transition $Tstart$ (which is part of each previously developed SRN model) is modified to include another output arc associated with place $Pinit$. When a token arrives in place $Pinit$, the software block is ready to operate on a new dataset. Transitions $Tvfail_0$, $Tvfail_1$, ... $Tvfail_N$ become enabled. The probability associated with each transition $Tvfail_i$ is $p_N(i)$, the probability that i out of the N variants produce an incorrect result. The firing of transition $Tvfail_i$ causes i tokens to be placed in $Ptotfail$. Place $Ptotfail$ represents the number of variants that will produce incorrect output on the current dataset. The number of tokens in place $Ptotfail$ is used to determine the variant failure probabilities in each SRN model. This is discussed in detail for each SRN model in the next section. When the software block completes execution on the current dataset (a token is moved to place $Pcompl$), all tokens in place $Ptotfail$ are removed by the firing of transition $Ttotdone$. This resets this subnet prior to the arrival of the next dataset.

6.4.3.1   RECOVERY BLOCK SRN

In the SRN model of the RB scheme, transitions Tne_i and Te_i are immediate transitions representing the correctness or incorrectness of variant i. These transitions are enabled only after $i-1$ variants have completed execution. Of these $i-1$ variants, #($Pmfail$) produced incorrect results. The immediate transition probabilities for Te_i and Tne_i incorporating common-mode failures are given by

$$prob(Te_i) \quad = \quad \frac{n_{totfail} - n_{fail}}{N - n_{vdone}}$$

$$= \quad \frac{\#(Ptotfail) - \#(Pmfail)}{N - (i-1)}$$

and

$$prob(Tne_i) = 1 - prob(Te_i)$$

6.4.3.2   N-VERSION PROGRAMMING SRN

In the SRN model of the NVP scheme, out of the N available variants #($Ptotfail$) variants produce incorrect results. The voter diagnosis is dependent on the number of the N variants producing incorrect output. If less than half of the variants produce correct output (that is if #($Ptotfail$) $< N/2$), then the vote should be positive. However, similar errors may cause the voter to diagnose a false positive when less than half of the variants produce a correct output. In addition, the implementation of the voter may be incorrect (e.g. the voter's variant error tolerance may be too small) and the voter may diagnose a false negative even though more than half of the variants produced a correct output.

$$
\begin{aligned}
prob(Tfpos) \quad &= \quad prob(\text{at least half of variants were incorrect}) \times \\
&\qquad prob(\text{diagnosis on incorrect input is positive}) \\
prob(Ttneg) \quad &= \quad prob(\text{at least half of variants were incorrect}) \times \\
&\qquad (1.0 - prob(\text{diagnosis on incorrect input is positive})) \\
prob(Tfneg) \quad &= \quad prob(\text{less than half of variants were incorrect}) \times \\
&\qquad prob(\text{diagnosis on correct input is negative}) \\
prob(Ttpos) \quad &= \quad prob(\text{less than half of variants were incorrect}) \times \\
&\qquad (1.0 - prob(\text{diagnosis on correct input is negative}))
\end{aligned}
$$

The variant probabilities used in the above equations are given by

$$prob(\text{at least half of variants are incorrect}) = 1_{\#(Ptotfail)>=N/2}$$

$$prob(\text{less than half of variants are incorrect}) = 1_{\#(Ptotfail)<N/2}$$

6.4.3.3   N SELF-CHECKING PROGRAMMING WITH ACCEPTANCE TEST SRN MODEL

In the SRN model of the NSCP with acceptance test, a token in place $Pavar$ enables transitions Te, which indicates an incorrect variant result, and transition Tne, which indicates a correct variant result. The number of previously completed and diagnosed variants is $\#(Pctneg) + \#(Pcfneg)$. The number of these variants which produced incorrect results is $\#(Pctneg)$. The probability that the variant represented by a token in place $Pavar$ produces an incorrect result is

$$
\begin{aligned}
prob(Te) &= \frac{n_{totfail} - n_{fail}}{N - n_{vdone}} \\
&= \frac{\#(Ptotfail) - \#(Pctneg)}{N - (\#(Pctneg) + \#(Pcfneg))}
\end{aligned}
$$

and

$$
prob(Tne) = 1 - prob(Te)
$$

6.4.3.4   N SELF-CHECKING PROGRAMMING WITH COMPARISON ALGORITHM SRN MODEL

Similarly, in the SRN model of the NSCP with comparison tests, a token in place $Pavar$ enables transitions $Te1$, $Te2$, and Tne. The firing of transition $Te1$ indicates that one variant in the pair produced an incorrect output while the other variant produced a correct output. The firing of transition $Te2$ indicates that both variants in the pair produced incorrect output. The firing of transition Tne indicates that both of the variants in the pair produced correct output.

The number of variant pairs that have completed execution and diagnosis is given by $\#(Pctneg) + \#(Pcfneg)$; the number of variants that have completed execution is therefore $2 \times (\#(Pctneg) + \#(Pcfpos))$. Of the variant pairs that have completed, the number of pairs where at least one variant did not produce correct output is given by $\#(Pmerr)$.

The probability neither variant produces incorrect output is

$$
\begin{aligned}
prob(Tne) &= \left(1.0 - \frac{n_{totfail} - n_{fail}}{N - n_{vdone}}\right) \times \left(1.0 - \frac{n_{totfail} - n_{fail}}{N - (n_{vdone} + 1)}\right) \\
&= \left(1.0 - \frac{\#(Ptotfail) - \#(Pmerr)}{N - 2 \times (\#(Pctneg) + \#(Pcfneg))}\right) \times \\
&\quad \left(1.0 - \frac{\#(Ptotfail) - \#(Pmerr)}{N - 2 \times (\#(Pctneg) + \#(Pcfneg)) - 1}\right)
\end{aligned}
$$

The probability both variants produce incorrect output is

$$
\begin{aligned}
prob(Te2) &= \frac{n_{totfail} - n_{fail}}{N - n_{vdone}} \times \frac{n_{totfail} - (n_{fail} + 1)}{N - (n_{vdone} + 1)} \\
&= \frac{\#(Ptotfail) - \#(Pmerr)}{N - 2 \times (\#(Pctneg) + \#(Pcfneg))} \times \\
&\quad \frac{\#(Ptotfail) - \#(Pmerr) - 1}{N - 2 \times (\#(Pctneg) + \#(Pcfneg)) - 1}
\end{aligned}
$$

Table 6.1 Error characteristics for $N = 1$ variant case

Category	Obs. Frequency	Computed Probability
No Errors	0.8549	0.8549
One Error	0.1451	0.1451

Table 6.2 Error characteristics for $N = 2$ variant case

Category	Obs. Frequency	Computed Probability
No Errors	0.8053	0.791833
One Error	0.1691	0.196034
Two Errors	0.0256	0.112133

The probability that one of the two variants produce incorrect output and the other produces correct output is

$$prob(Te1) = 1.0 - prob(Tne) - prob(Te2)$$

6.5 NUMERICAL RESULTS

In this section, we analyze the SRN for each software fault tolerant scheme. We compute steady state, transient, cumulative, and sensitivity measures for safety, reliability, and performance using the same SRN definitions. We vary parameters such as the number of variants N, variant execution rates, decider execution rates, as well as the distribution of failed variants for separate and common-mode failures. The flexibility of the SRN model makes this analysis quite easy.

6.5.1 Parameterizing the Model

In order to obtain numerical results, we need to select parameter values for the variant and decider execution rates, the decider failure probabilities, and the distribution of common-mode failures. We choose realistic values for the execution rates, as well as the decider failure probabilities. The common-mode failure distribution is obtained from experimental data obtained by Lyu and He [Lyu93]. This experimental data was also used in reliability analysis of fault tolerant software systems by Dugan and Lyu [Dug93b, Dug93a].

The execution rate of each variant is chosen to be $\mu = 1.0$. The execution rate of the AT is $\mu_{at} = 100 \times \mu$. The execution rate of the voter is $\mu_{voter} = 10 \times \mu$. The execution rate of the comparison algorithm is $\mu_{comp} = 50 \times \mu$.

The results of the experiment by Lyu and He are shown in Tables 6.1, 6.2, 6.3, and 6.4 for $N = 1,2,3,$ and 4 respectively. These results are used to account for common-mode variant failure. In each table, the number of variant errors (category), the observed frequency (or probability) of exhibiting that number of variant errors, and the computed frequency (assuming separate failures) is given. The observed frequency data provides the probability mass function $p_N(\cdot)$ used to account for common-mode failures. In our numerical study, we can compare the model results obtained using the common-mode failures indicated by this

Table 6.3   Error characterists for the $N = 3$ variant case

Category	Obs. Frequency	Computed Probability
No Errors	0.7426	0.74532
One Error	0.2360	0.230172
Two Errors	0.0202	0.0236942
Three Errors	0.0012	0.000813037

Table 6.4   Error characteristics for the $N = 4$ variant case

Category	Obs. Frequency	Computed Probability
No Errors	0.65052	0.657793
One Error	0.30889	0.29047
Two Errors	0.03303	0.0480998
Three Errors	0.00747	0.00354
Four Errors	0.00008	$9.77001E-5$

experimental data to separate failures. Separate variant failures are modeled by assuming that each variant fails independently with a probability computed using the common-mode $p_N(\cdot)$ pmf. The $p_N(\cdot)$ probability mass function for the separate failure case is binomial with parameter $p = prob$(variant failure).

Experimental data is available only for $N = 1$ through 4. In our numerical study, we compute the separate failure probability mass function for $N > 4$ to be a binomial distribution using the same value for parameter p as in the $N = 4$ case.

Next, we consider the decider failure probabilities for the acceptance test, voter, and comparison algorithm. We assume that the AT diagnoses a false positive with probability 0.002 and a false negative with probability 0.001. The probability that the voter diagnoses a false positive is 0.0005 and a false negative is 0.0001. The probability that the comparison algorithm diagnoses a false positive is 0.0001 and a false negative is 0.0002. These probabilities could be generalized. For example, the probability that the voter in an N-version programming scheme produces a false positive or false negative may depend on the number of variants which produce incorrect output. The same observation holds for the comparison algorithm in the N-self checking programming scheme. This dependence could be incorporated in the SRN. In the NVP SRN model, we maintain the number of variants that produced incorrect results in place $Ptotfail$ (therefore in the state space description) when the voter diagnosis probabilities are computed. In the NSCP with comparison algorithm SRN, we maintain the number of variants in the pair that produced incorrect by either placing the token in place $Pe1$ (indicating one of the two variants failed), place $Pe2$ (indicating both of the two variants failed), or place Pne (indicating neither of the two variants failed). Since the information is available, state dependent failure probabilities could be used to make the comparison algorithm diagnosis probabilities dependent on this status.

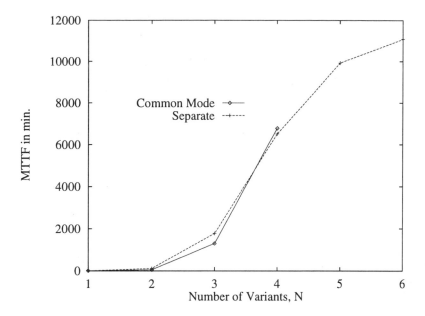

Figure 6.8 $MTTF$ of a NSCP with acceptance test as a function of the number of variants

6.5.2   Reliability Measures

Reliability measures include the system unreliability, $UR(t) = 1 - R(t)$, which is the probability that the system fails prior to time t, and the mean time to failure, $MTTF$.

First, we examine how the mean time until system failure, $MTTF$, is affected by the number of variants available in the software block. The $MTTF$ calculation is accomplished using the expected accumulated reward until absorption. Each non-absorbing state i is assigned the reward rate $r_i = 1$. Each absorbing state i is assigned the reward rate $r_i = 0$. In our SRN models, absorbing states are those with a token in either place $Pdetect$ or $Pundetect$. The $MTTF$ is then computed by

$$MTTF = \sum_{i \in \Omega_T} r_i \int_0^\infty P_i(\tau)d\tau$$

In Figure 6.8, the mean time to failure of the NSCP block with acceptance test error diagnosis is shown. We examine how the $MTTF$ calculation differs for separate failures and common-mode failures. At $N = 1$, the $MTTF$ is the same in each case. At $N = 2$ and $N = 3$, we see that the separate failure computation is optimistic. This is intuitive, since we expect common-mode failures to decrease block reliability. At $N = 4$, the $MTTF$ of the separate failure computation is pessimistic. This non-intuitive result occurs because in this case, the probability that one or two variants out of the four variants fail is less in the case of separate failure mode than in the common-mode case (as shown in Table 6.4). In general, we would not expect this to be true if the sample size of the experiment were increased. For both the separate failure case and the common-mode failure case, the $MTTF$ increases significantly with the number of variants.

Next, the unreliability of the N self-checking programming block with comparison algorithm for error diagnosis is plotted in Figure 6.9. The unreliability, $UR(t) = 1 - R(t)$, is the

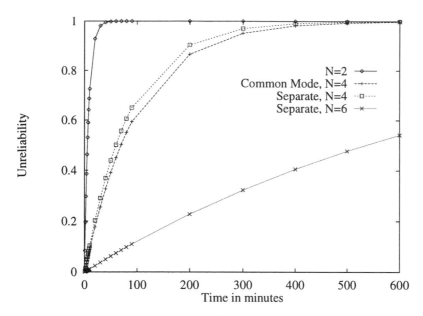

Figure 6.9   Failure probability of NSCP with comparison algorithm as a function of time

probability that a token arrives at either place $Pdetect$ or place $Pundetect$ by time t. The reliability, $R(t)$, of each model is computed using transient analysis. If $P_i(t)$ is the probability that the software block is in state i at time t then the reliability is computed simply by summing over the probability that the software block is in any state where there are no tokens in either place $Pdetect$ or $Pundetect$.

$$R(t) = \sum_{i \in \Omega_T : \#(Pdetect)=0 \wedge \#(Pundetect)=0} P_i(t)$$

$R(t)$ is determined by first performing transient analysis of the SRN to determine $P_i(t)$. Then the reward rates for each state are defined: $r_i = 1$ if i is an operational state (a state with no tokens in either place $Pundetect$ or $Pdetect$) and $r_i = 0$ otherwise. The reliability is simply the expected reward at time t.

$$R(t) = \sum_{i \in \Omega_T} r_i P_i(t)$$

The unreliability is plotted for $N = 2$, where (due to the fact that the comparison algorithm operates on two variant outputs at a time) the separate failure case is stochastically identical to the common-mode failure case. Next, the unreliability is plotted for $N = 4$ and 6. Only $N = 4$ data is available for common-mode failures. We see that reliability improves significantly by increasing N from 2 to 6.

6.5.3   Safety Measures

In safety analysis, the distinction between undetected and detected failures is most significant. Only undetected failures are unsafe. Detected failures are viewed as an alternate (and safe) way to complete an execution of the software block. The measures of interest in safety analysis

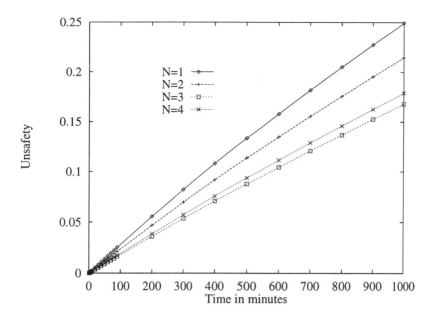

Figure 6.10 Probability of an unsafe failure in a RB as a function of time assuming common-mode failures

include, $S(t)$, the probability an undetected error occurs by time t and $MTTUF$, the mean time to an undetected failure.

A slight modification of the SRN models is needed to compute the safety measures. Detected failures and successful software block completion are both safe executions of the software block. This is accomplished the SRN model by modifying each transition into place $Pdetect$ so that it goes instead to place $Pcompl$. This is the *only* modification to the SRN that is needed to generate safety measures. After making this modification, the computation of $S(t)$ and $MTTUF$ follow the same procedures as the computation of $R(t)$ and $MTTF$ respectively.

Figure 6.10 shows the probability of unsafe failure in a recovery block as a function of time, $US(t) = 1.0 - S(t)$. The software block is considered to be in a safe state whenever there is no token in place $Pundetect$. The safety distribution, $S(t)$ is computed using the transient solution vector. The block safety is computed simply by summing over the probability that the software block is in any state where there are no tokens in $Pundetect$.

$$S(t) = \sum_{i \in \Omega_T : \#(Pundetect)=0} P_i(t)$$

This is easily computed once the transient analysis of the (modified) SRN produces $P_i(t)$. The reward rates for each state are defined: $r_i = 1$ if i is a safe state (a state with no tokens in place $Pundetect$) and $r_i = 0$ otherwise. The block safety is simply the expected reward at time t.

$$S(t) = \sum_{i \in \Omega_T} r_i P_i(t)$$

The complement of block safety, $US(t) = 1.0 - S(t)$, is computed for the recovery block strategy assuming common-mode failures. We see that as N increases from 1, to 2, and to 3,

162   TOMEK and TRIVEDI

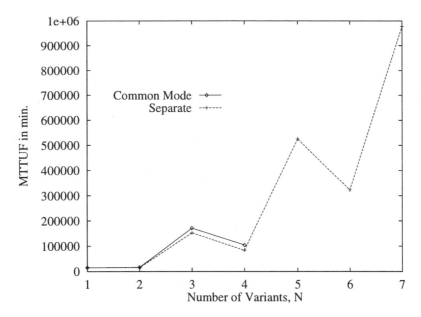

Figure 6.11   Mean time until an undetected failure in an NVP block as a function of the number of variants

the safety of the block increases. As N increases from 3 to 4, the safety decreases slightly. This is again due to experimental sampling. We expect that the unsafety of the block would decrease as N increases.

Figure 6.11 shows the mean time until an unsafe failure in an NVP block as a function of the number of variants. The $MTTUF$ is computed using the expected accumulated reward until absorption which was used to compute the $MTTF$. Each non-absorbing state i is assigned the reward rate $r_i = 1$. Each absorbing state i is assigned the reward rate $r_i = 0$. In our SRN models, absorbing states are those with a token in place $Pundetect$. (Recall that the modification made to the nets to facilitate safety analysis prevents a token from arriving in place $Pdetect$.) The $MTTUF$ is then computed by

$$MTTUF = \sum_{i \in \Omega_T} r_i \int_0^\infty P_i(\tau)d\tau$$

In Figure 6.11, we plot the mean time until an unsafe failure in an NVP block for both common-mode and separate failures. The saw toothed nature of the graph is due to the NVP strategy requirement that an output is diagnosed to be correct only if more than half of the variants produce the same output.

6.5.4   Performance Measures

The performance measures we compute include $E[D(t)]$, the number of datasets processed prior to time t and $E[D]$, the number of datasets processed prior to failure. We examine how the expected number of datasets is affected by the number of variants available in the system. In Figure 6.12, the expected number of dataset processed in a RB as a function of the number of variants is shown. The expected number of datasets is computed by assigning a positive

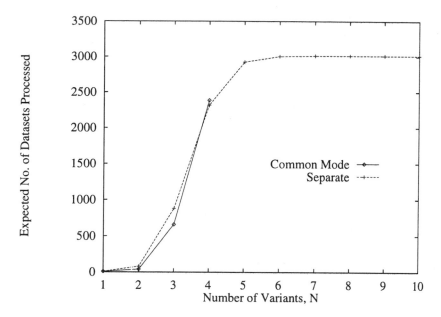

Figure 6.12   Expected number of datasets processed in a RB as a function of the number of variants

reward to each state where there is a token in place Pm_1 and zero reward in all other states. Since the expected sojourn of a token in place Pm_1 is $1/\text{rate}(Tm_1)$, the reward assigned to states where there is a token in place Pm_1 is the rate of transition Tm_1.

$$E[D] = \sum_{i \in \Omega_T} r_i \int_0^\infty P_i(\tau)\,d\tau$$

We observe in this graph, that as N increases beyond five variants, the increase in the expected number of datasets is small.

In Figure 6.13, the expected number of datasets in an NVP block is shown as a function of time. The expected number of datasets processed until time t, $E[D(t)]$, is computed using the same reward definitions as were used in the computation of $E[D]$.

$$E[D(t)] = \sum_{i \in \Omega_T} r_i \int_0^t P_i(\tau)\,d\tau$$

The expected number of datasets is computed for $N = 1,3,5,7$, and 9. In the case $N = 1$, the common-mode and separate failure cases are stochastically identical. We see that as N increases, the expected number of datasets processed over time continues to increase. This is due to the reduction in the probability of software block failure as N increases.

6.6   CONCLUSIONS

In this chapter, we explored the capability of stochastic reward nets (SRNs) to model fault tolerant software techniques. The software fault tolerance techniques we considered are N-

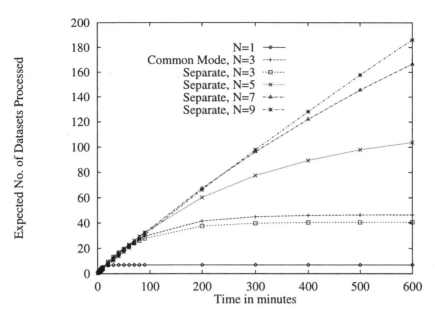

Figure 6.13   Expected number of datasets processed in an NVP block as a function of time

version programming, recovery blocks, and N self-checking programming. SRNs are well suited to allow for concise expression of each software fault tolerance technique. Associated with these techniques are various dependencies. We have shown that model structure and state dependent transition probabilities allow common-mode and separate failures to be easily modeled. In addition, since SRNs are equal in their modeling power to Markov reward models (MRMs), the wide range of steady state, transient, cumulative, and sensitivity measures available for MRMs, were shown to easily obtained for SRNs. We numerically demonstrated that safety, reliability, and performance measures were easily obtained for the above three software fault tolerance techniques using SRNs.

ACKNOWLEDGEMENTS

The work of K.S. Trivedi was supported in part by the National Science Foundation under Grant CCR-9108114.

REFERENCES

[Ajm84]   M. Ajmone-Marsan, G. Conte, and G. Balbo. A class of generalized stochastic Petri nets for the performance evaluation of multiprocessor systems. *ACM Transactions on Computer Systems*, 2(2):93–122, May 1984.

[And81]   T. Anderson and P.A. Lee. *Fault Tolerance-Principles and Practice*. Prentice Hall, 1981.

[Avi85]   A. Avižienis. The N-version approach to fault-tolerant software. *IEEE Transactions on Software Engineering*, SE-11(12):1491–1501, December 1985.

[Bea78]   M. D. Beaudry. Performance related reliability for computer systems. *IEEE Transactions on Computers*, C-27(6):540–547, June 1978.

[Chi85]   G. Chiola. A software package for the analysis of generalized stochastic Petri net models. In *Proceedings of the International Workshop on Timed Petri Nets*, pages 136–143, Los Alamitos, CA, July 1985. IEEE Computer Society Press.

[Cia92]   G. Ciardo, A. Blakemore, P. F. Chimento, J. K. Muppala, and K. S. Trivedi. Automated generation and analysis of Markov reward models using stochastic reward nets. In Carl Meyer and R. J. Plemmons, editors, *Linear Algebra, Markov Chains, and Queueing Models, IMA Volumes in Mathematics and Applications*, volume 48, Heidelberg, 1992. Springer-Verlag.

[Cia90]   G. Ciardo, R. Marie, B. Sericola, and K. S. Trivedi. Performability analysis using semi-Markov reward processes. *IEEE Transactions on Computers*, C-39(10):1251–1264, 1990.

[Cia89]   G. Ciardo, J. Muppala, and K. Trivedi. SPNP: stochastic Petri net package. In *Proceedings of the International Workshop on Petri Nets and Performance Models (PNPM '89)*, pages 142–150, Los Alamitos, CA, December 1989. IEEE Computer Society Press.

[Cou91]   J.A. Couvillion, R. Freire, R. Johnson, W.D. Obal, M.A. Qureshi, M. Rai, W.H. Sanders, and J.E. Tvedt. Performability modeling with ultrasan. *IEEE Software*, 8(5):69–80, September 1991.

[Dug93a]   Joanne Bechta Dugan and Michael R. Lyu. System-level reliability and sensitivity analyses for three fault-tolerant system architectures. In *Proceedings of the Fourth IFIP Working Conference on Dependable Computing for Critical Applications (DCCA 4)*, December 1993.

[Dug93b]   Joanne Bechta Dugan and Michael R. Lyu. System reliability analysis of an N-version programming application. In *Proceedings of the International Symposium on Software Reliability Engineering*, November 1993.

[Flo91]   Gérard Florin, C. Fraize, and Stéphane Natkin. Stochastic Petri nets: properties, applications and tools. *Microelectronics and Reliability*, 31(4):669–697, 1991.

[How71]   R. A. Howard. *Dynamic Probabilistic Systems, Vol.II: Semi-Markov and Decision Processes*. John Wiley & Sons, New York, 1971.

[Ibe90]   O.C. Ibe and K.S. Trivedi. Stochastic Petri net models of polling systems. *IEEE Journal on Selected Areas in Communications*, 8(10), December 1990.

[Ibe89]   O. C. Ibe, K. S. Trivedi, A. Sathaye, and R. C. Howe. Stochastic Petri net modeling of VAXcluster system availability. In *Proc. International Conference on Petri Nets and Performance Models*, Kyoto, Japan, December 1989.

[Lap90]   J. Laprie, J. Arlat, C. Béounes, and K. Kanoun. Definition and analysis of hardware- and software-fault-tolerant architectures. 23(7), July 1990.

[Lyu93]   Michael R. Lyu and Yu-Tao He. Improving the N-version programming process through the evolution of a design paradigm. *IEEE Transactions on Reliability*, June 1993.

[Mol82]   M. K. Molloy. Performance analysis using stochastic Petri nets. *IEEE Transactions on Computers*, C-31(9):913–917, September 1982.

[Nat80]   S. Natkin. *Reseaux de Petri stochastiques*. PhD thesis, CNAM-Paris, June 1980.

[Pet81]   J. L. Peterson. *Petri Net Theory and the Modeling of Systems*. Prentice-Hall, Englewood Cliffs, NJ, USA, 1981.

[Puc90]   G. Pucci. On the modeling and testing of recovery block structures. In *Proceedings of the Twentieth International Symposium on Fault Tolerant Computing (FTCS 20)*, pages 356–363, Newcastle upon Tyne, UK, 1990.

[Puc92]   Geppino Pucci. A new approach to the modeling of recovery block structures. *IEEE Transactions on Software Engineering*, SE-18(2):356–363, February 1992.

[Ran75]   B. Randell. System structure for software fault tolerance. *IEEE Transactions on Software Engineering*, SE-1(2):220–232, June 1975.

[Tom94]   Lorrie A. Tomek, Varsha Mainkar, Robert Geist, and Kishor S. Trivedi. Reliability modeling of life-critical, real-time systems. *IEEE Proceedings, Special Issue on Real-Time Life-Critical Systems*, 82(1), January 1994.

[Tom91]   L. A. Tomek and K. S. Trivedi. Fixed point iteration in availability modeling. In M. Dal Cin, editor, *Proceedings of the Fifth International GI/ITG/GMA Conference on Fault-Tolerant Computing Systems*, pages 229–240. Springer-Verlag, Berlin, September 1991.

7

Checkpointing and the Modeling of Program Execution Time

VICTOR F. NICOLA

University of Twente, Netherlands

ABSTRACT

Checkpointing is a commonly used technique for reducing the execution time of long-running programs in the presence of failures. With checkpointing, the status of the program under execution is saved intermittently. Upon the occurrence of a failure, the program execution is restarted from the most recent checkpoint rather than from the beginning. Due to its overhead, checkpointing may not always be beneficial, and, if it is, an optimal checkpointing strategy may be determined so as to minimize the expected execution time or to maximize the probability of the execution time not exceeding a critical limit. In this chapter we consider several models of checkpointing and recovery in a program in order to derive the distribution of program execution time or its expectation. We make important extensions to some existing results as well as introduce and analyze new models. It is shown that the expected execution time increases linearly (exponentially) with the processing requirement in the presence (absence) of checkpointing. Furthermore, these models can be used to compare different checkpointing strategies and to determine an optimal interval between checkpoints. Throughout the chapter, and whenever appropriate, we attempt to relate to other work in the existing literature.

7.1 INTRODUCTION

Fault-tolerance is a much desired feature of long-running software applications that may arise in a variety of contexts, such as numerically intensive computational physics, numerical optimization problems, simulation of complex systems, complex queries in large relational databases, and others. The reliability of such applications may be compromised due to external transient faults, such as power failure, disk failure, processor failure, and other types of system malfunctions, or due to permanent faults, such as those internal to the program itself. Techniques for fault-tolerance (see, for example, [And81] and Chapters 1 to 4 of this book) can be used to enhance the reliability of such applications, however, often at the expense of a performance degradation and/or additional resources. For example, adding a restart capability after repair (or replacement) will guarantee the successful completion of the program in the presence of failures [Ran75, Puc92]. However, such a restart capability does not guard against excessive run times due to repeated failures followed by prohibitive reprocessing. The execution time of a program is defined as the time to complete computation, including repairs and restarts after failures. This also includes additional overhead required by the fault-tolerance procedure, if any. The execution time is an important metric which is commonly used to evaluate and compare the performance of different fault-tolerance procedures in software applications. It is well known (see, for example, [Dud83, Nic86]) that, in the presence of random failures (and a restart capability), the expected execution time of a fault-tolerant software (or a program) typically grows exponentially with its processing requirement. This is due to failures which cause the program to restart from its beginning (thus losing all useful processing done thus far.) Checkpointing is a commonly used technique in fault-tolerant software applications and long-running programs to enhance their reliability and to increase their computational efficiency (see, e.g., [Cha72a, Cha72b, You74].) Checkpointing consists of intermittently saving the current state of program execution in a reliable storage, so that when a (transient) failure occurs, [1] the program execution may restart from the most recent checkpoint, rather than from its beginning (thus losing only a part of the useful processing done thus far.)

With checkpointing, the expected execution time of a program typically grows only linearly with its processing requirement (see, for example, [Dud83, Kul90].) After a failure, the process of reloading the program status saved at the most recent checkpoint is often called a *rollback*. (Note that the rollback time may be conveniently added to the repair time for the purpose of analysis.) The reprocessing of the program, starting from the most recent checkpoint and until the point just before the failure, is often called a *recovery* process.

Clearly, more checkpoints means less reprocessing after failures. If checkpoints were cost-less, then the execution time would reduce monotonically with the number of checkpoints in the program. However, usually there is checkpointing overhead and, therefore, a trade-off exists. In other words, there is usually an optimal number (or frequency) of checkpoints which optimizes a certain performance measure. For example, in a production environment, a likely objective would be to minimize the expected execution time. In a real-time environment, the likely objective is to maximize the probability of the execution time not exceeding a given hard deadline.

Over the years, there has been a huge body of literature covering a wide range of issues related to checkpointing and recovery in a variety of systems. These issues range from architectural and implementation aspects to functional and performance considerations. There

---

[1] We assume that a failure is detected as soon as it occurs. In practice, a latency may exist between the failure occurrence and its detection [She75]. Failure detection requires the use of a continuous error-checking mechanism, however, checkpointing can also be used for the detection of latent failures [Pra89]. A latent failure may not be detected during program execution, which could result in an erroneous computation [Shi87]. Otherwise, a latency between failure occurrence and detection may cause the program to restart from an earlier checkpoint or from the beginning. In [Kor86], a model is considered in which one or more recovery procedures (namely, instruction retries, program rollbacks to earlier checkpoints and program restarts) may be used depending on the length of the detection latency.

is no way to cover all these aspects in a single chapter or even a single book. In fact, in the domain of performance related issues and over the past two decades, there has been a great number of papers, too many to list. Most of these papers deal with the modeling and analysis of various checkpointing strategies at the system level (as opposed to that at the program level.) It should be mentioned, however, that there are many issues that are common to checkpointing and rollback recovery at the system and the program levels. As an example of system level checkpointing, one may consider a transaction-oriented database system [Hae83, Reu84, Ver78]. In such a system, checkpoints are inserted between transactions according to some strategy, with the objective of enhancing the overall reliability/integrity of the database as well as improving an overall system performance measure, such as the system availability (see [Cha75a, Cha75b, DeS90, Don88, Gel79, Gel90, Lec88, Loh77, Mik79, Nic83a, Nic83b, Shn73, Tan84] and others) or the mean response time of a transaction (see [Bac81a, Bac81b, Dud84, Gel78, Kul90, Nic83a, Nic83b, Nic86, Nic90b] and others.) Far less is reported on checkpointing at the program level and its effects on program performance (see [Bog92, Bro79, Cof88, Dud83, Gei88, Gra92, Kul90, Kri84, Leu84, Shi87, Tou84, Upa86, Upa88] and others.)

The main focus in this chapter is the modeling of checkpointing at the program level and the analysis of the program execution time. Therefore, in Section 7.2 we will briefly review some of the work relevant to this particular focus. However, we would like to direct the reader's attention to the closely related work at the system level (some references are included in this chapter.) We also consider some useful models of program performance in the presence of failures, without and with checkpointing. In Section 7.3, we describe the basic model and consider program execution in the presence of failures and without checkpointing. Then, under common basic assumptions, we analyze the program execution time with different checkpointing strategies. In the process, we extend previous models and introduce new ones. In Section 7.4, we consider a model with fixed (deterministic) productive time between checkpoints. Models with generally distributed productive time between checkpoints are considered in Section 7.5. A model with a random checkpointing strategy is analyzed in Section 7.6. In Section 7.7, we conclude with a summary and possible directions for further research.

7.2   RELATED WORK

In this section we give a brief overview of existing literature related to the modeling and performance analysis of checkpointing and recovery strategies at the program level. This literature coverage is neither exhaustive nor complete, but it is intended to provide an adequate background to help the reader place the present treatment of the subject in its proper context.

In most strategies, checkpoints are scheduled with respect to the productive time (or the progress of computation), i.e., excluding the time spent in repair and reprocessing after failures. [2] In particular, because of their established optimality (under fairly general assumptions) with respect to some commonly used criteria, strategies with a deterministic productive time between checkpoints have received a considerable attention from analysts and practitioners (see, e.g., [Bro79, Dud83, Gei88, Gra92].) However, in practice, it is not always possible to place checkpoints equally spaced in a program, as this depends to a large extent on the

---

[2] For a more complete discussion on checkpoint insertion based on the progress of computation in a program, the reader is referred to [Lon92].

structure of the program (see, e.g., [Cha72b, Lon92].) Furthermore, for certain criteria and/or accurate assumptions about the system, the optimal checkpointing strategy is not necessarily equidistant. For example, in [Tan84], it is demonstrated that, for a Weibull failure distribution, "equicost" checkpointing achieves a higher system availability than an equidistant strategy. In an "equicost" strategy, a checkpoint is performed whenever the expected reprocessing cost is equal to the checkpointing cost. For Poisson failures, this strategy results in equidistant checkpoints. However, for (more typical) increasing failure rate distributions, the frequency of checkpoints increases with the time since the last failure. Another example is in [Shi87], where the possibility of incorrect program execution due to latent errors is considered. The objective is to minimize the expected execution time, subject to the constraint of keeping the probability of correct execution higher than a specified level. An optimal strategy suggests that checkpointing should be performed more frequently towards the end of the program. Such a strategy increases the probability of detecting latent errors before the end of the program, while minimizing the expected execution time. Therefore, it is also of interest to consider checkpointing strategies other than the equidistant. In particular, a few authors have considered checkpointing strategies based on a dynamic optimization approach (see, e.g., [Mag83, Tou84].) Others (as in [Nic86]) considered a non-deterministic (e.g., exponential) productive time between checkpoints to obtain the distribution of the program execution time in the presence of failures and checkpointing.

In [Bro79], a model is considered to obtain the expected execution time of a program with and without checkpointing. In [Dud83], a program is divided into equal parts and checkpoints are performed only after the execution of each program part (including repetitions due to Poisson failures.) The execution time of program parts (including the checkpointing time at the end of each part) are independent and identically distributed random variables, the sum of which is the total program execution time. In [Dud83], the distribution of the program execution time is derived and the optimal number of checkpoints which minimizes its expectation is determined. Recently, the same model is considered in [Gra92] and it is suggested that the optimal number of checkpoints be determined based on the distribution of the program execution time, rather than its expectation. In [Gei88], a system with a constraint on the repair time is considered. An expression is derived to compute the probability of completing a program, having a given processing requirement, with equally spaced checkpoints. A constraint on the operational time before program completion is also considered.

In other papers, different approaches are followed with the Poisson failures assumption relaxed and checkpoints arbitrarily placed in the program. For example, in [Leu84], an algorithm is proposed to compute the distribution of the program execution time. Then, numerical optimization is suggested to determine the optimal placement of checkpoints in the program.

For age dependent failures, the distribution of program execution time is derived in [Cof88], assuming that the system is "as-good-as-new" after each checkpoint. With this assumption, the end of each checkpoint constitutes a renewal point, thus simplifying the analysis. They show that equally spaced scheduling of checkpoints is optimal when minimizing the expected execution time or the tail of its distribution, and also when maximizing the probability of completing the program in the presence of permanent failures. Age dependent failures have also been considered in models of checkpointing in database systems (see, for example, [Gel90, Sum89, Tan84].)

In [Tou84], a stochastic dynamic programming approach is considered to determine the optimal placement of checkpoints between tasks of given (arbitrary) lengths in a program, so as to minimize the total expected program execution time. An integer programming approach is considered in [Mag83].

General models for the analysis of the program execution time have been considered, in the presence of failures, degradation and repair, but not with checkpointing (see [Gav62, Kul87, Nic86, Nic87] and others.) In these models, the occurrence of a failure may result in no loss or in a complete loss of all the work done on the program, as opposed to a partial loss of the work in the presence of program checkpoints. A similar approach is followed in [Kul90] to model and analyze the program execution time with random (Poisson) failures and checkpointing.

A random checkpointing strategy makes sense in situations when it is not possible to schedule (insert) checkpoints at the program level, or when the decision to perform a checkpoint depends on the (non-deterministic) execution environment. Consider, for instance, "dynamic" checkpoint insertion schemes [Li90], in which a real-time (system) clock is polled to decide if a checkpoint is due. Clock granularity and the workload on the system can result in different checkpoint locations for different execution runs of the same computation. Another situation is when "global" checkpointing schemes are used in concurrent processing environments (see, e.g., [Kan78, Tha86].) In such cases, checkpoint operations (on behalf of the program) may be triggered at another application level or at the system level. For example, the system may trigger a checkpoint (on behalf of some or all running application programs) whenever it is lightly loaded or in response to certain events. In situations such as the above, checkpoints are not scheduled (inserted) at the program level, and, therefore, can be viewed to occur randomly (in a way, just like failures.) With random checkpointing strategies, it is obvious that checkpoints may occur not only during useful processing, but also during reprocessing subsequent to failures. In general, the possibility of checkpointing during reprocessing is of much interest, since it guards against prohibitive reprocessing caused by repeated failures in long recovery periods. This is particularly advantageous in typical situations where the frequency of failures is high during recovery. A model that takes into account the above features of random checkpointing is considered in [Kul90].

In the remainder of this chapter, we consider some useful models of program performance in the presence of failures, without and with commonly used checkpointing strategies. In order to carry out the analysis under, more or less, the same basic assumptions, it was necessary to extend some existing models and to introduce new models which are not considered previously. From these models we derive the distribution of the program execution time and/or its expectation. This makes it possible to assess whether checkpointing is beneficial and, if so, determine the optimal number (frequency) of checkpoints in a given program.

7.3   PROGRAM EXECUTION WITHOUT CHECKPOINTING

In this section we consider the execution of a program with a given processing requirement (as measured by the computation time on a failure-free system) in the presence of failures. We assume that the program is equipped with a fault-tolerance mechanism that enables it to restart after failures. Without checkpointing, the program has to be restarted form its beginning every time a failure occurs. The execution of the program will eventually complete, when, for the first time, its entire processing requirement is completed without failures. The program execution time is defined as the time elapsed from the beginning of its execution until its completion (including repairs and reprocessing after failures.)

Let x be the processing requirement of the program, and let $T(x)$ be its execution time.

(Note that the program processing requirement is identical to its execution time under failure-free environment.) Let us assume that failures occur according to a Poisson process at rate γ. This is a commonly used and accepted assumption, particularly when failures are caused by many different and independent sources. As in most previous work, we also assume that failures are detected as soon as they occur. Following a failure, there is a repair time, denoted by the random variable R. Without loss of generality, we assume that no failures may occur during the repair time R. Clearly, due to the randomness of the failure/repair process, $T(x)$ is a random variable, even though the processing requirement x is fixed.

For a random variable, say R, we denote its probability distribution function (CDF) by $F_R(t) = P(R \le t)$, its probability density function (pdf) by $f_R(t)$, and its Laplace-Stieltjes transform (LST) by $\phi_R(s) = E(e^{-sR}) = \int_{t=0}^{\infty} e^{-st} f_R(t) \, dt$. Similarly, for $T(x)$, we denote its CDF by $F_T(t,x)$, its pdf by $f_T(t,x)$, and its LST by $\phi_T(s,x)$. The following result has been established in various forms in the literature, either directly (see, e.g., [Dud83, Goy87, Gra92]) or as a special case of a more general result (see, e.g., [Kul87, Nic86].) It gives a closed form expression for the LST of the program execution time, $T(x)$, in the presence of failures. We include a proof for the purpose of illustrating the arguments, which may be used to establish other results in this chapter.

THEOREM 1. Without checkpointing, the LST of the program execution time in the presence of failures is given by

$$\phi_T(s,x) = \frac{(s+\gamma)e^{-(s+\gamma)x}}{s+\gamma(1-\phi_R(s)(1-e^{-(s+\gamma)x}))}. \tag{7.1}$$

Proof: Let H be the time to the first failure after starting program execution, then conditioning on $H = h$, we have

$$T(x)|_{H=h} = \begin{cases} x, & \text{if } h \ge x \\ h + R + T(x), & \text{if } h < x. \end{cases}$$

If $h \ge x$, then the program will complete in x units of time. If $h < x$, then a failure occurs before the completion of the program. In this case, there is a repair time R after which the program execution is restarted from its beginning, thus, again, requiring x units of uninterrupted processing time to complete. Writing the LST of $T(x)$, we have

$$\phi_T(s,x)|_{H=h} = E(e^{-sT(x)}|H=h) = \begin{cases} e^{-sx}, & \text{if } h \ge x \\ e^{-sh}\phi_R(s)\phi_T(s,x), & \text{if } h < x. \end{cases}$$

Unconditioning on H, we get

$$\phi_T(s,x) = \int_{h=0}^{\infty} \phi_T(s,x)|_{H=h} \, \gamma e^{-\gamma h} \, dh$$

$$= e^{-(s+\gamma)x} + \frac{\gamma\phi_R(s)\phi_T(s,x)(1 - e^{-(s+\gamma)x})}{s+\gamma},$$

from which Equation 7.1 follows directly. □

The LST in Equation 7.1 can be inverted numerically or by inspection to obtain the pdf $f_T(t,x)$. A closed form expression for $f_T(t,x)$ can be found in [Dud83]. However, in most cases, numerical inversion is necessary and can be carried out using one of many procedures for the numerical inversion of Laplace transforms (see, e.g., [DeH83, Gar88, Jag82, Kul86].) The first and higher moments of $T(x)$ can be obtained from its LST. Of particular interest is the expected program execution time, $E(T(x))$, which is given in the following corollary.

COROLLARY 1. Without checkpointing, the expected program execution time in the presence of failures is given by

$$E(T(x)) = (\frac{1}{\gamma} + E(R))(e^{\gamma x} - 1). \tag{7.2}$$

Proof: Follows directly from the LST in Equation 7.1, using the relation $E(T(x)) = \frac{-\partial \phi_T(s,x)}{\partial s}|_{s=0}$. It can also be obtained by following arguments similar to those of Theorem 1. □

Note that $E(T(x))$ grows exponentially with the processing requirement x.

Denote by $A(x)$ the expected fraction of productive time during program execution, i.e., $A(x) = x/E(T(x))$, and let A be the steady-state system availability, defined as the long run fraction of time the system is available of productive processing. Clearly, $A(x) \leq 1$ is a program (task) oriented measure, which, for sufficiently large x, approaches the system oriented measure A.

In the following sections, we consider the use of checkpointing in a program to avoid excessive execution times due to restarts in the presence of failures. We examine the effect of checkpointing on the distribution of program execution time and its expectation. In Sections 7.4 and 7.5 we analyze strategies for which the distribution of productive time between checkpoints is known; namely, deterministic and general, respectively. In Section 7.6 we consider a random checkpointing strategy.

7.4   EQUIDISTANT CHECKPOINTING

The optimality of checkpointing strategies with deterministic (fixed) productive time between checkpoints has been established at both, the system and the program, levels. For example, in [Gel79] it was shown to maximize the steady-state system availability, and in [Cof88] it was shown to minimize the expected program execution time and also the tail of its distribution. Therefore, this is an important class of checkpointing strategies, which, also because of its intuitive appeal and simplicity, has often been considered by system analysts and designers.

7.4.1   The Model

In this section, we analyze a strategy with a deterministic productive time between checkpoints. It is assumed that the program can be divided into equal parts, and that a checkpoint is placed at the end of each program part (except, maybe, the last program part.) For this model, the analysis of the program execution time has been considered in many papers (see, e.g., [Dud83, Gei88, Cof88, Gra92].) In [Gei88, Cof88], failures during a deterministic checkpoint duration were taken into account.

We use the same notation as in Section 7.3, with the added assumption that checkpoint duration is a random variable C, with a CDF $F_C(t)$, a pdf $f_C(t)$, and a LST $\phi_C(s) = E(e^{-sC})$. Unlike most previous models, we take into account the possibility of failures during checkpointing. A failure during a checkpoint causes a rollback to (i.e., a restart from) the previous checkpoint. Here we remark that regardless of how many times a program part (say, the i-th part) is repeated, the duration of its checkpoint remains fixed (say, c_i, where c_i is a realization of the random variable C.) We assume that failures occur according to a Poisson process at the same rate γ, also during checkpointing.

7.4.2   The Execution Time with Equidistant Checkpoints

In this section we derive the LST of the execution time of a program, when checkpoints are equally spaced with respect to the productive processing time. We also obtain an expression for its expectation and discuss the optimization with respect to the number of checkpoints in the program.

Let x be the total processing requirement of the program, which is divided into, say, n equal parts, and denote by $T(x, n)$ its total execution time. Note that there is a checkpoint at the end of each program part, except the last, thus a total of $n - 1$ checkpoints. The following theorem gives an expression for the LST of $T(x, n)$.

THEOREM 2. With $n - 1$ equidistant checkpoints, the LST of the program execution time in the presence of failures is given by

$$
\phi_T(s, x, n) = \left[\frac{(s + \gamma)\phi_C(s + \gamma)e^{-(s+\gamma)x/n}}{s + \gamma(1 - \phi_R(s))(1 - \phi_C(s + \gamma)e^{-(s+\gamma)x/n}))} \right]^{n-1}
$$

$$
\times \left[\frac{(s + \gamma)e^{-(s+\gamma)x/n}}{s + \gamma(1 - \phi_R(s))(1 - e^{-(s+\gamma)x/n}))} \right]. \tag{7.3}
$$

Proof: Each of the first $n - 1$ program parts requires $x/n + C$ units of un-interrupted processing time to complete. The execution times of the first $n - 1$ program parts are independent and identically distributed (i.i.d) random variables, each is given by $T(x/n + C)$. Note that the checkpoint duration C is a random variable; however, it is fixed for a given program part. Following similar steps as those used in the proof of Theorem 1, we obtain the following for the LST of $T(x/n + C)$

$$\phi_T(s, x/n + C) = \frac{(s+\gamma)\phi_C(s+\gamma)e^{-(s+\gamma)x/n}}{s+\gamma(1-\phi_R(s)(1-\phi_C(s+\gamma)e^{-(s+\gamma)x/n}))}.$$

The last program part requires x/n units of un-interrupted processing time (it does not include a checkpoint), and its execution time is given by $T(x/n)$. The LST of $T(x/n)$ is obtained directly from Equation 7.1

$$\phi_T(s, x/n) = \frac{(s+\gamma)e^{-(s+\gamma)x/n}}{s+\gamma(1-\phi_R(s)(1-e^{-(s+\gamma)x/n}))}.$$

The total program execution time is the sum of n independent random variables (corresponding to the execution times of the n parts.) The first $n-1$ of which are identically distributed and having the LST $\phi_T(s, x/n + C)$, and the last one having the LST $\phi_T(s, x/n)$. It follows that

$$\phi_T(s, x, n) = [\phi_T(s, x/n + C)]^{n-1} [\phi_T(s, x/n)],$$

and hence Equation 7.3. $\square$

The LST in Equation 7.3 can be inverted by inspection or numerically to obtain the pdf $f_T(t, x, n)$. The first and higher moments of $T(x, n)$ can be obtained from its LST. Of particular interest is the expected program execution time, $E(T(x, n))$, which is given in the following corollary.

COROLLARY 2. With $n-1$ equally spaced checkpoints, the expected program execution time in the presence of failures is given by

$$E(T(x, n)) = (\frac{1}{\gamma} + E(R)) \left[(n-1)(\phi_C(-\gamma)e^{\gamma x/n} - 1) + (e^{\gamma x/n} - 1) \right]. \qquad (7.4)$$

Proof: The proof follows directly from $E(T(x, n)) = \frac{-\partial \phi_T(s, x, n)}{\partial s}|_{s=0}$, or by following the same arguments as in Theorem 2. $\square$

Assuming that $E(T(x, n))$ is a non-concave function of n (related convexity properties have been discussed in [Cof88]), then equidistant checkpointing is beneficial only if $E(T(x, 2)) < E(T(x, 1)) = E(T(x))$, i.e., $e^{\gamma x/2}(\phi_C(-\gamma) + 1 - e^{\gamma x/2}) < 1$. Since C is a non-negative random variable, $\phi_C(-\gamma) \geq 1$, and the above inequality does not hold for $x \to 0$, i.e., checkpointing is not beneficial for a sufficiently small x.

If we fix the length of each program part to some constant, say, τ, then increasing the program processing requirement x (provided that $n = \frac{x}{\tau}$ remains an integer) would mean increasing the number of checkpoints in the program ($n-1$). In this case, Equation 7.4 may be written as follows

$$E(T(x,x/\tau)) = (\frac{1}{\gamma} + E(R)) \left[(\frac{x}{\tau} - 1)(\phi_C(-\gamma)e^{\gamma\tau} - 1) + (e^{\gamma\tau} - 1) \right]. \qquad (7.5)$$

Note that, for a fixed τ, $E(T(x,x/\tau))$ grows only linearly with the total program processing requirement x. (Recall that, without checkpointing, $E(T(x))$ grows exponentially with x, see Equation 7.2.)

Let $\hat{\tau}$ be the optimal length of a program part which minimizes the expected program execution time. It can be shown that $E(T(x,x/\tau))$ is a convex function of τ, and, hence, $\hat{\tau}$ can be determined by (numerically) solving the equation $\frac{d}{d\tau}(E(T(x,x/\tau))) = 0$.

For a sufficiently large x, we have the following approximation

$$E(T(x,x/\tau)) \approx (\frac{1}{\gamma} + E(R))(\phi_C(-\gamma)e^{\gamma\tau} - 1)\frac{x}{\tau}. \qquad (7.6)$$

An approximation to $\hat{\tau}$ can be determined by solving the equation $\phi_C(-\gamma)e^{\gamma\hat{\tau}}(1-\gamma\hat{\tau}) = 1$. It is interesting to note that $\hat{\tau}$ is independent of x, however, it does depend on the failure rate γ and the distribution of checkpoint duration, through its LST $\phi_C(-\gamma)$. For a sufficiently small γ, further approximation yields the following simple expression for the optimal inter-checkpoint interval $\hat{\tau} \approx \frac{1}{\gamma}\sqrt{2(1 - \frac{1}{\phi_C(-\gamma)})}$. Let $\hat{n} = \lfloor \frac{x}{\hat{\tau}} \rfloor$, then the optimal number of checkpoints is given by $max(0, \hat{n} - 1)$.

7.5 CHECKPOINTING IN MODULAR PROGRAMS

It is not always possible to place checkpoints equally spaced in a program, as this depends to a large extent on the structure of the program. In practice, many checkpoint placement schemes are based on the modularity of computation in a program (see, e.g., [Cha72b, Lon92].) This is due to the fact that the end of modules often constitute natural points to perform acceptance tests and to place checkpoints at a relatively low cost. For such schemes, there are only some (candidate) points in the program where checkpoints may be placed. (In [Tou84], the problem of optimal placement of checkpoints at such points is considered.) For example, a program may be composed of several modules or blocks (each requiring a random processing time to complete) and checkpoints may be placed only at the end of each module, except the last one. In such cases, the productive time between checkpoints (corresponding to the processing requirement of one or more modules) is a random variable. If the distribution of this random variable is known (by means of measurements, approximations, or otherwise), then it is of much interest to use it in models for the analysis of the program execution time.

In this section we consider a new model for the analysis of the program execution time in the presence of failures, with generally distributed productive time between checkpoints. More specifically, the model we consider here is the same as that in Section 7.4, except that the productive time between checkpoints (τ) is assumed to be generally distributed (rather than deterministic) with a CDF $F_\tau(t)$, a pdf $f_\tau(t)$, and a LST $\phi_\tau(s)$. This corresponds to placing checkpoints in a program at the end of modules having generally distributed processing time requirement.

There are two measures of interest here. The first is the execution time of a program consisting of, say, n modules; we denote this by $T_{mod}(n)$. The second is the execution time to complete a given amount of productive processing, say, x; which, as before, is denoted by $T(x)$. The analysis in this section is carried out to derive the expectation of the these two measures; however, the same approach can also be used to derive their distributions.

7.5.1 The Execution Time of a Modular Program

In this section we consider a model for the execution time of a modular program with checkpoints. The analysis of this model is useful for the evaluation of schemes in which checkpoints are placed at the program level, and based on the modularity of its computation. In the following theorem we give the expected execution time of a program consisting of n modules, each requiring an independent and identically (generally) distributed productive processing time and ending with a checkpoint (no checkpoint is placed at the end of the last module.)

THEOREM 3. With modular checkpointing, the expected execution time of a program consisting of n modules in the presence of failures is given by

$$E(T_{mod}(n)) = (\frac{1}{\gamma} + E(R)) \left[(n-1)(\phi_C(-\gamma)\phi_\tau(-\gamma) - 1) + (\phi_\tau(-\gamma) - 1) \right]. \quad (7.7)$$

Proof: Follows directly from Equation 7.4 of Corollary 2, after replacing the productive time between checkpoints, x/n, by τ and unconditioning on τ. □

For a deterministic productive time between checkpoints such that $\tau = x/n$, $\phi_\tau(-\gamma) = e^{\gamma x/n}$ and Equation 7.7 reduces to Equation 7.4. The following corollary specializes the above result to the case when the productive time between checkpoints is exponentially distributed with a mean equal to α^{-1}. In this case $f_\tau(t) = \alpha e^{-\alpha t}$ and $\phi_\tau(s) = 1/(\alpha + s)$.

COROLLARY 3. For exponential productive time between checkpoints, Equation 7.7 reduces to

$$E(T_{mod}(n)) = (\frac{1}{\gamma} + E(R)) \left[(n-1)(\frac{\phi_C(-\gamma)}{\alpha - \gamma} - 1) + (\frac{1}{\alpha - \gamma} - 1) \right]. \quad (7.8)$$

Proof: Direct substitution of $\phi_\tau(-\gamma) = \frac{1}{\alpha - \gamma}$ in Equation 7.7. □

Note that, for checkpointing in a given modular program (as considered here), optimization with respect to the number of modules (n) is not straightforward. This is due to the fact that, in general, changing n also implies a change in the distribution of the processing requirement of each module ($F_\tau(t)$).

7.5.2 The Execution Time of a Given Processing Requirement

In this section we consider the execution time of a given amount of productive processing in a program, with a checkpoint placed at the end of each module. This model is a generalization of that in Section 7.4, since here we assume that the productive processing between checkpoints is generally distributed (rather than deterministic). The analysis of this model is useful for the evaluation of non-deterministic checkpointing schemes, in which the productive processing times between checkpoints are independent and identically distributed random variables. In the following theorem we give the expected execution time to complete x units of productive processing time.

THEOREM 4. With generally distributed productive time between checkpoints, the expected execution time to complete x units of productive processing time in the presence of failures is given by the solution of the following integral equation

$$E(T(x)) = (\frac{1}{\gamma} + E(R)) \left[\phi_C(-\gamma) \int_{h=0}^{x} e^{\gamma h} dF_\tau(h) + e^{\gamma x}(1 - F_\tau(x)) - 1 \right]$$

$$+ \int_{h=0}^{x} E(T(x - h)) dF_\tau(h). \tag{7.9}$$

Proof: Let H be the productive time between checkpoints, then conditioning on $H = h$, we have

$$E(T(x))|_{H=h} = \begin{cases} (\frac{1}{\gamma} + E(R))(e^{\gamma x} - 1), & \text{if } h \geq x \\ \\ (\frac{1}{\gamma} + E(R))(\phi_C(-\gamma)e^{\gamma h} - 1) + E(T(x - h)), & \text{if } h < x. \end{cases}$$

If $h \geq x$, then there are no checkpoints during the execution of x units of productive time. From Equation 7.2, it follows that the expected execution time is given by

$$E(T(x)) = (\frac{1}{\gamma} + E(R))(e^{\gamma x} - 1).$$

If $h < x$, then a checkpoint will occur before completing x units of productive time. In this case, the expected execution time to complete h units of productive time and C units of checkpointing time is given by (note that, although C is a random variable, it is fixed for a given checkpoint)

$$E(T(h + C)) = (\frac{1}{\gamma} + E(R))(\phi_C(-\gamma)e^{\gamma h} - 1).$$

After the checkpoint, h units of productive time are completed and the expected remaining execution time is given by $E(T(x - h))$.

Unconditioning on H, we get $E(T(x)) = \int_{h=0}^{\infty} E(T(x))|_{H=h} \, dF_\tau(h)$, from which Equation 7.9 follows. $\square$

For a deterministic productive time between checkpoints such that $\tau = x/n$, it can be easily shown that Equation 7.9 reduces to Equation 7.4. The following corollary specializes the above result to the case when the productive time between checkpoints is exponentially distributed with a mean equal to α^{-1}.

COROLLARY 4. For exponential productive time between checkpoints, an explicit solution for Equation 7.9 is given by

$$E(T(x)) = (\frac{1}{\gamma} + E(R)) \left(\frac{\gamma + \alpha(\phi_C(-\gamma) - 1)}{(\alpha - \gamma)^2} \right)$$

$$\times \left(\alpha(\alpha - \gamma)x + \gamma(e^{-(\alpha - \gamma)x} - 1) \right). \tag{7.10}$$

Proof: Substituting for $dF_\tau(h) = \alpha e^{-\alpha h} dh$ and for $F_\tau(x) = (1 - e^{-\alpha x})$ in Equation 7.9, we get

$$E(T(x)) = (\frac{1}{\gamma} + E(R)) \left(\frac{\gamma + \alpha(\phi_C(-\gamma) - 1)}{\alpha - \gamma} \right) (1 - e^{-(\alpha - \gamma)x})$$

$$+ \alpha \int_{h=0}^{x} E(T(x - h))e^{-\alpha h} dh.$$

Define the Laplace transform $\tilde{T}(w) = \int_{x=0}^{\infty} e^{-wx} E(T(x)) dx$. After changing the order of integration in the above equation and some manipulation, we get

$$\tilde{T}(w) = (\frac{1}{\gamma} + E(R)) \left(\frac{\gamma + \alpha(\phi_C(-\gamma) - 1)}{(\alpha - \gamma)^2} \right)$$

$$\times \left(\frac{\alpha(\alpha - \gamma)}{w^2} + \gamma(\frac{1}{w + \alpha - \gamma} - \frac{1}{w}) \right).$$

Inverting $\tilde{T}(w)$ with respect to w yields Equation 7.10. $\square$

Note that, for $\alpha = 0$ (i.e., no checkpointing), $E(T(x))$ from Equation 7.10 reduces to $(\frac{1}{\gamma} + E(R))(e^{\gamma x} - 1)$, in agreement with Equation 7.2. For a sufficiently large x, it can be shown that $E(T(x))$ is a convex function of α and that $\frac{dE(T(x))}{d\alpha}|_{\alpha=0} < 0$, i.e., checkpointing is beneficial. It can also be shown that the optimal checkpointing rate is higher than the failure rate γ. For a large x, and in the particularly interesting range, namely, $\alpha > \gamma$, we obtain the following approximation for $E(T(x))$

$$E(T(x)) \approx (\frac{1}{\gamma} + E(R)) \left(\frac{\gamma + \alpha(\phi_C(-\gamma) - 1)}{(\alpha - \gamma)} \right) \alpha x. \tag{7.11}$$

In the above approximation, $E(T(x))$ is a linear of x. Also, an approximation to the optimal checkpointing rate $\hat{\alpha}$ is independent of x and is given by

$$\hat{\alpha} \approx \gamma \left(1 + \sqrt{\frac{\phi_C(-\gamma)}{(\phi_C(-\gamma) - 1)}} \right). \tag{7.12}$$

Substituting for $\hat{\alpha}$ from Equation 7.12 in Equation 7.11 yields an approximation for the minimum expected execution time when x is large

$$E(T(x)) \approx (\frac{1}{\gamma} + E(R))\gamma x \left(1 + 2(\phi_C(-\gamma) - 1) + 2\sqrt{\phi_C(-\gamma)(\phi_C(-\gamma) - 1)} \right). \tag{7.13}$$

The above approximations provide good estimates for a practical range of parameter values.

7.6   RANDOM CHECKPOINTING

In Section 7.2, we have described some situations in which checkpointing at the program level may be considered to occur randomly. For example, using an external trigger (e.g., a real-time clock [Li90] or a change in the system's workload) to determine checkpoint locations can result in non-deterministic checkpoint placements (relative to the computational progress) for different executions of the same program. As a consequence of non-determinism (or randomness), checkpointing may also occur during recovery (reprocessing) after failures. Since failures are usually more likely to occur during recovery, this is an important feature that is worthwhile considering in a checkpointing strategy. This feature is taken into account in [Kul90] for modeling and analysis of random checkpointing.

7.6.1   The Model

In this section we describe a model of random checkpointing in a program that we consider for analysis. As in [Kul90], it is assumed that the system, on which the program is being executed, can be in one of three states; namely, *operational* (includes reprocessing), *checkpointing*, or *under-repair* (excludes reprocessing.) In this model, it is important to note that the two components of recovery time (i.e., repair and reprocessing) are separated in two states; namely, repair time in the under-repair state and reprocessing time which constitutes a part of the operational state. When the system is in the operational state, failures and checkpoints occur according to a Poisson process at rates γ and α, respectively. A failure takes the system to the under-repair state for a random repair time R (excludes reprocessing), after which the system returns to the operational state, and the program is restarted from the most recent checkpoint. A checkpoint takes the system to the checkpointing state for a random checkpointing time C, after which the system returns to the operational state, and the program execution continues. At a checkpoint, the status of the program is saved, so that all useful processing done thus far is never lost again.

In this section, we extend the model in [Kul90] to allow for the possibility of failures (at the same rate γ) during checkpointing. A failure in the checkpointing state takes the system to the under-repair state for a random repair time R, after which the system returns to the operational state, and the program is restarted from the previous (successful) checkpoint.

Unlike the models considered in Sections 7.4 and 7.5, in the present model, it is appropriate to assume that subsequent checkpoints (including those next to a failed checkpoint) have different durations (i.e., different i.i.d. realizations of the random variable C.)

7.6.2 The Execution Time of a Given Processing Requirement

In this section we consider the execution time of a given amount of productive processing in a program with random checkpointing. We follow a similar approach as that in [Kul90] to derive the LST of the execution time and its expectation. We also discuss the minimization of the expected execution time with respect to the checkpointing rate α.

Let $\acute{C}$ be a random variable which denotes the holding time in the checkpointing state; it is the minimum of the two random variables, C and the time to next failure (the latter being exponentially distributed with a mean γ^{-1}.) It can be shown that the LST of $\acute{C}$ is given by

$$\phi_{\acute{C}}(s) = \frac{\gamma + s\phi_C(s+\gamma)}{s+\gamma}. \tag{7.14}$$

It follows that the expected holding time in the checkpointing state is given by $E(\acute{C}) = (1 - \phi_C(\gamma))/\gamma$.

In the presence of random failures and checkpointing, let $T(x)$ be a random variable which denotes the execution time of a program that requires x units of processing time. In the following theorem we give a closed form expression for the LST $\phi_T(s,x)$. We give only a starting recursive relation for $T(x)$ leading to the final result. The complete proof follows similar steps as those in [Kul90].

THEOREM 5. With random checkpointing, the LST of the program execution time in the presence of failures is given by

$$\phi_T(s,x) = \left\{ \left[\frac{\gamma + \alpha\phi_{\acute{C}}(s)(1 - \phi_C(\gamma))}{s + \alpha + \gamma} \right] \phi_R(s)(1 - e^{(s+\alpha+\gamma)x}) \right.$$

$$\left. + e^{(s+\alpha+\gamma)x}) \right\}^{1 - \frac{\alpha\phi_{\acute{C}}(s)\phi_C(\gamma)}{s+\alpha+\gamma - \left[\gamma + \alpha\phi_{\acute{C}}(s)(1-\phi_C(\gamma)) \right]\phi_R(s)}}. \tag{7.15}$$

Proof: Let H be the holding time in the operational state until the first event (a failure or a checkpoint), then conditioning on $H = h$, we have

$$T(x)|_{H=h} = \begin{cases} x, & \text{if } h \geq x \\ h + \acute{C} + T(x-h), & \text{if } h < x \text{ and event is a successful checkpoint} \\ h + \acute{C} + R + T(x), & \text{if } h < x \text{ and event is a failed checkpoint} \\ h + R + T(x), & \text{if } h < x \text{ and event is a failure.} \end{cases}$$

If $h \geq x$, then the program will complete in x units of time. If $h < x$ and the event is a checkpoint, then there is a holding time $\acute{C}$ in the checkpointing state, followed by one of two possibilities. If the checkpoint is successful (with a probability $\phi_C(\gamma)$), then program execution continues with $x - h$ units of productive processing time remaining to complete. Otherwise, the checkpoint fails (with a probability $(1 - \phi_C(\gamma))$), and the system spends R time units in repair before restarting the program, with x units of productive processing time remaining to complete. If $h < x$ and the event is failure, then the system spends R time units in repair before restarting the program, with x units of productive processing time remaining to complete.

The proof can be completed by unconditioning on H (using $f_H(h) = (\alpha + \gamma)e^{-(\alpha+\gamma)h}$) and following similar steps as those in [Kul90]. $\square$

The LST in Equation 7.15 can be inverted numerically to obtain $f_T(t,x)$. The first and higher moments of $T(x)$ can be obtained from its LST. Of particular interest is the expected program execution time, $E(T(x))$, which is given in the following corollary.

COROLLARY 5. With random checkpointing, the expected program execution time in the presence of failures is given by

$$E(T(x)) = a((\alpha + \gamma)x + \ln b(x)), \tag{7.16}$$

with

$$a = \frac{1 + \alpha E(\acute{C}) + (\alpha(1 - \phi_C(\gamma)) + \gamma)E(R)}{\alpha\phi_C(\gamma)},$$

and

$$b(x) = \frac{\alpha\phi_C(\gamma) + (\alpha(1 - \phi_C(\gamma)) + \gamma)e^{-(\alpha+\gamma)x}}{\alpha + \gamma}.$$

Proof: Follows directly from the LST in Equation 7.15, using the relation $E(T(x)) = \frac{-\partial\phi_T(s,x)}{\partial s}\big|_{s=0}$. $\square$

Again, checkpointing is beneficial only if $E(T(x))$ is less than the expected execution time without checkpointing, i.e., only if $E(T(x)) < (\frac{1}{\gamma} + E(R))(e^{\gamma x} - 1)$. This inequality may not hold for a sufficiently small x. For a sufficiently large x, $b(x)$ approaches $\frac{\alpha\phi_C(\gamma)}{(\alpha+\gamma)}$, which, for a small γ, approaches 1. In this case, $E(T(x))$ may be approximated by the following linear function of x,

$$E(T(x)) \approx a(\alpha + \gamma)x. \tag{7.17}$$

It follows that, for large x, an approximation to the optimal checkpointing rate $\hat{\alpha}$, which minimizes $E(T(x))$, is independent of x and is given by

$$\hat{\alpha} \approx \sqrt{\frac{\gamma(1 + \gamma E(R))}{E(\acute{C}) + (1 - \phi_C(\gamma))E(R)}}. \tag{7.18}$$

Substituting for $\hat{\alpha}$ from Equation 7.18 in Equation 7.17 yields an approximation for the minimum expected execution time for large x

$$E(T(x))|_{\alpha=\hat{\alpha}} \approx \frac{x}{\phi_C(\gamma)} \left(\sqrt{1 + \gamma E(R))} + \sqrt{\gamma(E(\dot{C}) + (1 - \phi_C(\gamma))E(R))} \right)^2. \quad (7.19)$$

The above approximations are quite useful as they could provide very good estimates for a practical range of parameter values.

7.7 CONCLUSIONS

Techniques for fault-tolerance are usually designed with their main goal is to satisfy certain dependability requirements of the system. This is often done at the expense of additional cost and/or degraded performance. It is therefore important to evaluate fault-tolerance procedures not only based on their dependability aspects [Lap84] but also based on their cost/performance aspects (some dependability and performance evaluation techniques [Tri82] are discussed in chapters 5 and 6 of this book).

Checkpointing is a commonly used technique for fault-tolerance in a variety of software applications and information systems. It involves intermittently saving sufficient information, which is used to avoid a complete loss of useful processing (work) at the occurrence of a transient failure. Typically, the main goal of checkpointing is twofold: to satisfy the reliability requirements of the system in the presence of failures, and to do so with a minimum performance sacrifice. If checkpoints were without a cost, then more checkpoints would mean meeting the reliability requirements at a better performance. However, this is rarely the case, and there is typically a trade off, i.e., there is an optimal checkpointing strategy (frequency) which optimizes an appropriate performance measure. In information (database) systems, the objective is usually to maintain the integrity of information, while maximizing its long run availability. In software applications, the objective is usually to maintain the correctness of a long executing program, while minimizing its expected execution time or keeping it within acceptable bounds.

In this chapter, our main focus has been the modeling of checkpointing and rollback recovery in a program. We have considered some basic models for the analysis of the program execution time in the presence of failures, with some commonly used checkpointing strategies; namely, the (well-known) equidistant strategy, a strategy used in modular programs and what we call "random" strategy. The latter maybe used to model strategies such as "global" checkpointing [Kan78] or "dynamic" checkpoint insertion schemes [Li90]. In all models considered in this chapter, we have assumed that failures may occur not only during recovery, but also during checkpointing (resulting in a rollback to the previous successful checkpoint), thus making an important extension to some existing models. We have also introduced and analyzed a new model for checkpointing in modular programs, where checkpoints may be placed only at the boundaries between program modules. The processing time requirement of a program module is assumed to be generally distributed. Although we have assumed a homogeneous Poisson failure process, most of the analysis can be carried out for other failure distributions; however, the final results may no longer turn out to be explicit or appear in a compact form. (A model with age dependent failures is considered in [Cof88].) The results of our analysis include closed form expressions for the LST (Laplace Stieltjes transform) of the program execution time and/or its expectation. The first and higher moments can be directly determined from the derivatives of the LST; however, numerical inversion of the LST is usually necessary to obtain the complete distribution of the program execution time. A conclusion which generally holds is that, with checkpointing, the expected execution time of a program grows only linearly (instead of exponential growth without checkpointing) with its processing requirement. It is noted that checkpointing may not always be beneficial, particularly for programs with sufficiently small processing requirement. Otherwise, there is usually an optimal (with respect to some criterion) checkpointing frequency, which can be determined either analytically or numerically. For programs with sufficiently large processing requirement, the optimal checkpointing frequency, which minimizes the expected execution time, is independent of the program processing requirement and is equal to the optimal checkpointing frequency which maximizes the long run system availability.

Needless to say, with much already accomplished, still there are many useful extensions and practical problems that need to be addressed. A dynamic programming approach to the modeling and analysis of checkpointing and recovery has been considered at the program level [Tou84] and at the system level [Lec88], and it typically yields an algorithmic solution. This approach is very promising and should be explored further, as it is capable of handling more realistic models with less restrictive assumptions.

In most previous work, as well as here, it has been assumed that failures are detected as soon as they occur. In reality, a failure may go undetected, leading to incorrect execution of the program. Or, as often is the case, there is a latency between failure occurrence and detection, which may cause the program to rollback to earlier checkpoints. Some models have considered these effects, for example, when combining checkpointing with instruction retries [Kor86], also in real-time [Shi87] and concurrent processing [Tha86] environments. It is of much interest to better understand the impact of such a latency in various systems and under different scenarios.

Also when tolerated, failures are likely to cause some sort of system degradation (for example, the unavailability of some processors in a multi-processor system). This may affect the processing (or reprocessing) speed after failures and until further repair action is taken to bring the system back to its full processing capacity. In some systems, another possible scenario is that checkpointing may be performed in the background, thus allowing productive processing (perhaps at a lower speed) to continue during checkpointing. It is certainly important to consider checkpointing models that take into account such a degradable/repairable or concurrent behavior, as this will largely influence the optimal checkpointing strategy. Models such as those considered in [Kul90] and in Section 7.6 of this chapter may be extended by adding more states with appropriate rewards (corresponding to processing speeds) to account for such behaviors.

Many other complications and problems arise if the program is running in a concurrent or a distributed environment (see [Cha85, Jon90, Lon91, Str85] and many others.) On the other hand, parallel (or multi-processor) computing systems provide hardware redundancy which can be exploited to achieve fault-tolerance with less performance degradation. In these systems, the same program is run on more than one processor. Checkpoints are used to detect failures (by comparing the states of the processors) and to reduce recovery time. Roll-forward recovery schemes have been suggested to take advantage of this hardware redundancy (see, for example, [Lon90, Pra92].) Similarly, software redundancy schemes can be used to achieve fault-tolerance by masking software (program) failures (see [Avi85, Tso87].) So far, only little has been done to model program checkpointing and recovery schemes and to understand their effects in such contexts (see, e.g., [Koo87, Nic90a, Shi84, Ziv93].)

Finally, there is growing interest and need for developing robust and effective checkpointing/recovery schemes at different levels of software applications running on various architectures and platforms. It is also apparent that these schemes are becoming increasingly complex and sophisticated, thus requiring more research and analysis to help abstract the main issues and understand the various trade-offs that are typically involved in their design.

REFERENCES

[And81]   T. Anderson and P. Lee. *Fault Tolerance—Principles and Practice*. Prentice-Hall, Englewood Cliffs, New Jersey, 1981.

[Avi85]   A. Avižienis. The N-version approach to fault-tolerant software. *IEEE Transactions on Software Engineering*, SE-11(12):1491–1501, 1985.

[Bac81a] F. Baccelli. Analysis of a service facility with periodic checkpointing. *Acta Informatica*, 15(1):67–81, 1981.

[Bac81b] F. Baccelli and T. Znati. Queueing algorithms with breakdowns in database modeling. In F.J. Kylstra, editor, *Performance '81*, pages 213–231. North-Holland, Amsterdam, 1981.

[Bog92]   L.B. Boguslavsky, E.G. Coffman, E.N. Gilbert, and A.Y. Kreinin. Scheduling checks and saves. *ORSA Journal on Computing*, 4(1):60–69, 1992.

[Bro79]   A. Brock. An analysis of checkpointing. *ICL Technical Journal*, 1(3), 1979.

[Cha72a] K.M. Chandy and C.V. Ramamoorthy. Rollback and recovery strategies. *IEEE Transactions on Computers*, C-21(2):137–146, 1972.

[Cha72b] K.M. Chandy and C.V. Ramamoorthy. Rollback recovery strategies for computer programs. *IEEE Transactions on Computers*, C-21(6):546–556, 1972.

[Cha75a] K.M. Chandy, J.C. Browne, C.W. Dissly, and W.R. Uhrig. Analytic models for rollback and recovery strategies in database systems. *IEEE Transactions on Software Engineering*, SE-1(1):100–110, 1975.

[Cha75b] K.M. Chandy. A survey of analytic models for rollback and recovery strategies. *Computer*, 8(5):40–47, 1975.

[Cha85]   K.M. Chandy and L. Lamport. Distributed snapshots: determining global states of distributed systems. *ACM Transactions on Computer Systems*, 3(1):63–75, 1985.

[Cof88]   E.G. Coffman and E. N. Gilbert. Optimal strategies for scheduling checkpoints and preventive maintenance. AT&T Bell Laboratories, Murray Hill, New Jersey, 1988.

[DeH83]   F.R. De Hoog, J.H. Knight, and A.N. Stokes. An improved method for numerical inversion of Laplace transforms. *SIAM Journal of Statistical Computing*, 3(3):357–366, 1983.

[DeS90]   E. de Souza e Silva and H.R. Gail. Analyzing scheduled maintenance policies for repairable computer systems. *IEEE Transactions on Computers*, C-39(11):1309–1324, 1990.

[Don88]   L. Donatiello, V. Grassi, and S. Tucci. Availability distribution of rollback recovery systems. In G. Iazeolla, P.J. Courtois, and O.J. Boxma, editors, *Mathematical Computer Performance and Reliability*, pages 489–502. North Holland, Amsterdam, 1988.

[Dud83]   A. Duda. The effects of checkpointing on program execution time. *Information Processing Letters*, 16(5):221–229, 1983.

[Dud84]   A. Duda. Performance analysis of the checkpoint-rollback-recovery system via diffusion approximation. In G. Iazeolla, P.J. Courtois, and A. Hordijk, editors, *Mathematical Computer Performance and Reliability*, pages 315–327. North-Holland, Amsterdam, 1984.

[Gar88]   B.S. Garbow, G. Giunta, and J.N. Lyness. Software for an implementation of Weeks method for the inverse Laplace transform problem. *ACM Transactions on Mathematical Software*, 14(2):163–170, 1988.

[Gav62]   D.P. Gaver. A waiting line with interrupted service including priorities. *Journal Royal Statistical Society*, B-24:73–90, 1962.

[Gei88]   R. Geist, R. Reynolds, and J. Westall. Checkpoint interval selection in critical task environment. *IEEE Transactions on Reliability*, R-37(4):395–400, 1988.

[Gel78]   E. Gelenbe and D. Derochette. Performance of rollback recovery systems under intermittent failures. *Communications of ACM*, 21(6):493–499, 1978.

[Gel79]   E. Gelenbe. On the optimum checkpoint interval. *Journal of ACM*, 26(2):259–270, 1979.

[Gel90]   E. Gelenbe and M. Hernandez. Optimum checkpoints with age dependent failures. *Acta Informatica*, 27:519–531, 1990.

[Goy87]   A. Goyal, V.F. Nicola, A.N. Tantawi, and K.S. Trivedi. Reliability of systems with limited repairs. *IEEE Transactions on Reliability*, R-36(2):202–207, 1987.

[Gra92]   V. Grassi, L. Donatiello, and S. Tucci. On the optimal checkpointing of critical tasks and transaction-oriented systems. *IEEE Transactions on Software Engineering*, SE-18(1):72–77, 1992.

[Hae83]   T. Haerder and A. Reuter. Principles of transaction-oriented database recovery. *ACM Computing Surveys*, 15(4):287–317, 1983.

[Jag82]   D.L. Jagerman. An inversion technique for the Laplace transform. *Bell System Technical Journal*, 61(8):1995–2002, 1982.

[Jon90]   D.B. Johnson and W. Zwaenepoel. Recovery in distributed systems using optimistic message logging and checkpointing. *Journal of Algorithms*, 11:462–491, 1990.

[Kan78]   K. Kant. A model for error recovery with global checkpointing. *Information Sciences*, 30:58–68, 1978.

[Koo87]   R. Koo and S. Toueg. Checkpointing and rollback-recovery for distributed systems. *IEEE Transactions on Software Engineering*, SE-13(1):23–31, 1987.

[Kor86]   I. Koren, Z. Koren, and S.Y.H. Su. Analysis of a class of recovery procedures. *IEEE Transactions on Computers*, C-35(8):703–712, 1986.

[Kri84]   C.M. Krishna, K.G. Shin, and Y.-H. Lee. Optimization criteria for checkpoint placements. *Communications of ACM*, 27(10):1008–1012, 1984.

[Kul86]   V.G. Kulkarni, V.F. Nicola, R.M. Smith, and K.S. Trivedi. Numerical evaluation of performability and job completion time in repairable fault-tolerant systems. *Proc. Sixteenth International Symposium on Fault-Tolerant Computing*, pages 252-257, 1986. IEEE Computer Society Press.

[Kul87]   V.G. Kulkarni, V.F. Nicola, and K.S. Trivedi. The completion time of a job on multimode systems. *Advanced Applied Probabilities*, 19:932–954, 1987.

[Kul90]   V.G. Kulkarni, V.F. Nicola, and K.S. Trivedi. Effects of checkpointing and and queueing on program performance. *Communications in Statistics: Stochastic Models*, 6(4):615–648, 1990.

[Lap84]   J.C. Laprie. Dependability evaluation of software systems. *IEEE Transactions on Software Engineering*, SE-10(11):701–714, 1984.

[Lec88]   P. L'ecuyer and J. Malenfant. Computing optimal checkpointing strategies for rollback and recovery systems. *IEEE Transactions on Computers*, C-37(4):491–496, 1988.

[Leu84]   C.H.C. Leung and Q.H. Choo. On the execution of large batch programs in unreliable computing systems. *IEEE Transactions on Software Engineering*, SE-10(4):444–450, 1984.

[Li90]   C.C. Li and W.K. Fuchs. CATCH: compiler-assisted techniques for checkpointing. *Proc. Twentieth International Symposium on Fault-Tolerant Computing*, pages 74-81, 1990. IEEE Computer Society Press.

[Loh77]   G.M. Lohman and J.A. Muckstadt. Optimal policy for batch operations: backup, checkpointing, reorganization and updating. *ACM Transactions on Database Systems*, 2(3):209–222, 1977.

[Lon90]   J. Long, W.K. Fuchs, and J.A. Abraham. A forward recovery strategy using checkpointing in parallel systems. *Proc. Nineteenth International Conference on Parallel Processing*, pages 272–275, 1990.

[Lon91]   J. Long, W.K. Fuchs, and J.A. Abraham. Implementing forward recovery using checkpointing in distributed systems. In J.F. Meyer and R.D. Schlichting, editors, *Dependable Computing for Critical Applications 2*, pages 27–46. Springer-Verlag, New York, 1991.

[Lon92]   J. Long, W.K. Fuchs, and J.A. Abraham. Compiler-assisted static checkpoint insertion. *Proc. Twenty-Second International Symposium on Fault-Tolerant Computing*, pages 58–65, 1992. IEEE Computer Society Press.

[Mag83]   J.M. Magazine. Optimality of intuitive checkpointing policies. *Information Processing letters*, 17(8):63–66, 1983.

[Mik79]   N. Mikou and S. Tucci. Analyse et optimisation d'une procedure de reprise dans un systeme de gestion de donnees centralisees. *Acta Informatica*, 12(4):321–338, 1979.

[Nic83a] V.F. Nicola and F.J. Kylstra. A Markovian model, with state-dependent parameters, of a transactional system supported by checkpointing and recovery strategies. In P.J. Kuhn and K.M. Schulz, editors, *Messung, Modellierung und Bewertung von Rechensystemen*, pages 189-206. Springer-Verlag, New York, 1983.

[Nic83b] V.F. Nicola and F.J. Kyls ra. A model of checkpointing and recovery with a specified number of transactions between checkpoints. In A.K. Agrawala and S.K. Tripathi, editors, *Performance '83*, pages 83–100. North-Holland, Amsterdam, 1983.

[Nic86] V.F. Nicola. A single server queue with mixed types of interruptions. *Acta Informatica*, 23:465–486, 1986.

[Nic87] V.F. Nicola, V.G. Kulkarni, and K.S. Trivedi. Queueing analysis of fault-tolerant computer systems. *IEEE Transactions on Software Engineering*, SE-13(3):363–375, 1987.

[Nic90a] V.F. Nicola and A. Goyal. Modeling of correlated failures and community error recovery in multiversion software. *IEEE Transactions on Software Engineering*, SE-16(3):350–359, 1990.

[Nic90b] V.F. Nicola and J.M. van Spanje. Comparative analysis of different models of checkpointing and recovery. *IEEE Transactions on Software Engineering*, SE-16(8):807–821, 1990.

[Pra89] D.K. Pradhan. Redundancy schemes for recovery. Technical Report TR-89-cse-16, Electrical and Computer Engineering Department, University of Massachusetts, Amherst, MA, 1989.

[Pra92] D.K. Pradhan and N.H. Vaidya. Roll-forward checkpointing scheme: concurrent retry with non-dedicated spares. *Proc. IEEE Workshop on Fault-Tolerant Parallel and Distributed Systems*, pages 166–174, 1992.

[Puc92] G. Pucci. A new approach to the modeling of recovery block structures. *IEEE Transactions on Software Engineering*, SE-18(2):159–167, 1992.

[Ran75] B. Randell. System structure for software fault tolerance. *IEEE Transactions on Software Engineering*, SE-1(6):220–232, 1975.

[Reu84] A. Reuter. Performance analysis of recovery techniques. *ACM Transactions on Database Systems*, 9(4):526–559, 1984.

[She75] J.J. Shedletsky and E.J. McCluskey. The error latency of a fault in a combinational digital circuit. *Proc. Fifth International Symposium on Fault-Tolerant Computing*, pages 210–214, 1975. IEEE Computer Society Press.

[Shi84] K.G. Shin and Y.-H. Lee. Evaluation of error recovery blocks used for cooperating processes. *IEEE Transactions on Software Engineering*, SE-10(11):692–700, 1984.

[Shi87] K.G. Shin, T. Lin, and Y.-H. Lee. Optimal checkpointing of real-time tasks. *IEEE Transactions on Computers*, C-36(11):1328–1341, 1987.

[Shn73] B. Shneiderman. Optimum database reorganization points. *Communications of ACM*, 16(6):362–365, 1973.

[Str85] R.E. Strom and S. Yemini. Optimistic recovery in distributed systems. *ACM Transactions on Computer Systems*, 3(3):204–226, 1985.

[Sum89] U. Sumita, N. Kaio, and P.B. Goes. Analysis of effective service time with age dependent interruptions and its application to optimal rollback policy for database management. *Queueing Systems: Theory and Applications*, volume 4, pages 193–212, 1989.

[Tan84] A.N. Tantawi and M. Ruschitzka. Performance analysis of checkpointing strategies. *ACM Transactions on Computer Systems*, 2(2):123–144, 1984.

[Tha86] S. Thanawastien, R.S. Pamula, and Y.L. Varol. Evaluation of checkpoint rollback strategies for error recovery in concurrent processing systems. *Proc. Sixteenth International Symposium on Fault-Tolerant Computing*, pages 246–251, 1986. IEEE Computer Society Press.

[Tou84] S. Toueg and O. Babaoglu. On the checkpoint selection problem. *SIAM Journal on Computing*, 13(3):630–649, 1984.

[Tri82] K.S. Trivedi. *Probability and Statistics with Reliability, Queueing and Computer Science Applications*. Prentice-Hall, Englewood Cliffs, New Jersey, 1982.

[Tso87] K.S. Tso and A. Avizienis. Community error recovery in N-version software: a design study with experimentation. *Proc. Seventeenth International Symposium on Fault-Tolerant Computing*, pages 127–133, 1987. IEEE Computer Society Press.

[Upa86] J.S. Upadhaya and K.K. Saluja. Rollback and recovery strategies for computer programs. *IEEE Transactions on Software Engineering*, SE-12(7):546–556, 1986.

[Upa88]   J.S. Upadhaya and K.K. Saluja. An experimental study to determine task size for rollback recovery systems. *IEEE Transactions on Computers*, C-37(7):872–877, 1988.

[Ver78]   J.S. Verhofstad. Recovery techniques for database systems. *Computing Surveys*, 10(2):167–195, 1978.

[You74]   J.W. Young. A first order approximation to the optimum checkpoint interval. *Communications of ACM*, 17(9):530–531, 1974.

[Ziv93]   A. Ziv and J. Bruck. Analysis of checkpointing schemes for multiprocessor systems. Research Report RJ 9593 (83791), IBM Research Division, Almaden, CA, 1993.

8

The Distributed Recovery Block Scheme

K.H. (KANE) KIM

University of California, Irvine

ABSTRACT

The *distributed recovery block* (DRB) scheme is an approach for realizing both hardware fault tolerance (HFT) and software fault tolerance (SFT) in real-time distributed and/or parallel computer systems. Since the initial formulation in 1983 of the basic structuring and operating principles by the author, the scheme has been steadily expanded with supporting testbed-based demonstrations and the expansion is still continuing. In this chapter, the basic principles of the DRB scheme, the implementation techniques established, and some of the demonstrations conducted, are briefly reviewed. The abilities for real-time detection and recovery for intentionally injected hardware faults and software faults were demonstrated but the experimental works have not yet gone far enough to test the abilities for tolerating unforeseen software faults. The limitations of the DRB scheme as well as major issues remaining for future research are also discussed.

8.1 INTRODUCTION

The *distributed recovery block* (DRB) scheme is an approach for realizing both hardware fault tolerance (HFT) and software fault tolerance (SFT) in real-time distributed and/or parallel computer systems. Since the initial formulation in 1983 of the basic structuring and operating principles [Kim84a], the scheme has been steadily expanded with supporting testbed-based demonstrations and the expansion is still continuing.

It uses a *pair of self-checking processing nodes* (PSP) structure together with both the software implemented internal audit function and the watchdog timer (WDT) to facilitate real-time HFT. For facilitating real-time SFT, the software implemented internal audit function and multiple versions of a real-time task software which are structured via the *recovery block*

Software Fault Tolerance, Edited by Lyu
© 1995 John Wiley & Sons Ltd

scheme [Hor74, Ran75, Lee78, Ran94] and executed concurrently on multiple nodes within a PSP structure, are employed.

The DRB scheme has been established with emphasis on the following three aspects.

(1) The target applications are of the real-time application type. Therefore, techniques which incur excessive overhead or yield excessive fault latency or recovery time have been consciously avoided.

(2) The target systems in which the DRB scheme will be used, are primarily *distributed computer systems* (DCS's) and *parallel computer systems*.

(3) The faults to be dealt with are both hardware faults and software faults. Therefore, the DRB scheme has been developed in such a form that proven HFT techniques can be easily integrated into the DRB scheme.

The decision to focus on real-time applications was made early on due to our belief that the significant advances achieved by computer industry in late 1970's and 80's pushed the issue of HFT in non-real-time or soft-real-time systems off the list of critical research topics. The emphasis on developing techniques applicable to DCS's and parallel computer systems was also based on our decision to be in line with technology evolution trends. In early 1980's, it was already safe to say that all future real-time application systems of moderate to large sizes and complexities would contain DCS's and some of these DCS's would in turn contain parallel computer systems as subsystems.

The emphasis on handling not just hardware faults but also software faults was based on our recognition that while the computer manufacturers succeeded in getting the issue of HFT under control, no similar progresses were made in the area of SFT. In spite of the hopes spread widely in the software engineering research community in 1970's, it became clear by early 1980's that production of largely error-free real-time software of non-trivial sizes was as distant a goal as ever, certainly not achievable before the entry into the 21st century.

In this chapter, the basic principles of the DRB scheme, the implementation techniques, and some of the demonstrations conducted, are briefly reviewed. The abilities for real-time detection and recovery for intentionally injected hardware faults and software faults were demonstrated but the experimental works have not yet gone far enough to test the abilities for tolerating unforeseen software faults. The limitations of the DRB scheme as well as major issues remaining for future research are also discussed.

8.2 NON-NEGLIGIBLE FAULT SOURCES AND DESIRABLE RECOVERY CAPABILITIES

8.2.1 Hardware Faults

Both permanent hardware faults, e.g., the crash of a processing node (consisting of one or more processors, local memory, communication, and other peripheral components), and temporary malfunction of hardware components are non-negligible potential causes for appearance of incorrect computational results. These faults are among the types of faults which DRB scheme was designed to handle, although the essential core of the scheme alone does not have the best coverage of such faults. However, the DRB scheme provides a flexible structure into which various proven HFT techniques [Avi71, Car85, Toy87], e.g., *triple modular redundancy* (TMR), *pair of comparing pairs* (PCP) used in Stratus computer series [Wil85], *error correcting code* (ECC), etc., can be easily incorporated.

8.2.2 Software Faults

During 1980's and even in late 1970's major computer system vendors have succeeded in producing fault-tolerant and yet economic modules of substantial complexity, thereby enabling production of "cost-competitive" computer systems with significant HFT capabilities and opening a sizable market for fault-tolerant computing. Therefore, the remaining challenge is in the problem of tolerating design faults, primarily in the software domain. Besides the problems related to incomplete or inconsistent specifications of computation requirements, there are largely two ways in which software faults arise. One major source for software faults is the selection of inadequate or insufficient algorithms which do not cover all realistically possible application situations. The other major source for software faults is the error in converting a selected algorithm into a program for a specific execution environment. Avoiding software faults is particularly difficult in real-time DCS's. Formal verification of designed algorithms or implemented programs has not yet advanced to the point where the absence of any error in sizable real-time software can be verified by a machine even with a moderate amount of assistance from human verifiers. Rapid progress in this formal verification technology is not likely to occur before we are well into the 21st century.

In a DCS, an algorithm may involve concurrency and distributed segments. A frequently occurring class of design faults are the *integration faults*. When a large number of modules are assembled into a DCS, the system developer often overlooks the possibilities of the system entering inconsistent states. This is due to the functional complexity of the integrated system. Individual components meet their specifications but the specifications are often incomplete, if not inaccurate, with respect to their integration with others. Therefore, it is nearly impossible to avoid such integration design faults in developing large-scale DCS's.

8.2.3 Generic Forward Recovery and Action-Level Fault Tolerance

In real-time applications, any computation results sent to the environment or the passage of real time can not be recalled. Therefore, the room for using *backward recovery* in a beneficial way is rather severely limited. This is not to say that old state information is not needed in recovery. A design issue here is how and what part of the recorded old state information can be utilized in achieving *forward recovery*.

A highly desirable forward recovery technique is one of a generic type. In the absence of generic forward recovery schemes, the design of fault-tolerant real-time computer systems will remain as a highly artistic error-prone discipline. Many *exception handling* approaches that have appeared in literature are examples of highly application-specific forward recovery schemes. Such approaches assume localization of the damage (due to the fault) to a very small area within the system, e.g., one or two program variables.

More generic forward recovery schemes which are capable of dealing with a broader range of fault conditions and more widely spread damages include the DRB scheme, the voting N-version programming (NVP) scheme [Avi75, Avi85], the PSP scheme, the TMR scheme, etc.

In addition, the degree of recovery achieved by an adopted forward recovery scheme is of great importance. The most desirable type of computer systems for use in safety-critical applications are those that have the capability of *action-level fault tolerance*, i.e., accomplishing critical actions (output actions of critical real-time tasks as specified) successfully in spite of component failures. Therefore, techniques for realizing action-level fault tolerance aim for

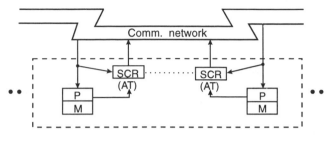

PSP-Structured Computing Station

Figure 8.1 A PSP station

much higher degree of dependability than those aimed for merely aborting some tasks and cleansing system states upon component failures. Both the DRB scheme and the voting NVP scheme mentioned above are action-level fault tolerance schemes.

8.3 BASIC PRINCIPLES OF THE DRB SCHEME

The development of the DRB scheme started with a view of a real-time DCS as an interconnection of *computing stations*, where a computing station refers to a processing node (hardware and software) dedicated to the execution of one or a few application processes. Some computing stations may perform system resource management functions only. The DRB scheme is a technology for constructing highly fault-tolerant computing stations. As mentioned in Section 8.1, the DRB scheme is a composition of two component technologies: the *pair of self-checking processing nodes* (PSP) scheme and the *recovery block* (RB) scheme.

8.3.1 The PSP Scheme

The essence of the PSP scheme is to use two copies of a *self-checking computing component* in the form of a *primary-shadow* pair [Kim93a] as shown in Figure 8.1.

A computing component is said to be *self-checking* if it possesses the capability of judging the reasonableness of its computation results. The internal audit logic represented as AT in Figure 8.1 for checking the computation results in a processing node can be implemented with or without special hardware support. A well known case of the PSP scheme implemented with a special internal audit hardware mechanism is the *pair of comparing pairs* (PCP) scheme used in the Stratus system [Wil85]. A generic software approach for the internal audit logic is to provide a run-time assertion or an acceptance test routine [Hor74, Ran75, Yau75].

The PSP scheme imposes a restrictive constraint on the structure of a computing component. Each computing component iterates computation cycles and each cycle is *two-phase structured*. That is, each cycle consists of an input acquisition phase and an output phase. During an input acquisition phase, the component may take one or more data input actions along with data transformation actions but no output action. Analogously, during an output phase, input actions are prohibited and one or more data output actions are allowed.

Basically, the PSP structure is adopted to facilitate parallel replicated execution of real-time tasks without incurring excessive overhead related to synchronization of the two partner nodes in the same PSP-structured computing station. Figure 8.2 illustrates a PSP-station in a local area network (LAN) based DCS. Here the self-checking function is implemented in the form of an acceptance test routine. For the sake of simplicity in discussion, Figure 8.2 depicts the special case where the following assumption holds:

(A1) The arrival rate of data items is such that each time a data item arrives, no other data items are being processed.

Node A is the initial *primary* node and node B is the initial *shadow* node within this computing station. Each of the partner nodes in a PSP station is assumed to contain its own local database which keeps persistent information used during more than one task cycle. Both nodes obtain input data from the multicast channel (built on a system-wide multi-access communication network). The next step for the primary node A is to inform the shadow node B of the ID of the data item that the former received (or selected in general) for processing in the current task cycle. This step is not essential in this special case subject to (A1). Node A and B process the data item and perform their self-checking concurrently by using the same acceptance test routine. Since node A passes the test, it delivers the results to both the successor computing station(s) and node B, and then starts the next task cycle. By receiving the output from node A, node B detects the success of node A and, if node B has also succeeded in its acceptance test, it too starts the next task cycle.

Suppose that the PSP-structured computing station in Figure 8.3 is the successor station. Nodes C and D process the data received from node A and perform their self-checking concurrently but this time the primary node C fails in passing the acceptance test or crashes during the processing of the data item whereas the shadow node D passes. Node D will learn the failure of node C by noticing the absence of output from node C. Node D then becomes a new primary and delivers its task execution results to both its successor computing station(s) and node C. Meanwhile, node C, if alive, attempts to become a new useful shadow node by making a retry of the processing of the saved data item. If node C passes the self-checking test this time, it can then continue as a useful shadow node and proceeds to the next task cycle.

In many applications, assumption (A1) does not hold. It is thus necessary to provide input data queues in each node within a PSP station. Each node may contain multiple input data queues corresponding to multiple data sources. Therefore, it is important for the partner nodes in a PSP station to ensure that they process the same data item in each task execution cycle. This is the main reason why the step of reporting the ID of the selected data item is taken by the primary node in Figure 8.2 and also in Figure 8.3. The gap between the time the primary node acquires a new input data item and the time the shadow node acquires a copy should be within a reasonable bound, certainly not to exceed a task execution cycle of the primary node by much. In addition, in typical DCS's with multicast channels, receiving data and placing them into input data queues within each node is handled by an independent unit (often called a LAN processor) operating concurrently with the main processor(s) in the node executing the application task(s).

8.3.2   The Algorithm Redundancy Component of the DRB Scheme

In order to support handling of not only hardware faults but also software faults, the above primary-shadow PSP scheme can be extended by incorporating the approach of using multiple versions of the application task procedure. Such versions are called *try blocks*. The extended scheme is the *distributed recovery block* (DRB) scheme and it uses the recovery block language construct to support the incorporation of try blocks and acceptance test [Hor74, Ran75, Ran94].

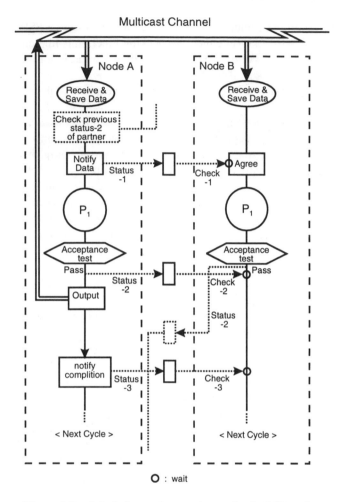

Figure 8.2   A fault-free task execution cycle of a PSP station

As seen in Chapter 1, Section 1.3, the syntax of recovery block is as follows: *ensure T by B₁ else by B₂ ⋯ else by Bₙ else error.* Here, *T* denotes the *acceptance test* (AT), B_1 the *primary try block*, and B_k, $2 \leq k \leq n$, the *alternate try blocks*. All the try blocks are designed to produce the same or similar computational results. The acceptance test is a logical expression representing the criterion for determining the acceptability of the execution results of the try blocks. A try (i.e., execution of a try block) is thus always followed by an acceptance test. If an error is detected during a try or as a result of an acceptance test execution, then a rollback-and-retry with another try block follows.

In the DRB scheme, a recovery block is replicated into multiple nodes forming a *DRB computing station* for parallel redundant processing. In most cases a recovery block containing just two try blocks is designed and then assigned to a pair of nodes as depicted in Figure 8.4. A try not completed within the maximum execution time allowed for each try block due to hardware faults or excessive looping is treated as a failure. Therefore, the acceptance test can be viewed as a combination of both *logic* and *time* acceptance tests.

As shown in Figure 8.4, the roles of the two try blocks are assigned differently in the

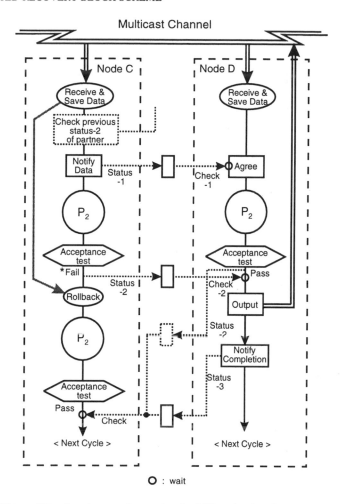

Figure 8.3   A task execution cycle of a PSP station involving a failure

two nodes. The governing rule is that *the primary node tries to execute the primary try block whenever possible whereas the shadow node tries to execute the alternate try block*. Therefore, primary node X uses try block *A* as the first try block initially, whereas shadow node Y uses try block *B* as the initial first try block. Until a fault is detected, both nodes receive the same input data, process the data by use of two different try blocks, and check the results by use of the acceptance test concurrently.

If the primary node fails and the shadow node passes its own acceptance test, the shadow immediately delivers its processing results to the successor computing stations. The two nodes then exchange their roles, i.e., the shadow assumes the primary's role. In case the shadow node fails, the primary node is not disturbed. Whichever node fails, the failed node attempts to become an operational shadow node without disturbing the (new) primary node; it attempts to roll back and retry with its second try block to bring its application computation state including local database up-to-date.

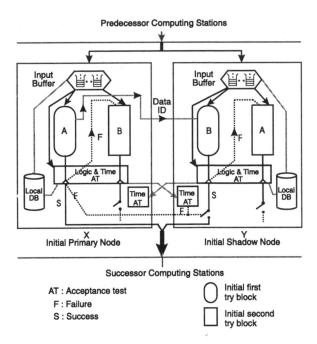

Figure 8.4   A DRB computing station

8.3.3   The Types of Faults Covered

In order to analyze the types of faults covered by the DRB scheme, it is useful to view a DRB station as consisting of three types of components : processing nodes (including a recovery block running), communication network, and processing-node-to-network links. In general, each component may exhibit two types of fault symptoms observable outside the component :

(1) *omission failures* (some expected outputs are never produced) of which special cases include continuous omission failures exhibited by crashed nodes and
(2) *faulty value output*.

The probability of a faulty value output being caused by the communication network or a node-network link can be reduced to a negligible level by incorporating relatively inexpensive mechanisms such as an error-correcting code scheme. A self-checking component structure is adopted to reduce the probability of a faulty value being output from the component. Internal audit mechanisms make a component to exhibit omission failures instead of outputting faulty values. An acceptance test is used in the DRB scheme as such an internal audit mechanism. Also, the damaging effects of omission failures of the communication network or a node-network link can be mitigated by the supplementary capabilities embedded in the sender and receiver computing components for detection of such communication failures and subsequent retry.

The DRB scheme is capable of real-time recovery from the omission failures of processing nodes and preventing faulty value output actions of processing nodes to the extent determined by the detection coverage of the acceptance test mechanism. The tolerated omission failures of a node in a DRB station include those caused by

(1) a fault in the internal hardware of a DRB station,

(2) a design defect in the operating system running on internal processing nodes of a DRB station, or

(3) a design defect in some application software modules used within a DRB station.

8.3.4 Strengths and Limitations

The DRB scheme has the following major useful characteristics:

a) Forward recovery can be accomplished in the same manner regardless of whether a node fails due to hardware faults or software faults;

b) The recovery time is minimal since maximum concurrency is exploited between the primary and the shadow nodes;

c) The increase in the processing turnaround time is minimal because the primary node does not wait for any status message from the shadow node;

d) The cost-effectiveness and the flexibility are high because

(d1) a DRB computing station can operate with just two try blocks and two processing nodes and

(d2) the two try blocks are not required to produce identical results and the second try block need not be as sophisticated as the first try block.

On the other hand, the DRB scheme imposes some restrictions on the use of the recovery block scheme. A recovery block to be used in the DRB scheme should be two-phase structured. That is, the computation segment encapsulated within a recovery block should consist of one input acquisition phase and one output phase. During the input phase, the recovery block must not involve any output step (i.e., sending computation results to the outside) while it may involve multiple input steps. Similarly, during the output phase, the recovery block may involve multiple output steps but not a single input step. This restriction is essential to prevent interdependency among different DRB stations for recovery from being formed.

More seriously, we can not even predict how effective the use of acceptance test routines and alternate algorithm implementations will be in achieving SFT. We simply do not understand enough about the nature of software faults in real-time DCS's. They are simply the only kinds of efforts of a general and systematic nature which a system designer can make with the hope of realizing SFT. In other words, use of software redundancy is the only systematic conceivable approach toward the goal of SFT and the acceptance test routines and alternate algorithm implementations are the two most fundamental types of software redundancy. Also, the recovery block structure is the most flexible and yet easily understandable and traceable structure for incorporation of software redundancy among all known structures. Therefore the underlying philosophy of the DRB scheme behind its adoption of the recovery block scheme as a component is simply to provide the most flexible structure which makes it easy for system designers to insert software redundancy into. Only future experimental studies will provide some indications of how effective system designers' redundant design efforts can be in achieving real-time SFT; this is not to imply that past experimental efforts did not produce some encouraging indicators but rather to point out that they have not produced cases sufficiently convincing to the general public.

8.3.5   Major Design Parameters

Three basic design parameters that must be chosen carefully to obtain a cost-effective DRB station, and that may be impacted by the types of communication architectures used, are the following.

(1) Mechanisms for ensuring input data consistency

Suppose each of the two fault-free partner nodes in a DRB station picks a new data item for the same task execution cycle. If these two data items have the same ID, then the two nodes are said to be preserving input data consistency. Complications can arise if the links between some nodes and the communication network are not reliable; certain data messages may arrive at one partner node but not at the other partner node. In general, it is necessary to take actions that explicitly ensure input data consistency.

(2) Mechanisms for sharing acceptance test results

The shadow node in a DRB station needs to learn the acceptance test result of its primary partner node with an acceptable delay. On the other hand, it is not essential in principle for the primary node to know the acceptance test result of the shadow node because as long as the primary node does not fail, it alone can satisfactorily meet the application requirements.

(3) Mechanisms for reliable communication of result data messages

Successful delivery of the result data message by the primary node to the successor computing station(s) must be confirmed by both partner nodes in the producer DRB station. In case of a failure, the primary node must learn it and then either make a retry for delivery or give up and become a new shadow node. (This means that the inability of a primary node to successfully deliver its computation result to at least one node in each successor computing station is treated as a failure of the primary node in performing a processing cycle. Upon such a failure the node attempts to become a new shadow node with the assumption that its partner node will detect the failure and become a new primary node.) The shadow node must also learn it so that it can decide whether or not to deliver its own result data message. This means that delivery of a result data message by the primary node must be followed by a reply with an acknowledgment message(s) by the successor computing station(s).

8.4   IMPLEMENTATION TECHNIQUES

8.4.1   Recursive Shadowing

The basic scheme described in Section 8.3 can easily be extended for use in configuring a DRB station consisting of more than two processing nodes and more than two try blocks. One of the most natural approaches is the *recursive shadowing* approach which is to treat the third node as a shadow node for the team of the first two nodes as depicted in Figure 8.5 [Kim91].

Node Z in the figure will normally use try block C as its primary try block and deliver its results only when both X and Y fail to produce acceptable results in time. Nodes X and Y behave like a single functional node with respect to interfacing with their shadow node Z. They must share responsibilities for providing their status information to node Z at various points as well as responsibilities for understanding the "useful/useless shadow" status of node Z. If node X or Y crashes, then it can be replaced by node Z and thus the computing station can start functioning as an ordinary two-node DRB station. Similarly, crash of node Z will result in the computing station functioning as an ordinary two-node DRB station. If both X and Y fail at their acceptance tests but are alive, then node Z becomes the new primary node

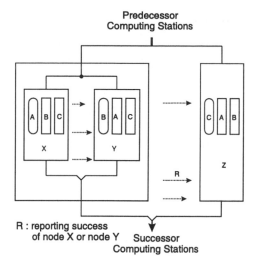

Figure 8.5   Recursive shadowing in the DRB scheme (adapted from [Kim91])

and one of the two failed nodes (X and Y) should become the new secondary node (a shadow for node Z) and the other should become the third node (a shadow for the team of Z and the secondary node).

In an n-node DRB station, the n-th node functions as a shadow for the team of the first $n - 1$ nodes. In the case of configuring a DRB station with two try blocks and three processing nodes, then the station structure will be essentially the same as that in Figure 8.5 except for the fact that node Z uses try block A as its first try block. A natural consequence of this recursive shadowing organization is the modest increase in the implementation complexity as the number of nodes used in a DRB station increases.

8.4.2   Virtual DRB (VDRB) Stations

When there are not enough nodes in a DCS to form dedicated DRB stations encapsulating all critical tasks in a given real-time application, an option worth exploring is to use the same node-pair to form multiple *virtual DRB* (VDRB) stations. Each of the VDRB stations hosted on the same node-pair is functionally equivalent to a DRB station when it is in execution using a time slice of the node-pair. Figure 8.6 illustrates a case of structuring VDRB stations.

An interesting requirement imposed on each node-pair supporting multiple VDRB stations is that the task schedulers on both partner nodes must schedule the executions of *virtual nodes* (i.e., constituent nodes of VDRB stations) such that the executions of *partner virtual nodes* (belonging to the same VDRB station) are maximally overlapped in time.

8.4.3   Supervisor Station

In a DCS consisting of multiple DRB stations, it is essential to incorporate a supervisor station [Hec91, Kim93a] or its decentralized equivalent. The supervisor station is in general responsible for the following:

(1) Detection of node crashes,

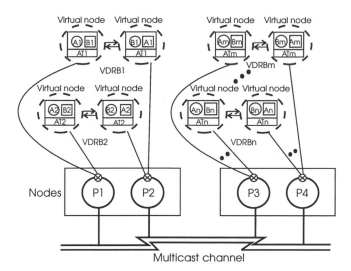

Figure 8.6   Virtual DRB stations

(2) Detection of misjudgments by the nodes in DRB stations about the status of their partner nodes (due to the faults occurring in communication links), and

(3) Network reconfiguration including task redistribution.

The first demonstration of the basic DRB scheme combined with the supervisor station was made by Hecht *et al* [Hec89, Hec91]. Often it is useful to structure the supervisor station itself in the form of a DRB station. Also, some of these functions, e.g., detection of node crashes, can be decentralized [Kop89, Mor86]. Research is currently active in this area.

The supervisor station can also detect the occurrence of a situation where the shadow node temporarily lags more than one task execution cycle behind the primary node. To do this will require the shadow node to periodically announce its progress.

8.4.4   LAN Based Systems vs. Highly Parallel Multicomputer Network (HPM) Based Systems

Since the DRB scheme is a technique for realizing a "hardened" real-time computing station and since both real-time computer systems based on highly parallel multi-computer networks (HPM's) and those based on LAN's can also be structured in the natural form of interconnections of real-time computing stations, the application fields of the DRB scheme cover both HPM based applications and LAN based applications. On the other hand, the differences in interconnection structures and mechanisms between the HPM's and the LAN's can have impacts on the approaches for implementation of DRB computing stations.

In LAN based systems, the inter-node communication costs are greater and the costs of providing redundant communication paths are greater. Therefore, the overhead of ensuring input data consistency at the beginning of each task cycle as well as the overhead for status exchange between the partner nodes is much greater in LAN based systems than in HPM based systems. On the other hand, the difference in communication time costs between an one-to-one message communication and a broadcast or multicast of a message in LAN-based system is relatively small whereas it is significant in HPM based systems. Also, in some HPM's, nodes may be connected via shared memory modules. In such HPM based systems, data queues hosted on shared memory modules serve as communication media between DRB stations as well as between partner nodes belonging to the same DRB stations. Therefore, noticeable differences exist between efficient implementations of the primary-shadow cooperating protocols (as well as in the protocols for interaction between the supervisor station and a DRB station) in LAN based systems and those in HPM based systems [Hec91, Kim91, Kim93a, Kim94a].

8.4.5 Acceptance Tests (AT's)

Since the emergence of the recovery block scheme, the quality of the acceptance test has been a subject of continuous debates. Experiences gathered so far on the design costs and the fault detection effectiveness of the acceptance tests are still inadequate. A number of useful principles in deriving cost-effective acceptance tests have been identified [Hec86, Ran94]. In the author's laboratory, we have taken the view that in real-time applications design of effective acceptance tests based on physical laws or apparent boundary conditions existing in application environments is much easier than producing effective acceptance tests in many non-real-time data processing applications. For example, in an aircraft control system, the variables representing acceleration and rate of change of acceleration are not expected to indicate that the pitch attitude has changed faster than at a certain rate, e.g., from level to pointing straight down in 1/50 of a second [Hec80].

As mentioned before, timing tests are essential parts of the acceptance tests in real-time systems. In addition, some hardware-implemented fault detectors are nowadays cost-effective candidates for incorporation in any sizable real-time computer systems. Such hardware detectors can significantly reduce the burden imposed on the software-implemented acceptance tests. For example, an extension of the DRB scheme under which each of the nodes (primary and shadow) in a DRB station is implemented in the form of a comparing processor-pair has important attractive characteristics . Such an augmented DRB station should exhibit much shorter *detection latency* for most hardware faults (since comparison in a processor-pair occurs every instruction cycle or internal bus cycle) than a DRB station with no such augmentation does. In such an augmented DRB station, only some rare types of hardware faults and software faults will escape the guards set by the comparing processor-pair mechanism and will have to be detected by the software-implemented acceptance test with concomitant larger detection latencies.

8.4.6 Incorporation of Complimentary HFT Techniques

One way to classify fault tolerance techniques is as follows.

(Class A): *Detection by Hardware AND Recovery management by Hardware.*
Examples include the TMR scheme and the PCP scheme.
(Class B): *Detection by Hardware AND Recovery management by Software.*
Examples include a combination of the comparing processor-pair scheme and the forward recovery exception handler scheme, a combination of hardware detectors and the recovery block scheme without the software-implemented acceptance test, and a combination of hardware detectors and the DRB scheme without the software-implemented acceptance test.

(Class C): *Detection by Software (with optional assistance of Hardware) AND Recovery management by Software.*

Examples include the recovery block scheme, the PSP scheme, the DRB scheme, and a combination of the software-implemented internal audit function (or the run-time assertion) approach and the exception handler scheme.

The class-C scheme with hardware detectors include class-B schemes as special cases. The DRB scheme can be used as such a scheme. The DRB scheme can also be combined with a class-A scheme.

8.4.7   Implementation Techniques for the Algorithm Redundancy Part

The approaches for designing alternate try blocks to be used in DRB stations are no different from those used in the recovery block scheme [Hor74, Ran75, Ran94] except that there are two-phase structuring restrictions discussed in Section 8.3.4. In designing alternate try blocks, exploitation of data structure diversity is a useful principle to follow. Also, the principles of developing diverse versions used in the NVP scheme are fully useful in designing alternate try blocks [Avi88].

8.5   EXPERIMENTAL VALIDATIONS OF REAL-TIME RECOVERY

Since the initial formulation of the DRB concept in 1983, several demonstrations of the performance of the scheme in practical application contexts were conducted. For example, several experiments involved application of the DRB scheme to adjacent computing stations in real-time parallel processing multi-computer testbeds. Other experimental applications of the DRB scheme to LAN based systems were also reported and several more advanced application developments are under way in several research organizations. In this section, a few representative examples are briefly reviewed.

8.5.1   Demonstrations of the DRB Scheme with Parallel Processing
Multi-computer Testbeds

The experiment carried out by the author and his colleagues initially at the University of South Florida (USF) and later at the University of California, Irvine (UCI) in mid-1980's [Kim89], was aimed for validating primarily the real-time recovery capability and the formulated implementation approach of the DRB scheme and secondarily the ability of the DRB scheme to detect and recover from the unforeseen design faults. While the experiment confirmed the real-time recovery capability and the implementation approach but came short of meeting the secondary, much more difficult objective.

The network configuration used is depicted in Figure 8.7. This network facility has been named the Macro-Dataflow Network (MDN). Each node in the MDN is a Z8000-based single-board microcomputer called the OEM-Z8000. The connection medium used between nodes is a two-port buffer memory developed in house and consisting of two independent memory banks of 16K bytes each. Nodes can exchange data through a two-port buffer memory nearly at the rate of local (on-board) memory access. A software nucleus implemented on each node supports concurrent programs consisting of asynchronous processes communicating through

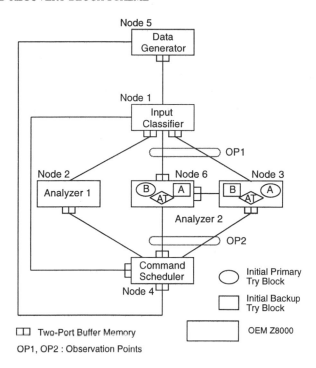

Figure 8.7   The parallel computing network configuration used for experimentation of the DRB scheme (adapted from [Kim89])

monitors, in particular, the programs written in the Extended Concurrent Pascal language [Bri77, Kim84b].

The distributed application program executed on the MDN during the experiment was written in Extended Concurrent Pascal. The distributed functions of this program are indicated in Figure 8.7. The DRB scheme was incorporated into nodes 3 and 6 (performing the Analyzer-2 function). Node 5 (Data generator) simulates a real-time device which generates stimulus data sent to the rest of the network and accepts the response (command). The remaining five data processing nodes contain an *input (i.e., stimulus data) classification process*, various *analysis processes*, constituting the intelligence of the solution algorithm, and a *control command scheduler process* that delivers the network's response to the real-time device. The stimulus data from Node 5 are first handled by the input classification process which distributes inputs to the rest of the network. The command scheduler process honors requests from various analysis processes to schedule commands for the real-time device.

The "travel times" of data sets passing through a computing station were measured to determine the execution overhead caused by the introduction of the DRB scheme into the network. As a part of facilitating this measurement, "observation points" were established in the network. When a data set arrives at the designated observation point in the network, the node stamps the real-time and saves a copy of the time-stamped data in its local memory. When enough measured data is obtained, the time-stamped data is transferred to another computer system for data analysis. The observation points are usually established at the points where the nodes are ready to send messages to the successor nodes and also at the points where the nodes have received messages.

In this experiment, two observation points were set up in the network. Figure 8.7 shows these points established in the network. Observation point 1 (OP1) is set up where the primary and shadow nodes have taken the data set from the queue buffers connected to the predecessor node. Observation point 2 (OP2) is set up where both nodes are ready to put the result data sets into the queue buffers connected to the successor node.

During experimentation, faults were injected to examine their impacts on system performance. The types of faults studied include: 1) total node failure (simulated by node reset); 2) transient hardware faults simulated by random changes in the contents of certain memory locations; and 3) software faults such as infinite looping, arithmetic overflow, etc. The recovery block incorporated into nodes 3 and 6 in Figure 8.7 was written in Extended Concurrent Pascal and executed on an OEM-Z8000 microcomputer with a clock rate of 4M-Hz.

The DRB execution overhead consists of interprocess communication among nodes and the execution of the acceptance test. The overhead was evaluated by comparing the delay between OP1 and OP2 in the case of using the DRB against the delay in the case without the DRB. The gap between the two delays is the execution time increase due to the incorporation of the DRB. The average execution time increase measured was approximately 30 ms (milliseconds). Moreover, measurements were taken in instances where arithmetic overflows occurred in the primary node and the fast recovery capabilities of the DRB scheme were exercised. We noted that the fault occurrences and subsequent recovery actions did not cause any visible degradation of the system performance. Again, in the absence of fault, the execution time increase is caused mainly by the execution of the acceptance test and the communication of the acceptance test success to the backup node.

Considering the inefficient implementation language (Extended Concurrent Pascal), and the slow processor (4 M-Hz Z8001) used, the amount of execution time increase mentioned above is at least 20 times higher than that expected in the systems built with current off-the-shelf hardware and software tools. For example, use of a processor running at 20 M-Hz will result in speedup by a factor of 5. Use of a more efficient language (C or an assembly language in the extreme case) will result in additional speedup by a factor of about 4.

Figure 8.8 shows the case where the primary node is reset, resulting in the crash of the node. Later an arithmetic overflow occurs in the remaining node. The recovery from the first fault (the crash of the primary node) took about 60 ms. This recovery time is largely a function of the timeout period used in the DRB. When the second fault (the arithmetic overflow) occurred in the remaining node after the crash of the first node, the node had no choice but to roll back and retry with try block B. Therefore, the recovery time was very high, i.e., about 290 ms, as shown in the figure. Again, the recovery time can be easily reduced by a factor of 20 by implementing real application systems with current off-the-shelf tools.

The data discussed above was one indicator that the DRB scheme could be used in many real-time applications with tolerable amounts of time overhead.

Other experiments conducted with different parallel processing machines were reported in [Kim89, Kim91].

8.5.2   Demonstrations of the DRB Scheme with LAN Based DCS's

Another major validation of the DRB scheme was conducted by a small company located in Los Angeles (SoHaR, Inc). They extended the DRB scheme for use in real-time local area PC networks for nuclear reactor control applications and produced a product prototype [Hec89, Hec91]. This was also the first demonstration of the basic DRB scheme combined with the

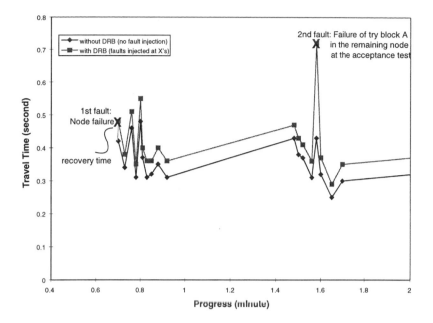

Figure 8.8   Data travel time measured (adapted from [Kim89])

supervisor station scheme. Figure 8.9 depicts a high level view of the product prototype developed.

This validation work confirmed the logical soundness of the implementation model of the DRB scheme augmented with the supervisor station scheme as well as the real-time recovery capability. However, it also came short of validating the the ability of the DRB scheme to detect and recover from the unforeseen design faults.

Quite a few other experimental applications of the DRB scheme to LAN based real-time DCS's have been performed [Arm91, Fra91, Kim94a] and some more are currently underway.

8.6 ISSUES REMAINING FOR FUTURE RESEARCH

8.6.1 Validation of Software Fault Detection and Recovery

While the potential of the DRB scheme, the recovery block scheme, and the NVP scheme for detecting and recovering from software faults has been widely recognized in the research community, the mission of demonstrating this capability in convincing application contexts still remains to be accomplished. Successful accomplishment of this mission will require long-term persistent research effort since use of artificially injected faults will be an invalid approach. The application system used also needs to be of considerable complexity since otherwise the convincing cases of software fault occurrences are not likely to be encountered [Hua93]. In parallel with such experimental efforts, the work on analytical modeling and

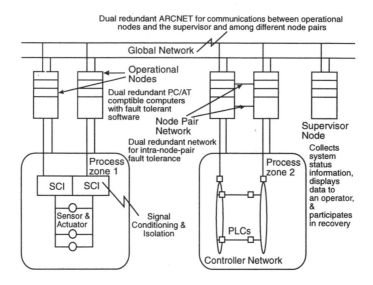

Figure 8.9   The DRB-based fault-tolerant LAN architecture developed by SoHaR, Inc.

evaluation of the potential has been under way (e.g., [Dug94]) and produced some useful insights into the nature of software fault tolerance .

8.6.2   Integration with Real-time Network Configuration Management (NCM)

As mentioned in Section 8.4.3, some functions, if not all, of the supervisor station can be decentralized. The functions of the supervisor stations are all related to real-time network configuration management (NCM). This area is not mature yet. However, rapid progresses are expected in the next several years. Cost-effective integration of the DRB scheme and the emerging real-time NCM techniques is an important issue for future research in design of fault-tolerant real-time DCS's.

8.6.3   Adaptation of the DRB Scheme to Object Based Systems

Object-oriented structuring is now a firmly established principle not only in generic software engineering but also in development of real-time computer systems [Bih89, Kop90, Kim94b]. Efficient adaptation of the DRB scheme to object-oriented DCS structures is thus a meaningful subject for future research.

8.6.4   Handling of Faults Crossing DRB Station Boundaries

Since it is not practical to assume that the acceptance tests will have perfect fault detection coverage in all applications, it will be meaningful in some applications to consider what supplementary mechanisms can be provided to handle such faults crossing DRB station boundaries. Some promising approaches have been proposed [Bes81, And83, Anc90, Kim93b] but demonstrations of the effectiveness of the approaches have lagged behind and will require considerable amount of efforts in the future. Also, firm establishment of such schemes is required to address the issue of tolerating integration faults mentioned in Section 8.2.2 to a greater extent than that to which the DRB scheme addresses.

8.7 CONCLUSIONS

The DRB scheme is a cost-effective approach of basic nature for realizing both hardware fault tolerance (HFT) and Software fault tolerance (SFT) in real-time distributed and/or parallel computer systems. A reasonably rich set of implementation techniques have been established and thus the DRB scheme is a practical technology available for use in a broad range of real-time safety critical applications. However, further research, especially on the issues discussed in Section 8.6, is needed to realize the full potential of the DRB scheme.

ACKNOWLEDGEMENTS

The work reported here was supported in part by US Navy, NSWC Dahlgren Division under Contract No. N60921-92-C-0204, in part by the University of California MICRO Program under Grant No. 93-080, and in part by a grant from Hitachi Co., Ltd.

REFERENCES

[Anc90]   M. Ancona, G. Dodero, V. Gianuzzi, A. Clematis, and E.B. Fernandez. A system architecture for fault tolerance in concurrent software. *IEEE Computer*, 23–32, October 1990.

[And83]   T. Anderson and J.C. Knight. A framework for software fault tolerance in real-time system. *IEEE Transactions on Software Engineering*, 355–364, May 1983.

[Arm91]   L.T. Armstrong and T.F. Lawrence. Adaptive fault tolerance. In *Proc. 1991 NSWC Systems Design Synthesis Technology Workshop*, Silver Spring, September 1991.

[Avi71]   A. Avižienis, G. Gilley, G.C. Mathur, D. Rennels, J.A. Rohr, and D.K. Rubin. The STAR (self testing and repairing) computer: an investigation of the theory and practice of fault-tolerant computer design. *IEEE Transactions on Computers*, C-20(11):1312–1321, November 1971.

[Avi75]   A. Avižienis. Fault tolerance and fault intolerance: complementary approaches to reliable computing. In *Proc. 1975 International Conference on Reliable Software*, pages 458–464, Los Angeles, April 1975.

[Avi85]   A. Avižienis. The N-version approach to fault-tolerant software. *IEEE Transactions on Software Engineering*, SE-11(12):1491–1501, December 1985.

[Avi88]   A. Avižienis, M.R. Lyu, and W. Schuetz. In search of effective diversity: a six-language study of fault-tolerant flight control software. In *Proc. 18th International Symposium on Fault-Tolerant Computing*, pages 15–22, Tokyo. IEEE Computer Society Press.

[Bes81]   E. Best and B. Randell. A formal model of atomicity in asynchronous systems. *Acta Informatica*, Springer-Verlag, 16:93–124, 1981.

[Bih89]   T. Bihari, P. Gopinath, and K. Schwan. Object-oriented design of real-time software. In *Proc. 10th Real-Time Systems Symposium*, pages 194–201, 1989. IEEE Computer Society Press.

[Bri77]   P. Brinch Hansen. *The Architecture of Concurrent Programs*. Prentice Hall, 1977.

[Car85]   W.C. Carter. Hardware fault tolerance. Chapter 2 in T. Anderson, editor, volume 1 of *Resilient Computing Systems*, pages 11–63, 1985. Wiley-Interscience.

[Dug94]   J.B. Dugan and M.R. Lyu. System-level reliability and sensitivity analyses for three fault-tolerant system architectures. In *Proc. 4th International Working Conference on Dependable Computing for Critical Applications*, IFIP 10.4 Working Group, pages 295–307, January 1994.

[Fra91]   J.S. Fraga, V. Rodrigues, and E.S. Silva. A language approach to implementation of the distributed recovery block schemes. In *Proc. 13th. CBC Conference on Computer Sciences*, Gramado, Brazil, August 1991.

[Hec80]   H. Hecht. Issues in fault-tolerant software for real-time control applications. In *Proc. 4th International Computer Software and Applications Conference (COMPSAC)*, pages 603–607, October 1980. IEEE Computer Society Press,

[Hec86]   H. Hecht and M. Hecht. Fault-tolerant software. Chapter 10 in D.K. Pradhan, editor, volume 2 of *Fault-Tolerant Computing: Theory and Techniques*. Prentice Hall, 1986.

[Hec89]   M. Hecht, J. Agron, and S. Hochhauser. A distributed fault tolerant architecture for nuclear reactor control and safety functions. In *Proc. 1989 Real-Time Systems Symposium*, pages 214–221, December 1989. IEEE Computer Society Press.

[Hec91]   M. Hecht et al. A distributed fault tolerant architecture for nuclear reactor and other critical process control applications. In *Proc. 21st International Symposium on Fault-Tolerant Computing*, Montreal, June 1991, pages 462–469. IEEE Computer Society Press.

[Hor74]   J.J. Horning, H.C. Lauer, P.M. Melliar-Smith, and B. Randell. A program structure for error detection and recovery. *Lecture Notes in Computer Science*, 16:171–187, Springer-Verlag, New York, NY, 1974.

[Hua93]   Y. Huang and C.M.R. Kintala. Software implemented fault tolerance: technologies and experience. In *Proc. 21st International Symposium on Fault-Tolerant Computing*, pages 2–9, June 1993. IEEE Computer Society Press.

[Kim84a] K.H. Kim. Distributed execution of recovery blocks: an approach to uniform treatment of hardware and software faults. In *Proc. 4th International Conference on Distributed Computing Systems*, pages 526–532, May 1984. IEEE Computer Society Press.

[Kim84b] K.H. Kim. Evolution of a virtual machine supporting fault-tolerant distributed processes at a research laboratory. In *Proc. 1st International Conference on Data Engineering*, pages 620–628, Los Angeles, April 1984. IEEE Computer Society Press.

[Kim89]   K.H. Kim and H.O. Welch. Distributed execution of recovery blocks: an approach to uniform treatment of hardware and software faults in real-time applications. *IEEE Transactions Computers*, pages 626–636, May 1989.

[Kim91]   K.H. Kim and B.J. Min. Approaches to implementation of multiple DRB stations in tightly coupled computer networks and an experimental validation. In *Proc. 15th International Computer Software and Applications Conference (COMPSAC 91)*, pages 550–557, Tokyo, September 1991. IEEE Computer Society Press.

[Kim93a] K.H. Kim. Structuring DRB computing stations in highly decentralized Systems. In *Proc. International Symposium on Autonomous Decentralized Systems*, pages 305–314, Kawasaki, March 1993. IEEE Computer Society Press.

[Kim93b] K.H. Kim. Design of loosely coupled processes capable of time-bounded cooperative recovery: the PTC/SL scheme. *Computer Communications*, 16(5):305–316, May 1993.

[Kim94a] K.H. Kim, L.F. Bacellar, K. Masui, K. Mori and R. Yoshizawa. Modular implementation model for real-time fault-tolerant LAN systems based on the DRB scheme with a configuration supervisor. In *Computer System Science & Engineering*, 9(2):75–82, April 1994.

[Kim94b] K.H. Kim and H. Kopetz. A real-time object model RTO.k and an experimental investigation of its potentials. In *Proc. 18th International Computer Software and Applications Conference (COMPSAC 94)*, Taipei, IEEE Computer Society Press, November 1994.

[Kop89]   H. Kopetz, G. Grunsteidl, and J. Reisinger. Fault-tolerant membership service in a synchronous distributed real-time system. In *Proc. International Working Conference on Dependable Computing for Critical Applications*, IFIP 10.4 Working Group, pages 167–174, Santa Barbara, August 1989.

[Kop90]   H. Kopetz and K.H. Kim. Temporal uncertainties in interaction among real-time objects. In *Proc. 9th Symposium on Reliable Distributed Systems*, pages 165–174, Huntsville, October 1990. IEEE Computer Society Press.

[Lee78]   P.A. Lee. A reconsideration of the recovery block scheme. *Computer Journal*, 21(4):306–310, November 1978.

[Mor86]   K. Mori. Autonomous decentralized software structure and its application. In *Proc. Fall Joint Computer Conference*, pages 1056–1063, Dallas, November 1986.

[Ran75]   B. Randell. System structure for software fault tolerance. *IEEE Transactions on Software Engineering*, pages 220–232, June 1975.

[Ran94]   B. Randell and J. Xu. The evolution of the recovery block concept. *Chapter 1 in this book*.

[Toy87]   W.N. Toy. Fault-tolerant computing. A Chapter in *Advances in Computers*. volume 26, pages 201–279. Academic Press, 1987.

[Wil85]   D. Wilson. The STRATUS computer system. Chapter 12 in T. Anderson, editor, volume 1 of *Resilient Computing Systems* pages 45–67. Wiley-Interscience, 1985.

[Yau75]   S.S. Yau and R.C. Cheung. Design of self-checking software. In *Proc. International Conference on Reliable Software*, pages 450–457, 1975.

9

Software Fault Tolerance by Design Diversity

PETER BISHOP

Adelard, England

ABSTRACT

This chapter reviews the use of software diversity, and especially multi-version programming, as a means of improving system reliability and safety. It considers the theoretical and experimental research undertaken in this field together with some of the more pragmatic issues in implementing diversity. Some alternatives to multi-version programming are also considered. The author concludes that software diversity is a viable option for improving reliability, and the extra costs could well be justifiable in an overall project context. However it is not the only option, and better results might be obtained by employing diversity at a higher level.

9.1 INTRODUCTION

Diversity as a basic concept has been around for many years as reflected in the old adage of "Do not put all your eggs in one basket". A more concrete example of this approach can be given in the Manhattan Project when the first nuclear pile was being constructed. In this case, the diverse shut-down system was a man with an axe who could cut a rope to release the shutdown rods.

Generally speaking, diversity is a protection against *uncertainty*, and the greater the uncertainty (or the greater the consequences of failure), the more diversity is employed. This concept of 'defense in depth' is reflected in, for example, aircraft control systems and nuclear plant protection. At the general systems engineering level, diversity is an established approach for addressing critical applications. Such an approach tends to utilize sub-systems that are functionally different (e.g. concrete containment, shutdown rods, boronated water, etc.). Even when subsystems perform a broadly similar function, the implementation technology can differ (e.g. using discrete logic or a computer system).

With the advent of computers, N-version software diversity has been proposed [Avi77] as a means of dealing with the uncertainties of design faults in a computer system implementation. Since that time there have been a number of computer systems which are based on the diverse software concept including railway interlocking and train control [And81], Airbus flight controls [Tra88], and protection of the Darlington nuclear reactor [Con88].

The main question to ask is "does software diversity buy you more reliability?". From a systems engineering viewpoint, if the software diversity is ineffective or too costly, there may be alternative design options at the systems engineering level that are more cost-effective. The remainder of this chapter will attempt to address this question, by summarizing research in this area, reviewing the practical application of diversity, and discussing where diversity can be most effectively applied.

9.2   N-VERSION PROGRAMMING RESEARCH

The key element of N-version programming approach is *diversity*. By attempting to make the development processes diverse it is hoped that the versions will contain diverse faults. It is assumed that such diverse faults will minimize the likelihood of coincident failures. A much stronger assumption is that 'ideal' diverse software would exhibit *failure independence*. In this model the probability of simultaneous failure of a pair of programs A and B is simply $Pf_A.Pf_B$ where Pf is the probability of failure for a program execution.

Over the years a range of experiments have been mounted to test these underlying assumptions. The experiments have examined factors that could affect the diversity of the development process, including:

- independent teams
- diverse specification and implementation methods
- management controls

The common features in all these experiments are the use of independent teams to produce diverse programs, followed by acceptance testing the diverse versions, and some form of comparison testing (either against each other or against a 'golden' program) to detect residual faults and estimate reliability. Table 9.1 summarizes some typical N-version experiments.

The performance of N-version programming has been assessed by a number of different criteria, including:

- diversity of faults
- empirical reliability improvement
- comparison with the independence assumption

Some of the main results in these areas will be discussed below:

9.2.1   Fault Diversity

Most of the early research in this area [Dah79, Gme80, Vog82, Kel83, Dun86] focused on analyzing the software faults produced and the empirical improvement in reliability to be gained from design diversity.

Table 9.1 Summary of some N-version programming experiments

Experiment	Specs	Languages	Versions	Reference
Halden, Reactor Trip	1	2	2	[Dah79]
NASA, First Generation	3	1	18	[Kel83]
KFK, Reactor Trip	1	3	3	[Gme80]
NASA/RTI, Launch Interceptor	1	3	3	[Dun86]
UCI/UVA , Launch Interceptor	1	1	27	[Kni86a]
Halden (PODS), Reactor Trip	2	2	3	[Bis86]
UCLA, Flight Control	1	6	6	[Avi88]
NASA (2nd Gen.) Inertial Guidance	1	1	20	[Eck91]
UI/Rockwell, Flight Control	1	1	15	[Lyu93]

One common outcome of these experiments was that a significant proportion of the faults were similar, and the major cause of these common faults was the specification. Since faults in the design and coding stages tended to be detected earlier, quite a high proportion of specification-related faults were present in the final program versions. For example in the KFK experiment, 12 specification faults were found out of a total of 104, but after acceptance testing 10 specification-related faults were still present out of a total of 18. The major deficiencies in the specifications were incompleteness and ambiguity which caused the programmer to make incorrect (and potentially common) design choices (e.g. in the KFK experiment there were 10 cases where faults were common to two of the three versions).

An extreme example of this general trend can be found in the Project on Diverse Software (PODS) [Bis86]. The project had three diverse teams (in England, Norway and Finland) implementing a simple nuclear reactor protection system application. With good quality control and experienced programmers *no design-related faults were found* when the diverse programs were tested back-to-back. All the faults were caused by omissions and ambiguities in the requirements specification. However, due to the differences in interpretation between the programmers, five of the faults occurred in a single version only, and two common faults were found in two versions.

Clearly any common faults limit the degree of reliability improvement that is possible, and it would certainly be unreasonable to expect failure independence in such cases. Some of the experiments have incorporated diverse specifications [Kel83, Bis86] which can potentially reduce specification-related common faults. In general it was found that the use of relatively formal notations was effective in reducing specification-related faults caused by incompleteness and ambiguity. The value of using diverse specifications on a routine basis is less obvious; the performance in minimizing common design faults is uncertain, and there is a risk that the specifications will not be equivalent. In practice, only a single good specification method would be used unless it could be shown that diverse specifications were mathematically equivalent.

The impact of the programming language has also been evaluated in various experiments such as [Dah79, Bis86, Avi88]. In general fewer faults seem to occur in the strongly typed, highly structured languages such as Modula 2 and Ada while low level assembler has the worst performance. However the choice of language seems to bear little relationship to the incidence of common specification-related or design-related faults, or the eventual performance the programs after acceptance testing.

In recent years there has been a focus on the 'design paradigm' for N-version programming to improve the overall quality and independence of the diverse developments [Avi88, Lyu93].

This is discussed in detail in Chapter 2, but one important feature of the model is the protocol for communication between the development teams and the project co-ordinator. When a problem is identified in the specification, a revision is broadcast to all teams and subsequently followed-up to ensure that the update has been acted upon. This helps to remove specification-related faults at an earlier stage. It is of course important to have a good initial specification since the project co-ordinator can become very overloaded. This situation was observed in the NASA experiment [Kel88] where there was an average of 150 questions per team compared with 11 questions per team in [Lyu93].

The first experiment using this paradigm (the UCLA Six Language Experiment) [Avi88] found only two specification-related common faults (out of a total of 93 faults). These were caused by procedural problems (illegible text and failure to respond to a specification change) and the paradigm was modified to eliminate these problem. In the following experiment [Lyu92, Lyu93], no specification-related faults were found after acceptance testing. The acceptance testing applied was far more extensive than earlier experiments and a lower number of residual faults were found compared with earlier experiments (e.g. around 0.5 faults/KLOC after one acceptance test, 0.05 after both acceptance tests). This is a significant improvement on around 3 faults/KLOC for the Knight and Leveson experiment and 1 fault/KLOC for the NASA experiment.

Perhaps the most important improvement to be noted is the reduction in identical or very similar faults. Table 9.2 shows how many similar faults were created during program development of some experiments, including both common implementation faults and specification faults. Table 9.2 also shows the *fault span* (the number of versions in which the same fault exists).

Table 9.2   Distribution of similar faults in some experiments

Experiment	Similar faults	Max fault span	Versions
Knight and Leveson	8	4	27
NASA	7	5	20
UCLA Flight Control	2	2	6
UI/RI Flight Control	2	2	12

One way of interpreting these results is to assess the capability of a set of diverse versions to mask faults completely. This can be done by computing the odds (in a gambling sense) that a randomly chosen tuple of program versions will contain a majority of fault-free versions.

If we assume that, after development, there is a probability p of a fault-free program, then it is easy to show that the chance of a fault-masking triple is:

$$p^2(3 - 2p)$$

So where the chance of a fault-free version is 50%, the chance of creating a fault-masking triple is also 50%. The odds of fault masking triples are computed in Table 9.3 for a number of experiments based on the quoted number of fault-free versions.

Note that Table 9.3 computes the probability of selecting a failure-masking triple from an arbitrarily large population of versions. This does not correspond exactly to the number of failure masking triples that can be constructed from the finite set of versions available in the experiments. For example in the UI/RI (AT2) case, 100% of triples are failure-masking.

The above analysis works on the pessimistic assumption that all faulty versions contain

Table 9.3   Computed odds of fault masking triples

Experiment	Versions	Fault-free	Fault-masking triple (%)
Knight and Leveson	27	6	12.6
NASA	20	10	50.0
UI/RI (AT1)	12	7	68.4
UI/RI (AT2)	12	11	98.0

similar faults that cannot be masked. If however the odds of faults being dissimilar are incorporated, then the chance of a fault-masking triple is increased. For example in the Knight and Leveson experiment, the maximum fault span is 4 in 27 programs. If we assume the probability of dissimilar or no faults to be 85% (23:27) the odds of selecting a fault-masking triple would increase to 94%.

In the NASA experiment, the largest fault span is 5 (out of 10 faulty versions). Using a figure of 75% for the odds of a version that is fault-free or dissimilar, the odds of failure masking triple increase to 84%. This estimate is probably an upper bound since dissimilar faults do not guarantee dissimilar failures, so complete masking of failures is not guaranteed.

Similar analyses can be performed for a fail-safe pair (a configuration that is often used in shutdown systems). In this case, a fail-safe action is taken if either version disagrees, so the pair is only unsafe if both versions are faulty. This would occur with probability $(1 - p)^2$, which means that the risk of unsafe pair can be up to 3 times less than the risk of a non-masking triple. Some example figures are shown in Table 9.4:

Table 9.4   Fail-safe probability analysis

Prob. version Fault-free	Prob. of Fault-masking Triple	Prob. of Fail-safe Pair
0.5	0.50	0.75
0.75	0.84	0.94
0.9	0.97	0.99

The use of odds for such applications is rather problematic, and might not be regarded as an acceptable argument especially where the software is safety-related. A more convincing argument could be made if it could be demonstrated that reliability is improved even when the majority of versions are faulty. The improvement that can actually be achieved is determined by the degree of failure dependency between the diverse versions, and this topic is discussed in the following section.

9.2.2   Evaluation of Failure Dependency

One strong assumption that can be made about diversity is that the failures of diverse versions will be independent. An experimental test of the assumption of independence was reported in [Kni86a, Kni86b]. In this experiment, a set of 27 programs were implemented to a common Missile Launch Interceptor specification. This experiment rejected the failure independence assumption to a high confidence level. Furthermore, these dependent failures were claimed to be due to *design faults only*, rather than faults in the specification. Analysis of the faults within the 27 programs showed that programmers tended to make similar mistakes.

Obviously the specification would be a potential source of similar mistakes and hence dependent failures, but specification was claimed to not to affect the outcome. The main justifications for this claim were careful independent review and that fact that it had built on the experience of an earlier experiment [Dun86].

At the time there was some dispute over the results of this experiment, particularly over the realism of an experiment which used students rather than professional software developers. However, the results of the empirical study were supported by a theoretical analysis of coincident failure [Eck85] which showed that, if mistakes were more likely for some specific input values, then dependent failures would be observed. This theory was later refined [Lit89] to show that it was possible to have cases where dependent failures occurred *less frequently* than predicted by the independence assumption. The underlying idea here is that the 'degree of difficulty' distribution is not necessarily the same for all implementors. If the distribution can be altered by using different development processes, then failures are likely to occur in different regions of the input space, so the failures could in principle be negatively correlated.

Another experimental evaluation of failure dependency was made in a follow-up to the PODS project [Bis87]. Rather than testing for independence, this experiment measured the *degree of dependency* between the faults in early versions of the PODS programs (which contained both specification- and implementation-related faults).

The experiment used modified versions of the original PODS programs where individual faults could be switched on, so it was possible to measure the individual and coincident failure rates of all possible fault pairs and make comparisons with the independence assumption. For comparison purposes a *dependency factor* D was defined as the ratio of actual coincident failure rate to that predicted by the independence assumption, i.e.:

$$D = P_{ab}/(P_a.P_b)$$

The observed distribution of dependency factors for the fault pairs is summarized in Figure 9.1. In this diagram independent fault pairs would have a dependency factor of unity. In practice, the distribution of dependency factors ranged from strong positive correlation to strong negative correlation. These extreme values were well beyond the calculated 95% confidence limits for the independence assumption.

On analysis, it was found that the strongly negatively correlated failures occurred between similar functions in the two diverse programs, however the faults exhibited a *failure bias* on a binary value. In one program the failure (when it occurred) produced a '1', while in the other program, the failure value was always '0'. This meant that coincident failures would never occur because one function was always correct when the diverse function was faulty. Such biased failures are an interesting example of a specific mechanism which could result in negatively correlated failures.

Most of the positively correlated (high dependency factor) fault pairs were related to the known common mode faults caused by problems in the requirements specification. However some strange clusters of high dependency fault pairs were observed which could not be accounted for by the known common mode faults (see the high dependency 'plateaus' in Figure 9.1). On examination, two of the high dependency plateaus were associated with failures on the same single-bit output, but it was difficult to explain the very similar levels of dependency, as there was little or no commonality between the input data variables, the faults, or the observed failure rates.

Eventually it was found that these common dependency levels were caused by 'error masking' [Bis89]. The single-bit output value was determined by an 'OR' of several logical

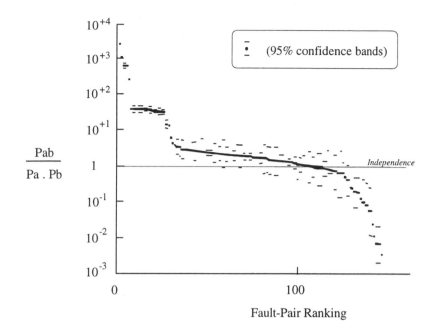

Figure 9.1 Dependency factors for PODS fault pairs

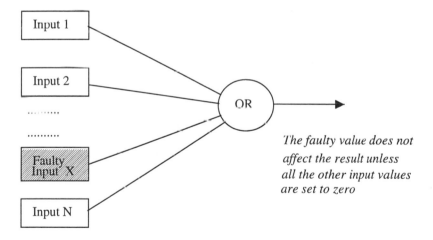

Figure 9.2 Error masking with OR logic

conditions as shown in Figure 9.2. This meant that an incorrectly calculated condition value could not be observed at the output unless all the other logical conditions were zero. This masking of internal errors causes dependent failures to be observed *even if the internal error rates are independent.*

The OR gate tends acts as a common 'shutter' for the internal errors and will tend to open simultaneously on both versions because it is controlled by common program input values. This 'shutter effect' results in correlation of the externally observed failures; high internal error rates have low externally observable failure rates (due to shutter closure), but exhibit high coincident failure rates (when the shutter opens).

In the case of the OR gate, it can be shown that for independent internal failures, the dependency factor approximates to $1/P0$, where $P0$ is the probability of observing a zero (logical false) at the OR output in a fault-free program. This dependency level is not affected by the error rates of the internal faults, which explains why the plateau of similar dependency factors were observed.

This error masking effect is a general property of programs. Any output variable whose computation relies on masking functions is likely to exhibit dependent failures in diverse implementations. Simple examples of masking functions are AND gates, OR gates, MAX and MIN functions or selection functions (IF .. THEN .. ELSE, case, etc.). In all these functions it is possible to identify cases where a faulty input value can be masked by the remaining inputs to yield a correct result. In fact any N to M mapping function is capable of some degree of masking provided M is smaller, so this phenomenon will occur to some extent in all programs.

Interestingly, the Launch Interceptor example contains a large number of OR gates within its specification (see Figure 9.3). The failure masking process for the Launch Interceptor conditions (LICs) is somewhat different from the PODS example, but analysis indicates that dependency factors of one or two orders of magnitude are possible [Bis91]. In experimental terms therefore, the Launch Interceptor example could be something of a 'worst case' in terms of the degree of error masking that might be anticipated.

The more recent experiments by NASA, UCLA and UI/RI have also attempted to estimate reliability improvement. In these examples, there is very little scope for error masking. For example the RSDIMU inertial measurement system [Kel88] has a limited number of inputs and performs arithmetic computations which have limited potential for masking. This is also true for the aircraft automatic lander example [Avi88]. If error masking were the only source of dependency, low coincident failure rates might be expected. In practice, the reliability improvements for arbitrary triples were still limited by dependent failures.

The NASA program versions contained significant numbers of near-identical design and specification-related faults (largely caused by misunderstanding of the specification or by a lack of understanding of the problem). This affected the achieved reliability very markedly and a statistically unbiased estimation of the reliability showed that the average failure rate of a triple was only 4 times lower than a single version.

However the variability in improvement is very wide. Depending on the operating mode, between 60% to 80% of triples successfully masked *all* failures. This is not too surprising since 50% of the triples contain only one faulty version (as discussed in the previous section). Of the remaining triples, some provided reliability improvements of possibly one order of magnitude, but the others (containing a high proportion of similar faults) exhibited very modest improvements (e.g. 10% of the triples gave a 20% reduction or less).

While common faults were the major cause of poor performance, it is interesting to note that two dissimilar faults lead to high levels of coincident failure. This may again be an inherent feature of the program function (but unrelated the error masking effect). In the NASA experiment there is one function called the Fault Detection and Isolation (FDI) module. This module is responsible for detecting faulty sensors so that subsequent modules can compute the acceleration using the remaining 'good' sensors. The two dissimilar faults affected this module. A fault in this module should cause too many (or too few) sensors to be used. In either circumstance the computed result will disagree with the 'golden' value. The significant feature is that failures in the faulty versions are likely to coincide with a change in the failure

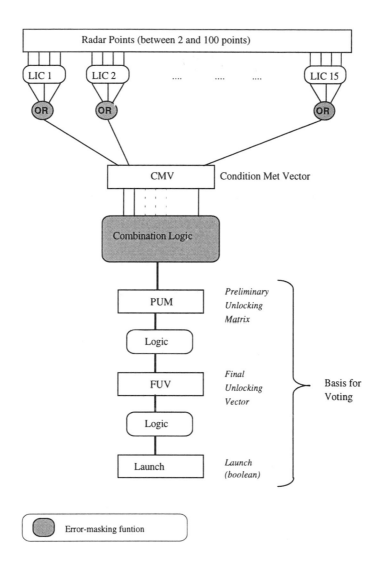

Figure 9.3   The Launch Interceptor application

status of a sensor. This would cause a 'burst' of coincident failures (even if the reasons for the sensor diagnosis errors differ).

The reliability improvements achieved in the UI/RI flight controller example are somewhat better. Using the versions obtained after acceptance test 1 (AT1), the reliability improvement for an average triple was around 13. This estimate did not include the error correction capability of the voting system. If this is included the average reliability improvement factor is increased to around 58.

The improved performance is largely the result of better quality programs containing fewer common faults which spanned fewer program versions. While there is no direct analysis of the distribution of reliability improvements over the triples, there is likely to be a significant amount of variability. It is known that at least 68% of triples must mask all failures (from the earlier fault distribution analysis), while the triples with similar faults (under 10%) are likely to exhibit only modest improvements. The remaining triples might exhibit quite large reliability improvements. In principle the improvement might approach that predicted by the independence assumption (as they did in PODS), but other sources of dependency such as the mechanism discussed in the NASA experiment could limit the gains.

The main lesson to be learned from these experiments is that the performance of N-version is seriously limited if common faults are likely. The most probable sources are likely to be common implementation mistakes (e.g. omitted cases or simple misunderstanding of the problem) together with omissions and ambiguities in the specification. These factors need to be closely controlled to minimize the risks and the diverse programming paradigm seems to have made an important contribution. The risks could be further reduced if it possible to predict where such common faults are likely to occur so that more effort can be devoted to these areas. The use of metrics to identify 'tough spots' in the program functions [Lyu94] seems to be a promising approach.

9.3 PITFALLS IN THE DESIGN OF N-VERSION EXPERIMENTS

When N-version programming experiments are performed it is quite easy to introduce common mode failures as an inherent feature of the experimental design. It is important that the experimenter should be aware of these risks. This section gives some examples of experimental design problems which are partly based on the author's own experience on the PODS project.

9.3.1 Faulty Acceptance Tests and Golden Programs

In diversity experiments, the individual programs are normally subjected to acceptance tests before being checked for failure dependency. In subsequent testing, failures are normally established by comparing the results produced by the diverse version against those from a 'golden' program. In the STEM project [Bis87] (a follow-up to PODS) early versions of the PODS programs were tested back-to-back *without an acceptance test*. Surprisingly, the eventual 'silver' programs produced by this process differed from the original 'perfect' PODS programs. On analysis it was found that the common acceptance test used in PODS was faulty (i.e. there was a misinterpretation of the requirements when defining the test data). All the PODS teams 'corrected' their programs to meet the acceptance test, and hence introduced two common mode faults.

On reflection this common mode mechanism is fairly obvious; the acceptance test is essentially just another diverse program which might fail to implement the specification correctly. Excessive reliance on this single 'program' would obviously compromise diversity.

This might have implications for other experiments. In quite a few experimental designs, the acceptance test data is generated by a 'golden' program. In this case, if a fault is activated while generating the acceptance test data, the programs are likely to be modified to mirror this fault (which would typically be an alternative interpretation of the specification). If the golden program is used in subsequent operational testing such faults will be undetectable. This detracts from the experiment, but the remaining population of observable faults should be realistic examples (even if they are reduced in number). The more interesting case is where a golden program contains a fault but *does not* reflect this in the acceptance test data. In subsequent operational tests it would be possible to observe an apparent coincident failure of *all* the diverse programs. In reality, it is the golden program that has failed, but the apparent effect is a fault that spans all program versions. Fortunately, this situation should be relatively easy to spot and, to my knowledge, this effect has not been reported in the literature.

The only exception to these two extreme scenarios can be found in the Knight and Leveson experiment. The experiment used 200 *randomly generated* test data sets as the acceptance tests for the 27 programs. The risk here is that, since the test data is different for each program version, a fault in golden program could be reflected in some test sets but not in the others. Any program version using a test set that did not reflect the golden program fault would subsequently be deemed to contain the same common fault.

Of course this is not a problem if the golden program and the specification are consistent, but there is some evidence that they are not. The major source of dependent failures in the Launch Interceptor experiment is related to one particular function (embodied in Launch Interceptor conditions 3 and 10). In the published requirements specification, the tests for LICs 3 and 10 are *directional* — testing whether a third point represents a change of direction (or turn) of greater than a specified angle from the direction specified by the first two points [Kni86a]. This would certainly make sense in testing for valid missile tracks where very sharp turns would be unlikely. However, the description of the test 'failure' in the main body of the paper talks in terms of *collinearity* where the three points have to be in approximately a straight line [Kni86a]. Such a definition would permit a second case where the missile performs a 180 degree turn. The 'faulty' programs omitted the 180 degree turn case.

This discrepancy could be explained if the golden program implemented a collinearity test while the requirement specified an 'angle of turn' test. In a subsequent analysis of the faults [Bri90], only three of the 27 programs seem to contain this particular 'omission' (Programs 3, 8 and 25), but around 10 of the programs contain faults associated with incorrect implementations of the 'omitted' case.

Under an hypothesis of 'induced common mode', 24 of the 27 programs were 'corrected' to agree with the golden program, leaving 3 which attempted to implement the specified behavior for LICs 3 and 10. This particular scenario would possible if the probability of observing a 'missing case' failure was around 0.01 per test case. This is quite credible if 90% to 95% of the internal errors in LICs 3 and 10 are masked.

In addition, the need for all 27 programs to be 'corrected', either at the acceptance test stage or in subsequent testing, could result in a high proportion of faults being found in LICs 3 and 10 simply due to incorrect modifications. This is particularly likely if the programmer has to infer the change from the test failures rather than an explicit specification.

It is impossible to be sure whether this particular problem actually occurred in the Knight and Leveson experiment, but it does serve to illustrate that quite subtle sources of induced common mode can exist in an apparently straightforward experimental design.

9.3.2 Diversity and Voting

Many experimenters have noted 'discrepancies' where diverse software disagrees but there is no apparent fault. The discrepancies generally arise because there are differences in computational precision and the choice of algorithm. Discrepancies were certainly noted in the PODS experiment. Fortunately they were quite rare so it was possible to perform a manual analysis to determine whether the discrepancy was symptomatic of a genuine fault. The discrepancies were infrequent because the comparison scheme included a tolerance band so that differences in the computation of analogue values could be accepted. However, this was not a complete answer because the analogue values had to be compared with thresholds in order to determine to value of certain binary outputs (such as the trip signal). It is therefore possible for one program to compute a value above the threshold and another program to be below the threshold and hence disagree. This event was infrequent in PODS (a few per million) because there were only 3 or 4 comparisons of this type and the 'error band' was small because the calculations were straightforward. Using the design paradigm discussed in chapter 2, such key decision points (cc-points) should be identified from the functional specification and be voted upon (e.g. so that a single voted value is compared with the threshold).

If an experiment permits inconsistent comparisons, this can be a source of apparent common mode failure (especially in large scale-experiments). Let us suppose that a value (as computed by the golden program) is close to a threshold. On average around half the programs would compute values on the other side of the threshold *and would be deemed to fail simultaneously*. So even if all the programs are 'correct' in the sense that they conform to the specification with adequate precision, the experiment would observe a high proportion of coincident failures.

Other experiments (such as the aircraft landing example) explicitly include cc-points and voting within tolerance bands so that this problem is overcome. In such examples, consistency is very important because data from past cycles is reused and so the effect of an inconsistent comparison (and the associated dependent failures) can persist for many subsequent executions cycles.

Like PODS, the Knight and Leveson example does not contain cc-points. However the Launch Interceptor specification requires a large number of comparisons — up to 1500 values have to be computed and compared against thresholds on every execution cycle. There was an attempt to ensure consistency by requiring all programmers to use single precision floating point and a REALCOMPARE function that limited the accuracy of all comparisons (including those used in algorithms) to 6 decimal digits. This requirement does not improve comparison consistency, and can increase the size of the 'error band' for the computed values (especially where algorithms make heavy use of the REALCOMPARE function).

It is not obvious what effect inconsistent comparisons had on the overall experiment. It is notable that in a subsequent analysis of the faults [Bri90], at least 13 of the 45 faults are associated with accuracy problems caused by using different algorithms. Under a different voting scheme these might not have been regarded as faults, so the failure and the associated failure dependency would have been removed.

9.4   PRACTICAL APPLICATION OF N-VERSION PROGRAMMING

In addition to the research work undertaken to assess the potential for reliability improvement, it is also necessary to examine other issues that could affect the decision to adopt N-version programming. Some of the key areas are examined below.

9.4.1   Maintaining Consistency

N-version programming can impose additional design constraints in order to deal with the diversity in computation. The problems of dealing with such differences in computed values were noted in [Bri89]. The main difficulty is that, within some given precision, there can be multiple correct answers — any of the answers would be acceptable but to maintain consistency, one should be chosen. This is particularly important where the program reaches a decision point where alternative but incompatible actions may be taken. A simple example of this is a railway interlocking system — two equally acceptable alternatives are to stop one train and allow the other to pass or vice versa, but the choice must be agreed. Furthermore when there are a number of related outputs (such as a set of train interlock outputs) it is not sufficient to take a vote on individual values — a consistent set of values must be selected. Without such arrangements it is, in principle, possible for all the diverse programs to make valid but divergent choices. In order to achieve consistency, diverse programs must implement voting arrangements before all key decision points. This enforced commonality could compromise the diversity of the individual designs.

The above discussion shows that design constraints have to be imposed in order to implement consistent comparisons when decisions are based on numerically imprecise data. It is therefore easiest to apply diversity in applications where such indeterminacy either does not exist or does not affect any key decisions. Fortunately quite a few safety-related applications fall into this category. For example, railway interlocking depends on binary status values (e.g. signal on or off) which are not indeterminate. Reactor protection systems may base their decisions on numerical calculations, but internal consistency is not needed to maintain safety. In borderline conditions, either a trip or no-trip action would be acceptable, and the only effect of small discrepancies would be to introduce a small delay until reactor conditions changed. The same argument applies to the launch interceptor application; in practice the discrepancies would only delay a launch by a few execution cycles since fresh data is arriving continuously. Many continuous control applications could, in principle, operate without cc-points. This is possible because most control algorithms are self-stablizing and approximate consistency can be maintained by the feedback of the data from the plant.

At present, most of the industrial applications of design diversity fall into the class where consistent comparisons are not a major issue. For example the rail interlocking system [Hag87] operates on binary data, while the Airbus controller [Bri93] is an example of continuous control where consistency is checked within some window. Actually the Airbus design utilizes the concept of a diverse self-checking pair — one diverse computer monitors the other and shut-down occurs if the diverse pair disagrees outside some window. On shut-down the functions are taken over by other self-checking pairs (with a different mix of software functions). The CANDU reactor protection system utilizes two diverse computer systems that trigger separate shutdown mechanisms [Con88] so no voting is required at all between the diverse systems.

In more complex systems, it is undeniable that standardized intermediate voting points would have to be identified in order to prevent divergent results. The voting schemes used in such cases are very similar to those that would be required for a parallel redundant system and would be essential in any case in order to maintain system availability. It is not clear how much these voting constraints compromise design diversity — most of the observed faults in diversity experiments seem to occur in specific functional modules and are related to the programmers knowledge or specification difficulties.

9.4.2   Testing

One potentially cost-saving feature of diversity is the capability for utilizing back-to-back testing to reduce the effort in test design. Experiments have shown that this form of testing is as effective as alternative methods of fault detection; in a re-run of PODS using back-to-back testing, 31 out of 33 unique faults were found [Bis87]. The remaining 2 faults were found by back-to-back testing with final 'silver' programs against the original 'golden' PODS programs. Of these two faults one was a minor computation error which was within the specified tolerance, and the other might not be a fault at all (given a quite reasonable interpretation of the specification). The cross-check also revealed a common fault in the original 'perfect' programs caused by the use of an incorrect acceptance test.

Back-to-back tests on the Launch Interceptor programs were shown to detect the same number of faults (18 out of 27) as alternative, more labour-intensive, methods [Lev90]. An earlier experiment on a different program example [Lev88] also found that back-to-back testing was as good as any alternative method at detecting faults (123 out of 270). The lower detection performance of these two experiments compared with the PODS re-run might be partly explained by a difference in procedure; in the PODS re-run, any discrepancy resulted in an analysis of *all three programs*, while in the other two experiments fault detection was defined to require a successful majority vote. In this context a 'vote' assumes that if one program disagrees with the other two and the outvoted program is actually correct, the fault is unrevealed. The use of voting rather than a straight comparison as the detection test can therefore leave two-fold common faults or three-fold distinct faults undetected. Another procedural difference was that the PODS programs were re tested after fault removal, which helps to reveal faults masked by the prior faults so the fault detection efficiency progressively improves.

One of the problems encountered in such testing is deciding when a true failure has occurred; as noted earlier there can be small differences in computation which result in discrepancy. Are these discrepancies really faults? In actual real-time operation, such minor differences are likely to be resolved soon afterwards (e.g. if the nuclear power level increased a bit more, or another radar echo is received). So, viewed in relation to the real-world need, the system performs its function. Conventional engineering uses the concept of acceptable 'tolerances', and perhaps it would be fruitful if such concepts could be used more widely software engineering.

9.4.3 Cost of Implementation

In general, the development and maintenance costs for three-fold diversity could be twice that of a single development and less than double for two-fold diversity [Bis86, Hag87, Vog94]. The increases are not directly proportional to the number of diverse versions because some savings can be made on shared activities (such as requirements specification and the provision of test environments).

If the use of diversity doubled the cost of the whole project, then this could well be an impediment to the practical application of design diversity. However in making such choices we have to examine the overall cost implications to the project:

1. For some applications, only a small part of the functionality is safety critical. For example in the Ericsson railway interlocking system [Hag87], the majority of the system is concerned with quite complex computations to make train control decisions. The control commands are submitted to the interlocking software and it is only the interlocking software which is diversely implemented.
2. Some industries are subject to official regulation (e.g. aircraft and nuclear power). In these industries, the costs of *demonstrating safety* can far outweigh the development costs. For example the Sizewell 'B' nuclear power station computer-based protection system has absorbed over 500 man-years of effort in safety assessment [Bet92, War93], and this

does not include any lost income associated with licensing delays. In such circumstances, diversity (although not necessarily software diversity) has been used to make a more convincing safety case.

3. Acceptable alternatives to diversity may also increase the cost. For example, formal methods can be used to prove that a program meets its specification. This might give a high confidence that there are no software design faults. However such development approaches require highly specialized and expensive staff, and there are still residual risks of faults in the proof process, the compiler and the underlying hardware.

9.5   ALTERNATIVES TO N-VERSION PROGRAMMING

This chapter has concentrated on N-version programming, but the diversity concept can be utilized in others ways. The well-known recovery block method [Ran75] is excluded from this discussion since it has been described in detail in Chapter 1.

One interesting idea is the comparison of data derived from an *executable specification* with the behavior of the final implemented program [Blo86]. In this case the specification is a mathematically formal description which can be executed (albeit rather slowly) to generate test cases which can be compared with the actual behavior of the implemented program. This has the advantages of back-to-back testing, without the necessity for a full implementation of a second diverse version.

Another highly novel approach to diversity has been suggested in recent years, and this is *data diversity* [Amm88]. The basic idea here is that the *same program* can be utilized, but run several times with different input data, and then the results are combined using a voter. Part of the motivation behind this approach is the observation that faults tend to manifest themselves as contiguous areas in the input space, and this appears to be a general phenomenon [Fin91, Bis93]. Selecting a set of values increases the chance that some of the inputs values will avoid the defect. For some of the simpler application functions, it is possible to define analytic transformations which use very different values from the intended input value (e.g. using the half angle formulae for sine and cosine function).

A similar concept was also proposed as a means of obtaining a reliable test 'oracle' [Lip91]. The method relies on identifying functions where it is possible to derive the same result using random offsets from the intended input value. For example, a linear function $P(x)$ could be calculated as $P(x + r) - P(r)$, where r is a randomly selected offset which can range over the whole input space. The function is then tested to establish a modest level of reliability using randomly selected numbers (e.g. 100 tests). Given some bound on the failure rate p for random execution, arbitrary levels of reliability can be obtained by repeated computation using randomized offsets followed by a majority vote. This reliability estimate is not affected by localized defects because the actual sample values are spread evenly over the entire input space, so n randomized computations which agreed imply that the result is correct with probability $1 - p^n$. The main problem is to identify functions that are *randomly testable* over the whole input domain. This is not as restrictive as it first appears and it can be shown that conventional modulo 2 integer arithmetic (e.g. addition and multiplication) can be utilized, and also functions constructed using these basic operators (e.g. polynomials and the Fast Fourier Transform function). The method is also applicable to functions of rational numbers (and by implication floating point numbers) provided the precision is doubled to accommodate the inherent round-off effects. While this procedure has been proposed as a basis for generating off-line test data, it could also be used to implement on-line fault tolerance.

The data diversity strategy using very large random perturbations seems to be limited to 'well-behaved' programs or sub-programs where there is some concept of a continuous function over the whole input space. This could exclude important classes of programs such those which use Boolean logic, or switch between alternative functions under differing circumstances.

The use of small random perturbations about the input value combined with a voting mechanism could be effective, although the need for consistent comparison applies equally to data diversity as N-version diversity — so it would be most easily used on systems where the comparison requirements are minimal. The actual reliability enhancement achieved experimentally by such an approach depends on the shape and distribution of defects within the program. Recent work on defect shapes [Bis93] has indicated that, in a multi-dimensional space, the defect can have quite large internal dimensions even when the failure probability is small. However, empirical observations and a related theoretical argument suggest that the shapes will tend be defined by the program function (e.g. bounded by equivalence domain boundaries) and also suggest that the defect will be a hypersurface which is 'thin' in the direction normal to the surface. With sufficiently large perturbations it should in principle be possible to 'straddle' such defects.

Data diversity is an attractive concept since only a single version of the program is required. In its strongest form (using large perturbations) mathematically well-founded arguments can be made for very large reliability improvements (assuming the only faults are design faults). The main problem lies in extending its applicability over a sufficient wide range to be practically useful. The weaker form, using small perturbations, may only exhibit modest reliability improvements, but could be used in a range of practical applications. The author is not aware of any industrial application that uses this concept.

9.6 CONCLUSIONS

Almost from the beginning, it was recognized that N-version programming was vulnerable to common faults. The primary source of common faults arose from ambiguities and omissions in the specification. Provided the difficulties with the specification were resolved, it was hoped that the implementation faults would be dissimilar and exhibit a low level of coincident failure (possibly approaching the levels predicted under the independence assumption). The Knight and Leveson experiment did a service to the computing community as a whole by showing that failure independence of design faults cannot be assumed (although there are some doubts about certain aspects of their experimental design).

This result is backed up by later experiments and qualitative evidence from a number of sources which show that common design mistakes can be made. Also, from a theoretical standpoint, it has been shown that any variation in the degree of difficulty for particular input values will result in failure dependency. Furthermore the error masking phenomenon has been identified as an explicit mechanism that will cause failure dependency.

This may paint too gloomy a picture of the potential for N-version programming, because:-

- Back-to-back testing can certainly help to eliminate design faults, especially if some of the intermediate calculations can be exposed for cross-checking.

- The problems of failure dependency only arise if a majority of versions are faulty. If good quality controls are introduced the risk of this happening can be reduced significantly.

This latter point is supported by the results of recent experiments indicating that the chance of a fault-free version can range from 60% to 90%. In addition, good quality conventional development processes can deliver software with fault densities between 1 and 0.1 faults/KLOC. In this scenario, with small applications, the probability of having multiple design faults can be quite low, and so two fault-free diverse programs will have no problem out-voting the single faulty one.

This is essentially a gambling argument — and it might be reasonable to ask whether you would bet your life on the outcome; however you can only compare this with the alternative — betting your life on a single program. The relative risks are identical with a 50% probability of a fault-free version and the residual risk only moves slowly in favor of a diverse triple as the probability increases (3 times less risk at 90%, 30 times less at 99%).

This argument presupposes that the chance of a fault-free program would be the same in either case. However N-version programming could improve the probability through extensive back-to-back testing, while a single version could benefit if the same resources were devoted to greater testing and analysis. The main argument in favor of N-version programming is that it can also give protection against dissimilar faults, so absolute fault-freeness is not required in any one version — just dissimilarity. This is a less stringent requirement which should have a marked effect on the odds of obtaining an (almost) failure-free system.

Based on its potential for intensive testing and the capability for outvoting dissimilar faults, I would regard N-version programming as a useful safeguard against residual design faults, but my main concern is whether software diversity is justifiable in the overall system context. I would argue that the key limitation to reliability is the *requirements specification*. N-version programming can have benefits in this area because the specification is subjected to more extensive independent scrutiny; however this is only likely to reveal inconsistencies, ambiguities and omissions. The system as a whole would still be vulnerable if the wrong requirement was specified. Excessive reliance on software diversity may be a case of diminishing returns (i.e. high conformity to the wrong specification). So it might make more sense to utilize diversity at a higher level (e.g. a functionally diverse protective system) so that there is some defense-in-depth against faults in the requirements.

Nevertheless in systems where there are no real options for functional diversity, and the requirements are well-established (e.g. railway interlocking), then N-version programming seems to be a viable option. Perhaps paradoxically, the greatest confidence can be gained from the use of diversity when there is only a low probability of design faults being present in the software. So software diversity is not an alternative to careful quality control — both methods are necessary to achieve high levels of reliability.

REFERENCES

[Amm88]   P.E. Amman and J.C. Knight. Data diversity: an approach to software fault tolerance. *IEEE Transactions on Computers*, 37(4) April 1988.

[And81]   H. Anderson and G. Hagelin. Computer controlled interlocking system. *Ericsson Review*, (2), 1981.

[Avi77]   A. Avižienis and L. Chen. On the implementation of N-version programming for software fault tolerance during Execution. In *Proc. the First IEEE-CS International Computer Software and Applications Conference (COMPSAC 77)*, Chicago, November 1977.

[Avi88]   A. Avižienis, M.R. Lyu and W. Schuetz. In search of effective diversity: a six language study of fault tolerant flight control software. In *Eighteenth International Symposium on Fault Tolerant Computing (FTCS 18)*, Tokyo, June 1988.

[Bet92]   A.E. Betts and D. Wellbourne. Software safety assessment and the Sizewell B applications. *International Conference on Electrical and Control Aspects of the Sizewell B PWR*, 14-15 September 1992, Churchill College, Cambridge, organized by Institution of Electrical Engineers, IEE, 1992.

[Bis86]   P.G. Bishop, D.G. Esp, M. Barnes, P. Humphreys, G. Dahll and J. Lahti. PODS — a project on diverse software, *IEEE Transactions on Software Engineering*, SE-12(9), 1986.

[Bis87]   P.G. Bishop, D.G. Esp, F.D. Pullen, M. Barnes, P. Humphreys, G. Dahll, B. Bjarland, H. Valisuo. STEM — project on software test and evaluation methods. In *Proc. Safety and Reliability Society Symposium (SARSS 87)*, Manchester, Elsevier Applied Science, November 1987.

[Bis89]   P.G. Bishop and F.D. Pullen. Error masking: a source of dependency in multi-version programs. In *Dependable Computing for Critical Computing Applications*, Santa Barbara, August 1989.

[Bis91]   P.G. Bishop and F.D. Pullen. Error masking: a source of dependency in multi-version programs. *Dependable Computing and Fault Tolerant Systems*, volume 4 of *Dependable Computing for Critical Applications*, (ed. A. Avižienis and J.C. Laprie), Springer Verlag, Wien-New York, 1991.

[Bis93]   P.G. Bishop. The variation of software survival times for different operational profiles. In *Proc. FTCS 23*, Toulouse, June 1993. IEEE Computer Society Press.

[Blo86]   R.E. Bloomfield and P.K.D. Froome. The application of formal methods to the assessment of high integrity software. *IEEE Transactions on Software Engineering*, SE-12(9), September 1986.

[Bri89]   S.S. Brilliant, J.C. Knight and N.G. Leveson. The consistent comparison problem. *IEEE Transactions on Software Engineering*, 15, November 1989.

[Bri90]   S.S. Brilliant, J.C. Knight and N.G. Leveson. Analysis of faults in an N-version software experiment. *IEEE Transactions on Software Engineering*, 16(2), February 1990.

[Bri93]   D. Brire and P. Traverse. AIRBUS A320/A330/A340 electrical flight controls — A family of fault-tolerant systems. In *Proc. 23rd International Symposium on Fault-Tolerant Computing (FTCS-23)*, pages 616–623, Toulouse, France, June 1993. IEEE Computer Society Press.

[Con88]   A.E. Condor and G.J. Hinton. Fault tolerant and fail-safe design of CANDU computerized shutdown systems. *IAEA Specialist Meeting on Microprocessors important to the Safety of Nuclear Power Plants*, London, May 1988.

[Dah79]   G. Dahll and J. Lahti. An investigation into the methods of production and verification of highly reliable software. In *Proc. SAFECOMP 79*.

[Dun86]   J.R. Dunham. Experiments in software reliability: life critical applications. *IEEE Transactions on Software Engineering*, SE-12(1), 1986.

[Eck91]   D.E. Eckhardt, A.K. Caglayan, J.C. Knight, L.D. Lee, D.F. McAllister, M.A. Vouk and J.P.J. Kelly. An experimental evaluation of software redundancy as a strategy for improving reliability. *IEEE Transactions on Software Engineering*, SE-17(7):692–702, 1991.

[Eck85]   D.E. Eckhardt and L.D. Lee. A theoretical basis for the analysis of multi-version software subject to coincident failures. *IEEE Transactions on Software Engineering*, SE-11(12), 1985.

[Fin91]   G. Finelli. NASA software failure characterization experiments. *Reliability Engineering and System Safety*, 32, 1991.

[Gme80]   L. Gmeiner and U. Voges. Software diversity in reactor protection systems: an experiment. In R. Lauber, editor, *Safety of Computer Control Systems*. Pergamon, New York, 1980.

[Gme88]   G. Gmeiner and U. Voges. Use of diversity in experimental reactor safety systems. In U. Voges, editor, *Software Diversity in Computerized Control Systems*. Springer Verlag, 1988.

[Hag87]   G. Hagelin. Ericsson system for safety control. In U. Voges, editor, *Software Diversity in Computerized Control Systems*. Springer Verlag, 1988.

[Kel83]   J.P.J. Kelly and A. Avižienis. A specification-oriented multi-version software experiment. In *Thirteenth International Symposium on Fault Tolerant Computing (FTCS 13)*, Milan, June 1983.

[Kel88]   J.P.J. Kelly, D.E. Eckhardt, M.A. Vouk, D.F. McAllister, and A. Caglayan. A large scale second generation experiment in multi-version software: description and early results. In *Eighteenth International Symposium on Fault Tolerant Computing (FTCS 18)*, Tokyo, June 1988.

[Kni86a]   J.C. Knight and N.G. Leveson. An experimental evaluation of the assumption of independence in multiversion programming. *IEEE Transactions on Software Engineering*, SE-12, January 1986.

[Kni86b]   J.C. Knight and N.G. Leveson. An empirical study of the failure probabilities in multi-version software. In *Proc. FTCS 16*, Vienna, July 1986.

[Lev90]   N.G. Leveson, S.S. Cha, J.C. Knight and T.J. Shimeall. The use of self checks and voting in software error detection: an empirical study. *IEEE Transactions on Software Engineering*, SE-16(4), April 1990.

[Lev88]   N.G. Leveson and T.J. Shimeall. An empirical exploration of five software fault detection methods. In *Proc. SAFECOMP 88*, Fulda Germany, November 1988.

[Lip91]   R.J. Lipton. New directions in testing. *DIMACS Series in Discrete Mathematics and Computer Science* (American Mathematical Society), volume 2, 1991.

[Lit89]   B. Littlewood and D. Miller. Conceptual modelling of coincident failures in multi-version software. *IEEE Trans on Software Engineering*, SE-15(12):1596–1614, 1989.

[Lyu92]   M.R. Lyu. Software reliability measurements in an N-version software execution environment. *Proc. International Symposium on Software Reliability Engineering*, pages 254–263, October 1992.

[Lyu93]   M.R. Lyu and Y. He. Improving the N-version programming process through the evolution of a design paradigm *IEEE Transactions on Reliability*, 42(2):179–189, June 1993.

[Lyu94]   M.R. Lyu, J-H. Chen, A. Avižienis. Experience in metrics and measurements for N-version programming, *International Journal of Reliability, Quality and Safety Engineering*, 1(1), March 1994.

[Ran75]   B. Randell. System structure for software fault tolerance. *IEEE Transactions on Software Engineering*, SE-1, June 1975.

[Tra88]   P. Traverse. Airbus and ATR system architecture and specification. In U. Voges, editor, *Software Diversity in Computerized Control Systems*. Springer Verlag, 1988.

[Vog82]   U. Voges, F. French and L. Gmeiner. Use of microprocessors in a safety-oriented reactor shutdown system. In *Proc. EUROCON*, Lyngby, Denmark, June 1982.

[Vog94]   U. Voges. Software diversity, *Reliability Engineering and System Safety*, (43), 1994.

[War93]   N.J. Ward. Rigorous retrospective static analysis of the Sizewell B primary protection system software, *Proc. SAFECOMP 93*, Springer Verlag, 1993.

10

Software Fault Tolerance in the Application Layer

YENNUN HUANG and CHANDRA KINTALA
AT&T Bell Laboratories

ABSTRACT

By software fault tolerance in the application layer, we mean a set of application level software components to detect and recover from faults that are not handled in the hardware or operating system layers of a computer system. We consider those faults that cause an application process to crash or hang; they include application software faults as well as faults in the underlying hardware and operating system layers if they are undetected in those layers. We define four levels of software fault tolerance based on availability and data consistency of an application in the presence of such faults. We describe three reusable software components that provide up to the third level of software fault tolerance. Those components perform automatic detection and restart of failed processes, periodic checkpointing and recovery of critical volatile data, and replication and synchronization of persistent data in an application software system. These components have been ported to a number of UNIX[2] platforms and can be used in any application with minimal programming effort.

Some telecommunications products in AT&T have already been enhanced for fault-tolerance capability using these three components. Experience with those products to date indicates that these modules provide efficient and economical means to increase the level of fault tolerance in a software system. The performance overhead due to these components depends on the level and varies from 0.1% to 14% based on the amount of critical data being checkpointed and replicated.

---

[1] This is an expanded version of the paper "Software Implemented Fault Tolerance: Technologies and Experience" in *Proceedings of 23rd Intl. Symposium on Fault Tolerant Computing (FTCS-23)*, Toulouse, France, pages 2–9, June 1993.

[2] UNIX is now a registered trademark of X/Open Co.

10.1 INTRODUCTION

There are increasing demands to make the application software systems we build today more tolerant to faults. From a user's point of view, fault tolerance has two dimensions: *availability* and *data consistency* of the application. For example, users of telephone switching systems demand continuous availability whereas bank teller machine customers demand the highest degree of data consistency. Safety critical real-time systems such as nuclear power reactors and flight control systems need highest levels in both availability and data consistency. Most other applications have lower degrees of requirements for fault-tolerance in both dimensions; see Figure 10.1. But, the trend is to increase those degrees as the costs, performance, technologies and other engineering considerations permit.

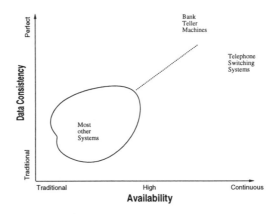

Figure 10.1 Dimensions of fault tolerance

Availability and data consistency in an application is traditionally provided through fault-tolerant hardware and operating system used by the application for its execution. New trends are emerging in the marketplace that are changing this tradition. Standard commercial hardware and operating systems are becoming highly reliable, distributed and inexpensive to the extent that they are now off-the-shelf commodity items. New application software systems are increasingly networked and distributed, i.e. mostly client-server systems. Many of those applications are also built from reusable components whose sources are unknown to the application developers. Due to this complexity in application software, the proportion of failures due to faults in the application software is increasing. The *End-to-End* type of arguments imply that one needs fault tolerance in the application software itself to handle such failures. Also, as the society's dependence on such diverse and distributed applications grows, demands for more reliable and yet economical fault-tolerant software will grow.

In this paper, we discuss three cost-effective reusable software components, watchd, libft, and REPL, to raise the degree of fault tolerance in an application's availability and data consistency dimensions. We discuss the background concepts of software faults, failures and fault tolerance in Section 10.2 and then present a model for providing fault tolerance through software in Section 10.3. The three components are described in Section 10.4 and the experience with applications in using those technologies are discussed in Section 10.5, followed by some concluding remarks in Section 10.6.

10.2   BACKGROUND

10.2.1   Software Faults and Failures

Following Cristian [Cri91], we consider distributed software applications that provide a "service" to clients. The applications in turn use the services provided by the underlying operating or database systems which in turn use the computing and network communication services provided by the underlying hardware; see Figure 10.2.

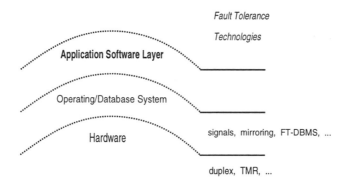

Figure 10.2   Layers of fault tolerance

Due to the complex and temporal nature of interleaving of messages and computations in distributed software systems, no amount of verification, validation and testing can eliminate all faults in an application and give complete confidence in the availability and data consistency of that application. So, those faults occasionally manifest themselves as failures, causing application processes to crash or hang. A process is said to be *crashed* if the working process image is no longer present in the system. A process is said to be *hung* if the process image is alive, its entry is still present in the process table but the process is not making any progress from a user's point of view.

Tolerating faults in such applications involves detecting a failure, gathering knowledge about the failure and recovering from that failure. Traditionally, these fault tolerance actions are performed in the hardware, operating or database systems used in the underlying layers of the application software. Hardware fault tolerance is provided using Duplex, Triple-Module-Redundancy or other techniques [Pra86]. Fault tolerance in the operating and database layers is often provided using replicated file systems [Sat90], exception handling [Shr85], disk shadowing [Bit88], transaction-based checkpointing and recovery [Nan92], and other system routines. These methods and technologies handle faults occurring in the underlying hardware, operating and database system layers only.

Increasing number of faults are however occurring in the application software layer causing application processes to crash or hang [Sie92]. Software, unlike hardware, has no physical properties. So, the only kind of faults it has are design and coding faults. Due to the permanent nature of such design faults, it has been generally assumed that the failures caused by software faults are also permanent. This belief led to the use of design diversity for supporting fault tolerance. With design diversity, if a module cannot provide its service, then another module which has a different design is used to provide the required service. The two well known methods for design diversity are the recovery block approach (see Chapter 1), and the N-version programming approach (see Chapter 2).

However, the failures exhibited by those software faults can be *transient*, i.e. the failure may not recur if the software is reexecuted on the same input [Gra91, Wan93]; this is a frequently used technique in hardware to mask transient hardware failures. Sullivan and Chillarege [Sul92] also showed that a large percentage of software errors are triggered by peak conditions in workload, exception handling and timing. Such errors are likely to disappear when the software is reexecuted after a certain amount of clean-up and reinitialization [Ber92]. This is because the behavior of a program, especially a client server application running on a distributed system, depends not only the input data and message contents but also on the timing and interleaving of messages, shared variables and other "state" values in the operating environment of the application [Cri91, Hua94].

10.2.2   Software Fault Tolerance

It is possible to detect a software failure and restart the application at a checkpointed state through operating system facilities, as in IBM's MVS [Sie92]. In their chapter on *End-to-End Arguments* [Sal84], Saltzer et. al. claim that such hardware and operating system based methods to detect and recover from software failures are necessarily incomplete. They show that fault tolerance cannot be complete without the knowledge and help from the endpoints of an application, i.e., the application software itself has to be engaged to provide complete end-to-end fault tolerance. We claim that such hardware and operating system based methods, i.e. services at a lower layer detecting and recovering from failures at a higher layer, may also be inefficient. For example, file replication on a mirrored disk through a facility in the operating system is more inefficient in execution time and space usage than replicating only the "critical" files of the application in the application layer since the operating system has no internal knowledge of that application. Similarly, generalized checkpointing schemes in an operating system checkpoint entire in-memory data of an application whereas application-assisted methods checkpoint only the critical data [Lon92, Bak92].

A common but misleading argument against embedding checkpointing, recovery and other fault tolerance schemes inside an application is that such schemes are not efficient or reliable because they are coded by application programmers. We claim that well-tested and efficient fault tolerance methods can be built as libraries or reusable software components that can be linked into an application and that they are as efficient as some of the operating system based methods. They may not be as transparent to the application as the other methods but they are much more portable across many hardware and operating system platforms since they are in the application layer. All the three components discussed in this chapter are efficient, reliable and portable across many platforms.

The above observations lead to our notion of software fault tolerance as:

> a set of software components executing in the application layer of a computer system to detect and recover from faults that are not handled in the underlying hardware or operating system layers.

We consider all faults that cause an application process to crash or hang which include software faults as described earlier as well as faults in the underlying hardware and operating system layers if they are undetected in those layers. Thus, if the underlying hardware and operating system are not fault-tolerant due to performance/cost trade-offs or other engineering considerations in an application system, then that system's availability can be increased cost effectively through software fault tolerance components described in this chapter.

10.3 MODEL

For simplicity in the following discussions, we consider only client-server based applications running in a network of computers (nodes) in a distributed system[3]. Such an application has a server process and several client processes executing in the user level (application layer) on top of vendor supplied hardware and operating systems. To get services, client processes send messages to the server process. In each of those message processing steps, the server process performs the required computation and data processing and sends back a response if necessary. We sometimes call the server process *the application.* For fault tolerance purposes, the nodes in the distributed system are viewed as being in a circular configuration so that each node is a backup node for its left neighbor in that circular list. As shown in Figure 10.3, each application is executing primarily on one of the nodes in the network, called the primary

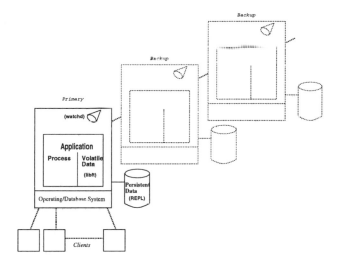

Figure 10.3 Model for software fault tolerance in the application layer

node for that application. Each executing application has *process text* (the compiled code), *volatile data* (variables, structures, pointers and all the bytes in the static and dynamic memory segments of the process image) and *persistent data* (the application files being referred to and updated by the executing process).

10.3.1 Modified Primary-Site Approach

We modify the primary-site approach to software fault tolerance [Als76] slightly in our model. In the primary site approach, the service to be made fault tolerant is replicated at many nodes,

---

[3] These discussions also apply to other kinds of applications. Indeed, the components described in the next section have been used in compute-intensive non-distributed applications.

one of which is designated as primary and the others as backups. All the requests for the service are sent to the primary site. The primary site periodically checkpoints its state on the backups. If the primary fails, one of the backups takes over as primary. This model for fault tolerance has been analyzed for frequency of checkpointing, degree of service replication and the effect on response time by Huang and Jalote [Hua89, Hua92]. This model is slightly modified, as described below, to build the three technologies described in this chapter.

- Each node has its left (or right) neighbor in the circular configuration designated as a backup node.
- The application is active only on its primary node; the application is inactive (i.e. process image is available but not executing) on its backup node.
- A watchdog process (called watchd in our technologies), is running on the primary node watching for application crashes or hangs.
- Another watchdog process is running on the backup node watching for primary node crashes.
- A routine (supplied by libft library in our technologies) is periodically checkpointing the critical volatile data in the application and logging the client messages to the application between checkpoints.
- A replication mechanism (called REPL in our technologies) is running on the primary and the backup nodes to duplicate application's persistent data on the backup node.
- When the application on the primary node crashes or hangs, it is restarted on the primary node, if possible, or on the backup node, otherwise.
- The application is restored to its latest possible internal state before the failure using the checkpointed data structures and message log.
- The application is connected to the replicated files on the backup node if the application restarts on the backup.

Observe that these software fault tolerance tasks can be used in addition to other methods such as N-version programming [Avi85] or recovery blocks [Ran75] inside an application program. Observe also that the application process on the backup node need not be running until it is started by the watchdog process and hence there are no consistency and concurrency concerns; this is unlike in the process-pair model [Gra91] where the backup process is actively running even during normal operations.

10.3.2   Levels of Software Fault Tolerance

The degree to which the above software fault tolerance tasks are used in an application determines the availability and data consistency of that application. It is, therefore, useful to establish a classification of the different levels of software fault tolerance. We define the following 4 levels based on our experience in AT&T. Applications illustrating these levels are described in Section 10.5.

Level 0: *No tolerance to faults in the application software:*
In this level, when the executing application process dies or hangs, it has to be manually restarted from an initial internal state. The application may leave its data in an incorrect or inconsistent state due to the timing of the crash and may take a long time to restart due to elaborate initialization procedures.

Level 1: *Automatic detection and restart:*
When the application dies or hangs, the error is detected and the application is restarted

from an initial internal state on the same processor, if possible, or on a backup processor if available. In this level, the internal state of the application is not saved and, hence, the process restarts at the initial internal state. As stated above, restart along with reinitialization is slow. The restarted internal state may not reflect all the messages that have been processed in the previous execution, and therefore, may not be consistent with the persistent data. The difference between Levels 0 and 1 is that the detection and restart are automatic in Level 1, and therefore, the application availability is higher in Level 1 than in Level 0.

Level 2: *Level 1 plus periodic checkpointing, logging and recovery of internal state:*
In addition to what is available in Level 1, the internal state of the application process is periodically checkpointed, i.e. the critical volatile data is saved, and the messages to the application are logged. After a failure is detected, the application is restarted at the most recent checkpointed internal state and the logged messages are reprocessed to bring the application close to the state at which it crashed. The application availability and volatile data consistency are higher in Level 2 than those in Level 1.

Level 3: *Level 2 plus persistent data recovery:*
In addition to what is available in Level 2, the persistent data of the application is replicated on a backup disk connected to a backup node, and is kept consistent with the data on the primary node throughout the normal operation of the application. In case of a fault and resulting recovery of the application on the backup node, the backup disk brings the application's persistent data as close to the state at which the application crashed as possible. The data consistency of the application in Level 3 is higher than that in Level 2.

Level 4: *Continuous operation without any interruption:*
This level of fault tolerance in software guarantees the highest degree of availability and data consistency as required, for example, in safety critical real-time systems. Often, this is provided by replicated processing of the application on "hot" spares, such as the recovery block in Chapter 1 or the N-version software in Chapter 2. The technologies we describe in this chapter do not provide this level of fault tolerance and hence we do not recommend them to be exclusively used in such applications.

10.4 TECHNOLOGIES

Sometimes, the fault tolerance tasks described in the previous section are individually implemented in an application in an *ad hoc* manner. We developed three generic and reusable components (watchd, libft and REPL)[4] to embed those tasks in any application with minimal programming effort.

10.4.1 Watchd

10.4.1.1 PROCESS RECOVERY

Watchd is a watchdog daemon process that runs on a single machine or on a network of machines. It continually watches the life of a local application process by periodically sending a null signal to the process and checking the return value to detect whether that process is alive or dead. It detects whether that process is hung or not by using one of the following two methods specified by the application. In the first method, watchd sends a null message to

---

[4] watchd, libft and REPL are registered trademarks of AT&T Bell Laboratories.

the local application process using IPC (Inter Process Communication) facilities on the local node and checks for a response. If watchd cannot make the connection, it waits for some time (specified by the application) and tries again. If it fails after the second attempt, watchd interprets the failure to mean that the process is hung. In the second method, the application process sends a heartbeat message to watchd periodically and watchd periodically checks the heartbeat. If the heartbeat message from the application is not received by a specified time, watchd assumes that the application is hung. Libft provides the function hbeat() for applications to send heartbeats to watchd. The hbeat() function has an argument whose value specifies the duration for the next heartbeat to arrive.

When it detects that the application process crashed or hung, watchd recovers that application at an initial internal state or at the last checkpointed state. The application is recovered on the primary node if that node has not crashed, otherwise on the backup node for the primary as specified in a configuration file. If libft is also used, watchd sets the restarted application to process all the logged messages from the log file generated by libft.

10.4.1.2   PROCESSOR RECOVERY

Watchd also watches one neighboring watchd (left or right) in a circular fashion to detect node failures; this circular arrangement is similar to the adaptive distributed diagnosis algorithm [Bia91]. When a node failure is detected, watchd can execute user-defined recovery commands and reconfigure the network. Observe that neighboring watchds cannot fully differentiate between node failures and link failures. In general, this is the problem of attaining common knowledge in the presence of communication failures which is provably unsolvable [Hal90]. However, to minimize the problem, watchd can use two communication links for polling a neighboring node. Only when it can not reach the neighboring node by both links, watchd reports a node failure; an example is given in Section 10.5, Level 3.

10.4.1.3   SELF RECOVERY

Watchd also watches itself. A self-recovery mechanism is built into watchd in such a way that it can recover itself from an unexpected software failure. When watchd finishes initialization, it forks a backup watchd. The backup watchd executes a loop and keeps polling the primary watchd. If the primary watchd fails, the backup watchd breaks the polling loop and resumes the primary watchd's task by itself becoming the primary. It also spawns a new backup watchd for watching itself, the new primary watchd. If the backup watchd fails, the primary watchd gets a signal from operating system since the backup watchd is always a child process of the primary watchd.

Watchd also facilitates restarting a failed process, restoring the saved values and reexecuting the logged events and provides facilities for remote execution, remote copy, distributed election, and status report production.

10.4.2   Libft

Libft is a user-level library of C functions that can be used in application programs to specify and checkpoint critical data, recover the checkpointed data, log events, locate and reconnect to a server, do exception handling, do N-version programming (NVP), and use recovery block techniques.

10.4.2.1   FUNCTIONS

`Libft` provides a set of functions, described below, to specify critical volatile data in an application. Those critical data items are allocated in a reserved region of the virtual memory and are periodically checkpointed. The reserved region is saved using a single system call to the memory copy function (`memcpy()`); we thus avoid traversing complex, application-dependent data structures. When an application does a checkpoint, its critical data is saved on the primary and backup nodes. Unlike other checkpointing methods [Lon92], the overhead in our checkpointing mechanism is minimized by saving only critical data and avoiding data-structure traversals. This idea of saving only critical data in an application is analogous to the Recovery Box concept in Sprite [Bak92].

Data structure checkpointing, recovery, fault-tolerant network communication and file operations are done using the following functions in `libft`.

- `ft_start()` reserves a block of critical memory. The function takes two arguments — the size of the critical memory and the file name for checkpoint data. When in recovery, `ft_start()` restores the data structures from the critical memory in reserved address space.
- `t_critical()` declares critical global variables along with an `id` to identify the thread that made the call; function `critical()` is similar to `t_critical()` without the identifier. Both functions take a list of variables and their sizes as input arguments.
- `t_checkpoint()` and `checkpoint()` save the values of critical variables and the critical memory onto a file.
- `t_recover()` and `recover()` restore the values of critical variables and critical memory.
- `ftmalloc()`, `ftcalloc()` and `ftrealloc()` are used to allocate space from the critical memory and function `ftfree()` is used to free space to critical memory.
- `getsvrloc()`, `getsvrport()`, `ftconnect()` and `ftbind()` are used by clients to locate server processes and reconnect to servers in a network environment.
- `ftfopen()`, `ftfclose()`, `ftcommit()` and `ftabort()` help in committing and aborting file updates. Files updated using `ftfopen()` can be committed only by calling `ftfclose()` or `ftcommit()`. Therefore, in the case of process rollback recovery, file updates can be rolled back to the last commit point.

`Libft` also provides `ftread()` and `ftwrite()` functions to automatically log messages. When the `ftread()` function is called by a process in a normal condition, the data are read from a channel and automatically logged on a file. The logged data then are duplicated and logged by the `watchd` daemon on a backup machine. The replication of logged data is necessary for a process to recover from a primary machine failure. When the `ftread()` function is called by a process which is recovering from a failure in a recovery situation, the input data are read from the logged file before any data can be read from a regular input channel. Similarly, the `ftwrite()` function logs output data before they are sent out. The output data is also duplicated and logged by the `watchd` daemon on a backup machine. The log files created by the `ftread()` and `ftwrite()` functions are truncated after a `checkpoint()` function is successfully executed. Using functions `checkpoint()`, `ftread()` and `ftwrite()`, one can implement either a sender-based or a receiver-based logging and recovery scheme [Jal89]. There is a slight possibility that some messages during the automatic restart procedure may get lost. If this is a concern to an application, an additional message synchronization mechanism can be built into the application to check and retransmit lost messages.

The exception handling, NVP and recovery block facilities are implemented using C macros and standard C library functions. These facilities can be used by any application without changing the underlying operating system or adding new C preprocessors.

Speed and portability are primary concerns in implementing libft. The libft checkpoint mechanism is not fully transparent to programmers as in the Condor system [Lit88]. However, libft does not require a new language, a new preprocessor or complex declarations and computations to save data structures [Gra91]. The sacrifice of transparency for speed has been proven to be useful in some projects to adopt libft. The installation of libft doesn't require any change to a UNIX-based operating system; it has been ported to several platforms.

Watchd and libft separate fault detection and volatile data recovery facilities from the application functions. They provide those facilities as reusable components which can be combined with any application to make it fault tolerant. Since the messages received at the server site (active node) are logged and only the server process is recovered in this scheme, the consistency problems that occur in recovering multiple processes [Jal89] are not issues in this implementation.

10.4.2.2   EXAMPLE

The following program is an example of a server program using libft library for check-pointing. The server program reads a number from a client and pushes the number onto the top of a stack. The stack is implemented using a linked list.

```
#include <ft.h>
...
struct llist {
    int data;
    struct llist *link;
    ...
}
...
main(){
    struct llist *pHead=NULL, *ptmp;
    int s, indata;
    ...
    ft_start("/tmp/exampl",16384);
    critical(&pHead, sizeof(pHead),0);
    ...
    for (;;) {
        ...
        if (in_recovery()) recover(INFILE);
        if (application decides to checkpoint due to
            a change in its state) checkpoint(INFILE);
        ...
        s=accept(..);
        read(s,indata,MaxLen);
        ptmp=(struct llist *) ftmalloc(sizeof(struct llist));
        ptmp->link=pHead;
```

```
        ptmp->data=indata;
        pHead=ptmp;
        . . .
    }
}
```

The critical data in the above program is the stack itself; to save it, the pointer to the top of the stack, pHead, and the stack size are declared to be critical. To save the contents of the stack, the stack elements are assigned from the critical memory. A critical memory of size 16K bytes is created by the ft_start() function. The size of the critical memory can be dynamically increased as needed. in_recovery() function returns 1 or 0 indicating whether the program is in recovery state.

10.4.2.3   OTHER CONSTRUCTS

Libft provides C-style constructs to do N-version programming, recovery block, exception handling and program retry block. All the constructs are implemented using macros. Therefore, no new C preprocessor or compiler is needed. The syntax of each construct is listed below.

Recovery block:

```
#include <ftmacros.h>
. . .
ENSURE(accept-test) {
        primary block;
} ELSEBY {
        secondary block 1;
} ELSEBY {
        secondary block 2:
}
. . .
ENSURE;
```

In the above program, accept-test is a condition statement which should return 0 if the condition fails.

N-version programming:

```
#include <ftmacros.h>
. . .
NVP
VERSION{
        block 1;
        SENDVOTE(v-pointer, v-size);
}
VERSION{
        block 2;
        SENDVOTE(v-pointer, v-size);
}
. . .
```

```
ENDVERSION(timeout,v-size);
if (!agreeon(v-pointer)) error_handler();
ENDNVP;
```

The `v-pointer` is a pointer to a critical variable containing recovery block's output data to be voted upon. Function `SENDVOTE()` sends that data to a voting registrar. The function `agreeon()`, the default registrar, returns 1 if a majority of the returned data agree. In this case, the result of the voting is stored in the function argument. Otherwise, function `agreeon()` returns 0.

Exception handling:

```
#include <ftmacros.h>
...
exception name1, ...;
TRY
    statements;
EXCEPT(name1) {
    handler routine 1;
}
EXCEPT(name2) {
    handler routine 2;
}
...
ENDTRY;
```

To raise an exception, `THROW(name)` construct is used.

Retry block:

```
#include <ftmacros.h>
...
START(max_no) {
    statements;
}
FINISHBY(post-condition);
```

The program stops if the retry block can not satisfy the `post-condition` after max_no of retries.

10.4.3 REPL

REPL file replication technology provides facilities for on-line replication of user specified files on a backup node. The implementation of REPL uses a shared library to intercept file system calls, as in nDFS [Fow93], and is built on top of UNIX file systems. So, it runs entirely in the application layer and requires no change to the underlying file system or operating system. Speed, robustness and replication transparency are the overriding goals in the design and implementation of REPL.

10.4.3.1 COMPONENTS

REPL technology contains two parts — a shared library librepl.a and a REPL system of processes to run on the primary and backup nodes. Applications are linked with librepl.a library. The library intercepts all the system calls that operate on the specified critical files of that application, generates file update messages and routes those systems calls to the underlying file system on the primary as in a normal system call. The REPL system on the primary transports the generated file update messages to the REPL system on the backup host using the available transport mechanisms such as sockets. The REPL system on the backup host receives and logs the update messages from the primary and performs the corresponding updates on the backup files asynchronously. The shared library can be linked with the application either dynamically if the underlying UNIX supports dynamic shared libraries (e.g., Sun's OS 4.3 and higher, Solaris IRIX 5.1 and higher) or can be linked with the application during compilation. Thus, REPL has five major components; see Figure 10.4. They are:

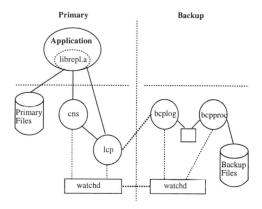

Figure 10.4 Software architecture of REPL

- librepl.a, the shared library that intercepts file system calls from the application,
- cns, the connection server on the primary; it creates a child process, lcp, maintains a file descriptor for that connection to lcp and sends that file descriptor to the application,
- lcp, the child process of cns; it opens a connection to bcplog on the backup host, receives data corresponding to the intercepted file system operations in the application from librepl.a, sends messages about those update operations to bcplog,
- bcplog, the backup log server that receives update messages from lcp on primary and logs them onto a log file and
- bcpproc, the backup process server that reads the log file, processes the update messages and performs those operations on the backup files.

10.4.3.2 PRIMARY FAILURE RECOVERY

watchd and libft together detect and recover failures of any of those components in REPL. If the primary node fails or the application running on the primary fails, then watchd and libft recover the application on the backup node as explained in the previous section. The recovered application on the backup node gets access to the replicated files. REPL itself uses `watchd` and `libft` for fault detection and recovery from failures in its mechanism. If one of the components of REPL fails (i.e. a software failure in REPL) or if the backup file system fails, then REPL recovers itself from such failures as explained below. A crashed backup file system, after it is repaired, can catch up with the primary file system without appreciably slowing down the applications running on the primary. The failure and the recovery are transparent to applications and users.

10.4.3.3   BACKUP FAILURE RECOVERY

If the backup node fails, `watchd` running on the primary detects the failure in about 20 seconds and sends a signal (`SIGPIPE`) to `lcp`. Then, `lcp` creates a local log file, `ftopenlog`, and writes all the incoming data to the log file while the backup node is down. After the backup node is repaired and rebooted, `watchd`, `bcplog` and `bcpproc` are restarted on the backup. The new `bcplog` sends a signal to the `lcp` on the primary node, and forces the `lcp` to connect to the new `bcplog`. Once the connection is established, `lcp` sends new file update messages to that `bcplog`. In addition, the backup `bcpproc` gets the logged file, `ftopenlog`, from the primary node and then processes the update messages on the backup file system in order to catch up with state of the primary file system. While the backup node is down, if the size of the `ftopenlog` file becomes too large, `lcp` stops logging the operations and puts a flag at the beginning of the log file. When the backup node is rebooted and `bcpproc` is restarted, `bcpproc` copies all the critical files from the primary node. At the same time, `bcplog` logs the updates coming from the primary node. When the file copy is complete, `bcpproc` processes the log files created by `bcplog` to catch up with the primary file system. Eventually, all the log files are processed and the recovery is complete. We assume that the relative loads on the primary and backup nodes are such that they can process these file recovery operations without appreciable degradation of the normal application processing.

10.5   EXPERIENCE

Fault tolerance in some of the telecommunications network management products in AT&T has been enhanced using `watchd`, `libft` and REPL. Experience with those products to date indicates that these technologies are indeed economical and effective means to increase the level of fault tolerance in application software. The performance overhead due to these components depends on the level of fault tolerance, the amount of critical volatile data being checkpointed, frequency of checkpointing, and the amount of persistent data being replicated. The overhead varies from 0.1% to 14%. We describe some of those products to illustrate the availability, flexibility and efficiency in providing software fault tolerance through these 3 components. To protect the proprietary information of those products, we use generic terms and titles in the descriptions.

10.5.1   Example 1

Level 1 - Failure detection and restart using `watchd`:

  Application C monitors and analyzes data in a special purpose on-line billing system on AT&T's network. Application C uses `watchd` to check the "liveness" of some service daemon processes in C at 10 second intervals. When any of those processes fails, i.e. crashes or hangs, watchd restarts that process at its initial state. It took 2 people 3 hours to embed and configure watchd for this level of fault tolerance in application C.

Another example is a cross-connection system which consists of several processes using shared memory for interprocess communication. One of these processes is a writer process which may modify some data structures in the shared memory and the others are reader processes which only read the data structures. Because of a hideous software bug, there is a slight chance that a reader may be reading a data structure while the writer is modifying it (e.g., manipulating the pointers for inserting a new data node). Consequently, the reader may receive a segmentation violation fault if the reader happens to read the pointer (a byte) while the writer is modifying it. In such a case, the reader will be rolled back and restarted by *watchd*. Once the reader is restarted, it will access the same pointer again. This time, however, the read operation will succeed because the writer has finished the modification.

Other potential uses of this kind of fault tolerance are in in general purpose local area computing environments for state-less network services such as lpr, fingerd or inetd daemons. Providing higher levels of fault tolerance in those services would be unnecessary.

10.5.2   Example 2

Level 2 - Failure detection, checkpointing, restart and recovery using watchd *and* libft:

Application N maintains a certain segment of the 800 number call routing information on a Sun server; maintenance operators use workstations running N's client processes communicating with N's server process using *sockets*. The server process in N was crashing or hanging for unknown reasons. During such failures, the system administrators had to manually bring back the server process, but they could not do so immediately because of the UNIX delay in cleaning up the socket table. Moreover, the maintenance operators had to restart client interactions from an initial state. Replacing the server node with fault tolerant hardware would have increased their capital and development costs by a factor of 4. Even then, all their problems would not have been solved; for example, saving the client states of interactions. Using watchd and libft, system N is now able to tolerate such failures. Watchd also detects primary server failures and restarts it on the backup server. Location transparency is obtained using getsvrloc() and getsvrport() calls in client programs and ftbind() in server program. Libft's checkpoint and recovery mechanisms are used to save and recover all critical data. Checkpointing and recovery overheads are below 2%. Installing and integrating the two components into the application took 2 people 3 days. This application is running on 5 maintenance centers across the country.

10.5.3   Example 3

Level 3 - Failure detection, checkpointing, replication, restart and recovery using watchd, libft *and* REPL:

Application *U* is a real-time telecommunication network element which collects data from a switch, filters that data and stores them on a disk for several days. Other off-line operations systems access the stored data for billing and various other purposes. In addition to the previous requirements for fault tolerance, this product needed to get its persistent files on-line immediately after recovery of the failed application on a backup node. During normal operations on the primary server, REPL replicates all the critical persistent files on a backup server with an expected overhead of less than 14%. When the primary server fails, watchd starts the application U on the backup node and automatically connects it to the backup disk on which the persistent files were replicated. To distinguish a node failure from a link failure, watchd was configured to use an ethernet and a datakit connection for polling; see Figure 10.5. A fail-over takes place only when watchd on the backup site can not poll the

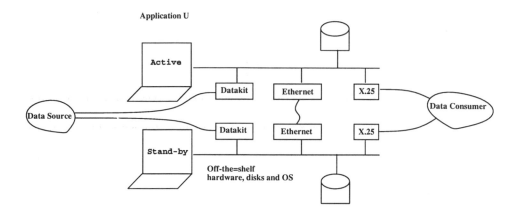

Figure 10.5   Architecture of application U

primary site using both ethernet and datakit connections. The fail-over takes about 30 seconds to complete.

10.5.4   Other Possible Uses

The three software components, watchd, libft and REPL, can be used not only to increase the level of fault-tolerance in an application, as described above, but also to aid in other operations unrelated to fault-tolerance as described below.

- *On-line upgrading of software:* One can install a new version of software for an application without interrupting the service provided by the older version. This can be done by first loading the new version on the backup node, simulating a fault on the primary and then letting watchd dynamically move the service location to the backup node. This method assumes that the two versions are compatible at the application level client-server protocol.
- *Using checkpoint states and message logs to aid in debugging distributed applications:* In libft, all the checkpointed states, i.e. values in the critical data, and message logs can optionally be saved in a journal file. This journal can be used to aid in analyzing failures in distributed applications.

10.6   CONCLUSIONS

We defined a role, a taxonomy and tasks for software fault tolerance in the application layer based on availability and data consistency requirements of an application. We then described three software components, watchd, libft, and REPL to perform these tasks. These three components are flexible, portable and reusable; they can be embedded in any UNIX-based application software to provide different levels of fault tolerance with minimal programming effort. [5]

Experience in using these three components in some telecommunication products has shown that these components indeed increase the level of fault tolerance with acceptable increases in performance overhead.

ACKNOWLEDGMENTS

Many thanks to Lawrence Bernstein who suggested defining levels for fault tolerance, provided leadership to transfer this technology rapidly and encouraged using these components in a wide range of AT&T products and services. The authors have benefited from discussions, contributions and comments from several colleagues, particularly, Rao Arimilli, David Belanger, Marilyn Chiang, Glenn Fowler, Kent Fuchs, Pankaj Jalote, Robin Knight, David Korn, Herman Rao and Yi-Min Wang.

REFERENCES

[Als76]   P. A. Alsberg and J. D. Day. A principle for resilient sharing of distributed services. In *Proc. of 2nd International Conference on Software Engineering*, pages 562–570, October 1976.

[Avi85]   A. Avižienis. The n-version approach to fault-tolerant software. *IEEE Transactions on Software Engineering*, 11(12):1491–1501, 1985.

[Bak92]   M. Baker and M. Sullivan. The recovery box: using fast recovery to provide high availability in the UNIX environment. In *Proc. of Summer USENIX*, pages 31–43, June 1992.

[Ber92]   L. Bernstein. On software discipline and the war of 1812. *ACM Software Engineering Notes*, 18, October 1992.

[Bia91]   R. Bianchini, Jr. and R. Buskens. An adaptive distributed system-level diagnosis algorithm and its implementation. In *Proc. of 21st International Symposium on Fault-Tolerant Computing (FTCS-21)*, pages 222–229, July 1991.

[Bit88]   D. Bitton and J. Gray. Disk shadowing. In *Proc. of 14th Conference on Very Large Data Bases*, pages 331–338, September 1988.

[Cri91]   H. Cristian. Understanding fault-tolerant distributed systems. *Communications of the ACM*, 34(2):56–78, 1991.

[Fow93]   G. S. Fowler, Y. Huang, D. G. Korn and H. Rao. A user-level replicated file system. In *Proc. of Summer USENIX*, pages 279–290, June, 1993.

[Gra91]   J. Gray and D. P. Siewiorek. High-availability computer systems. *IEEE Computer*, 24(9):39–48, 1991.

[Hal90]   J. Y. Halpern and Y. Moses. Knowledge and Common Knowledge in a Distributed Environment. *Journal of the ACM*, 37(3):549–587, 1990.

[Hua89]   Y. Huang and P. Jalote. Analytic models for the primary site approach to fault-tolerance. *Acta Informatica*, 26:543–557, 1989.

[Hua92]   Y. Huang and P. Jalote. Effect of fault tolerance on response time — analysis of the primary site approach. *IEEE Transactions on Computers*, 41(4):420–428, 1992.

[Hua94]   Y. Huang, P. Jalote and C. M. R. Kintala, Two techniques for transient software error Recovery. In M. Banâtre and P. A. Lee (Eds.), *Hardware and Software Architectures for Fault Tolerance: Experience and Perspectives*, Lecture Notes in Computer Science, No. 774, Springer Verlag, pages 159–170, 1994.

[Jal89]   P. Jalote. Fault tolerant processes. *Distributed Computing*, 3:187–195, 1989.

---

[5] As of this writing (October 1994), these three components have been used within AT&T and are also available from Tandem Computers Incorporated as a product named HATS (High-Availability Transforming Software). Interested readers should contact the authors ([cmk,yen]@research.att.com) or Tandem Computers for further information.

[Lit88]   M. Litxkow, M. Livny, and M Mutka. Condor — a hunter of idle workstations. In *Proc. of 8th International Conference on Distributed Computing Systems*, IEEE Computer Society Press, June 1988.

[Lon92]   J. Long, W. K. Fuchs and J. A. Abraham. Compiler-assisted static checkpoint insertion. In *Proc. of 22nd International Symposium on Fault-Tolerant Computing (FTCS-22)*, pages 58–65, July 1992.

[Nan92]   A. Nangia and D. Finker. Transaction-based fault-tolerant computing in distributed systems. In *Proc. of 1992 IEEE Workshop on Fault-tolerant Parallel and Distributed Systems*, pages 92–97, July 1992.

[Pra86]   D. K. Pradhan (ed.). *Fault-Tolerant Computing: Theory and Techniques*, volumes 1 and 2, Prentice-Hall, 1986.

[Ran75]   B. Randell. System structure for software fault tolerance. *IEEE Transactions on Software Engineering*, SE-1(2):220–232, 1975.

[Sal84]   J. H. Saltzer, D. P. Reed and D. D. Clark. End-to-end arguments in system design. *ACM Transactions on Computer Systems*, 2(4):277–288, 1984.

[Sat90]   M. Satyanarayanan. Coda: a highly available file system for a distributed workstation environment. *IEEE Transactions on Computers*, C-39:447–459, 1990.

[Shr85]   S. K. Shrivastava (ed.). *Reliable Computer Systems*, Chapter 3, Springer-Verlag, 1985.

[Sie92]   D. P. Siewiorek and R. S. Swarz. *Reliable Computer Systems Design and Implementation*, Chapter 7, Digital Press, 1992.

[Sul92]   M. Sullivan and R. Chillarege. A comparison of software defects in database management systems and operating systems. In *Proc. of 22nd International Symposium on Fault-Tolerant Computing (FTCS-22)*, pages 475–484, June 1992.

[Wan93]   Y. M. Wang, Y. Huang and W. K. Fuchs. Progressive retry for software error recovery in distributed systems. In *Proc. of 23rd International Symposium on Fault-Tolerant Computing (FTCS-23)*, pages 138–144, June 1993.

11

Software Fault Tolerance in Computer Operating Systems

RAVISHANKAR K. IYER and INHWAN LEE
University of Illinois at Urbana-Champaign

ABSTRACT

This chapter provides data and analysis of the dependability and fault tolerance for three operating systems: the Tandem/GUARDIAN fault-tolerant system, the VAX/VMS distributed system, and the IBM/MVS system. Based on measurements from these systems, basic software error characteristics are investigated. Fault tolerance in operating systems resulting from the use of process pairs and recovery routines is evaluated. Two levels of models are developed to analyze error and recovery processes inside an operating system and interactions among multiple instances of an operating system running in a distributed environment.

The measurements show that the use of process pairs in Tandem systems, which was originally intended for tolerating hardware faults, allows the system to tolerate about 70% of defects in system software that result in processor failures. The loose coupling between processors which results in the backup execution (the processor state and the sequence of events occurring) being different from the original execution is a major reason for the measured software fault tolerance. The IBM/MVS system fault tolerance almost doubles when recovery routines are provided, in comparison to the case in which no recovery routines are available. However, even when recovery routines are provided, there is almost a 50% chance of system failure when critical system jobs are involved.

11.1 INTRODUCTION

The research presented in this chapter evolved from our previous studies on operating system dependability [Hsu87, Lee92, Lee93a, Lee93b, Tan92b, Vel84]. This chapter provides data and analysis of the dependability and fault tolerance of three operating systems: the Tan-

Software Fault Tolerance, Edited by Lyu

dem/GUARDIAN fault-tolerant system, the VAX/VMS distributed system, and the IBM/MVS system. A study of these three operating systems is interesting because they are widely used and represent the diversity in the field. The Tandem/GUARDIAN and VAX/VMS data provide high-level information on software fault tolerance. The MVS data provide detailed information on low-level error recovery. Our intuitive observation is that GUARDIAN and MVS have a variety of software fault tolerance features, while VMS has little explicit software fault tolerance.

Although an operating system is an indispensable software system, little work has been done on modeling and evaluation of the fault tolerance of operating systems. Major approaches for software fault tolerance rely on design diversity [Ran75, Avi84]. However, these approaches are usually inapplicable to large operating systems as a whole due to cost constraints. This chapter illustrates how a fault tolerance analysis of actual software systems, performing analogous functions but having different designs, can be performed based on actual measurements. The chapter provides the information of how software fault tolerance concepts are implemented in operating systems and how well current fault tolerance techniques work. It also brings out relevant design issues in improving the software fault tolerance in operating systems. The analysis performed illustrates how state-of-the-art mathematical methods can be applied for analyzing the fault tolerance of operating systems.

Ideally, we would like to measure different systems under identical conditions. The reality, however, is that differences in operating system architectures, instrumentation conditions, measurement periods, and operational environments make this ideal practically impossible. Hence, a direct and detailed comparison between the systems is inappropriate. It is, however, worthwhile to demonstrate the application of modeling and evaluation techniques using measurements on different systems. Also, these are mature operating systems that are slow-changing and have considerable common functionality. Thus, the major results can provide some high-level comparisons that point to the type and nature of relevant dependability issues.

Topics discussed include: 1) investigation of basic error characteristics such as software fault and error profile, time to error (TTE) and time to recovery (TTR) distributions, and error correlations; 2) evaluation of the fault tolerance of operating systems resulting from the use of process pairs and recovery routines; 3) low-level modeling of error detection and recovery in an operating system, illustrated using the IBM/MVS data, and 4) high-level modeling and evaluation of the loss of work in a distributed environment, illustrated using the Tandem/GUARDIAN and VAX/VMS data.

The next section introduces the related research. Section 11.3 explains the systems and measurements. Section 11.4 investigates software fault and error profile, TTE and TTR distributions, and correlated software failures. Section 11.5 evaluates the fault tolerance of operating systems. Section 11.6 builds two levels of models to describe software fault tolerance and performs reward analysis to evaluate software dependability. Section 11.7 concludes the chapter.

11.2   RELATED RESEARCH

Software errors in the development phase have been studied by researchers in the software engineering field [Mus87]. Software error data collected from the DOS/VS operating system during the testing phase was analyzed in [End75]. A wide-ranging analysis of software error data collected during the development phase was reported in [Tha78]. Relationships between the frequency and distribution of errors during software development, the maintenance of the developed software, and a variety of environmental factors were analyzed in [Bas84]. An approach, called *orthogonal defect classification*, to use observed software defects to provide feedback on the development process was proposed in [Chi92]. These studies attempt to tune the software development process based on error analysis.

Software reliability modeling has been studied extensively, and a large number of models have been proposed (reviewed in [Goe85, Mus87]). However, modeling and evaluation of fault-tolerant software systems are not well understood, although several researchers have provided analytical models of fault-tolerant software. In [Lap84], an approximate model was derived to account for failures due to design faults; the model was also used to evaluate fault-tolerant software systems. In [Sco87], several reliability models were used to evaluate three software fault tolerance methods. Recently, more detailed dependability modeling and evaluation of two major software fault tolerance approaches—recovery blocks and N-version programming—were proposed in [Arl90].

Measurement-based analysis of the dependability of operational software has evolved over the past 15 years. An early study proposed a workload-dependent probabilistic model to predict software errors based on measurements from a DEC system [Cas81]. A study of failures and recovery of the MVS/SP operating system running on an IBM 3081 machine addressed the issue of hardware-related software errors [Iye85]. A recent analysis of data from the IBM/MVS system investigated software defects and their impact on system availability [Sul91]. A discussion of issues of software reliability in the system context, including the effect of hardware and management activities on software reliability and failure models, was presented in [Hec86]. Methodologies and advances in experimental analysis of computer system dependability over the past 15 years are reviewed in [Iye93].

11.3 MEASUREMENTS

For this study, measurements were made on three operating systems: the Tandem/GUARDIAN system, the VAX/VMS system, and the IBM/MVS system. Table 11.1 summarizes the measured systems. These systems are representative of the field in that they have varying degrees of fault tolerance embedded in the operating system. The following subsections introduce the three systems and measurements. Details of the measurements and data processing can be found in [Hsu87, Lee92, Lee93b, Tan92b, Vel84].

Table 11.1 Measured systems

HW/SW System	Architecture	Fault-Tolerance	Workload
Tandem/GUARDIAN	Distributed	Single-Failure Tolerance	1) Software Development 2) Customer Applications
IBM 3081/MVS	Single	Recovery Management	System Design/Development
VAXcluster/VMS	Distributed	Quorum Algorithm	1) Scientific Applications 2) Research Applications

11.3.1   Tandem/GUARDIAN

The Tandem/GUARDIAN system is a message-based multiprocessor system built for on-line transaction processing. High availability is achieved via single-failure tolerance. A critical system function or user application is replicated on two processors as the primary and backup processes, i.e., as process pairs. Normally, only the primary process provides service. The primary sends checkpoints to the backup so that the backup can take over the function on a failure of the primary. A software failure occurs when the GUARDIAN system software detects nonrecoverable errors and asserts a processor halt. The "I'm alive" message protocol allows the other processors to detect the halt and take over the primaries which were executing on the halted processor.

A class of faults and errors that cause software failures was collected. Two types of data were used: human-generated software failure reports (used in Section 11.4.1 and Section 11.5.1) and on-line processor halt logs (used in Section 11.4.2, Section 11.4.4, and Section 11.6.1). Human-generated software failure reports provide detailed information about the underlying faults, failure symptoms, and fixes. Processor halt logs provide near-100% of reporting and accurate timing information on software failures and recovery.

The source of human-generated software failure reports is the Tandem Product Report (TPR) database. A TPR is used to report all problems, questions, and requests for enhancements by customers or Tandem employees concerning any Tandem product. A TPR consists of a header and a body. The header provides fixed fields for information such as the date, customer and system identifications, and brief problem description. The body of a TPR is a textual description of all actions taken by Tandem analysts in diagnosing a problem. If a TPR reports a software failure, the body also includes the log of memory dump analyses performed by Tandem analysts. Two-hundred TPRs consisting of all reported software failures in all customer sites during a time period in 1991 were used.

The processor halt log is a subset of the Tandem Maintenance and Diagnostic System (TMDS) event log maintained by the GUARDIAN operating system. Measurements were made on five systems—one field system and four in-house systems—for a total of five system-years. Software failures are rare in the Tandem system, and only one of the in-house systems had enough software failures for a meaningful analysis. This system was a Tandem Cyclone system used by Tandem software developers for a wide range of design and development experiments. It was operating as a beta site and was configured with old hardware. As such, it is not representative of the Tandem system in the field. The measured period was 23 months.

11.3.2   IBM/MVS

The MVS is a widely used IBM operating system. Primary features of the system are reported to be efficient storage management and automatic software error recovery. The MVS system attempts to correct software errors using recovery routines. The philosophy in the MVS is that for each major system function, the programmer envisions possible failure scenarios and writes a recovery routine for each. It is, however, the responsibility of the installation (or the user) to write recovery routines for applications. The detection of an error is recorded by an operating system module.

Measurements were made on an IBM 3081 mainframe running the IBM/MVS operating system. The system consisted of dual processors with two multiplexed channel sets. Time-stamped, low-level error and recovery data on errors affecting the operating system functions were collected. During the measurement period, the system was used primarily to provide a time-sharing environment to a group of engineering communities for their daily work on system design and development. Two measurements were made. The measurement periods were 14 months and 12 months. The source of the data was the on-line error log file produced by the IBM/MVS operating system.

11.3.3 VAX/VMS

A VAXcluster is a distributed computer system consisting of several VAX machines and mass storage controllers connected by the Computer Interconnect (CI) bus organized as a star topology [Kro86]. One of the VAXcluster design goals is to achieve high availability by integrating multiple machines in a single system. The operating system provides the cluster-wide sharing of resources (devices, files, and records) among users. It also coordinates the cluster members and handles recoverable failures in remote nodes via the Quorum algorithm.

Each operating system running in the VAXcluster has a parameter called VOTES and a parameter called QUORUM. If there are n machines in the system, each operating system usually sets its QUORUM to $\lfloor n/2 + 1 \rfloor$. The parameter VOTES is dynamically set to the number of machines currently alive in the VAXcluster. The processing of the VAXcluster proceeds only if VOTES is greater than or equal to QUORUM. Thus, the VAXcluster functions like an $\lfloor n/2 + 1 \rfloor$-out-of-n system.

The two measured VAXclusters had different configurations. The first system, VAX1, was located at the NASA Ames Research Center, a typical scientific application environment. It consisted of seven machines (four 11/785's, one 11/780, one 11/750, and one 8600) and four controllers. The data collection periods for the different machines in VAX1 varied from 8 to 10 months (from October 1987 through August 1988). The second system, VAX2, was located at the University of Illinois, an academic research and student application environment. It consisted of four machines (two 6410's, one 6310, and one 11/750) and one controller. The data collection period was 27 months (from January 1989 through March 1991). The source of the data was the on-line error log file produced by the VAX/VMS operating system.

11.4 BASIC ERROR CHARACTERISTICS

In this section, we investigate basic error characteristics using the measured data. These include fault and error profile, time to error (TTE) and time to recovery (TTR) distributions, and correlated software failures.

11.4.1 Fault and Error Classification

Collection of software faults and errors identified naturally reflect the characteristics of the software development environment. Many studies attempted to tune the software development process by analyzing the faults identified during the development phase [Tha78, End75, Bas84]. However, fault and error profiles of operational software can be quite different from those of the software during the development phase, due to the differences in the operational environment and software maturity. Therefore, it is necessary to investigate the fault and error profiles of operational software. Also, software fault and error categorization for the three measured operating systems is important because they are widely used operating systems. In order to be of value to the community at large, such a knowledge should be accumulated in a public domain database that is regularly updated. Results of such categorization can then be used for testing and for designing efficient on-line error detection and recovery strategies as well as for fault avoidance.

11.4.1.1 GUARDIAN

We studied the underlying causes of 200 Tandem Product Reports (TPRs) consisting of all software failures reported by users for a time period in 1991 [Lee93b]. Twenty-one of the 200 TPRs were due to nonsoftware causes. Underlying causes of these failures indicate that hardware and operational faults sometimes cause failures that look as though they are due to software faults. Our experience shows that determining whether a failure is due to software faults is not always straightforward. This is partly because of the complexity of the system and partly because of close interactions between software and hardware platforms in the system. In 26 out of the remaining 179 TPRs, analysts believed that the underlying problems were software faults but had not yet located the faults. These are referred to as *unidentified* problems.

Table 11.2 shows the results of a fault classification using 153 TPRs whose software causes were identified. The table shows both the number of TPRs and the number of unique faults. Differences between the two represent multiple failures due to the same fault. The numbers inside parentheses show a further subdivision of a fault class.

Table 11.2 Software fault classification in GUARDIAN

Fault Class	#Faults	#TPRs
Incorrect computation	3	3
Data fault	12	21
Data definition fault	3	7
Missing operation:	20	27
– Uninitialized pointer	(6)	(7)
– Uninitialized nonpointer variable	(4)	(6)
– Not updating data structure on the occurrence of event	(6)	(9)
– Not telling other processes about the occurrence of event	(4)	(5)
Side effect of code update	4	5
Unexpected situation:	29	46
– Race/timing problem	(14)	(18)
– Errors with no defined error handling procedures	(4)	(8)
– Incorrect parameter or invalid call from user process	(3)	(7)
– Not providing routines to handle legitimate but rare operational scenarios	(8)	(13)
Microcode defect	4	8
Other (cause does not fit any of the above class)	10	12
Unable to classify due to insufficient information	15	24
All	100	153

Table 11.2 shows what kinds of faults the developers introduced. In the table, the faults were ordered by the difficulty in testing and identifying them. "Incorrect computation" means

an arithmetic overflow or the use of an incorrect arithmetic function (e.g., use of a signed arithmetic function instead of an unsigned one). "Data fault" means the use of an incorrect constant or variable. "Data definition fault" means a fault in declaring data or in defining a data structure. "Missing operation" means that a few lines of source code were omitted. A "side effect" occurs when not all dependencies between software components are considered when updating software. "Unexpected situation" refers to cases in which software designers did not anticipate a potential operational situation and the software does not handle the situation correctly. Table 11.2 shows that "missing operation" and "unexpected situation" are the most common causes of TPRs. Additional code inspection and testing efforts can be directed to such faults.

A high proportion of simple faults, such as incorrect computations or missing operations, is usually observed in new software, while a high proportion of complex causes, such as unexpected situations, is usually observed in mature software. The coexistence of a significant number of simple and complex faults is not surprising, because the measured system is a large software system consisting of both new and mature components. Further, some customer sites run earlier versions of software, while other sites run later versions. Yet one would like to see fewer simple faults. The existence of a significant proportion of simple faults indicates that there is room for improving the code inspection and testing process.

A software failure due to a newly found fault is referred to as a *first occurrence*, and a software failure due to a previously-reported fault is referred to as a *recurrence*. Out of the 153 TPRs whose underlying software faults were identified, 100 were due to unique faults. Out of the 100 unique faults, 57 were diagnosed before our measurement period. Therefore, 43 new software faults were identified during the measurement period. That is, about 72% (110 out of 153) of the software failures were recurrences of previously-reported faults. Considering that a quick succession of failures at a site, failures likely to be due to the same fault, is typically reported in a single TPR, the actual percentage of recurrences can be higher. This shows that, in environments where a large number of users run the same software, software development is not the only factor that determines the quality of software. Recurrences can seriously degrade software dependability in the field. Clearly, the impact of recurrences on system dependability needs to be modeled and evaluated.

11.4.1.2   MVS

In MVS, software error data, such as the type of error detection (hardware and software), error symptom, severity, and the results of hardware and software attempts to recover from the problem, are logged by the system. The error symptoms provided by the system were grouped into classes of similar errors. The error classes were chosen to reflect commonly encountered problems. Six classes of errors were defined [Vel84]:

1. Control: indicates the invalid use of control statements and invalid supervisor calls.
2. I/O and data management: indicates a problem occurred during I/O management or during the creation and processing of data sets.
3. Storage management: indicates an error in the storage allocation/deallocation process or in virtual memory mapping.
4. Storage exceptions: indicates addressing of nonexistent or inaccessible memory locations.
5. Programming exceptions: indicates a program error other than a storage exception.

6. Timing: indicates a system or operator-detected endless loop, endless wait state, or violation of system or user-defined time limits.

Table 11.3 shows the percentage distribution of the errors during the measured period. On the average, the three major error classes are storage management (40%), storage exceptions (21%), and I/O and data management (19%). This result is probably related to the fact that a major feature of MVS is the multiple virtual storage organization. Storage management and I/O and data management are high-volume activities critical to the proper operation of the system. Therefore, one might expect their contributions to errors to be significant.

Table 11.3   Software error classification in MVS (measurement period: 14 months)

Error Type	Frequency	Fraction (%)
Control	22	5.5
Timing	29	7.3
I/O and Data Management	74	18.5
Storage Management	161	40.4
Storage Exceptions	82	20.6
Programming Exceptions	31	7.8
All	399	100.0

11.4.1.3   VMS

Software errors in a VAXcluster system are identified from "bugcheck" reports in the error log files. All software detected errors were extracted from bugcheck reports and divided into four types in [Tan92c]:

1. Control: problems involving program flow control or synchronization, for example, "Unexpected system service exception," "Exception while above ASTDEL (Asynchronous System Traps DELivery) or on interrupt stack," and "Spinlock(s) of higher rank already owned by CPU."
2. Memory: problems referring to memory management or usage, for example, "Bad memory deallocation request size or address," "Double deallocation of memory block," "Pagefault with IPL (Interrupt Priority Level) too high," and "Kernel stack not valid."
3. I/O: inconsistent conditions detected by I/O management routines, for example, "Inconsistent I/O data base," "RMS (Record Management Service) has detected an invalid condition," "Fatal error detected by VAX port driver," "Invalid lock identification," and "Insufficient nonpaged pool to remaster locks on this system."
4. Others: other software-detected problems, for example, "Machine check while in kernel mode," "Asynchronous write memory failure," and "Software state not saved during powerfail."

Table 11.4 shows the frequency for each type of software-detected error for the two VAXcluster systems. Nearly 13% of software-detected errors are type "Others," and almost all of them belong to VAX2. The VAX2 data showed that most of these errors were "machine check" (i.e., CPU errors). It seemed that the VAX1 error logs did not include CPU errors in the bugcheck category. A careful study of the VAX error logs and discussions with field engineers indicate that different VAX machine models may report the same type of error (in this case, CPU error) to different classes. Thus, it is necessary to distinguish these errors in the error classification. Most "Others" errors were judged to be nonsoftware problems.

Table 11.4 Software error classification in VMS (Measurement period: 10 months for VAX1 and 27 months for VAX2)

Error Type	Frequency (VAX1)	Frequency (VAX2)	Fraction (%), Combined
Control	71	26	50.0
Memory	8	4	6.2
I/O	16	44	30.9
Others	1	24	12.9
All	96	98	100.0

11.4.2 Error Distributions

Time to error (TTE) and time to failure (TTF) distributions provide the information on error and failure arrivals. Figure 11.1 shows the empirical TTE or TTF distributions fitted to analytic functions for the three measured systems. Here, a failure means a processor failure, not a system failure. An error is defined as a nonstandard condition detected by the system software. Due to the differences in semantics and logging mechanisms between the measured systems, a direct comparison of the distributions is not possible. But we can make high level observations that point to relevant dependability issues.

None of the distributions in Figure 11.1 fit simple exponential functions. The fitting was tested using the Kolmogorov-Smirnov or Chi-square test at the 5% significance level. This result conforms to the previous measurements on IBM [Iye85] and DEC [Cas81] machines. Several reasons for this nonexponential behavior, including the impact of workload, were documented in [Cas81].

The two-phase hyperexponential distribution provided satisfactory fits for the VAXcluster software TTE and Tandem software TTF distributions. An attempt to fit the MVS TTE distribution to a phase-type exponential distribution led to a large number of stages. As a result, the following multistage gamma distribution was used:

$$f(t) = \sum_{i=1}^{n} a_i g(t; \alpha_i, s_i) \tag{11.1}$$

where $a_i \geq 0$, $\sum_{i=1}^{n} a_i = 1$, and

$$g(t; \alpha, s) = \begin{cases} 0 & t < s, \\ \frac{1}{\Gamma(\alpha)}(t - s)^{\alpha-1} e^{-(t-s)} & t \geq s. \end{cases} \tag{11.2}$$

It was found that a 5-stage gamma distribution provided a satisfactory fit.

Figure 11.1b and Figure 11.1c show that the measured software TTE and TTF distributions can be modeled as a probabilistic combination of two exponential random variables, indicating

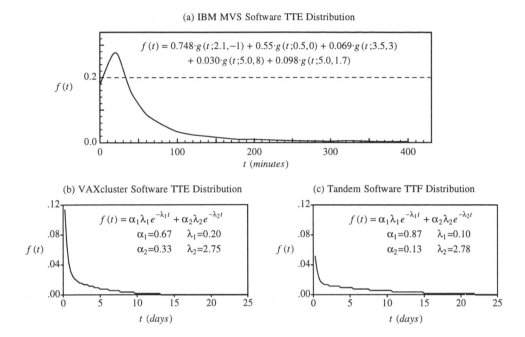

(a) IBM MVS Software TTE Distribution

$$f(t) = 0.748 \cdot g(t;2.1,-1) + 0.55 \cdot g(t;0.5,0) + 0.069 \cdot g(t;3.5,3)$$
$$+ 0.030 \cdot g(t;5.0,8) + 0.098 \cdot g(t;5.0,1.7)$$

(b) VAXcluster Software TTE Distribution

$$f(t) = \alpha_1 \lambda_1 e^{-\lambda_1 t} + \alpha_2 \lambda_2 e^{-\lambda_2 t}$$
$$\alpha_1 = 0.67 \quad \lambda_1 = 0.20$$
$$\alpha_2 = 0.33 \quad \lambda_2 = 2.75$$

(c) Tandem Software TTF Distribution

$$f(t) = \alpha_1 \lambda_1 e^{-\lambda_1 t} + \alpha_2 \lambda_2 e^{-\lambda_2 t}$$
$$\alpha_1 = 0.87 \quad \lambda_1 = 0.10$$
$$\alpha_2 = 0.13 \quad \lambda_2 = 2.78$$

Figure 11.1   Empirical software TTE/TTF distributions

that there are two dominant error modes. The higher error rate, λ_2, with occurrence probability α_2, captures both the error bursts (multiple errors occurring on the same operating system within a short period of time) and concurrent errors (multiple errors on different instances of an operating system within a short period of time) on these systems. The lower error rate, λ_1, with occurrence probability α_1, captures regular errors and provides an interburst error rate. Error bursts are also significant in MVS. They are not clearly shown in Figure 11.1a because each error burst was treated as a single situation, called a *multiple error*. (The characteristics of multiple errors and their significance are discussed in Section 11.6.2.)

The above results show that error bursts need to be taken into account in the system design and modeling. The inclusion of error bursts in a model can cause a stiffness problem which may require improved solution methods. Error bursts, which are near-coincident problems, can affect recovery/retry techniques because additional errors can hit the system while it is recovering from the first error. Hence design tradeoffs between performing a rapid recovery and a full-scale power-on-self-test (POST) need to be investigated.

Error bursts can also be repeated occurrences of the same software problem or multiple effects of an intermittent hardware fault on the software. Software error bursts have been observed in laboratory experiments reported in [Bis88]. This study showed that, if the input sequences of the software under investigation are correlated (rather than being independent), one can expect more "bunching" of failures than those predicted using a constant failure rate assumption. In an operating system, input sequences (user requests) are highly likely to be correlated. Hence, a defect area can be triggered repeatedly.

11.4.3 Correlated Software Failures

When multiple instances of an operating system interact in a multicomputer environment, the issue of correlated failures should be addressed. The data showed that about 10% of software failures in the VAXcluster and 20% of software failures in the Tandem system occurred on multiple machines concurrently. To understand these concurrent software failures on different machines, it is instructive to examine a real case of correlated failures in detail.

Figure 11.2 shows a scenario of correlated software failures. In the figure, Europa, Jupiter, and Mercury are machine names in the VAXcluster. A dashed line represents that the corresponding machine is in a failure state. At one time, a network error (net1) was reported from the CI (Computer Interconnect) port on Europa. This resulted in a software failure (soft1) 13 seconds later. Twenty-four seconds after the first network error (net1), additional network errors (net2,net3) were reported on the second machine (Jupiter), which was followed by a software failure (soft2). The error sequence on Jupiter was repeated (net4,net5,soft3) on the third machine (Mercury). The three machines experienced software failures concurrently for 45.5 minutes. All three software failures occurred shortly after network errors occurred, so they are network error related. Further analysis of the data revealed that the network-related software of the VAX/VMS is a potential software bottleneck in terms of correlated failures.

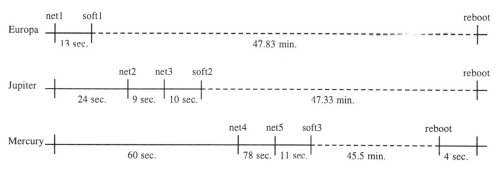

Note: soft1, soft2, soft3 — Exception while above asynchronous system traps delivery or on interrupt stack.
        net1, net3, net5 — Port will be re-started.   net2, net4 — Virtual circuit timeout.

Figure 11.2   A scenario of correlated software failures

The higher percentage of correlated software failures in the Tandem system is attributed to the architectural characteristics of the Tandem system. In the Tandem system, it is possible that a single software fault causes halts of two processors on which the primary and backup processes of the faulty software are executing. If the two halted processors control a disk that includes files needed by other processors on the system, additional software halts can occur on these processors. (In the Tandem system, a disk can typically be accessed by two processors via dual-port disk controllers.) This explains why there is a higher percentage of correlated software failures in the Tandem system.

Note that the above scenario is a multiple component failure situation. A substantial amount of efforts has been directed at developing general system design principles against correlated failures. Still, correlated failures exist due to design holes and unmodeled faults. Generally, correlated failures can stress recovery and break the protection provided by the fault tolerance.

It has been shown that even a low percentage of correlated failures can have a big impact on system dependability [Dug92, Tan92a]. Thus, correlated failures cannot be neglected.

11.4.4   Recovery Distributions

In MVS, time to recovery (TTR) is defined as the time difference between the operating system's departure from the normal state due to the detection of an error and its subsequent return to the normal state. The normal state means that no error recovery is pending, i.e., all previously-detected errors are resolved by the operating system. In GUARDIAN, TTR is defined as the time difference between a processor's going down due to software and its coming back on-line. VMS shares the definition of TTR with MVS, but the TTR data from VMS look closer to the GUARDIAN TTR data than the MVS TTR data. This is probably because VMS logs only serious software errors. About 80% of software errors logged resulted in a node failure in the measured VAXcluster systems.

Since each system has different recovery procedure and maintenance environment, it is inappropriate to compare the measured systems in terms of TTR distribution. Our intention is to understand and discuss the different recovery mechanisms and resulting recovery time characteristics in the three operating systems.

Figure 11.3a plots a spline-fit for the TTR distribution of multiple software errors in the MVS system. A multiple software error is an error burst consisting of different types of software errors. The TTR distribution for multiple software errors was studied because these errors have longer recovery times than other software errors and are more typical in terms of recovery process (see Table 11.13 in Section 11.6). Our analysis found that a three-phase hyperexponential function can be used to approximate the distribution, suggesting a multimode recovery process. Because most MVS software errors do not lead to system failures, the TTR for multiple errors is short, although these errors take the longest time to recover of all software errors.

Figure 11.3b and Figure 11.3c plot the empirical software TTR distributions for the VAXcluster and Tandem systems. Because of their peculiar shapes, the raw distributions are provided. In the VAXcluster (Figure 11.3b), most of the TTR instances (85%) are less than 15 minutes. This is attributed to those errors recovered by on-line recovery or automatic reboot without shutdown repair. However, some TTR instances last as long as several hours (the maximum is about 6.6 hours). These failures are, in our experience, probably due to a combination of software and hardware problems. Since the Tandem system does not allow an automatic recovery from a halt, its TTR distribution (Figure 11.3c) reflects the time to reload and restart by the operator.

Typically, analytical models assume exponential or constant recovery times. Our results show that this does not apply universally. None of the three TTR distributions is a simple exponential. For the MVS system, since the recovery is usually quick, a constant recovery time assumption may be suitable. For the VAXcluster and Tandem systems, neither exponential nor constant recovery time can be assumed. More complex multimode functions are needed to model these TTR distributions.

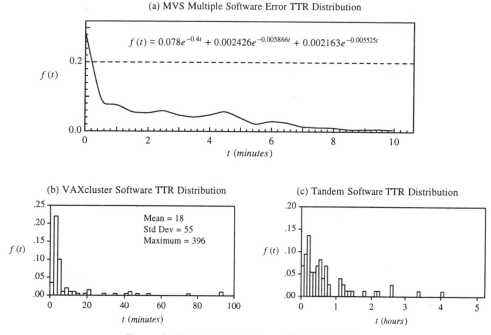

Figure 11.3 Empirical software TTR distributions

11.5 EVALUATION OF FAULT TOLERANCE

This section discusses the evaluation of the software fault tolerance achieved by the use of 1) process pairs in the Tandem/GUARDIAN operating system [Lee93b] and 2) recovery routines in the IBM/MVS operating system [Vel84]. Process pairs are an implementation of checkpointing and restart, which is a general approach developed in the context of distributed data management. Recovery routines are an implementation of exception handling.

The evaluation of process pairs focuses on the faults in the system software that cause processor failures. The evaluation of recovery routines focuses on software errors occurred in the system software. Clearly, the two evaluations cover different software fault spaces. As such, the results in this section should be regarded as what we can achieve by using process pairs and recovery routines, not as a comparison between the two techniques. Recovery routines and process pairs are techniques that can be used together.

While the Tandem/GUARDIAN and VAX/VMS operating systems rely on recovery routines to a certain degree, the data from these systems did not allow us to evaluate their effectiveness against software faults and errors. Also, the IBM/MVS and VAX/VMS operating systems do not have constructs for checkpointing and restart.

11.5.1 Evaluation of Process Pairs

It has been observed that process pairs allow the system to tolerate certain software faults [Gra85, Gra90]. That is, in many processor halts due to software faults, the backup of a failed primary can continue the execution. This is rather counter-intuitive because the primary and backup run the same copy of the software. The phenomenon was explained by the existence of subtle faults, often referred to as "transient" software faults, that are not exercised again on a restart of the failed software. Field software faults were not detected during the testing phase, and many of them could be transient in nature. Since the technique is not explicitly intended for tolerating software faults, study of field data is essential for understanding the phenomenon and for measuring the effectiveness of the technique against software faults.

Using human-generated field software failure reports in the Tandem system, [Lee93b] measured 1) the user-perceived ability of the Tandem system to tolerate faults in its system software due to the use of process pairs and 2) the detailed reasons for software fault tolerance. Recently, attempts have been made to use the transient nature of some software faults for tolerating such faults in user applications using checkpoint and restart [Hua93, Wan93].

11.5.1.1   MEASURE OF SOFTWARE FAULT TOLERANCE

There were 179 TPRs generated due to software faults during the measured period (see Section 11.4.1). Since each TPR reports just one problem, sometimes two TPRs are generated as a result of a multiple processor halt. There were five such cases, making a total of 174 software failures during the measured period. Table 11.5 shows the severity of the 174 software failures. A single-processor halt implies that the built-in single-failure tolerance of the system masked the software fault that caused the halt. We aggregated all multiple processor halts into a single group because, in the Tandem system, a double processor halt can potentially cause additional processor halts due to the system architecture (see Section 11.4.3). There was one case in which a software failure occurred in the middle of a system coldload.

Table 11.5   Severity of software failures

Severity	# Failures
Single processor halt	138
Multiple processor halt	31
During system coldload	1
Unclear	4
All	174

Here the term software fault tolerance (SFT) refers to the ability to tolerate software faults. Quantitatively, it was defined as

$$SFT = \frac{\text{number of software failures in which a single processor is halted}}{\text{total number of software failures}}. \qquad (11.3)$$

Thus, it represents the user-perceived ability of the system to tolerate faults in its system software specifically due to the use of process pairs.

Table 11.5 shows that process pairs can provide a significant level of software fault tolerance in distributed transaction processing environments. The measure of the software fault tolerance is 82% (138 out of 169). This measure is based on the reported software failures. The issue of underreporting was discussed in [Gra90]. The consensus among experienced Tandem engineers seems to be that about 80% of software failures do not get reported as TPRs and that most of them are single-processor halts. If that is true, then the software fault tolerance may be as high as 96%.

11.5.1.2   OUTAGES DUE TO SOFTWARE

We first focused on the multiple processor halts. For each multiple processor halt, we investigated the first two processor halts to determine whether the second halt occurred on the processor executing the backup of the failed primary process. In such cases, we also investigated whether the two processors halted due to the same software fault.

Table 11.6 shows that in 86% (24 out of 28, excluding "unclear" cases) of the multiple processor halts, the backup of the failed primary process was unable to continue the execution. In 81% (17 out of 21, excluding "unclear" cases) of these halts, the backup failed due to the same fault that caused the failure of the primary. In the remaining 19% of the halts, the processor executing the backup of the failed primary halted due to another fault during job takeover. While the level of software fault tolerance achieved with process pairs is high, it is not perfect. As a result, there is a chance that a single software fault in the system software can manifest itself as a multiple processor halt that the system is not designed against.

Table 11.6   Reasons for multiple processor halts

Reasons for Multiple Processor Halts	# Failures
The second halt occurs on the processor executing the backup of the failed primary	24
– The second halt occurs due to the same fault that halted the primary	(17)
– The second halt occurs due to another fault during job takeover	(4)
– Unclear	(3)
Not related to process pairs	4
– System hang	(1)
– Execution of faulty parallel software	(1)
– Random coincidence of two independent faults	(1)
– Single-processor halt, but system coldload was necessary for recovery	(1)
Unclear (insufficient information in TPR)	3

11.5.1.3   CHARACTERIZATION OF SOFTWARE FAULT TOLERANCE

The information in Table 11.5 poses the question of why the Tandem system loses only one processor in 82% of software failures and, as a result, tolerates the software faults that cause these failures. We identified the reasons for software fault tolerance in all single-processor halts and classified them into several groups. Table 11.7 shows that, in 29% of single-processor halts, the fault that causes a failure of a primary process is not exercised again when the backup reexecutes the same task after a takeover. This happens because some software faults are exposed on rare situations such as 1) a specific memory state (e.g., running out of buffer), 2) the occurrence of a single event or a sequence of asynchronous events during a vulnerable time window (timing), 3) race conditions or concurrent operations among multiple processes, or 4) the occurrence of an error. These situations are usually not repeated on the backup.

Table 11.7   Reasons for software fault tolerance

Reasons for Software Fault Tolerance	Fraction (%)
Backup reexecutes the failed task after takeover, but the fault that caused a failure of primary is not exercised by backup	29
– Memory state	(4)
– Timing	(7)
– Race or concurrency	(6)
– Error	(4)
– Others	(7)
Backup, after takeover, does not automatically re-execute the failed task	20
Effect of error latency	5
Fault affects only backup	16
Unidentified problem	19
Unable to classify due to insufficient information	12

The following is a real example of a fault that is exercised only in a specific memory state. The primary of an I/O process pair requested a buffer to serve a request. Due to the high activity in the processor executing the primary, the buffer was not available. But, due to a fault, the buffer management routine returned a "successful" flag, instead of an "unsuccessful" flag. The primary used the uninitialized buffer pointer, thinking that it was a valid one, and a halt occurred in the processor running the primary. The backup took over and served the same request, but the fault was not exercised again because buffer was available in the processor running the backup.

Table 11.7 also shows that, in 20% of single-processor halts, the backup of a failed primary process does not serve the failed request after a successful takeover. This is because some faults are exposed while the primary is handling requests that are important but are not automatically resubmitted to the backup on a failure of the primary. Examples of such requests are operator commands to reconfigure I/O lines. These requests are not automatically resubmitted to the backup because they are interactive tasks that can easily be resubmitted by the operator if a failure occurs. Also, some software faults are exposed while executing system functions that are important but do not run as process pairs. An example of such system functions is a utility program for on-line processor performance monitoring. Consider that the response time on a processor increases. Then the operator would run such a utility program. In this situation, it is not imperative to run the utility as process pairs, because there is no need to monitor a processor any longer if the processor fails. If the monitoring processor fails, then the operator can run the utility on another processor. In this case, the failed task does not survive the failure. But process pairs allow the other applications on the halted processor to continue to run. This is not a strict software fault tolerance but a side benefit of using process pairs. If these failures are excluded, the measure of software fault tolerance becomes 77%.

Another reason for the software fault tolerance is that some software faults cause errors that are detected after the service that caused the errors has finished successfully (see "effect of error latency" in Table 11.7). For example, a process overwrote words in a system data structure due to an uninitialized pointer when it served a request. The underlying fault was a missing operation, i.e., not initializing a pointer. The process that caused the error finished serving the request successfully, which was checkpointed successfully to its backup. (The error did not affect the service and was not a part of the checkpoint information.) After a while, another process in the same processor detected the error and asserted a halt. The backups of these processes continued the executions, but the service that caused the error was not repeated because the service was already provided. Differences between this case and the first group listed in Table 11.7 is that the software function that caused the failure of the primary did not have to be executed again in the backup.

Table 11.7 also shows that 16% of single-processor halts occur due to a failure of a backup process. This indicates that the software fault tolerance does not come free: the added complexity due to the implementation of process pairs introduces additional software faults in the system software. The measure of software fault tolerance (77%) estimated above can be adjusted again to 72% by excluding these failures. All unidentified failures were single-processor halts. This is understandable because these are due to subtle faults that are very hard to observe and diagnose. The reason why an unidentified problem caused a single-processor halt is unknown. Based on their symptoms, we speculate that a significant number of these were single-processor halts due to the effect of error latency.

11.5.1.4   DISCUSSION

The results in this section have several implications. First, process pairs are not explicitly designed for tolerating software faults. Our results show that a major reason for the measured software fault tolerance is the loose coupling between processors which results in the backup execution (the processor state and the sequence of events occurring) being different from the original execution. This confirms that there is another dimension for achieving software fault tolerance in distributed environments. The actual level of software fault tolerance achieved by the use of process pairs will depend on the level of differences between the original and backup executions. Each processor on a Tandem system has an independent processing environment, so the system naturally provides such differences. ([Gra85] discussed the advantages of using checkpointing, as opposed to lock-step operation, in terms of the ability to tolerate software faults.) The level of software fault tolerance achieved by the use of process pairs will also depend on the proportion of subtle faults in the software that are exercised only in rare processor states. While process pairs may not provide perfect software fault tolerance, the implementation of process pairs is not as prohibitively expensive as developing and maintaining multiple versions of large software programs.

Second, the results indicate that process pairs can also allow the system to tolerate nontransient software faults. This is because software failures can occur while executing important tasks that are not automatically resubmitted to the backup on a failure of the primary. In this case, the failed task does not survive, but process pairs allow the other applications on the failed processor to survive.

Third, it has been observed that short error latency with error confinement within a transaction is desirable [Cri82]. In actual designs, such a strict error confinement might be rather hard to achieve. In Tandem systems, the unit of error confinement is a processor, not a transaction [Gra85]. Errors generated by a transaction may be detected by another transaction. Interestingly, the data show that long error latency, when combined with error propagation across transactions, sometimes helps the system to tolerate software faults. This result should not be interpreted as long error latency or error propagation is a desirable characteristic. Rather, it should be interpreted as a side effect of the system software containing subtle faults.

Finally, an interesting question is: if process pairs are good, are process triples better? Our results show that process triples may not necessarily be better, since faults that cause double processor halts with process pairs may cause triple processor halts with process triples.

11.5.2   Evaluation of Recovery Routines

[Vel84] evaluated the effectiveness of recovery routines using error logs collected from an IBM/MVS operating system. Using job names (at error occurrence) supplied by the system, three groups of job functions were defined: *critical* (for system survival), *essential* (would degrade but not crash the system), and *nonessential* (to system survival). Table 11.8 evaluates the effectiveness of recovery routines in dealing with these jobs. The table shows that retries occurred on 43% of errors involving critical jobs and for 68% on essential jobs. Importantly, in over 50% of the cases where system-critical jobs are involved, task termination results. The task is a module of the critical jobs, and usually system termination (recall that this is defined as a failure) results. Similar, although slightly improved, figures are found for essential jobs. This points toward an inadequacy in recovery management, since one would like better recovery and far fewer task terminations when critical and essential jobs are involved.

Table 11.8   Recovery management

Job Criticality and Type of Recovery				
	Retry %	Task Termination %	Job Termination %	Frequency
Critical	43.3	53.0	3.7	402
Essential	68.6	23.5	7.8	51
Nonessential	24.8	51.9	23.3	592

(a)

Effectiveness of Recovery Routines			
	Recovery Routines Provided %	Failures (Recovery Routines Provided) %	Failures (Recovery routines Not Provided) %
Critical	65.7	44.3	80.4
Essential	78.4	20.0	72.7

(b)

Table 11.8 also shows that recovery routines were specified in about 65% of the errors where critical jobs were involved. In interpreting this table, recall that recovery is possible even when no recovery routine is provided through the recovery termination manager. The percentage of failures in cases where recovery routines were specified is 44%, compared to 80% when no recovery routine was specified. This appears to show that recovery routines have an effect in improving the system fault tolerance, but there is still considerable room for improvement. For essential jobs (where we expect degradation in service but not necessarily a system failure), the percentage of failures where recovery routines are specified drops to nearly 20%, compared to 72% when no recovery routines are specified. Thus, the recovery routines are doing a much better job of dealing with essential jobs than with critical jobs. In fact, one would like to see these figures reversed.

Table 11.9 relates the provision of recovery routines to the specified error classes when critical jobs are involved. (See Section 11.4.1 for the definition of error classes in MVS.) It is found that the recovery routines are most effective in dealing with storage management problems (an important feature of MVS). When no recovery routines are provided, the probability of a storage management failure is high (81%). The recovery routines are weakest in dealing with timing errors, I/O and data management errors, and programming exceptions. Thus, it appears that these are the particularly vulnerable areas of the system where further attention could be directed. To quantify the above figures, measures of fault tolerance were defined and evaluated.

Table 11.9 Effectiveness of recovery routines for critical jobs

Error Type	Frequency	Recovery Routine Provided %	Failures[**] (Recovery Routine Provided) %	Failures[**] (Recovery Routine Not Provided) %
Control	22	63.6	21.4	100.0*
Timing	29	82.8	100.0	100.0
I/O and Data Management	74	82.4	90.2	7.7
Storage Management	161	79.5	7.8	81.8
Storage Exceptions	82	18.3	46.7	92.5
Programming Exceptions	31	64.5	80.0	63.6
All	399	65.7	44.3	80.4

* The number of failures due to control errors were statistically insignificant.
** A failure means a job or task termination in critical jobs.

Here, the software fault tolerance (FT) (i.e., the probability of recovery given that a software error has occurred) is

$$FT = 1 - \frac{\text{number of failures}}{\text{total number of errors}} \qquad (11.4)$$

where the number of failures is the number of job/task terminations of critical jobs. This measure was evaluated for all errors and each error category defined in the operating system.

Table 11.10 presents the system fault tolerance under two conditions. It shows how well the system handles all problems, i.e., regardless of the type of job in control at the time of error. It also shows the fault-tolerance measure (FT) when a critical job was in control at the time of error, to quantify how well the system recovery management handles serious system problems. The overall system fault tolerance to a software error is found to be 0.88. Table 11.10 shows that the system is weak in dealing with errors occurring on critical jobs. It is seen that the system deals best with storage management and control problems. It is at its weakest in dealing with timing and exception errors. The figure for I/O and data management errors is rather low.

Table 11.10   Fault tolerance

Error Type	All Jobs	Critical Jobs
Control	0.80	0.50
Timing	0.90	0.00
I/O and Data Management	0.42	0.24
Storage Management	0.89	0.77
Storage Exceptions	0.63	0.16
Programming Exceptions	0.69	0.26
All	0.88	0.43

11.6   MODELING AND ANALYSIS

The previous sections discussed the fault tolerance of operating systems resulting from the use of process pairs and recovery routines, and basic error characteristics such as TTE and TTR distributions. This section investigates how all these factors affect system availability and completion of jobs, using Markov modeling and reward analysis. We build two levels of models using the data and conduct analyses to quantify the effects of errors and recovery on service loss and job completion. The low-level modeling focuses on error detection and recovery inside an operating system, while the high-level modeling deals with distributed systems in which multiple instances of operating systems interact. The IBM/MVS data are suited for illustrating the lower-level modeling, while the Tandem/GUARDIAN and VAX/VMS data are suited for illustrating the higher-level modeling and reward analysis. The two-level modeling and reward analysis not only allows us to evaluate software fault tolerance and software dependability, it also provides a framework for modeling complex software systems in a hierarchical fashion.

11.6.1   High-Level Modeling

In distributed environments such as the Tandem and VAXcluster systems, multiple instances of an operating system are running, and these instances form a single overall software system. In this subsection, each operating system instance is treated as a software element of the overall software system, and software fault tolerance is discussed at a high level. The modeling is illustrated using the Tandem/GUARDIAN and VAX/VMS data.

11.6.1.1   MODEL CONSTRUCTION

We constructed two-dimensional, continuous-time Markov models using the software error logs from the Tandem and VAXcluster systems. Figure 11.4 shows the model structure. In the model, the state $S_{i,j}$ represents that, out of a total of n operating systems, i copies are in an error state, j copies are in a failure state, and $(n - i - j)$ copies are running error-free. The state transition probabilities were estimated from the measured data. For example, the state transition probability from state $S_{i,j}$ to state $S_{i,j+1}$ was obtained from

$$p_{(i,j),(i,j+1)} = \frac{\text{observed number of transitions from state } S_{i,j} \text{ to state } S_{i,j+1}}{\text{observed number of transitions out of state } S_{i,j}} . \quad (11.5)$$

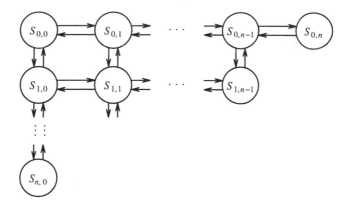

Figure 11.4 GUARDIAN and VMS software error/recovery model

11.6.1.2 REWARD FUNCTIONS

Performability models [Mey92] and reward models [Tri92] have been widely used to evaluate performance-related dependability measures in recent years. To evaluate the loss of service due to software errors, we define two reward functions for the Markov models. The first applies to a non-single-failure tolerant system, such as the VAXcluster, and the second applies to a single-failure tolerant system, such as the Tandem system.

A. NSFT (No Single-Failure Tolerance) Reward Function:

In a non-single-failure tolerant system, any recovery time spent on errors or failures results in degradation. Given a time interval ΔT, a reward rate for a single operating system is defined as

$$r(\Delta T) = W(\Delta T) / \Delta T, \tag{11.6}$$

where $W(\Delta T)$ denotes the useful service time provided by the operating system during the ΔT and is calculated by

$$W(\Delta T) = \begin{cases} \Delta T & \text{in normal state} \\ \Delta T - c\tau & \text{in error state} \\ 0 & \text{in failure state}, \end{cases} \tag{11.7}$$

where c is the number of raw errors occurring in the operating system during ΔT and τ is the mean recovery time for a single error. Thus, one unit of reward is given for each unit of time when the operating system is in the normal state. In an error state, the reward loss depends on the amount of time the operating system spends on error recovery. (If ΔT is less than $c\tau$, $W(\Delta T)$ is set to 0.) In a failure state, the reward is zero.

With the above definition, the reward rate for state $S_{i,j}$ in the model (Figure 11.4) is obtained from

$$r_{i,j} = 1 - \frac{i \cdot \bar{c}\tau + j}{n} \tag{11.8}$$

where $\bar{c}$ is the average number of errors occurring in an operating system per unit time, when the operating system is in an error state. Here each operating system failure causes degradation.

B. SFT (Single-Failure Tolerance) Reward Function:

The Tandem system allows recovery from minor errors and can also tolerate a single operating system failure without noticeable performance degradation. (During job takeover, application programs would experience a short delay, which is typically less than 10 seconds.) To describe the built-in single-failure tolerance, we modify the reward rate (Equation 11.8) as follows:

$$
r_{i,j} = \begin{cases} 1 - \frac{i \cdot \bar{c}\tau + j}{n} & if\ j = 0\ or\ j = n \\ 1 - \frac{i \cdot \bar{c}\tau + (j-1)}{n} & if\ 1 \le j \le (n-1)\ . \end{cases} \tag{11.9}
$$

Thus the first operating system failure causes no reward loss. For the second and subsequent failures, the reward loss is proportional to the number of these failures.

11.6.1.3   REWARD ANALYSIS

Given the Markov reward model described above, the expected steady-state reward rate, Y, can be estimated from [Tri92]

$$
Y = \sum_{S_{i,j} \in S} r_{i,j} \cdot \Phi_{i,j} \tag{11.10}
$$

where S is the set of valid states in the model and $\Phi_{i,j}$ is the steady-state occupancy probability for state $S_{i,j}$. The steady-state reward rate represents the relative amount of useful service the system can provide per unit time in the long run, and is a measure of service-capacity-oriented software availability. The steady-state reward loss rate, $(1-Y)$, represents the relative amount of service lost per unit time due to software errors. If we consider a specific group of errors in the analysis, the steady-state reward loss quantifies the service loss due to this group of errors.

Table 11.11 shows the estimated steady-state reward loss due to software, nonsoftware, and all problems for the Tandem and VAXcluster systems. It is seen that software problems account for 30% of the service loss due to all problems in the Tandem system, while they account for 12% of the service loss due to all problems in the VAXcluster system. This indicates that software is not a dominant source of service loss in the measured VAXcluster system, while software is a significant source of service loss in the measured Tandem system.

Table 11.11   Estimated steady-state reward loss

System	Measure	Software	Nonsoftware	Total
Tandem	$1 - Y$	.00007	.00016	.00023
	Fraction (%)	30.4	69.6	100
VAXcluster	$1 - Y$	.00077	.00565	.00642
	Fraction (%)	12.0	88.0	100

A census of Tandem system availability [Gra90] has shown that, as the reliability of hardware and maintenance improves significantly, software is the major source (62%) of outages in the Tandem system. It is inappropriate, however, to directly compare our number with Gray's because Gray's is an aggregate of many systems and ours is a measurement on a single system. Besides, the sources of the data and analysis procedures are different. Since our analysis is based on automatically generated event logs, some nonsoftware problems which require the replacement of faulty hardware can result in long recoveries and more reward loss. Also, because of the experimental nature of the measured Tandem system, nonsoftware problems due to operational or environmental faults may have been exaggerated. An operational or environmental fault can potentially affect all processors on the system.

11.6.1.4   WHAT DOES SINGLE-FAILURE TOLERANCE BUY?

The Tandem/GUARDIAN data allows us to evaluate the impact of built-in software fault tolerance on system dependability and to relate loss of service to different software components. We performed reward analysis using the two reward functions defined above (SFT and NSFT). The reward function defined in Equation 11.9 measures the reward loss under SFT. The reward function defined in Equation 11.8 allows us to determine the reward loss assuming no SFT. Difference between the two functions provides evaluation of the improvement in service due to the built-in single-failure tolerance. We evaluated the impact of six groups of halts on overall system dependability: all software halts, four mutually exclusive subsets of software halts, and all nonsoftware halts. The four subsets of software halts were formed based on the processes that were executing prior to the occurrences of software halts.

The first and the second columns of Table 11.12 show the estimated steady-state reward loss with and without SFT, respectively. The third column of the table shows what the fault tolerance buys, i.e., the decrease in reward loss due to the fault tolerance. It is seen that the single-failure tolerance in the measured system reduced the service loss due to software halts by approximately 90%. This clearly demonstrates the effectiveness of this fault tolerance mechanism against software failures and corroborates the results obtained in Section 11.5.1. The last row also shows that the single-failure tolerance reduced the service loss due to all nonsoftware halts by 92%.

Table 11.12   Estimated steady-state reward loss (Tandem)

Halt Group	With SFT		With NSFT		What fault tolerance buys: $\left(1 - \frac{Reward\ Loss_{SFT}}{Reward\ Loss_{NSFT}}\right)$
	Reward Loss	(%)	Reward Loss	(%)	
SW, all	0.00007	100	0.00062	100	89%
SW, interrupt handlers	0.00003	43	0.00023	37	87%
SW, memory manager	0.00004	57	0.00035	56	89%
SW, all others	0	0	0.00003	5	100%
SW, unknown	0	0	0.00001	2	100%
Non-SW, all	0.00016		0.00205		92%

SW = Software halts

The first column of Table 11.12 shows that nearly 100% of the service loss due to software halts with SFT was caused by the halts that occurred while the memory manager or an interrupt handler was executing. This indicates that some of these halts affected more than one operating system at the same time, while the rest of the software halts affected a single operating system. The software halts under interrupt handlers can occur for three reasons. First, they can occur due to bugs in interrupt handlers. Secondly, some problems are always detected during interrupt handling. For example, the failure of the "I'm alive" message protocol, which is a timeout in sending or receiving the "I'm alive" message, is detected at clock interrupt. Thirdly, sometimes an interrupt handler is called after a problem is detected by other routines. The software halts under the memory manager can occur due to bugs in memory management software or due to illegal requests from other processes.

11.6.2   Low-Level Modeling

This subsection discusses a low-level model that describes error detection and recovery inside an operating system. The model is illustrated using the IBM/MVS data. In the MVS operating system, when a program is abnormally interrupted due to an error, the supervisor routine gets control. If the problem is such that further processing can degrade the system or destroy data, the supervisor routine gives control to Recovery Termination Manager (RTM), an operating system module responsible for error and recovery management. If a recovery routine is available for the interrupted program, the RTM gives control to this routine before it terminates the program.

   More than one recovery routine can be specified for the same program. If the current recovery routine is unable to restore a valid state, the RTM can give control to another recovery routine, if available. This process is called *percolation*. The percolation process ends if either a routine issues a valid retry request or no more recovery routines are available. In the latter case, the executing program and its related subtasks are terminated. An error recovery can result in the following four situations:

- Resume Operation (Resume Op): The system successfully recovers from the error and returns control to the interrupted program.
- Task Termination (Task Term): The program and its related subtasks are terminated, but the system does not fail.
- Job Termination (Job Term): The job in control at the time of the error is aborted.
- System Damage (System Failure): The job or task that was terminated is critical for system operation. As a result of the termination, a system failure occurs.

11.6.2.1   MODEL CONSTRUCTION

Using the collected error and recovery data, we constructed a semi-Markov model that provides a complete view of the measured MVS operating system from error detection to recovery. The states of the model consists of eight types of error states (see Table 11.13) and four states resulting from error recoveries. Figure 11.5 shows the model. The Normal state represents that the operating system is running error-free. The transition probabilities were estimated from the measured data using Equation 11.5. Note that the System Failure state is not shown in the figure. This is because the occurrence of system failure was rare, and the number of observed system failures was statistically insignificant.

   Table 11.13 shows the waiting time characteristics of the normal and error states in the model. The waiting time for a state is the time the system spends in that state before making a transition. In the table, a multiple software error is defined as an error burst consisting of

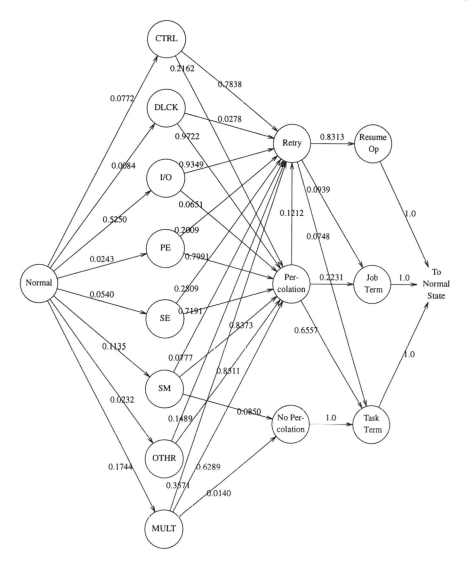

Figure 11.5 MVS Software error/recovery model

more than one type of software error. Table 11.13 shows that the duration of a single error is typically in the range of 20 to 40 seconds, except for DLCK (deadlock), OTHR (others), and MULT (multiple error). The average recovery time from a program exception is twice as long as that from a control error (21 seconds versus 42 seconds). This is probably due to the extensive software involvement in recovering from program exceptions. Table 11.13 clearly highlights the importance of incorporating multiple errors into a system model. The average duration of a multiple error is at least four times longer than that of any type of single error.

An error recovery can be as simple as a retry or as complex as requiring several percolations before a successful retry. The problem can also be such that no retry or percolation is possible. Figure 11.5 shows that about 83.1% of all retries are successful. The figure also shows that the operating system attempts to recover from 93.5% of I/O and data management errors

Table 11.13   Waiting time

State	# Observations	Mean Waiting Time (Sec.)	Standard Deviation
Normal (Error-Free)	2757	10461.33	32735.04
CTRL (Control Error)	213	21.92	84.21
DLCK (Deadlock)	23	4.72	22.61
I/O (I/O & Data Management Error)	1448	25.05	77.62
PE (Program Exception)	65	42.23	92.98
SE (Storage or Address Exception)	149	36.82	79.59
SM (Storage Management Error)	313	33.40	95.01
OTHR (Other Type)	66	1.86	12.98
MULT (Multiple Software Error)	481	175.59	252.79

and 78.4% of control related errors by retries. These observations indicate that most I/O and control related errors are relatively easy to recover from, compared to the other types of errors such as deadlock and storage errors. Also note that "No Percolation" occurs only in recovering from storage management errors. This indicates that storage management errors are more complicated than the other types of errors. The problem can also be such that no retry or percolation is possible.

11.6.2.2   MODEL EVALUATION

The dynamic behavior of the modeled operating system can be described by various probabilities. Given the irreducible semi-Markov model of Figure 11.5, the following steady-state probabilities were evaluated. The derivations of these measures are given in [How71].

- Transition probability (π_j): given that the system is now making a transition, the probability that the transition is to state j.
- Occupancy probability (Φ_j): at any point in time the probability that the system occupies state j.
- Mean recurrence time ($\bar{\Theta}_j$): mean recurrence time of state j.

The occupancy probability of the normal state can be viewed as the operating system availability without degradation. The state transition probability, on the other hand, characterizes error detection and recovery processes in the operating system. Table 11.14(a) lists the state transition probabilities and occupancy probabilities for the normal and error states. Table 11.14(b) lists the state transition probabilities and the mean recurrence times of the recovery and result states. A dashed line in the table indicates a negligible value (less than 0.00001).

Table 11.14(a) shows that the occupancy probability of the normal state in the model is 0.995. This indicates that in 99.5% of the time the operating system is running error-free. In the other 0.5% of time the operating system is in the error or recovery states. In more than half of the error and recovery time (i.e., 0.29% out of 0.5%), the operating system is in the multiple error state. An early study of the MVS error/recovery estimated that the average reward rate for the software error/recovery state is 0.2736 [Hsu88]. Based on this reward rate

Table 11.14   Error/recovery model characteristics

Measure	Normal State	Error State							
		CTRL	DLCK	I/O	PE	SE	SM	OTHR	MULT
π (%)	24.74	1.91	0.20	12.99	0.60	1.34	2.81	0.57	4.31
Φ (%)	99.50	0.016	—	0.125	0.0098	0.0189	0.036	—	0.291

(a)

Measure	Recovery State			Resultant State		
	Retry	Percolation	No Percolation	Resume Op	Task Term	Job Term
π (%)	17.04	8.45	0.30	14.14	7.12	3.48
$\overline{\Theta}(hr.)$	4.25	8.55	241.43	5.11	10.16	20.74

(b)

and the occupancy probability for the error/recovery state shown in the table (0.005), it can be estimated that the steady-state reward loss in the modeled MVS is 0.00363.

By solving the model (Figure 11.5), it is found that the operating system makes a transition every 43.37 minutes. Table 11.14 shows that 24.74% of all transitions made in the model are to the normal state, 24.73% of them are to error states (obtained by summing all the π's for all error states), 25.79% of them are to recovery states, and 24.74% of them are to result states. Since a transition occurs every 43 minutes, it can be estimated that, on the average, a software error is detected every three hours and a successful recovery (i.e., reaching the Resume Op state) occurs every five hours. This indicates that nearly 43% of all software errors result in user task/job terminations. Although these terminations do affect the user perceived reliability and availability, only a few (statistically insignificant number) of them lead to system failures. This result indicates that recovery routines in MVS are effective in avoiding system failures, but are not so effective in avoiding user job terminations.

11.7   CONCLUSIONS

In this chapter, we provided data and analysis of the dependability and fault tolerance for three operating systems: the Tandem/GUARDIAN system, the VAX/VMS system, and the IBM/MVS system. Measurements were made on these systems for substantial periods to collect software error and recovery data. Basic software error characteristics were investigated via fault and error classification and via the analysis of error distributions and correlations. Fault tolerance in operating systems resulting from the use of process pairs and recovery routines was evaluated. A two-level modeling and reward analysis were used to analyze and evaluate error and recovery processes inside an operating system and interactions among multiple instances of an operating system running in a distributed environment.

Process pairs in Tandem systems tolerate about 70% of defects in system software that result in processor failures. The loose coupling between processors which results in the backup execution (the processor state and the sequence of events occurring) being different from the original execution is a major reason for the measured software fault tolerance. The results indicate that the level of software fault tolerance achieved by the use of process pairs depend on differences between the original and backup executions and the proportion of subtle faults in the software.

The measurements in IBM/MVS showed that the system fault tolerance almost doubles when recovery routines are provided, in comparison to the case where no recovery routines are available. However, even when recovery routines are provided, there is almost a 50% chance of system failure when critical system jobs are involved. The system recovery routines are most effective in handling storage management problems (an important feature of MVS). Timing, I/O and data management, and exceptions are the main problem areas. The overall system availability is very high (0.995). From the user perspective, however, this is not quite so, since more than 40% of all software errors lead to user job/task termination. The above results show that a combination of recovery routines and process pairs—first try recovery routines to see if the failed process can be recovered locally and then switch over to the backup when the recovery routine fails— can be a viable approach for tolerating software faults.

Software errors tend to occur in bursts on all measured systems. Software TTE distributions obtained from the data are not simple exponentials. Both the VAXcluster and Tandem data demonstrated that software TTE distributions can be modeled by a two-phase hyperexponential random variable: a lower rate error pattern that characterizes regular errors, and a higher rate error pattern that characterizes error bursts and concurrent errors on multiple machines. The investigation of error correlations found that about 10% of software failures in the VAXcluster and 20% of software halts in the Tandem system occurs concurrently on multiple machines. It is suspected that the network-related software in the VAXcluster is a software reliability bottleneck, in terms of correlated failures.

It should be emphasized that the results of this study should not be interpreted as a direct comparison among the three measured operating systems, but rather an illustration of the proposed methodology. Differences in operating system architectures, instrumentation conditions, measurement periods, and operational environments make a direct comparison impossible. It is suggested that more measurements and analyses be conducted in a manner proposed here so that a wide range of information on software fault tolerance in computer operating systems is available.

ACKNOWLEDGMENTS

We thank Tandem Computers Incorporated, NASA AMES Research Center, and IBM Poughkeepsie for their assistance in collecting data from the Tandem, VAXcluster, and IBM machines, respectively. This research was supported by NASA under Grant NAG-1-613, in cooperation with the Illinois Computer Laboratory for Aerospace Systems and Software (ICLASS), by Tandem Computers, and by the Office of Naval Research under Grant N00014-91-J-1116.

REFERENCES

[Arl90]   L. Arlat, K. Kanoun, and J.C. Laprie. Dependability modeling and evaluation of software fault-tolerant systems. *IEEE Transactions on Computers*, 39(4):504–513, April 1990.

[Avi84]   A. Avizienis and J.P.J. Kelly. Fault tolerance by design diversity: concepts and experiments. *IEEE Computer*, pages 67–80, August 1984.

[Bas84] V. R. Basili and B. T. Perricone. software errors and complexity: an empirical investigation. *Communications of the ACM*, 22(1):42–52, Jan. 1984.

[Bis88] P.G. Bishop and F.D. Pullen. PODS revisited—a study of software failure behavior. In *Proc. 18th International Symposium on Fault-Tolerant Computing*, pages 2–8, 1988.

[Cas81] X. Castillo and D.P. Siewiorek. *A Comparable Hardware/Software Reliability Model*. PhD dissertation, Carnegie-Mellon University, July 1981.

[Chi92] R. Chillarege, I. S. Bhandari, J. K. Chaar, M. J. Halliday, D. S. Moebus, B. K. Ray, and M.-Y. Wong. Orthogonal defect classification—a concept for in-process measurements. *IEEE Transactions on Software Engineering*, 18(11):943–956, November 1992.

[Cri82] F. Cristian. Exception handling and software fault tolerance. *IEEE Transactions on Computers*, C-31(6):531–540, June 1982.

[Dug92] J.B. Dugan. Correlated hardware failures in redundant systems. In *Proc. 2nd IFIP Working Conference on Dependable Computing for Critical Applications*, February 1991.

[End75] A. Endres. An analysis of errors and their causes in system Programs. In *Proc. International Conference on Software Engineering*, pages 327–336, April 1975.

[Goe85] A.L. Goel. Software reliability models: assumptions, limitations, and applicability. *IEEE Transactions on Software Engineering*, SE-11(12):1411–1423, December 1985.

[Gra85] J. Gray. Why Do Computers Stop and What Can We Do About It? Tandem Technical Report 85.7, Tandem Computers Inc., June 1985.

[Gra90] J. Gray. A census of tandem system availability between 1985 and 1990. *IEEE Transactions on Reliability*, 39(4):409–418, October 1990.

[Hec86] H. Hecht and M. Hecht. Software reliability in the system context. *IEEE Transactions on Software Engineering*, SE-12(1):51-58, January 1986.

[How71] R.A. Howard. *Dynamic Probabilistic Systems*. John Wiley & Sons, Inc., New York, 1971.

[Hsu87] M.C. Hsueh and R.K. Iyer. A measurement-based model of software reliability in a production environment. In *Proc. 11th Annual International Computer Software & Applications Conference*, pages 354–360, October 1987.

[Hsu88] M.C. Hsueh, R.K. Iyer, and K.S. Trivedi. Performability modeling based on real data: a case study. *IEEE Transactions on Computers*, 37(4):478–484, April 1988.

[Hua93] Y. Huang and C. Kintala. Software implemented fault tolerance: technologies and experience. In *Proc. 23rd International Symposium on Fault-Tolerant Computing*, pages 2–9, June 1993.

[Iye85] R.K. Iyer and P. Velardi. Hardware-related software errors: measurement and analysis. *IEEE Transactions on Software Engineering*, SE-11(2):223–231, February 1985.

[Iye93] R.K. Iyer and D. Tang. Experimental Analysis of Computer System Dependability. Center for Reliable and High-Performance Computing Technical Report CRHC-93-15, Coordinated Science Laboratory, University of Illinois at Urbana-Champaign, June 1993.

[Kro86] N.P. Kronenberg, H.M. Levy and W.D. Strecker. VAXcluster: a closely-coupled distributed system. *ACM Transactions on Computer Systems*, 4(2):130–146, May 1986.

[Lap84] J.C. Laprie. Dependable evaluation of software systems in operation. *IEEE Transactions on Software Engineering*, SE-10(6):701–714, November 1984.

[Lee92] I. Lee and R.K. Iyer. Analysis of software halts in tandem system. In *Proc. 3rd International Symposium on Software Reliability Engineering*, pages 227–236, October 1992.

[Lee93a] I. Lee, D. Tang, R.K. Iyer, and M.C. Hsueh. Measurement-based evaluation of operating system fault tolerance. *IEEE Transactions on Reliability*, 42(2):238–249, June 1993.

[Lee93b] I. Lee and R.K. Iyer. Faults, symptoms, and software fault tolerance in the Tandem GUARDIAN90 operating system. In *Proc. 23rd International Symposium on Fault-Tolerant Computing*, pages 20–29, June 1993.

[Mey92] J.F. Meyer. Performability: a retrospective and some pointers to the future. *Performance Evaluation*, 14:139–156, February 1992.

[Mus87] J.D. Musa, A. Iannino, and K. Okumoto. *Software Reliability: Measurement, Prediction, Application*. McGraw-Hill Book Company, 1987.

[Ran75] B. Randell. System structure for software fault tolerance. *IEEE Transactions on Software Engineering*, SE-1(2):220–232, June 1975.

[Sco87] R.K. Scott, J.W. Gault, and D.F. Mcallister. Fault-tolerant software reliability modeling. *IEEE Transactions on Software Engineering*, SE-13(5):582–592, May 1987.

[Sul91]   M.S. Sullivan and R. Chillarege. Software defects and their impact on system availability—a study of field failures in operating systems. In *Proc. 21st International Symposium on Fault-Tolerant Computing*, pages 2–9, June 1991.

[Tan92a] D. Tang and R.K. Iyer. Analysis and modeling of correlated failures in multicomputer systems. *IEEE Transactions on Computers*, 41(5):567–577, May 1992.

[Tan92b] D. Tang and R.K. Iyer. Analysis of the VAX/VMS error logs in multicomputer environments—a case study of software dependability. In *Proc. 3rd International Symposium on Software Reliability Engineering*, pages 216–226, October 1992.

[Tan92c] D. Tang. *Measurement-Based Dependability Analysis and Modeling for Multicomputer Systems*. PhD dissertation, University of Illinois at Urbana-Champaign, Department of Computer Science, 1992.

[Tha78]   T. A. Thayer, M. Lipow, and E. C. Nelson. *Software Reliability*. North-Holland Publishing Company, 1978.

[Tri92]   K.S. Trivedi, J.K. Muppala, S.P. Woolet, and B.R. Haverkort. Composite performance and dependability analysis. *Performance Evaluation*, 14:197–215, February 1992.

[Vel84]   P. Velardi and R.K. Iyer. A study of software failures and recovery in the MVS operating system. *IEEE Transactions on Computers*, C-33(6):564–568, June 1984.

[Wan93]   Y. M. Wang, Y. Huang, and W. K. Fuchs. Progressive retry for software error recovery in distributed systems. In *Proc. 23rd International Symposium on Fault-Tolerant Computing*, pages 138–144, June 1993.

12

The Cost Effectiveness of Telecommunication Service Dependability

Y. LEVENDEL

AT&T Bell Laboratories

ABSTRACT

In switching software applications, service quality has traditionally been achieved by the combination of two strategies: high reliance on defect elimination and fault recovery/tolerance. In turn, defect elimination has proven to be costly in staffing, and the implementation of fault tolerance has resulted in high hardware costs, by exclusively relying on proprietary hardware and by using monolithic recovery techniques external to the applications to achieve high quality service. The driving force for this strategy were: no unscheduled downtime, deferred maintenance, easy restart when needed, and easy growth and de-growth. While these objectives are still attractive, they can today be achieved in a more cost-effective way by increased reliance on standard software fault recovery components distributed closer to and inside the applications, and by using hardware sparing recovery at the system level. A recent trend toward rapid software customization will limit traditional software recovery techniques where absolutely necessary to satisfy performance requirements.

12.1 INTRODUCTION

Electronic telephone switching systems are expected by telephone customers to satisfy high reliability requirements in order to assure high quality service. Ideally, the system is expected to perform continuous, uninterrupted operation, and in principle, switching systems are designed for long range continuous operation. In practice, however, target thresholds are set in the form of maximum allowable failure rate, and different sets of requirements are applied for different types of situations. Under these conditions, the products are subjected to the following requirements.

1. Operation without Catastrophic Failures
   In the USA, the system downtime is expected to be less than 1 hour for 20 years of continuous operation.
2. Operation without Non-catastrophic Failures
   The system is expected to provide call processing from beginning to end, but is allowed to interrupt at most 1 call in 10,000. Dial tone must be provided with a delay not to exceed 1 sec.
3. Non-intrusive Office Administration and Maintenance
   The data base, the software, and the system configuration can be changed under specific sets of circumstances without affecting call processing operation. These include: customer data modification, minor software updates, hardware growth, and hardware preventive maintenance and repairs.
4. Intrusive Office Provisioning
   During intrusive Office Provisioning, such as major software or hardware upgrades, it is acceptable for a customer not to be able to initiate new calls after the beginning of the provisioning operation. However, a strict requirement applies to calls in progress: they must be maintained as long as the customers desire during the entire provisioning operation.

A large number of additional requirements further specifies internal operating conditions, such as overload conditions, performance under limited hardware availability, fault propagation restrictions, etc.

Large systems, such as electronic telephone systems, are composed of a collection of hardware and software elements, each one with a certain degree of imperfection. A continuous analysis of field failures is essential to guide the effort of improving system performance. For the 5ESS®switch, the typical partition of field failures is given in Table 12.1 [1] [Cle86, Lev90a]. The proportions may vary from product to product and depend on product maturity. Also, the data in Table 12.1 must be first qualified by the fact that, with the exception of undesirable multiple counting, the data tend to represent the first occurrence of a failure, which is closer to fault enumeration.

Table 12.1   System failure attribution

Failure Type	Usual Rate	Mature Product
Hardware	30%-60%	22%
Software	20%-25%	1%
Procedure	30%	62%
Other	-	15%

Procedural errors which dominate mature systems may be due to personnel's inexperience, inadequate operations manuals or inconsistent behavior of multi-vendor equipment. Hardware failures dominate the other failure types. However, this does not reflect the current industry

---

[1] The rightmost column is the Federal Communication Commission Data for the 5ESS®Switch (Fourth Quarter 1992).

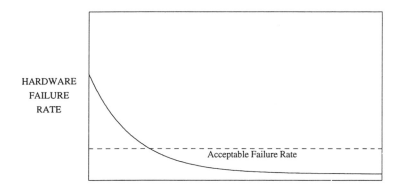

HARDWARE LIFE CYCLE

Figure 12.1   Hardware failure rate improvements

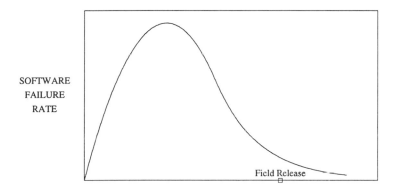

RELEASE LIFE CYCLE

Figure 12.2   Software failure rate improvements

experience in commercial hardware where the hardware failure rate is much lower [Har93]. This is mainly due to the fact that large segments of telephone switching hardware are highly proprietary and its reliability improvement process is slower than commercial hardware which is produced in larger quantities. Commercial hardware may reach higher dependability earlier than proprietary hardware. Over the product life cycle software defects represent a significant overhead.

Over the years, however, 5ESS®hardware failure rates have significantly dropped because of design improvements (Figure 12.1), and software quality improves even more rapidly (Figure 12.2). We use here the classic distinction between faults and failures [Lap92]. Actual field data can be found in a separate publication [Lev90a]. New releases of hardware or software may cause a resurgence of failures.

Recently, the Federal Communication Commission released outage statistics for the major telecommunication equipment suppliers in the US. As shown in Figure 12.3, the AT&T products surpass the products of its competitors by a significant margin. The outage data

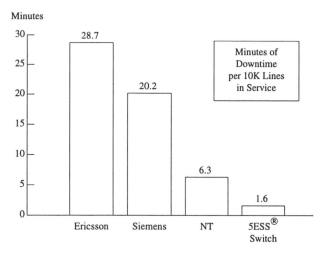

Figure 12.3   US outage data for major telecommunication suppliers (1992)

covers all causes (hardware, software, operator errors,...) is normalized to 10,000 telephone lines to provide a common scope of customer impact of the outages. In fact, it took a decade to achieve this result, and Figure 12.4 can testify that the road to success was not a simple one. 5E4, 5E5, 5E6, 5E7, and 5E8 are major successive releases whose development spanned most of the recent decade and which have had enough field exposure to justify the significance of field statistics.

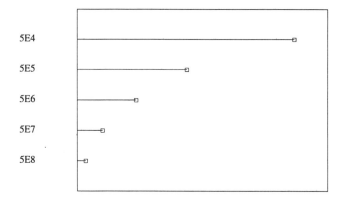

OUTAGES/10,000 LINES

Figure 12.4   A decade of system dependability improvements

The remainder of this chapter details how the improvement was achieved and outlines directions to a new step function in improving large system dependability. Section 12.2 studies the fault removal process in achieving the quality objectives in the past decade. Section 12.3 examines fault recovery mechanisms in improving system dependability. Remaining shortcomings are also discussed. New promising avenues are indicated in Section 12.4. Finally, Section 12.5 provides some conclusions.

12.2   TEN YEARS OF SOFTWARE DEPENDABILITY IMPROVEMENTS THROUGH FAULT REMOVAL

Traditional software quality improvement processes rely heavily on test-based debugging which has required immense effort and resources. A better understanding of the defect removal process is essential to reduce software development cost and increase its quality [Lyu95].

12.2.1   Modeling of the Defect Removal Process

In most software projects, the fault detection rate follows the profiles in Figure 12.5, where curves a, b and c represent a *successful* project, a *failing* project and a *bankrupt* project, respectively [Abe79]. The bankrupt nature of curve c originates from the fact that the fault detection rate decreases very slowly, indicating that the number of residual faults does not substantially change. The failing project of curve b is characterized by a high rate of field failures. All projects in Figure 12.5 are managed in such a way that the number of residual faults first increases ("destruction" phase) and then decreases ("reconstruction" phases). In the context of such a management strategy, project success (curve a) is an expensive task.

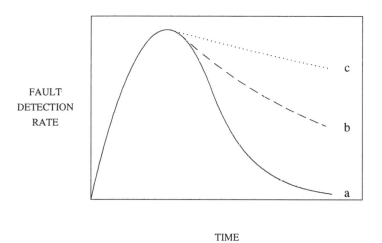

FAULT
DETECTION
RATE

TIME

Figure 12.5   Software fault detection rates

Evidently, the ability to forecast the behaviors of the fault finding rate is very attractive for project managers. However, software reliability growth models have been used and abused in this endeavor, and their use has not always led to satisfactory results. Good studies of reliability models and modelling can be found in the technical literature [Goe85, Mus87]. The industry has often been tempted to use software reliability growth models to track software quality improvement during the development process (cumulative detected faults, fault detection rate). While they were not intended as such, they may prove of some use after they are better understood.

12.2.1.1 SOFTWARE RELIABILITY GROWTH MODELS EVALUATION

A fundamental observation was made by B. Littlewood which significantly puts in question the validity of these models [Lit89]. He compared the forecasts of 7 models and discovered that 4 of them were consistently pessimistic (curve a in Figure 12.6) while 3 of them were consistently optimistic (curve b). The true field behavior being approximately in the middle between the two classes, a pragmatic solution was proposed to interpolate between the two groups (curve c).

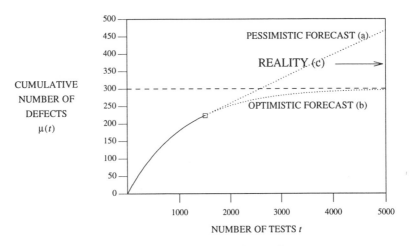

Figure 12.6   Two inadequate forecasts

While the interpolation is pragmatically attractive, it does not stand scientific rigor and may at best expose the limitations of the models.

In fact, the difficulty brought forth by Littlewood is not different from what practical field experience had already taught us about software reliability growth models. The optimistic models share their excessive reliance on preset fault density, namely these models assume a constant number of software defects known in advance. The pessimistic class is excessively driven by the derivative (fault finding rate) and will always overestimate the number of defects to be found.

The fault density driven models naturally tend to be more popular because the initial fault density is a parameter which can easily be derived from historical product data, and intuitively, it is very attractive to embed in a model readily available historical knowledge. A major drawback of this class of models is its optimism, namely the actual defect finding rate does not taper down when expected.

A possible practical instrument to model this effect is to introduce the *software revisiting rate*, β, which reflects the fact that for every defect fixed there will be a probability β to revisit the fix, because it which was either partial or incorrect. Curves a, b, and c in Figures 12.5 represent respectively a low, high and catastrophic effect of β. Practical measured values of the software revisiting rate range between 0.25 and 0.35. This seriously puts in question the assumption that, in most models, the revisiting rate is 0 [Goe85].

12.2.1.2   MODEL WITH SOFTWARE REVISIT RATE

As a result of the difficulties mentioned above and for benefits discussed below, a new model was developed [Lev87, Lcv89a, Lcv89b]. In addition to the initial fault density α and contrary to most models in the literature, the model presented here assumes a time-to-detection s, a non-zero defect repair time t, and a defect revisiting rate β, and is tightly coupled with the software production rate through the fault density and the defect detection time. The model with revisiting rate belongs to the "birth-death" family of models [Bai64, Kre83]. A good understanding of these parameters can provide the answers to the following questions:

1. How many defects are expected in the system at the time the system is delivered to the field? Is the system ready?
2. How many defects are expected in the future as a function of time after the system has been put in service? What is the expected failure rate as a function of time?
3. What is the required staffing profile needed to support the field deployment?

A — Defect Introduction, Detection and Removal during Software Development

During the development process, defects are introduced as a function of the size of the software being introduced or modified [Gaf84, Lip82]. The defects introduced at some point in time are discovered at later times and recorded as trouble reports. Critical defects and "ultra-visible" defects are discovered immediately, whereas latent defects remain in the system until they are exposed by the appropriate set of tests. The less critical and the less visible a defect is, the longer the defect will remain in the system undetected.

Without lowering the importance of achieving quality up front by better design practices [ATT86], it is important to consider the existence of software defects as a reality. As a matter of fact, the success of a development is largely determined by the programmers ability to eliminate defects in the speediest way [Abe79, Mon82]. Therefore, the software development process may be modeled as a defect removal process. Defect removal becomes the bottleneck of the design process. An important question becomes: when is system dependability high enough to release the system? [Dal88, Dal94, Lev89c, Lev90b, Lev91a, Mus89]

B — A Time Dependent Model

Calendar and execution time models [Goe85, Mus75] are common models for describing the dynamics of defect detection in large software projects.

Here, a calendar time model is developed. The model is based upon an incremental software introduction in the public domain. Every software increment is assumed to bring into the system a corresponding increment of defects. Tools have be developed to measure the incremental software deliveries (number of lines of code per incremental release).

The model developed here provides an analytical link between code introduction, fault detection and defect removal (Figure 12.7).

Given n lines of code, the number of defects appearing during time period i is described by

$$d_i = n\alpha e^{-s}\frac{s^i}{i!} \tag{12.1}$$

where α is the defect density per line of code. d_i is proportional to a Poisson distribution with mean time s. If we assume that the defect repair rate is described by a Poisson distribution with mean t, the removal rate of the $n\alpha$ defects introduced with n lines of code is described by the new Poisson distribution:

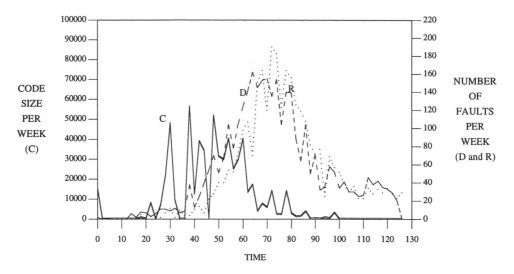

Figure 12.7   Code introduced (C), faults detected (D) and faults repaired (R)

$$r_i = n\alpha e^{-(s+t)} \frac{(s+t)^i}{i!} \tag{12.2}$$

which is the composition of two Poisson distributions, one with mean s and the other with mean t. In addition to the introduction of defects resulting from successive code submissions, each defect repair will require a revisiting of the software at the rate β, because of new defects reintroduction or incomplete repair, and the defect detection rate D_k for time period k becomes:

$$D_k = \alpha \sum_{i=0}^{k} n_{k-i} \gamma_i \tag{12.3}$$

for $0 \le k \le C$ and

$$D_k = \alpha \sum_{i=k-C}^{k} n_{k-i} \gamma_i \tag{12.4}$$

for $k > C$, where

$$\gamma_i = \sum_{j=0}^{\infty} \beta^j e^{-((j+1)s+jt)} \frac{((j+1)s+jt)^i}{i!} \tag{12.5}$$

Similarly, the defect removal is given by:

$$R_k = \alpha \sum_{i=0}^{k} n_{k-i} \phi_i \tag{12.6}$$

for $0 \leq k \leq C$ and

$$R_k = \alpha \sum_{i=k-C}^{k} n_{k-i}\phi_i \tag{12.7}$$

for $k > C$, where

$$\phi_i = \sum_{j=0}^{\infty} \beta^j e^{-(j+1)(s+t)} \frac{((j+1)(s+t))^i}{i!} \tag{12.8}$$

The median time m_D for D_k is given by the expression:

$$m_D = \frac{s + \beta t}{1 - \beta} + \frac{\sum_{i=0}^{C} i n_i}{\sum_{i=0}^{C} n_i} \tag{12.9}$$

Similarly, it can be shown that:

$$m_R = \frac{s + t + \beta t}{1 - \beta} + \frac{\sum_{i=0}^{C} i n_i}{\sum_{i=0}^{C} n_i} \tag{12.10}$$

Also, it appears that:

$$m_R - m_D = \frac{t}{1 - \beta} \tag{12.11}$$

Another important quantity is the predicted number of defects remaining to be fixed after time period T:

$$ERD_T = \alpha \frac{1}{1 - \beta} \sum_{i=0}^{C} n_i - \sum_{i=0}^{T} R_i \tag{12.12}$$

The estimated current defect number at time T, ECD_T, is an estimate of the level of defects currently in the system inclusive of the net open defect profile, NOD_T. The values of ECD_T make sense for $T \leq C$.

$$ECD_T = (1 - \beta)ERD_T \tag{12.13}$$

The testing process effectiveness, TPE_T, is the ratio:

$$TPE_T = \frac{\text{number of filtered defects found so far}}{\text{number of raw defects found so far}} \tag{12.14}$$

This ratio is a measure of the time spent on fixing real defects versus the time spent eliminating "false" defects. The testing process quality at time T (TPQ_T) is a measure of the success of the defect identification process so far. It is defined as:

$$TPQ_T = \frac{\text{number of defects found so far}}{\text{number of defects introduced so far}} \tag{12.15}$$

The previous formula becomes:

$$TPQ_T = \frac{\sum_{i=0}^{T} D_i}{\alpha \sum_{i=0}^{C} n_i + \beta \sum_{i=0}^{T} R_i}$$ (12.16)

The analytical model is fitted with the actual project data in Figures 12.7, and the resulting estimates are summarized in Table 12.2.

Table 12.2   Key parameters and variables (with defect reintroduction)

Defect Detection Time Constant s	17.2 Weeks
Defect Repair Time Constant t	4.7 Weeks
Code Delivery	589810 Lines
Initial Error Density α	0.00387 Defects per Line
Defect Reintroduction Rate β	33 Percent
Deployment Time T	Week 100
Estimated Remaining Defects ERD_T	664 Defects
Estimated Current Defects ECD_T	445 Defects
Testing Process Quality TPQ_T	90 Percent
Testing Process Efficiency TPE_T	60 Percent

The results above indicate that the time constants of the process for reliability improvement are very large, and therefore, it must be a very expensive process.

12.2.2   Process Control Deficiencies

An important question is that of establishing a more cost effective process control. However, two important deficiencies of the current software dependability improvement process may stand in the way:

A — Excessive Reliance on Back-end Quality Monitoring

One of the traditional software development process deficiencies is a tendency to be driven by emergency which in turn results in a back-end loaded process, namely heavy resources are invested late. The main disadvantages of a back-end loaded process are:

1. Large staff results in major inefficiencies.
2. There is no room for additional course corrections.

The solution to this problem resides in the institution of on-going quality gates to bring attention on difficulties as they occur instead of postponing them to the end of the process. The quality gates are distributed all along the development process.

B — Inadequate Operational Profile

A correct operational profile is a necessary condition for the validity of test data as a measure of quality and reliability. The operational profile [Mus87] represents the set of environment conditions which will guarantee that the test program is executed under realistic field conditions. Although the concept of operational profile is an elegant one, it may prove to be unusually difficult and often impossible to implement. A study of the telephone central offices was done in the US [Sys90] to determine the profile of the end-customers (features used) in each telephone central office. It became obvious that it would be impossible to accurately reflect all realistic situations. Instead, 9 canonical operational profiles were constructed (large metropolitan center, hospital, university, large business customer, etc.). A lab model was

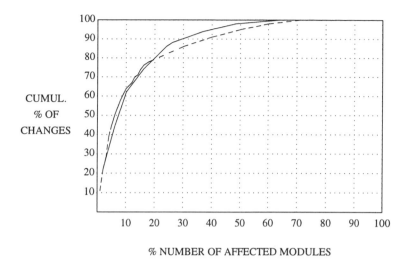

Figure 12.8   80 percent of the changes affect 20 percent of the modules

constructed for each model, but it proved extremely expensive to continuously maintain because of the need to assure consistency between large collections of data. The models proved equally prohibitively expensive to exercise in a meaningful way because they required large sets of automated tests. In practice, the automated test sets were too small, and the metrics derived from these tests tended to converge much before the product was ready for field, namely the fault finding rate of the automated tests became very low while the fault finding rate through manual testing was still too high for field release. In other words, the test metrics obtained by using the operational profile were *optimistic*. The reason for this result is the difficulty to execute an ever changing set of automated tests to avoid "tuning" the software for a limited experiment.

12.2.3   The Design Hole Conjecture

12.2.3.1   SOFTWARE ERROR CLUSTERING

Data collected under various circumstances demonstrate that software defects tend to concentrate in specific parts of the system. A typical distribution of software modifications against the number of software modules is given in Figure 12.8. Two typical subsystems in the 5ESS®system were selected (solid and dashed graphs). However, all the subsystems display a similar behavior, namely a large amount (80%) of the changes are concentrated in a small number (20%) of modules. These highly active modules during development will likely be the lingering cause of residual defects. This is in line with other studies [Gra92]. Although operational profiles could theoretically give more weights to active modules, deriving operational profiles for new additions to software is largely impractical.

There is a dual importance to the clustering of defects:

1. Eliminating clusters of defects is more economical than eliminating isolated defects.
2. The knowledge of the recent clustering information may be used as a guide to better position a test program in areas that are the likely sites of residual defects.

12.2.3.2   THE PRINCIPLE OF INCOMPLETENESS

Many quantitative theories of software reliability are based on defect enumeration, and they tend to consider bugs as discrete objects statistically distributed over the entire software space [Gaf84, Goe85, Lev87, Lev89a, Lev89b, Lip82]. In the classical prediction of residual defects, known bugs are subtracted from a preestimated quota (predicted total number of defects) regardless of the cause and nature of software defects. A different and alternative point of view, which is presented here, was developed by the author to alleviate difficulties encountered with traditional reliability models.

The mechanism that leads to software design errors is tightly related to the human factor, and must be analyzed from the point of view of human comprehension of complexity. During the software development process, corrections and improvements are performed, and new features are incrementally added. Each of these human interventions perturbs numerous system interactions. Since it is practically impossible for a single individual to comprehend the entire scope of possible interactions between modules that implement a feature, the programmers address a small fraction of the necessary software scope, and entire segments may be overlooked. At the beginning of the design process, the design is *incomplete*, and the debugging process is used to construct the missing areas. More obvious design segments and interactions are implemented earlier in the design process. Each large deficiency breaks down into many smaller ones. The design process stops when a compromise is reached between quality and cost. The software development process obeys two important rules:

The Impact of Complexity: *One large class of software bugs is caused by human inability to comprehend the design complexity within a finite time and cost.*

The Principle of Incompleteness: *Many Software bugs originate from design incompleteness. As the design matures, the missing design areas are progressively filled in, thus creating numerous smaller design deficiencies.*

The need for revisiting the same software for iterative repairs has been recognized in the industry as "fix-on-fix" or defect reintroduction [Lev90a]. The classical defect theories assume that the subsequent repairs are done to correct errors introduced in earlier repairs. The design hole hypothesis can offer one plausible cause of iterative code modification: the iterative code repairs can also be linked to incomplete designs in addition to erroneous repairs. A few definitions are now in order.

Definition 1: *Design Space or Scope*
   The design scope is the complete span of a design with its full intended functionality. The design scope corresponds to what is called *input space* in other contexts.
Definition 2: *Design Pass-Space*
   The design pass-space is the actual span of the correct part of the design. The design pass-space will generally be smaller than the design space.
Definition 3: *Design Fail-Space*
   The design fail-space is the complement of the design pass-space. It is the part of the design space that causes incorrect responses to legitimate inputs. It corresponds to the *fail space* in other contexts.
Definition 4: *Design Hole*
   A design hole is a subset of the design fail-space which is composed of closely related defects.

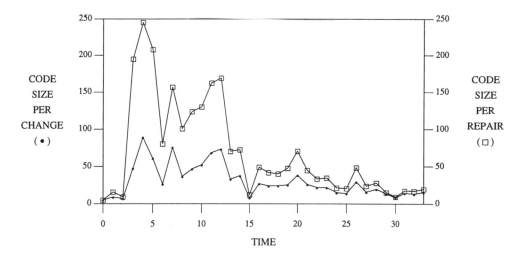

Figure 12.9   Code change size (in lines) per repair during development

12.2.3.3   DESIGN HOLE DISINTEGRATION

Statistical analysis of the way software development is done tends to confirm the theory of design holes and their disintegration. A repair generally contains multiple software changes due to the distributed nature of the system functionality. As can be seen in Figures 12.9, the size and the scope of changes progressively decreases as the design "converges," indicating a slow reduction of the design holes. Figure 12.9 shows that the number of changes per repair decreases with time from 4 to 1.2. This behavior is characteristic of all 5ESS®field releases.

12.2.4   The Manufacturization of the Testing Process

The size of large software systems often reaches millions of lines of source code that are developed by hundreds of programmers. By and large, the manufacturing of software does not adhere to robust disciplines, and recent advances in the software development methodology have not yet been widely accepted. Contrary to hardware manufacturing, software manufacturing is lacking the essential elements of statistical process control that have for decades been the attributes of other forms of manufacturing. Reduction of the variance is a key element in our ability to improve the quality of the testing process [Tag90].

Neither the theory of statistical manufacturing process control [Rya88] nor the statistical analysis of the software development [Goe85] are new. We show here a use of these techniques in the software development process [Lev91b].

12.2.4.1   THE ROLE OF TESTING: DEBUGGING OR PROCESS CONTROL

When testing is used strictly as a debugging mechanism, the execution of an exhaustive set of tests is required, and quality becomes dependent on mass inspection. Every possible situation needs to be explored, since testing will continue as long as there still exist bugs. *From the point of view of debugging, testing is aimed at proving that there are no more defects.* Projects that adopt this testing philosophy are bound to release defective products to the customer or incur extraordinary costs in a never ending quest for full test coverage. In fact, it is impossible to implement a test program that spans all possible situations.

When used for process control, testing helps identify the most defective areas first. As soon as an important defective area is found, testing is suspended and a corrective action is undertaken. *In the context of process control, testing is aimed at proving that there still are remaining defects.* This approach makes a more cost effective use of testing.

In practice, it is impossible to completely separate the two roles of testing and exclusively operate from one point of view or from the other, but, in reality, the tendency is to exclusively use testing for debugging purposes. Therefore, the question at hand is: "how does one refocus testing to serve as a process control mechanism?".

12.2.4.2   WHEN TO STOP TESTING?

The question: "when to stop testing?" can be asked in several contexts, and the answer is different depending on the situation.

Testing Purpose #1: *Assessing Software Quality by Fault Detection*
Question: *How long does one need to test for assessing software quality?*
Answer: *One can stop testing when enough tests have been executed to allow a determination of the software quality with high enough confidence.*
Testing Purpose #2: *Improving Software Quality by Fault Identification*
Question: *How long does one need to test for finding the software deficiencies?*
Answer: *One can stop testing when enough failure points have been generated to determine the likely source of the most important software deficiencies with high enough confidence.*
Testing Purpose #3: *Reaching Acceptable Software Quality*
Question: *How long does one need to test for reaching field quality?*
Answer: *One can stop testing when it can be determined with high enough confidence that the desired software quality is achieved.*

The remainder of this section focuses on developing a testing methodology that can serve as a process control mechanism, and help alleviate the difficulties addressed earlier. This testing methodology is used as a homing mechanism onto design holes, and it is combined with off-line debugging which is a cheaper alternative than testing defects one by one out of a system.

12.2.4.3   THE USE OF UNTAMPERED TEST METRICS FOR PROCESS CONTROL

The word "tampering" is often used in an ethical sense. Modifying information with the intent of defrauding represents an unethical form of tampering. In the context of this paper, tampering will be used in a systemic sense. In other words, systems that induce employees to distort failure data by providing them with unconscious incentives to do so practice "systemic tampering".
A — Unrepaired and Repaired Test Pass Rate
Commonly, software test programs are preset and run over several months. In a debugging-oriented test philosophy, the failing tests are repaired, rerun, and the testing operation ceases when "100% cumulative pass rate is reached". Unfortunately, the backlog of unrepaired known

defects is often used as the dominant measure of product quality. *Cumulative (repaired)* pass rate is computed as the sum of the initial *first pass (unrepaired)* pass rate and any correction due to repair of the faults that cause system failures during the initial execution. A 100% repaired pass rate can always be reached, no matter how low the initial pass rate was.

Our experience in the telecommunication industry has repeatedly shown that field quality does not correlate to the high level of system test cumulative pass rate (usually close to 100%) or, equivalently, to the small size of the backlog of unrepaired defects. This can be explained by the fact that system test programs represent at best a well-distributed small percentage of the universe of all reasonable system exercises. Obviously, improving the quality of a small sample will marginally affect the overall product quality.

In the hardware manufacturing process, mostly untampered failure data is used to control the process. The first pass pass rate (first pass yield) generated at a given test station is not recomputed to reflect the failure repairs. This fundamental ingredient allows the hardware manufacturing process managers to control the hardware production quality.

Giving to much importance to the cumulative pass rate is a typical example of systemic data tampering, since the project creates strong incentives for employees to speedily "improve" failure data by overemphasizing the measurement of residual unrepaired known defects. As a matter of fact, hasty repairs may in the long run adversely affect the product quality. The size of the backlog of unrepaired defects reflects the *project ability to fix known problems*, whereas the first pass pass rate reflects the *product quality*.

B — Cumulative Test Failures and Unrepaired Test Fail Rate

Often, the reliability of a software system is characterized by the instantaneous rate of failures and the cumulative number of failures. The *cumulative number of test failures* $\mu(t)$ can be modelled by the function

$$\mu(t) = \nu_0(1 - e^{-\frac{\lambda_0}{\nu_0}t})$$
(12.17)

where t is the testing time measured in testing hours [Kru89, Mus89] or in number of tests (Figure 12.10).

The derivative, $\lambda(t)$, of $\mu(t)$ is the *instantaneous rate of failure*

$$\lambda(t) = \lambda_0 e^{-\frac{\lambda_0}{\nu_0}t}$$
(12.18)

A special case of interest occurs when t is the number of tests executed. $\mu(t)$ becomes the *Cumulative Test Failures* and $\lambda(t)$ becomes the *Unrepaired Test Fail Rate*. Then, the first pass pass rate $p(t)$ is the complement of the derivative $\lambda(t)$, namely

$$p(t) = 1 - \lambda(t)$$
(12.19)

In other words, the derivative (slope) of $\mu(t)$ is a good indicator of product quality. A product will be acceptable if the derivative of $\mu(t)$ has a value below a given threshold. The model of Equation 12.17 is the simplest of a collection of published models. However, this will not affect the generality of our conclusions, since we are only interested in the slope of the curve regardless of its exact nature.

C — System Partitioning

Although many projects use uniform test metrics, practical experience has shown that software is not uniform in a given project. This observation yields a decomposition of software

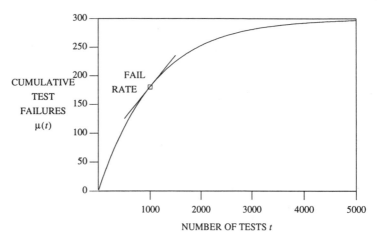

Figure 12.10   Cumulative test failures $\mu(t)$

into various functional areas for the purpose of testing and evaluation. First, a hierarchical decomposition may be considered (Table 12.3).

Table 12.3   Functional and testing hierarchy

FUNCTIONAL HIERARCHY	TEST HIERARCHY
Functional Area	*Evaluation Segment*
Complex Functionality	*Test Suite*
Functional Component	*Test Component*

Testing levels correspond to functional levels. A *Test Component* is an exercise that spans the smallest element of functionality, the functional component. For instance in telecommunication, the action of forwarding a call to another line is a test component. Generally, a test is a succession of steps that correspond to the execution of several functional components. A *Test Suite* is an ordered set of test components. An *Evaluation Segment* is a collection of test suites. Conceptually, a test suite can be considered as a traversal of functional modules.

D — Number of Test Suites for Detection Purposes: an Adaptive Test Program Size

The validity of the test results as a process control element depends on the size of the test sample which is determined by the desired level of confidence. The theory of sampling [Rya88] and random testing [Yar88] are well-established. For a given desired level of confidence, sample sizes can be determined using the variance of the test results.

A sample size between a few tens and a few hundreds is enough to approximate the incoming quality of a measured entity [Dem82, Mas89]. This test sample should be applied to a relatively homogeneous software functional area (evaluation segment). An example of using test sampling results for quality evaluation is given in Figure 12.11. The actual first pass pass rate p_s is computed as the sample size grows. p_{st} is the desired test suite pass rate target, and p_{st}^+ and p_{st}^- are the upper and lower 95% confidence levels, respectively. For a confidence level of 95%, p_{st}^+ and p_{st}^- are approximated by the following formulas:

$$p_{st}^+ = p_{st} + \frac{1.96\sigma}{n_s^{1/2}}$$

(12.20)

and

$$p_{st}^- = p_{st} - \frac{1.96\sigma}{n_s^{1/2}} \qquad (12.21)$$

where n_s is the number of test suites and $L = \frac{1.96\sigma}{n_s^{1/2}}$ is half the *ambiguity* interval. The level of confidence is inversely related to 2L (or the size of the variance). The variance σ is estimated by

$$\sigma = [p_{st}(1 - p_{st})]^{1/2} \qquad (12.22)$$

with a maximum value of 50%.

The upper and the lower confidence limits partition the graph of Figure 12.11 into three regions: the *acceptance region*, the *rejection region* and the *ambiguity region*. As soon as the number of tests drives the pass rate into the acceptance region or the rejection region, it is possible to stop testing with a definite conclusion about the product quality. A pass rate in the ambiguity region requires to continue testing until the pass rate reaches one of the two definite regions or until testing is no more economical. For a sample size of T or larger, the test results in Figure 12.11 probably indicate poor software quality.

It is important to notice that less tests are needed to assess both high and poor quality product than to assess marginal results (close to the target). This has a serious economic consequences towards the end of the development process: *more and more resources (tests) are needed to provide a reliable assessment of the product quality as quality increases unless the quality becomes very high* [Lev89c].

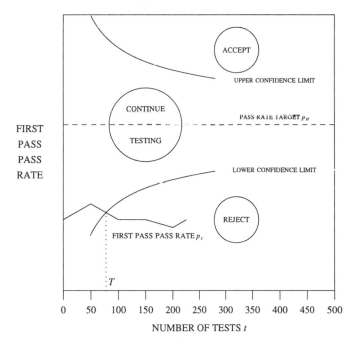

Figure 12.11 Sample size and confidence limits

The correctness of Equations 12.20 and 12.21 is predicated on the validity of the statistical distribution underlying the testing results (we have assumed a binomial distribution). However, our experience confirms the validity of statistical sample data analysis, even if the statistical distribution underlying the data is not well characterized. Specifically, actual values of the variance of the first pass pass rates were found to be very small for sample sizes of a few tens of tests. Alternate methods for adaptive (sequential) sampling have been documented for statistical control of manufacturing [Gra88].

E — System Functional Decomposition to Aid Fault Identification

The statistical method explained above can be applied to any evaluation segment. The test suite pass rate produces a "GO/NO GO" decision for the evaluation segment (fault detection). In case of a "NO GO" decision, an additional mechanism is needed to narrow down the problem to a lower level root cause, namely the functional component (fault identification). During test suite execution, a count is kept for both component test execution and fail rate. Equations 12.20 and 21 can be extended to component pass rates as well, yielding the following results.

$$P_{ct}{}^{+} = P_{ct} + \frac{1.96\sigma}{n_c{}^{1/2}} \tag{12.23}$$

and

$$P_{ct}{}^{-} = P_{ct} - \frac{1.96\sigma}{n_c{}^{1/2}} \tag{12.24}$$

where P_{ct} and n_c are the component pass rate target and the number of component tests executed, respectively.

The fail rates for the various modules of a typical project are provided in Figure 12.12. The relative concentration of failures indicates the relative quality of the software segments represented by test components (functional modules). A functional module with a high fail rate is likely to be affected by a "megabug". Isolating modules with potential megabugs is a cost effective way of improving quality.

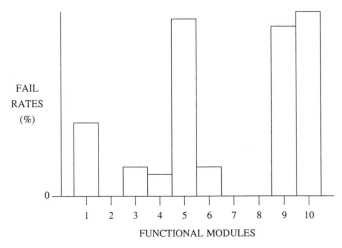

Figure 12.12   Failure data distribution against functional modules

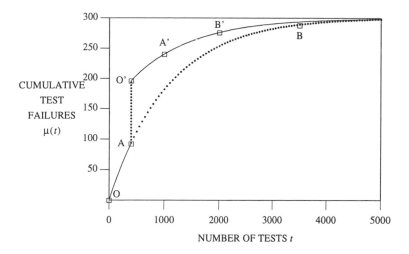

Figure 12.13 Cumulative test failures for a functional area

12.2.4.4   USE OF UNREPAIRED PASS RATE AS A PROCESS CONTROL METRIC

As discussed earlier in Section 12.2, error prevention methods are essential to lower the risk of field product quality to be too low. However, it is necessary to accept the reality of error correction and optimize its efficiency, since it is the last resort for protecting the customers interest. Also, appropriate analysis of the corrected errors can in the long run lead to error prevention.

A quality improvement methodology based on "megabug" identification and elimination is discussed next. Assume that a testing program has reached point A in the process of evaluating a given software functional area (Figure 12.13).

It was shown [Lev91a] that the instantaneous rate of failure $\lambda(t)$ (derivative of $\mu(t)$) is a good measure of quality. If the derivative of $\mu(t)$ at A is too high (the first pass pass rate is too low), then the software quality is too low. A possible solution consists of continued testing until the pass rate (derivative) is acceptable (point B on the dotted curve). This alternative requires the execution of a large number of new tests, $t_B - t_A$, and may be impractical. At this point, it is more appropriate to stop and examine a functional decomposition of the defect data. The results will guide the designer to reexamine the software design and repair large design holes. Redesigning defective areas results in jumping to point O' on a higher curve with a lower failure rate. The derivative at O' is again approximated by performing additional testing until point A'. This either yields an acceptable derivative or the distance to point B' with an acceptable derivative is smaller than the distance to an acceptable derivative on the original curve, namely

$$t'_B - t'_A < t_B - t_A \qquad (12.25)$$

If the derivative is not acceptable but the point with an acceptable one is close enough, then it is appropriate to reach the point by an additional testing program. This procedure may have to be repeated if $t'_B - t'_A$ is too large. The choice between the various alternatives should be based on an economic decision.

12.2.4.5   MANUFACTURIZATION OF THE SYSTEM TEST PHASE

This section describes the result of an experiment that was recently conducted in a software project for a large distributed system (5E6 release of the 5ESS$^{\circledR}$system). During this experiment, a "manufacturization" of the back end of the development process was implemented using most of the techniques described earlier. The software release included a substantial hardware architectural modification and spanned approximately one million of new and modified source code built on an existing base of several millions of source code. The data collected during the experiment [Sys90] provides the base for the analysis of the remainder of this section. Subsets of the data are provided in the sequence (Tables 12.4 to 12.7).

The early field failure rate for the recent release is 60% lower than the early field failure rate of previous releases and is 10% lower than the current field failure rate of the previous release after 15 months of field exposure. In addition, the frequent abortions of new software installations have practically disappeared.

A — Repetitions in a Manufacturing Process

In any manufacturing process, repetition is the key element that allows the application of statistical process control. Usually, the repetition happens along the time dimension, namely a new copy of the product is produced at regular intervals. However, space repetition is also used for process control. For instance, n production stations working in parallel constitute a space repetition, and the failure data produced by all the stations can be compared in order to identify and correct abnormal station behavior. In the case of time or space repetition, the repetition must be large enough to justify the use of statistics. *Conversely, the existence of space or time repetitions in a process allows its modelling as a "manufacturing" process.*

In software, there are several possible dimensions of meaningful repetition:

1. The various modules in a given software delivery represent a space repetition.
2. The implementation of all evaluation segments in a software delivery represents another type of space repetition.
3. The successive execution of test suites within a given evaluation segment represents a time repetition that maps directly to the second space repetition mentioned above.

The various forms of repetition happening at every phase of the software manufacturing process provide the base for the use of statistical methods to control this process and the transitions between its phases. The use of time and space repetitions is illustrated next.

B — The Manufacturization of System Test: a Case Study

The process used is described in Figure 12.14. Partitioning the features into 54 groups of features (evaluation segments ES_1 to ES_n) constituted space repetition. Grouping features into feature groups is essential for providing comparisons between groups of features and between features in the same group. Four successive evaluation intervals realized a time repetition. Time repetition is essential for measuring the rate at which the fail rate decreases and the software approaches field quality.

The implementation of the system test phase using the four subphases described in Figure 12.14 constitutes a manufacturing process within the system test phase.

C — The Economics of Quality Assessment

As discussed earlier, less tests are needed to assess the quality of software when the quality is far below or far above the acceptability threshold than close to it. This can be seen in Figure 12.11.

If the pass rate remains in the ambiguity region, more tests are executed, and several alternatives are available afterwards:

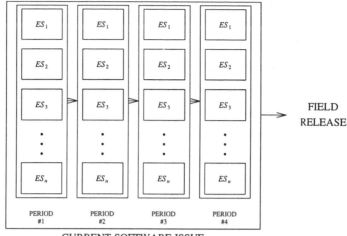

CURRENT SOFTWARE ISSUE

Figure 12.14   Manufacturization of system test

1. If the results are definitely in the acceptance region, stop testing
2. If the results are definitely in the rejection region, repair the software
3. If the results are still ambiguous, two possibilities are available:

   (a) Continue the test/repair cycle until the ambiguity is lifted
   (b) Stop testing and release the product anyway

Under alternative 3, the choice between pursuing and stopping testing depends on a cost/benefit tradeoff and a risk analysis. The pass rate is likely to remain around the ambiguity region until many tests are executed and the software repaired. At this point, the risk of releasing an imperfect product must be weighed against lost market opportunities before a decision is made. The difficulty originates from the fact that, in the ambiguity region, a few failure points are available to accelerate the product quality into the acceptance region.

D — System Evaluation using Evaluation Segments

It is important to note that the test suites in the four evaluation intervals must be distinctly different in order to provide an untampered view of the product quality. Along the four evaluation intervals, the testing results showed substantial improvements due to the identification and repair of design holes. The resulting first pass pass rates (FPPR) and failures per test (FPT) are given in Table 12.4.

Table 12.4   Quality improvements during the software manufacturing process

Period	#1	#2	#3	#4
FPPR	75%	80%	84%	90%
FPT	0.115	0.108	0.072	0.080

A closer look is now given to evaluation segments. As mentioned earlier, a test suite is composed of test components. The components that are critical to an evaluation segment are key to the evaluation segment. The non-critical ones may provide additional information for the evaluation of other evaluation segments for which they are critical. First pass pass rates (FPPR) for Period #1 are given in Table 12.5. The variance of the FPPR is much smaller for the component test pass rates than for the test suite pass rates.

Table 12.5   Test suite and test component pass rates

Feature Subset	Test Suite FPPR	Test. Comp. FPPR	Crit. Comp. FPPR
ES_1	86%	98%	94%
ES_2	96%	99%	99%
ES_3	67%	90%	89%
ES_4	75%	94%	97%
ES_5	72%	95%	94%
ES_6	92%	97%	98%
ES_7	90%	96%	96%
ES_8	71%	95%	90%
ES_9	97%	99%	98%
ES_{10}	86%	96%	98%
ES_{11}	76%	97%	87%
ES_{12}	91%	96%	88%
ES_{13}	67%	87%	89%
ES_{14}	92%	97%	97%

A further analysis of the FPPR of the critical components of an evaluation segment will help identify which functional module is most likely to be the site of a "megabug". In Table 12.5, the test suite FPPR for ES_{11} indicates a quality problem. The FPPR distribution for four critical components of feature set ES_{11} is given in Table 12.6. Critical components c_{i1} and c_{i2} definitely point at the cause of the quality problem. Note that critical component c_{i4} has a low FPPR. However, there were too few tests, and more tests were required for a good fault identification.

Table 12.6   Critical component FPPR for ES_{11}

Component	c_{i1}	c_{i2}	c_{i3}	c_{i4}
Tests	55	44	71	18
FPPR	87%	80%	100%	61%

The example of Table 12.6 is consistent with the observation [Dem82, Lev91a] that only a few tens of samples are sufficient to produce a good estimate of the product quality.

12.2.5   Are Testing Metrics Really Untamperable?

12.2.5.1   VARIANCE DUE TO HUMAN FACTOR

An experiment was conducted over a four-week period among 51 testers to assess the importance of human factor variance. Each tester was responsible for a different functionality, but all were told that the experiment would focus on individual fault finding rate. As expected fault finding rates started diverging significantly (Table 12.7), and a closer examination of the techniques used by individuals show an important pattern: all the individuals with the highest fault discovery rates had found a way to home onto software vulnerabilities by testing areas where the code had been recently significantly modified because of new features or significant recent deficiencies. By using a combination of "street wisdom " and actual software knowledge the most productive testers had been able to home in on design vulnerabilities ("design holes"). Operationally, the testers used a combination of black box (functional) testing and white box (code structure) testing.

Table 12.7   Testing results for a four-week period

TESTER IDENTIFICATION	PROBLEMS OPENED	REAL FAULTS
1	55	48
2	50	46
3	49	45
4	27	25
5	26	24
6	21	21
7	20	19
.	.	.
.	.	.
.	.	.
37	1	1
.	.	.
.	.	.
44	1	0
45	0	0
.	.	.
51	0	0

This experiment indicates the plausibility of the "design hole" hypothesis, namely an area of the software where a concentration of defects exists. In the neighborhood of a design hole, the probability of failing a test is the highest. In different terms, the test program is approaching an area of *software instability,* which acts like a *pole* in linear systems. Further research is required to better define and locate software instability. Testers 1-7 seem to have empirically homed on to design holes.

12.2.5.2   A NEW CHALLENGE FOR AN OLD TECHNOLOGY: HARNESS THE VARIANCE

It would be attractive to develop a theory of software stability (and instability) similar to the theory of linear systems stability. However, such a theory is not at hand. In the mean time, it is possible to develop testing instrumentation which enables "homing" on design holes [Cla92]. This instrumentation is a tool which emulates the experiment described in the previous section, namely directs the testing towards areas which detect more software errors by measuring the changes in fault finding rate: the larger the rate (faults/tests), the closer testing is to a design hole or instability. The purpose of testing then becomes that of maximizing the fault finding rate.

12.3 RECOVERY: A SUCCESSFUL BUT EXPENSIVE STRATEGY

The existence of recovery software is predicated on the assumption that it is impossible to deliver high quality hardware and software. It is the need for a system to operate correctly in the presence of these hardware or software faults that led to the development of large recovery software. In the 5ESS®switch, software development costs are an order of magnitude larger than hardware development costs, and 38% of this software deals with recovery. This represents a significant overhead cost directly related to the imperfections of hardware and software.

5ESS®recovery software has traditionally been partitioned into *Hardware Failure Recovery Software*, or in short *Fault Recovery Software*, and *Software Fault Recovery Software*, or *Software Integrity*. Of course, the boundary between the two is not totally unambiguous because some hardware failure may cause software corruptions without being clearly identifiable as hardware failures. For all AT&T switching products, the two segments of recovery software are regulated by recovery strategies and escalation levels [Cle86].

The recovery from hardware failures requires fault detection implements which are capable of rapidly identifying the presence of these failures and performing some degree of correction. At detection time, error data is automatically collected and stored so that it can be later analyzed. After error detection, a multi-level recovery strategy is used with an escalation policy, ultimately leading to resource swapping and system reconfiguration decisions based on alternate resource availability. In the case of the 5ESS®switch, several forms of redundancy are used in different parts of the system depending on the criticality of the function of each one of these parts (duplex, $m + k$,...). At the end of reconfiguration and after the system resumes operation, automatic troubleshooting is initiated in the suspected failing unit.

Two basic strategies are utilized for software fault recovery: dynamic error checking for very critical software, and data check for the remainder of the software. The data checks assume that a software error will ultimately manifest itself as a data error or inconsistency. Here too, an escalation strategy has been commonly used.

12.3.1 External Recovery Software Versus Embedded Hardware Recovery

Traditionally, hardware fault recovery has partially been embedded in the hardware while its software component was external to the application. The software fault recovery has essentially been external. Embedding recovery in the hardware has resulted in extremely high cost of hardware design and manufacturing goods. This is aggravated by the high proprietary nature of the hardware which prevents an economy of numbers and also affects software portability. The external nature of the recovery software makes it difficult to tune to specific applications and makes it vulnerable to inadequacies.

12.3.2 The Nature and Implications of Software Errors

As reported earlier [Cle86], several observations about software development are essential. Two software classes can be identified:

1. *High usage software*
   This is software which deals with delivering to the customer essential system functions which will be triggered by end customer requests. These include basic call processing, billing, system provisioning, customer data and office administration, etc.

2. *Low usage software*

This category includes software which is run infrequently and software triggered by unexpected events. Recovery software belongs to that category. Some parts of call processing may belong to low usage software depending on the selling patterns and service cost policies of the service providers.

High usage software is easier to test and will ultimately receive the highest exposure. Therefore, its quality improvement curve will be the steepest. Conversely, recovery software will be the most difficult to "train." Testing it thoroughly in laboratory is impossible, and its field exposure will be the lowest, making its reliability improvement curve the flattest.

Recovery software can be triggered by errors originating from hardware or software or can be run on a routine basis. For instance, defensive diagnostic software can be routinely run in sensitive hardware areas on a low priority basis when processing cycles are available. The same can be done for routine audits which examine the consistency of software and data.

Software failures may be primary or secondary. A software *primary* failure is a failure that originated from a single error in a segment of code. A software *secondary* failure is a failure that originated from an erroneous reaction of a segment of software to another imperfection in software or in hardware.

Example 1: A software bug in call processing causes a call to be interrupted. The system routines that are in charge of cleaning up the data structures associated with interrupted calls does its job correctly. The software bug is primary.

Example 2: As a result of a hardware failure, a segment of recovery software takes the wrong hardware unit out of service. This software error is a secondary failure to the original hardware failure.

Example 3: Recovery software exhibits a secondary failure as a result of a primary call routing error.

Example 4: As a result of a routine audit of system data, recovery software erroneously tears down all call processing in a community of 256 customers. This failure is primary in recovery software. Although such cases are possible, most of the field failures in recovery software are secondary failures.

As the product improves in the field, primary failures in hardware or in software outside the recovery software will become rarer and rarer, thus decreasing the exposure of the recovery software and slowing down its debugging. In conclusion, the recovery software is likely to remain with the highest fault density, because its improvement depends on field exposure, as for any other software.

12.3.3 Software Which Does Not Fail Does Not Exist

Table 12.8 summarizes the field fault densities (x) and the fault densities during development (y) for a given product release. This release was composed of a significant hardware configuration change and a large increment of software (850,000 lines of code). The results were measured over 4 years.

The development and field fault density [Lip82] are obtained by dividing the number of development and field errors by the size of the code. x/y is the *training ratio*.

The data in Table 12.8 demonstrate the high "training" experienced by the high usage software (upper segment of Table 12.8). It is therefore likely that the high usage software has significantly improved as a result of this "training." Conversely, the low usage software (lower segment of Table 12.8) receives poor field training and displays a significantly lower

Table 12.8 Development and field fault density comparison

Software Increment Size	Development Fault Density (y)	Field Fault Density (x)	Training Ratio x/y	Software Type
42069	0.0285	0.0072	0.2543	Preventive Maintenance
5422	0.0673	0.0210	0.3123	Billing
9313	0.0793	0.0277	0.3491	Field Update Software
14467	0.0265	0.0072	0.2741	System Growth
165042	0.1016	0.0053	0.0534	Hardware Fault Recovery
16504	0.0841	0.0020	0.0237	Software Fault Recovery
38737	0.1494	0.0058	0.0393	Hardware and Software System Integrity

training ratio. These measures clearly indicate serious problems with operational profile during software development.

12.3.4   Software Exposure and Software Improvement

The improvements of hardware and software (Figures 1 and 2) due to field exposure cause a rapid irrelevance of large amounts of recovery software. After a short interval in the field, the improvement of recovery software becomes very slow, postponing its maturation.

Most of the impact of fault recovery software occurs during system development, and helps maintain reasonable system cycling when the system has not yet reached field grade. In a laboratory experiment, system integrity software was turned off at various points during the development cycle to measure a global software quality metric. At the worse point in development (highest software failure rate in Figure 2), the system could not stay up beyond ten minutes without system recovery software. A few days before release the system remained up for one week before the experiment was stopped. In a sense, this indicates that a large part of the role of recovery software is aimed at maintaining a satisfactory design environment by allowing the system to run in the lab in spite of a relatively high number of hardware failures and software errors. It also allows to deliver to the field a product that is still imperfect. But, over a short period of time, the hardware and software reliability improvements make the recovery software somewhat irrelevant. However, when invoked, recovery software may exhibit secondary failures. Therefore, excessive reliance in the field on imperfect recovery software may prove to be more detrimental than it is beneficial since it is based on partially immature software, as exhibited in recent noted field incidents.

Given the decreasing number of field failure triggers, the time to significantly improve this software may go beyond the product useful life. Certainly, because of its sheer size (38% of the total software), large recovery software represents a costly strategy for achieving system dependability. On the other hand, since the cost of injecting failures in the laboratory prior to field release proves equally prohibitive, one cannot realistically avoid relying on field training of recovery software.

There also is a hidden cost of using "untrained" recovery software. Non-catastrophic, unattended errors will tend to absorb excessive hardware resources further increasing the cost to performance ratio of the hardware.

In conclusion, recovery software may end up serving as a placebo, in the best case, and being detrimental, in the worst case.

12.4   A MODERN STRATEGY FOR DESIGNING DEPENDABLE SYSTEMS

12.4.1   Low Cost Upfront Hardware Dependability

Some of the techniques explained below are consistent with Bernstein and Yuhas [Ber93]. An essential step of a better strategy for system dependability is to increase up front dependability of its components.

1. Increased Reliance on Off-the-shelf Components
   Excessive utilization of specialized designs causes excessive failure rates and excessive reliance on recovery software. Conversely, using commercial components will allow the system designers to "ride" on commercial quality and performance curves, achieving earlier hardware maturation. This in turn will allow lowering the investment in recovery software. The use of commercial hardware components brings with it the potential of increasing the usage of commercial processors and their software, furthering the dependability of the system components.
2. Decrease Reliance on Duplex Configurations
   With an increase in commercial computers dependability, it may be feasible to rely less on duplex recovery mode in favor of $m + k$ techniques which may be more economical.
3. System and Functionality Distribution
   Distribution of functionality allows to reduce system complexity and therefore decreases the cost of achieving reliability targets. This technique enhances the usability of off-the-shelf system components, and it also allows to better choose hardware quality (and cost) in a range of possibilities and limit the use of proprietary hardware where absolutely necessary:

   (a) Fault tolerant hardware for high performance application segments.
   (b) High availability commercial hardware for mid-range applications.
   (c) Regular commercial hardware for the remainder.

   Interestingly enough, this trend may already be emerging in telecommunication and will affect its economy in the same way computer distribution to the end-user's desk has affected computing.
4. Use of Client-server Model
   This model strengthens our ability to implement a choice of hardware attributes and makes it a better fit for a simplified recovery software because distribution creates smaller software segments with more robust boundaries between them, yielding a better software architecture [Bor93].

12.4.2   Low Cost Upfront Software Dependability

In the past, significant effort has been invested in formally constructing software [Bac78, Pry77]. However, these techniques have not yielded a lowering of software development costs and time-to-market, because they have transferred the complexity from software programming to software specifications.

Some progress has been achieved in the area of empirical software robustness methods [Bro95]. This work provided a prototype software development environment using object orientation which supports the concept of *Software Physical Design*, namely the boundaries of software components are given a certain amount of rigidity (physical design) similar to hardware components. This concept is implemented by requiring mapping of software components (objects) on processors during execution and communication exclusively performed by messaging. It is important to mention that robust recovery strategies can be implemented in a similar way by taking advantage of the partitioning provided by the software "physical design" [Bro95].

The resulting productivity increased by an order of magnitude, but the method fell short of a complete hardware analogy by not focusing on the software *Logic Design*, which can provide another dimension of software reuse. Indeed, as long as software technologies will remain *generic* in nature, software reuse will not be feasible on a large scale.

12.4.2.1   SOFTWARE ASSEMBLY SPEED AND CUSTOMIZATION

Without minimizing the need to improve current software production processes, it must be noted that today software production is largely a manual process. This is why the necessary additional breakthroughs can only be achieved by technological solutions which can in turn lead to the industrialization of the software production process. The essential ingredients to achieve upfront software dependability are:

1. Reusability of software components
2. Customization by software layering
3. Ease of software assembly and portability by using platforms

12.4.2.2   DOMAIN ANALYSIS AND SOFTWARE REUSE

It is interesting to analyze software technologies along two dimensions, expansion factor and degree of specialization. The expansion factor is a measure of the amount of object code generated by the invocation of a language high level construct. For instance, C++ may have an expansion factor 3 times larger than C. Larry Bernstein observed (private communication) that the expansion factor grows by an order of magnitude every 20 years, yielding commensurate productivity improvements. While recovery software principles have remained practically constant over the years, improvements in software technologies have continued to happen. Fundamentally, software engineers can now write software with a large "expansion factor" by using better languages and technologies. This improvement is based on an increase of the elementary language constructs which become larger reusable units. These techniques can improve the initial quality of software deliveries making the reliance on recovery software less necessary. Continued emphasis on initial software quality may prove to be a more economical route.

The second dimension, specialization, represents the degree to which a software technology is specially tailored for a given application. For instance, Finite State Machine (FSM) definition languages have expansion factors similar to C but a higher degree of specialization.

Figure 12.15 is a representative map of a few software technologies. The technologies at the bottom of the map are the most popular ones, and by and large, the upper region of the map is less popular. This probably illustrates one of the major differences between software applications and other engineering applications. Indeed, specialized technologies have been critical in bringing many application domains to the industrial age. For instance, manufacturing could not have become effective without specialized technologies. In a similar fashion, it is expected that specialization of software technologies will bring software applications to the industrial age, namely will provide high velocity and low cost. The *Domain of Opportunities* is the area of the map of Figure 12.15 which represents technologies with high expansion factor and high specialization. Although this area of the map is not heavily populated, it is expected that this area will become denser as software becomes less of an art and more of a technology.

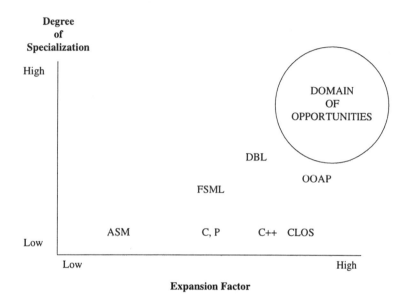

Figure 12.15   Software expansion factor and software specialization

The acronyms used in Figure 12.15 are given in Table 12.9.

Table 12.9   Sample of software technologies

ASM	Assembler
C	C Programming Language
P	Pascal Programming Language
C++	C++ Programming Language
CLOS	Common Lisp
FSML	Finite State Machine Programming Languages
DBL	Data Base Applications Languages
OOAP	Object Oriented Applications

As in any other industrial domain, specialization can occur only after thorough *Domain Analysis*. Much of the on-going work is predicated on the assumption that each application domain ought to yield its own flavor of specialization. Applications have ranged from telecommunication applications [Gac94, Kol92, Lev95] to general computing applications [Huy93].

12.4.2.3   RAPID CUSTOMIZATION AND SOFTWARE LAYERING

Our approach is to provide various degrees of software customization by creating three software layers defined in Table 12.10. The programming in each layer uses programming elements from the adjacent layer below and produces products which are used as elements in the adjacent layer above. Primitive capabilities are used to produce building blocks, and building blocks are used to produce services.

While the service layer allows service assembly and customization, additional customization can be achieved by providing programmability of the building blocks using lower level specialized primitive capabilities. This is expected to provide a simplification of the existing programming paradigms (C, C++,...) by harnessing specialization. As a result of higher specialization of all the layers, our approach moves our work to the domain of opportunities on the map of Figure 12.15. As a result of developing specialized software technologies, an advantageous relationship ought to appear between programming ease (velocity) and service revenue opportunity (Figure 12.16). The upper layer ought to be the easiest to program and produce the largest revenue. Conversely, the lower layer should be the stablest and the least rewarding to modify.

Table 12.10   Software assembly programming layers

PROGRAMMING LAYER	ELEMENTS USED	PRODUCTS LOCATION
SERVICE (GUI*)	BUILDING BLOCKS	SERVICE SOFTWARE
INTERMEDIATE (AOL**)	PRIMITIVE CAPABILITIES	BUILDING BLOCKS
PLATFORM	GENERIC SOFTWARE	PRIMITIVE CAPABILITIES

*GUI: Graphical User Interface
*AOL: Application Oriented Language

12.4.2.4   NETWORK EXECUTION PLATFORMS AND PRIMITIVE CAPABILITIES

The lower software layer provides primitive capability access for the software layer above it. In a sense, it acts as a specialized *Operating System* whose role is to interact both with the layer above it and with various network resources. The lower layer acts as a platform and its role is to facilitate the programming of the building blocks in the intermediate layer above it.

The Network Execution Platform is composed of a number of *Genies*, each one capable of providing support to the application software above it through a collection of primitive capabilities, and of communicating with the network through a hardware platform. Each genie is specialized to a specific domain of support. Examples are given next.

1. Signaling Genie: takes care of tracking and interpreting telecommunication signaling messages.
2. Network Functions Genie: invokes network resources and functions (for instance, executes I/O commands such as ASCII translation to voice or voice collection and storage).

PROGRAMMING PYRAMIDS

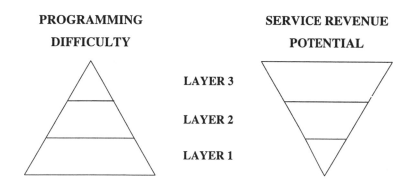

Figure 12.16 Programming difficulty and service revenue potential in software layers

3. Service Data Genie: accesses service description data bases.
4. System Integrity Genie: takes care of error recovery using hardware independent Recovery Software.

There are two merits of defining a Network Execution Platform: a) the hardware can be upgraded to track industry performance and cost curves, and b) different service domains can use the same platform as long as the necessary primitive capabilities are provided by the platform (Figure 12.17). The network execution platform is a client which can invoke resources, R_1,..., R_n, distributed on network servers.

12.4.2.5 INTERMEDIATE PROGRAMMING: CONSTRUCTION OF REUSABLE BUILDING BLOCK

In general, a robust service software assembly environment ought to provide simple technologies to program building blocks based on the availability of powerful platform functionalities as described in Section 12.4.2.4. The benefit of a simple programming paradigm over existing paradigms (i.e. finite state machines) is velocity of new building block construction. The power of the primitive capabilities provided by the network execution platform is the key to this simplicity.

In a typical telecommunication context, reusable robust software building blocks can be designed and reused to assemble more complex software which implements complete services. Typical building blocks represent often used capabilities such as Voice Message Storing, Synthetic Voice Prompting, Dial Tone Message Collection, Call Transfer, etc. The existence of these executable software building blocks allows to assemble and execute more complex functionality.

12.4.2.6   SERVICE SOFTWARE ASSEMBLY ENVIRONMENT AND NETWORK
           EXECUTION PLATFORM

Figure 12.17 represents a simplified system architecture capable of supporting the approach
described in Section 12.4.

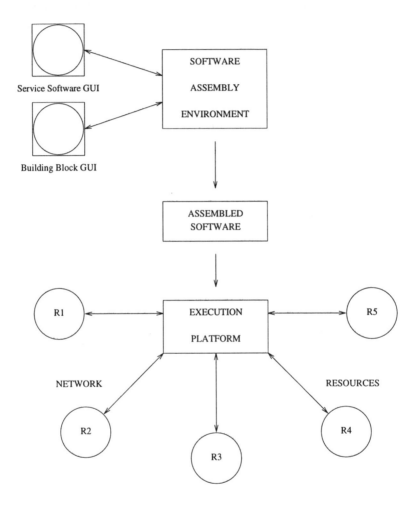

Figure 12.17   System architecture

The service Software Assembly Environment (SAE) is a two-layered programming environment including the service layer and the building block layer, each layer with its programming
paradigm, aided by Graphical User Interfaces (GUI). The software generated in the SAE is
shipped to the Network Execution Platform after having been adequately verified. The service
software is executed by the service manager which can access the network resources through
the genies in the network execution platform.

In addition, the language constructs drive both a *simulation* of the service under assembly
and the *production* of the software to be executed on the network execution platform.

12.4.2.7   MORE RELIANCE ON RECOVERY SOFTWARE METHODOLOGIES

In rethinking the recovery strategy, it is important to distribute it when appropriate and move it from hardware to software as much as possible. Coupled with an appropriate choice of "fault-tolerance quality," this allows the appropriate hardware cost and performance overhead choices.

As discussed in Chapter 10, Huang and Kintala [Hua93] recognize 4 levels of recovery:

- *Level 1*: detection and restart; data may still be inconsistent.
- *Level 2*: Level 1 plus periodic check of dynamic data and recovery of internal states.
- *Level 3*: Level 2 plus check and recovery of static data.
- *Level 4*: continuous operation by duplication (hot spares, etc.).

These authors experimented with fault tolerant software that can address levels 1,2 and 3, and recover from faults undetected by hardware. The method incurred a performance overhead of 0.1% to 14%. The strategy is composed of the following three components:

1. *A watchdog daemon process (watchd)* which watches the cycle of local application process, recovers to the last checkpoint or to a standard state, can watch other watchdogs and reconfigure the network, and can watch itself to a certain extent.
2. *A library of C-functions for fault tolerance (libft)* which can be used in application programming to specify checkpoints and establish the recovery strategy. They allow tuning of the performance/resilience ratio of the recovery.
3. *A multi-dimensional file system (nDFS)* which allows the replication of critical data and is built on top of UNIX, which lowers design costs.

As opposed to hardware recovery, these techniques allow transferring the design effort from designing a complex mechanism to that of designing a strategy that is easily implementable by "off-the-shelf" software components (libraries). Since these techniques lend themselves to some degree of "mechanization" in implementing recovery software, they can help tune the strategy with respect to the frequency and amount of dynamic data (as well as static data) to be recovered. This can also facilitate software portability, making hardware upgrades easier.

A more detailed description is provided in Chapter 10.

12.4.2.8   RECOVERY SOFTWARE BUILT IN REUSABLE COMPONENTS

The aforementioned strategy for rapid assembly of reusable software components requires to rethink and modernize the strategy for recovery from hardware failures and software errors. Indeed, it would make no sense to rapidly assemble service software if it had to take a considerable amount of time to provide the software dependability. Therefore, it is necessary to develop modular recovery software which can be built automatically during the software assembly process. Using more dependable components will release the fault tolerance designer from the need to worry about the internal behavior of the components as a result of faults, and focus instead on the system as a whole. In addition to the standard reliability techniques used in commercial products, it may be feasible to implement "boundary" hardware reliability techniques to aid system recovery.

In addition to using the aforementioned software recovery techniques, variable degrees of service dependability can be achieved by replicating on multiple platforms services and/or service resources, depending on their criticality [Bar93] and the economic value of the desired level of service dependability. Evidently, a successful application of service component replication depends on more rigorous application programming technologies.

12.5 CONCLUSIONS

Although traditional methodologies for designing large dependable software have been feasible in many industries (telecommunications, space, aeronautics, etc,), these methodologies have proven expensive, lengthy, and inflexible. In order to maintain leadership and competitiveness, software manufacturing will have to move toward industrialization which can be enabled by reusability of specialized software components for both operational and recovery softwares.

This chapter is based on the work of many engineers who, over the years, have made the 5ESS$^{\circledR}$switch a success. They have met the challenges of producing a very large system which has exceeded customers quality and availability expectations. The experience gained and the dependability improvements achieved over the years can now be embodied in a "leaner" recovery strategy more in line with the economic trends of the nineties.

ACKNOWLEDGEMENTS

I am deeply indebted to L.Bernstein whose challenging questions and insights have contributed to shape the viewpoints expressed here. My thanks also go to the team of Steel Huang which has produced some of the data used here.

REFERENCES

[Abe79]   J. Abe, K. Sakurama, and H. Aiso. An analysis of software project failures. In *Proc. of the 4th. International Conference on Software Engineering*, Munich, September 17-19, 1979.

[ATT86]   *Quality: Theory and Practice*, AT&T Technical Journal, 65(2), March 1986.

[Bac78]   J. Backus. Can programming be liberated from the von Neumann style? A functional style and its algebra of programs. *Communications of the ACM*, 21(8):613–641, 1978.

[Bai64]   N. T. J. Bailey. *The Elements of Stochastic Processes.* John Wiley & sons, 1964.

[Bar93]   Rod Bark. Fault-tolerant platforms for emerging telecommunications markets. In *Proc. of the Workshop on Hardware and Software Architectures For Fault Tolerance: Perspectives and Towards a Synthesis*, Le Mont Saint Michel, France, June 14–16 1993.

[Ber93]   L. Bernstein and C. M. Yuhas. To err is human; to forgive, fault tolerance. *SuperUserNewsletter*, International Data Group, July 1993.

[Bor93]   Andrea Borr and Carol Wilhelmy. Highly-available data services for UNIX client-server networks: why fault-tolerant hardware isn't the answer. In *Proc. of the Workshop on Hardware and Software Architectures For Fault Tolerance: Perspectives and Towards a Synthesis*, Le Mont Saint Michel, France, June 14-16 1993.

[Bro95]   D. Brown. Design of a highly available switching platform employing commercial components. In *Proc. 1995 International Communication Conference (ICC)*, Hamburg, Germany, 1995.

[Cla92]   K. C. Clapp, R. K. Iyer, and Y. Levendel. Analysis of large system black-box test data. Third International Symposium on Software Reliability Engineering, pages 94–103, October 1992. IEEE Computer Society Press.

[Cle86]   George F. Clement. Evolution of fault tolerant computing at AT&T. In *Proc. of the One-day Symposium on the Evolution of Fault Tolerant Computing*, pages 27–37, Baden, Austria, 1986.

[Dal88]   Siddhartha R. Dalal and C. L. Mellows. When should one stop testing software? *Journal of American Statistician Association*, 83:872–879, 1988.

[Dal94]   Siddhartha R. Dalal and Allen A. McIntosh. When to stop testing for large software systems with changing code. *IEEE Transactions on Software Engineering*, SE-20(4):318–323, April 1994.

[Dem82]   W. Edwards Deming. *Out of the Crisis*. Massachusetts Institute of Technology Center for Advanced Engineering Studies, 1982.

[Gac94]   Raymond Ga Coté. Desktop telephony. *Byte*, pages 151–154, March 1994.

[Gaf84]   J.E. Gaffney. Estimating the number of faults in code. *IEEE Transactions on Software Engineering*, SE-10(4):459–464, July 1984.

[Goe85]   Amrit L. Goel. Software reliability models: assumptions, limitations, and applications. *IEEE Transactions on Software Engineering*, SE-11(12):1411-1423, December 1985.

[Gra92]   Robert B. Grady. *Practical Software Metrics for Project Management and Process Improvement*, pages 60–61. Prentice Hall, Englewood Cliffs, NJ, 1992.

[Gra88]   E. L. Grant and R. S. Levenworth. *Statistical Process Control*. McGraw-Hill Book Company, 1988.

[Har93]   *Hardware and Software Architectures For Fault Tolerance: Perspectives and Towards a Synthesis*, Le Mont Saint Michel, France, June 14–16 1993.

[Hua93]   Yennun Huang and Chandra M. R. Kintala. Software implemented fault tolerance: technologies and experience. In *Proc. of the 23rd International Symposium on Fault Tolerant Computing (FTCS-23)*, Toulouse, France, June 22-23 1993.

[Huy93]   T. Huynh, C. Jutla, A. Lowry, R. Strom, and D. Yellin. The global desktop: a graphical composition environment for local and distributed applications. *IBM TJ Watson Technical Report 93-227*, November 1993.

[Kol92]   M. V. Kolipakam, G. Y. Wyatt, and S. Y. Yeh. Distributed telecommunication service architectures: design principles and evolution. In *Proc. of the 2nd International Conference on Intelligence in Networks*, pages 1–5, Bordeaux, 1992.

[Kre83]   W. Kremer. Birth-death and bug counting. *IEEE Transactions on Reliability*, R-32(1):37–46, April 1983.

[Kru89]   G. A. Kruger. Validation and further application of software reliability growth models. *Hewlett-Packard Journal*, pages 75–79, April 1989.

[Lap92]   J.C. Laprie, editor. *Dependability: Basic Concepts and Terminology*, volume 5 of *Dependable Computing and Fault-Tolerant Systems*. Springer Verlag, Wien-New York, 1992.

[Lev87]   Y. Levendel. Quality and reliability estimation for large software projects using a time-dependent model. In *Proc. of COMPSAC87*, pages 340–346, Tokyo, Japan, October 1987.

[Lev89a] Y. Levendel. Defects and reliability analysis of large software systems: field experience. In *Proc. of the Nineteenth International Symposium on Fault-Tolerant Computing*, pages 238–244, Chicago, June 1989.

[Lev89b] Y. Levendel. Quality and reliability estimation: a time-dependent model with controllable testing coverage and repair intensity. In *Proc. of the Fourth Israel Conference on Computer Systems and Software Engineering*, pages 175–181, Israel, June 1989.

[Lev89c] Y. Levendel. The manufacturing process of large software systems: the use of untampered metrics for quality control. *National Communication Forum*, Chicago, October 1989.

[Lev90a] Y. Levendel. Reliability analysis of large software systems: defect data modeling. *IEEE Transactions on Software Engineering*, February 1990.

[Lev90b] Y. Levendel. Large software systems development: use of test data to accelerate reliability growth. *First IEEE International Sympoium on Software Reliability Engineering*, Washington, DC, April 12-13 1990.

[Lev91a] Y. Levendel. Using untampered metrics to decide when to stop testing. In *TENCON91 Pre-conference Proc.*, volume II, pages 352–356, Delhi, August 1991.

[Lev91b] Y. Levendel. The manufacturization of the software quality improvement process. In *TENCON91 Pre-conference Proc.*, volume II, pages 362–366, Delhi, August 1991.

[Lev95]   Y. Levendel, and J. Lumsden. One-step service creation for intelligent networks applications. In preparation for *Proc. ISS95*.

[Lip82]   M. Lipow. Number of faults per line of code. *IEEE Transactions on Software Engineering*, SE-8(5):437–439, July 1982.

[Lit89]   B. Littlewood. *Forecasting Software Reliability*, Center for Software Reliability Report, The City University, London, February 1989.

[Lyu95]   Michael R. Lyu, editor. *McGraw-Hill Software Reliability Engineering Handbook*. McGraw-Hill Book Company, New York, New York, 1995.

[Mas89]   R. L. Mason, R. F. Gunst and J. L. Hess. *Statistical Design & Analysis of Experiments*. Wiley-Interscience, John Wiley and Sons, 1989.

[Mon82]   M. Monachino. Design verification system for large-scale LSI designs. *IBM Journal of Research and Development*, 26(1):89–99, January 1982.

[Mus75]   J. D. Musa. A theory of software reliability and its application. *IEEE Transactions on Software Engineering*, SE-1(3):312–327, September 1975.

[Mus87]   J. D. Musa, A. Iannino, and K. Okumoto. *Software Reliability: Measurement, Prediction, Application*. McGraw-Hill, 1987.

[Mus89]   J. D. Musa and A. F. Ackerman. Quantifying software validation: when to stop testing? *IEEE Software*, pages 19–27, May 1989.

[Pry77]   N. S. Prywes. Automatic generation of computer programs. *Advances in Computers*, volume 16, M. Rubinoff and M. Yovits, editors, pages 57–125, Academic Press, 1977.

[Rya88]   T. Ryan. *Statistical Methods for Quality Improvement*. Wiley-Interscience, John Wiley and Sons, 1988.

[Sys90]   *System Verification of the 5ESS®Switch (5E6 Generic)*. AT&T Internal Reports Nos. 1-4, January to June 1990.

[Tag90]   G. Taguchi and D. Clausing. Robust quality. *Harvard Business Review*, 90(1):65–75, January-February 1990.

[Yar88]   V. N. Yarmolik and S. N. Demidenko. *Generation and Application of Pseudorandom Sequences for Random Testing*. John Wiley and Sons, 1988.

13

Software Fault Insertion Testing for Fault Tolerance

MING-YEE LAI AND STEVE Y. WANG

Bell Communications Research

ABSTRACT

Fault tolerance of a telecommunications system is critical to provide high-quality services to users during abnormal conditions and failures. Insufficient design, implementation, and testing for fault tolerance could lead to significant outages, impacting millions of users for long hours, as seen in the recent Common Channel Signaling (CCS) and Internet networks outages. This chapter focuses on improving fault tolerance through testing. A clear testing methodology, supporting tools, and a concept of testing adequacy is essential to the completion of testing a large and complex telecommunications software. Toward this end, a methodology for testing of fault tolerance through Software Fault Insertion Testing (SFIT) is discussed. Those logical system components responsible for handling faults and providing services are defined as the *fault manager* and *service manager*, respectively. The goal is to reduce the complexity of testing a system by testing its fault manager. A notion of "testing adequacy" depending on the structure of the system is also proposed in the methodology as the basis to guide the selection of test cases. The proposed methodology is a systematic approach to testing fault tolerance of existing and new telecommunications systems. This methodology has been used in testing fault tolerance of various telecommunications systems with large scale software, such as circuit switches, digital cross connects, signal transfer points, and broadband switches. The experiences of applying the methodology are also discussed.

13.1 INTRODUCTION

Fault tolerance of a telecommunications system is critical to providing high-quality services to users during abnormal conditions and failures. Insufficient design, implementation, and testing for fault tolerance could lead to significant outages, impacting millions of users for long hours, as seen in the Common Channel Signaling (CCS) and Internet network outages [Coa93].

In 1992 and 1993, Federal Communications Commission (FCC) Network Reliability Council (NRC) conducted an extensive study that involved all major key telecommunications system suppliers, network providers, service providers, users, and research institutions in the industry and issued a report entitled *Network Reliability: A Report to the Nation* [NRC93]. In the report, more than 70% of outages in network elements (such as switches, digital cross connects, and signal transfer points) are attributable to software related problems.

There are three lines of defense against software faults: avoidance, elimination, and tolerance. Fault avoidance is achieved during the specification, design, and coding process of the software. Fault elimination is the responsibility of the testing and maintenance processes. Fault tolerance is a property of the deployed software that is designed to survive anticipated possible failures. Fault tolerance, which is complementary to fault avoidance and fault elimination, is indispensable to dependable telecommunications software. It enables graceful service degradation in the face of system failures.

In the NRC report, Software Fault Insertion Testing (SFIT)[1] [Li94, BCR93] was recommended *to be performed as a standard part of a telecommunications system supplier's development process* for improving fault tolerance. However, testing a large, complex system for fault tolerance is a daunting task. A clear testing methodology, supporting tools, and a concept of testing adequacy is essential to the completion of this task. In this chapter, a methodology for testing of fault tolerance through SFIT is discussed.

The main objective of SFIT is to test the fault tolerance capability through injecting faults into the system and analyze if the system can detect and recover from faults as specified by the system or anticipated by the customers of the system. This testing of "rainy-day" scenarios before system deployment can reduce or contain service impacts on the system customers in the presence of failure scenarios. The results from SFIT can lead to either fixing of individual software bugs or discovery of design deficiencies in system fault tolerance. With SFIT, several network-wide telecommunications outages (such as long-distance phone service disruption caused by tandem switch software in January 1990 and local-exchange phone service disruption caused by CCS signal transfer point software in June 1991), could be avoided.

There are several challenges in the pursuit of a methodology for testing fault tolerance.

1. **Complexity of telecommunications software** — A typical telecommunications system may contain millions of lines of source code. Moreover, the software complexity of these systems is growing while the public demands increased simplicity of use, functionality, and dependability at reduced costs.
2. **Dormancy of faults** — Some faults may lie dormant in the system without causing observable failure long after deployment. Those faults may only be triggered when a system is under extreme stress, abnormal use, or severe failures.
3. **Diversity of telecommunications systems** — National and international telecommunications networks are composed of products made by many vendors. This heterogeneity poses a challenge to find a generic methodology for testing fault tolerance.
4. **Constraint of resource availability** — A testing methodology should allow fault tolerance validation of a system by testing organizations that are independent of development.

---

[1] Also known as Software Fault Injection Testing (SFIT)

Independent testing may be limited in access to and understanding of proprietary internal information such as source code and in testing time.

13.2 TESTING FAULT TOLERANCE USING SOFTWARE FAULT INSERTION

13.2.1 Definition of Faults, Errors, and Failures

The International Federation for Information Processing (IFIP) Working Group 10.4 has defined [Lap92]:

- **Fault** — adjudged or hypothesized cause of an error.
- **Error** — part of system state that is liable to lead to failure. Manifestation of a fault in a system.
- **Failure** — deviation of the delivered service from compliance with the specification. Transition from correct service delivery to incorrect service.

Each fault may have the following associated attributes:

- Type: The classification that the fault belongs to. Example types are memory fault, logical fault, etc.
- Locality: The location of a fault in certain component. This is the most important characteristic. A fault in a risky component will inflict more serious damage on the system than the identical fault in a component incapable of affecting system performance.
- Latency: The time interval between insertion and observation of the fault.
- Frequency: The average occurrence of a fault over a given time interval.
- Severity: The magnitude of the fault's effect on system performance. Note that this attribute depends on the combination of the fault type and its locality. For example, the severity may vary for a fault type in two components with different degrees of criticality. A preliminary approach to assigning severity to faults is through error codes, whose severity degree is specified when the system is designed.
  The severity of a fault is classified into *critical, major,* or *minor* [BCR90], depending on whether the system can continue to function indefinitely without fixing them.

  - **Critical fault** — a fault that prevents the system or significant parts of it from functioning until it is fixed.
  - **Major fault** — a fault that prevents the system or significant parts of it from functioning, but there is a work-around that can be used for a limited period of time.
  - **Minor fault** — a fault that is neither critical nor major.

13.2.2 Why Use SFIT?

The fault tolerance capability of a typical telecommunications system is critical since it is responsible for rescuing the system from errors in the field. Therefore, it should be tested in a controlled and systematic way before deployment. To this end, SFIT has emerged as an important technique for at least two reasons:

- Failure acceleration: Testing fault tolerance by waiting for the occurrence of failures in the field is not desirable. By intentionally inserting faults to invoke the fault tolerance capability, one can achieve more thorough testing in a controlled environment and within a desirable time frame.

- Systematic testing: Without systematic testing and analysis, it is hard to know which fault may be activated in the field and which component of the system will respond to the error caused by the fault. By inserting faults designed to invoke a specific fault tolerance capability, one can test that functionality effectively in the testing environment.

13.2.3   Previous Work of SFIT

There has been considerable research [Seg88, Dil91, Ros93, Kao93, Hor92, Arl90, Arl92, Iye93, You93, Kan92, Avr92, Ech92] in the Software Fault Insertion Testing area. The major differences among them are mainly in target systems, fault types and method of injecting faults. The target systems range from real-time distributed dependable systems [Seg88, Avi87] to large-scale operating systems [Chi89]. The fault types injected into the target systems also vary greatly from simple memory bit faults to processor level and system/communication faults.

The insertion method applied to software is inspired by the success of hardware fault insertion testing in the expectation that this kind of testing can be used to evaluate the robustness and expose the deficiency of the tested software. Faults can be inserted through:

- Changing a predetermined portion of the source code to produce a syntactically correct but semantically incorrect mutant [Dem88]; or
- Applying a patch to the object code at a designated location [Lai92].

Because such insertion methods deal with source code or object code directly, they are called *code injection* methods. An example of code injection is to change and re-compile the software to produce a "pointer too large" or an "invalid input parameter" fault. Such an injection is possible in both the object and source code. Another example of code injection is through the use of patching tool. The source code or value of some data structure can be corrupted by patching the software or data.

Another injection approach, *state injection*, in contrast, is achieved through altering the state or behavior of a running system. More specifically, instead of injecting faults, a system-level fault "manifestation" is injected as an erroneous state. This fault state is intended to mimic the error produced by a fault. For example, data inconsistency, that is, a common error between two copies of data in a system, can be simulated by corrupting the data of either one. There are several methods for state injection:

1. Process-based: The injection is to be accomplished by a high-priority process modifying the state of the computation [Ros93]. This approach often needs support from the underlying operating system.
2. Debugger-based: Using the facilities of a debugger (e.g. dbx, gdb), errors can be injected to a running process through the composition of breakpointing, evaluating, and jumping.
3. Message-based: For message-oriented communication between two software components, the erroneous state can be created by disrupting message sequences using message-based tools.
4. Storage-based: Using the storage manipulation tools (for memory, disk, or tape), errors can be injected into the system by changing the value at some location of the storage hierarchy, which represents some system state.

5. Command-based: Using the commands from the craft interface or remote maintenance terminal, errors can be injected by changing the states of the system entities for operations, administration, maintenance, and provision.

Most reported studies using fault insertion were aimed at assessing the efficiency in handling faults of fault tolerance mechanisms. The focus of this chapter is on the testing methodology for eliminating design/implementation problems in the fault tolerance mechanisms and improve these mechanisms.

13.3 FAULT MANAGER

For conceptual simplicity, one can view the collection of software safeguard components (such as the network safeguard, node safeguard, and Operation, Administration and Maintenance (OA&M) software) that are dedicated to handle exceptions in a typical telecommunications system as a logical entity — *fault manager* . The other part of the system that provides services to users (such as feature software) can be viewed as another logical entity — *service manager*.

Under normal operation, the service manager provides services to users while the fault manager keeps constant surveillance on the health of the service manager, until an error situation is detected. The fault manager then takes action to get the service manager back to normal operation.

In this view, testing fault tolerance in a telecommunications system amounts to testing the fault manager. Software faults are inserted in the service manager to trigger the reaction in the fault manager.

In more details, the fault manager provides the following capabilities to ensure continuous service to customers: error detection, isolation, recovery, and reporting (DIRR).

- Error Detection — Detects errors through continuous monitoring, periodic tests, per-call tests, or other automatic processes. Software audits are considered as part of the error detection capability.
- Error Isolation — Isolates the error to its source, preferably to a single or a reasonable subset of components.
- Error Recovery — Recovers errors by automatic or manual actions such as retry, rollback, on-line masking, restart, reload, or re-configuration, to minimize the degradation of service.
- Error Reporting — Sends error messages to a display device, a logging device, or an Operations System (OS), describing the error, the place where the error is observed, and system reactions to the error.

Although the fault tolerance strategies employed in different products vary, one common aspect for complex systems is that the DIRR capabilities are rarely implemented in one centralized location physically. Usually, for both efficiency of error handling and convenience of implementation, DIRR capabilities are physically distributed in separate software components. These DIRR components, through cooperation and communication using a fault tolerance protocol, work as a single fault manager. It is nonetheless an important conceptual simplification to view DIRR functions of the fault manager as a *single logical* entity (even though some error detection capability is built-in the application). We take this logical view throughout this chapter.

Two major capabilities in the fault manager are focused in this chapter: error detection and error recovery. Error detection is the beginning of exception handling. Physically, errors can be detected either by an application or by an error detection task (or process). For example, the application system adopts some self-check logic to detect certain kinds of anomalous conditions and raises exceptions. Other errors beyond the self-check logic can be detected by some error detection task. For example, data inconsistency between two applications can be detected by an error detection task.

Recovery often takes several levels to restore the system to normal operation. In general, errors can be recovered by an application with self-recovery capability such as the recovery block [Hor74]. It is the objective of a robust system to take the least possible disruptive recovery action in the presence of errors. For example, a local low-level recovery action is preferred when devices or resources are hung. However, a system-wide recovery may be needed when the central processing unit is in an unrecoverable state. Even more drastically, when both the program and data are corrupted, a system reload from a backup device is needed as the last resort for system recovery.

13.4   CATEGORIZATION OF SOFTWARE FAULTS, ERRORS, AND FAILURES

Categorization of software faults, errors, and failures can achieve the following benefits:

- A set of generic faults, errors, and failures can serve as a partial adequacy checklist of common problems against the potential deficiency of fault handling.
- No matter how diversified the systems may be, they share similar user requirements and are susceptible to a set of common and generic faults, errors, or failures.
- Interacting with the fault manager through faults, errors, or failures from the service manager can generate realistic inputs to the fault manager for test execution and observation.

13.4.1   Fault Categorization

Fault categorization is an important research area for fault prevention, elimination, and fault tolerance. Fault categorization has been studied extensively for the purpose of fault prevention during development [Chi92].

This section emphasizes the fault categorization for fault tolerance (as opposed to fault categorization for fault prevention and elimination.) There are many sources for generic fault types. The first source of fault types comes from system architecture analysis [BCR92]. For example, analysis of the system architecture may show that in some situations the execution order of two actions is critical. Hence, the system may have a recovery strategy for handling the event of mis-ordering the execution of these actions. Thus a fault that disturbs the required order will test this recovery mechanism.

The second source of fault types is from the error code of the system. Ordinarily, a list of *error codes* is available for each telecommunications system software. These codes specify which errors may occur and how the errors are to be treated. These errors were anticipated at the time the software was created, and thus reveal the designer's view of errors likely to occur.

The third source of fault types is through root cause analysis of empirical data. Field data on failures and modification requests from the customers indicated that these faults were not anticipated by the software or its designers.

The following is a sample set of common single fault types from various sources. These fault types should be disjoint.

- Intra-module faults

  - Memory faults, such as illegal access, illegal write, pointer too large, array index out of range, memory not allocated, buffer overflow, buffer not allocated, or illegal reference to uninitialized variables.
  - Logic faults, such as undefined state, omitted cases in a case statement, erroneous control statement, wrong algorithm, and incorrect value in data or program (by fault patches, typing errors, or environmental factors).
  - Mutation faults, such as mutating the operators (arithmetic, boolean operators) and operands (counter not incremented/decremented, and incorrect global variables).

- Intermodule faults

  - Incorrect input, such as input value out of valid range and input in mismatched data type.
  - Incorrect output, such as invalid output value.
  - Incorrect sequence/timing, such as wrong message sequences between two modules, messages delayed for too long, and lack of concurrency control.

There is a large number of software faults in a complex system. A library of faults must be systematically refined or enhanced to represent the most important fault types. New fault types must be both realistic and generic and are orthogonal to the existing fault types in the library.

13.4.2 Error and Failure Category

An error or failure is caused by some faults triggered under certain conditions. There are several points that encourage the use of state injection of errors/failures over the code-injection method. In general, the fault manager responds directly to errors (as a result of faults). Thus, injection of errors or failures is a short-cut to fault injection if the error state in the state injection method is reachable by the code injection method with some sequence or combination of input/trigger events. Further, injection of a specific error/failure can provide a better focus on a specific functionality of the fault manager than injection of faults. Lastly, in a distributed environment, some complicated failure modes are caused by the interaction of multiple errors, where error/failure injection is easier to simulate these failure modes.

When we allow error or failure insertion as surrogates for faults, the fault latency may be shortened. For example, to simulate a crash of a processor, it would be easier to send a crash message than to insert faults into processes to actually crash the processor. The following is a sample set of common error/failure types based on field experiences.

- Process errors, such as deadlocks, live locks, process looping, process hung, and using too many system resources.
- Message errors, such as lost message, corrupted message, out-of-order messages, duplicated messages and timeout waiting for message.
- Operating system errors, such as job overflow (overloaded with processes), resources thrashing, wrong signal, and wrong acknowledgement.

- Data errors, such as corrupted data value and structure, data inconsistency, and data integrity violation.
- Hanging resources, such as hanging alarms, terminal, I/O, lines, trunks, and CPU errors.
- CPU or storage devices crash.
- Device or CPU overload.
- Network errors such as network congestion (traffic overflow), link oscillation, and routing error.
- Operational procedure errors, such as wrong data input from the operator, and incorrect maintenance procedures.

13.5   SFIT METHODOLOGY

Testing is time-consuming, especially testing for fault tolerance. To execute a test case, several steps, including test set-up, test execution, and system restoration are required. Some injected faults or errors/failures may change the system into a chaotic state that cannot be automatically recovered. In this case, manual restoration may be required.

SFIT is recommended to be performed at the system testing or acceptance testing during the testing life cycle. In this way, the system's overall reaction to faults/errors/failures can be observed and analyzed. However, in some cases, SFIT can also be performed at the unit testing level where the fault manager functionality resides in a local subsystem level.

Figure 13.1 shows the methodology used for SFIT. The methodology provides a systematic approach to validate the fault tolerance capability. The methodology consists of the following steps:

A — Pre-SFIT Steps:

1. Software Architecture Analysis [Eri93]. Before conducting SFIT, a sufficient knowledge of the software (including functions of some key software components, such as error recovery software subsystem) and its architecture is needed. This analysis is proactive and consists of three key parts:

   - service manager analysis: pinpoint potential risky areas based on (a) new and changed software components, (b) functionally critical components, (c) fault-prone software components, (d) low test coverage components, and (e) components with poor software attributes (such as the Non-Commentary Source Lines of code, fault density during the internal testing, design, and code complexity measurement). The output from the analysis includes fault/error type and insertion point in the service manager for the test cases.
   - fault manager analysis: analyze fault handling mechanisms, observation mechanisms, and module interactions within the fault manager (the analysis result can be represented in a graphic form).
   - fault manager/service manager interface analysis: analyze the error codes and their associated attributes (such as error description, severity, and recovery action routines) as well as the possible event sequences (consisting of error code and recovery action) across the interface.

2. Root Cause Analysis. Internal testing results and external field problems often can give a

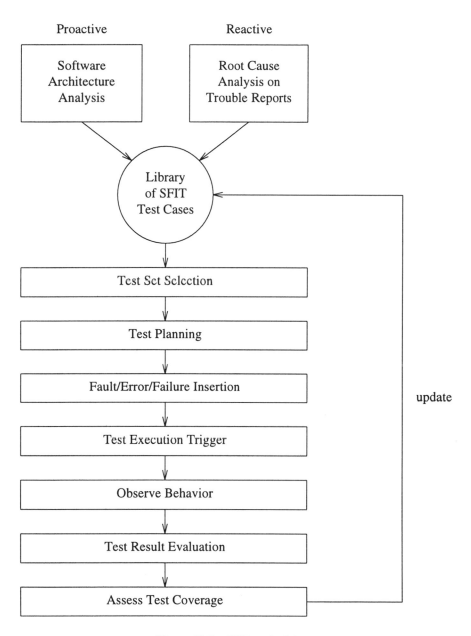

Figure 13.1   SFIT methodology

good indication of the product's reliability. Therefore, root cause analysis on the internal trouble reports and customer service reports can help the testing organization to identify common problems that need to be addressed in SFIT. Root cause analysis is more reactive; nevertheless, it can help to identify the area and type of faults/errors to be tested.

3. Test Set Selection. During the test set selection, the following two aspects need to be identified: properties/predicates to be checked for assessing the proper behavior of the Fault Manager in the presence of the injected faults (expected system behavior) and observations to be made to verify the assertion of the corresponding predicates (i.e, actual system behavior). Depending on different factors such as test coverage and available resources for testing, the test set needs to be selected before the actual SFIT testing. For coverage, the following criteria should be considered:

- Test cases that enhance the test coverage (see the discussion on the following step "assess test coverage" for more details).
- Test cases that simulate faults/errors that are similar to those that have occurred in the field as seen by customers.
- Test cases for faults/errors that have direct customer service impact.
- Test cases for high-profile faults/errors (for example, faults that catch the attention of the general public).

Another important factor for test set selection, is time available for testing. Since software fault insertion testing tends to be destructive, the time required to restore the system back to normal condition plays an important part. Therefore, if fault latency and the time required to recover from each software fault are taken into consideration, one may see that test set selection is a scheduling problem to maximize the testing in a given amount of time. While this approach is useful from a project management point of view (i.e., the project manager can allocate appropriate resources to conduct SFIT), it is difficult to measure the time required to prepare each test and the time the system will take to react and recover from each inserted fault.

4. Test Planning. After the test set has been selected, testing needs to be planned. For example, test scripts need to be prepared based on the selected test set. For code-based injection, software patches need to be prepared in advance. For state-based injection, appropriate tools need to be allocated to change the state of the system. If testing is to be performed at a remote location, proper links and expert support should be established ahead of time. Background traffic needs to be planned for test cases to simulate user's typical operation profile or abnormal traffic conditions.

B — SFIT Steps:

1. Fault/Error/Failure Insertion. With all the test cases available, this step involves the actual insertion of faults, errors or failures. The location of faults or errors should be identified during this step. Depending on the insertion method used (e.g., process-based, debugger-based, or message-based), the corresponding tools can be used to insert the faults/errors/failures.
2. Test Execution Trigger. A fault in the system may not be activated when it is inserted into the system. Therefore, the test trigger needs to be set during this step to activate the inserted faults. This test execution trigger can be used to reduce the natural dormancy of faults. Triggers could be input values from the users, internal and external events, or messages.
3. Observe Behavior. This step observes the system reaction to the inserted faults or errors within a specified time frame.

C — Post-SFIT Steps:

1. Test Result Evaluation. Test results can provide insights on two aspects. First, the test result can reveal the effectiveness of the test cases. Second, the test result can reveal the weakness of the system's fault tolerance capability. The test result evaluation step can help to eliminate less effective test cases and identify areas for improvements for the system's fault tolerance capability.

2. Assess Test Coverage. Although complete testing coverage with SFIT is not economically possible, a notion of test coverage adequacy is essential to the confidence in the fault tolerance of a system. The criteria for test coverage adequacy consist of:

   - Coverage of the fault, error, and failure types in the library.
   - Functional coverage of the fault manager (test all functionalities in the fault manager).
   - Structural coverage of the fault manager (test all branches in the fault manager).
   - Coverage of the risky components in the service manager.
   - Coverage generated from a fault tree analysis of the software [Lev91].

   Thorough testing for these sorts of faults will constitute adequate testing of the fault manager of a telecommunications system. A test stopping rule may be specified by choosing an appropriate level of adequacy. Of course, setting a stopping rule short of complete adequacy is risky.

3. Update SFIT Test Case Library. A library of common and generic faults, errors, and failures along with their attributes (such as frequency of occurrence or severity) should be collected and stored. This library of faults, errors, and failures can be used to define test input for fault tolerance testing. The library will be updated periodically. In addition, faults designed to test for the rare, unusual, and severe fault tolerance conditions of the system will be added to the repository. These faults can be garnered from an analysis of system architecture and an understanding of the potential weaknesses of the fault manager. Together, the generic fault types and unusual fault types will, as our understanding grows, constitute an *adequacy* criterion for fault tolerance testing.

The details of these steps are described in [BCR92].

13.5.1   SFIT for Subsequent Software Releases

Telecommunications systems grow both in size and complexity. However, the growth is usually in the service manager and less in the fault manager area after the system has been operational in the field for years and its fault manager matures. One may ask why testing the slow changing fault manager for subsequent releases given that the system's fault tolerance capabilities have been tested in the previous release. The reasons for conducting SFIT for new releases are:

- Interaction of the service manager and the fault manager may be different for the new release because of the new or changed parts in the service manager and the fault manager.
- The reaction of the fault manager to the same inserted faults may be different in new releases because of new interactions between inserted faults and latent faults from the new release.
- New services may need some enhancement in the fault manager. For example, new ISDN services may need new audit functions in the fault manager to check the sanity of ISDN-related data structures.

- When a system's outage frequency and downtime do not meet customers' requirements, improvements on the fault manager over releases are essential.

13.6   SAMPLE SFIT TEST PLANS

The purposes of establishing a sample set of SFIT test plans are:

- This set of generic test plans can be used to develop detailed test cases for specific telecommunications products.
- This set of generic test plans can be further refined to improve the test quality as we gain experience with software fault insertion testing.
- This set of generic test plans can be used for repeated testing for future software releases.

In the rest of this section, we concentrate on the sample test plans for recovery actions and audit functions.

13.6.1   Test Plan for Recovery Actions

Service recovery for a typical telecommunications system means the automatic or manual protection actions taken to minimize degradation of service. Actions should be taken in the meantime to identify the cause of the trouble and repair it. Based on Bellcore's Operations Technology Generic Requirements (OTGR) [BCR91], the service recovery strategies for call processing based network elements shall be such that stable calls are protected and then transient calls are protected. The automatic service recovery should be considered before manual service recovery. Section 4 of the OTGR lists complete service recovery requirements. The following list is a sample of SFIT test plans for recovery routines. This list is broken down to generic recovery routines, call-processing specific recovery routines, database management recovery routines, memory management recovery routines, inter-process communication recovery routines, and network management recovery routines.

A — Generic Recovery:

1. Insert a fault and trigger it to invoke the service recovery action to see if it performs automatic recovery as designed.
2. Insert a fault and trigger it to invoke automatic service recovery and check if stable calls are maintained. For transient calls, the automatic service recovery should be satisfactorily completed, without the customer being made aware that a fault exists.
3. For each level or recovery, insert a fault and trigger it to invoke the appropriate recovery action. Observe the system's reaction to see if it performs as designed. For example, faults that have minor impact to the system's operation may result in small and local level of recovery while faults that have serious service impact will result in more drastic reaction such as a large restart or reload of the software generic.
4. Insert a fault to test if the system provides automatic escalation of service recovery. Analyze and observe if the system can do the following:

   - Restore both hardware and software to a known state
   - Allow call/message processing to resume at a safe point
   - Successively encompass more software and hardware than the previous lower level

- Restrict use of the levels that are service-affecting. In particular, levels affecting stable calls and recent change data shall require manual action. All other levels shall be allowed automatically.

5. Insert a fault so that manual service recovery is required. Test to see if multiple levels of initialization and reconfiguration capabilities are available to supplement automatic recovery capabilities.

B — Call-Processing Specific Recovery:

1. For systems that offer local recovery other than system-wide recovery actions, insert a fault to test each local recovery area to see if the system reacts as designed.

C — Database Management Recovery:

1. Insert transaction aborted failures to verify that the Database Management System's (DBMS) recovery mechanisms work as designed.
2. Insert locking conflict detection or resolution failures to verify that the DBMS's recovery mechanisms work as designed.
3. Insert time-out failures to verify that the DBMS's recovery mechanisms work as designed.

D — Memory Management Recovery:

1. Insert memory operation errors to verify that the memory management's error recovery is as designed.

E — Inter-Process Communication Recovery:

1. Insert message errors to verify that the integrity of the system is maintained as designed.

F — Network Management Recovery:

1. For network management functions, insert a fault to corrupt the network management function parameters to observe the adequacy of fault handling in the network. Example of parameters are:

   - Network performance parameters such as Answer-Seizure Ratio (ASR), percentage of overflow (%OFL), seizures per circuit per hour (SCHP), bits per circuit per hour (BCH), and route load (occupancy).
   - Exchange parameters such as exchange input load, code sender/receiver route load, and processor load.
   - Trunk route and destination performance parameters such as route overflow (congestion), route load, route blocking, route answer-seizure ratio, and route disturbance-seizure ratio (DSR).

2. Changeover Procedure: Insert a fault in the software to shift traffic from a failed link to a standby good link (e.g., CCS changeover software)
3. Link Restoration Procedure: Insert a fault in the software handling restoration from a failed link (e.g., CCS Signaling Link Restoration)
4. Transfer Prohibited Procedure: Insert a fault in the software handling transfer prohibited procedure (e.g., CCS TFP procedure).
5. Transfer Allowed Procedure : Insert a fault in the software handling transfer allowed procedure (e.g., CCS TFA procedure).

6. Transfer Controlled Procedure: Insert a fault in the software handling transfer controlled procedure (e.g., CCS TFC procedure).
7. Traffic Flow Control Procedure: Insert a fault in the software handling signaling traffic flow control procedure (e.g., CCS signaling traffic flow control procedure).

13.6.2   Test Plan for Audit Functions

There are a variety of audit programs in telecommunications system software that are used to examine the validity of programs and data, provide protection against memory errors, and generate alarms and printouts for trouble resolution. Bellcore's OTGR requirements (Section 4) highlights the general audit guidelines that include the following:

• Audit programs should run continuously to check data and programs for correctness and consistency, and to detect all data errors so errors can be corrected before affecting service.
• Audit programs that cannot run continuously shall run at least periodically.
• Audit programs to check for non-critical errors shall run at least periodically.
• Audit programs shall not detract from the quality of service.
• Audit programs shall correct detected errors or initialize the data to a state that would allow normal call or message processing to continue.
• Audit programs shall provide a record of detected errors and switching network element corrective actions.
• It shall be possible to manually inhibit selected audit programs and to have these inhibits reported periodically.
• The switching network element shall provide a notification when it has inhibited audits.
• The switching network element should provide a periodic automatic reminder of all active trouble detection inhibits.

There are many audit techniques that can be used in audit programs. The following are some examples:

• Redundant Software Checking.
• Overwriting of Temporary Memory.
• Image Checking.
• Consistency Checking.
• Range Check.
• Duration Check.
• Data Definition Check.
• Input/Output Check.
• Checksumming.
• Limbo States Detection.
• Point-to, Point-back Check.
• Initialization.

These general audit techniques are to help ensure the quality of individual customer service and maintain the sanity of the telecommunications software. Below is a sample set of test plans for software audits and system audits.

1. Software Audits

   (a) Physical audits on programs. Insert a fault to create a bit fault in either the program or data area to see if the bit fault will be detected (for example, through checksumming) and corrected by the audit program as designed.

   (b) Physical audits on data. Insert a fault such as data inconsistency or data integrity violation to see if the audit program can detect it.

   (c) Memory faults. Insert a fault to create illegal memory access, illegal write, pointer too large, array index out of range, memory not allocated, buffer overflow, buffer not allocated, or illegal reference to uninitialized variables to see the audit program can detect the fault.

   (d) Logical audits on residual design errors, operator input and output errors, translation errors, etc. Insert a fault to test logical errors that can be detected by techniques such as range check or duration check. Observe and analyze the system behavior to see if it reacts as designed.

2. System Audits

   (a) Call processing. Insert a fault to test the progress of call processing for individual calls.

   (b) Call completion. Insert a fault to test the audit program to see if it monitors the call completion rate.

   (c) Equipment. For hardware equipment such as lines, trunks, code senders and receivers, or disk storage, create a fault to simulate a hardware problem (such as device hanging) to see if the audit program can detect it.

   (d) Operating system. For memory allocation, queues, and buffers, create a fault to corrupt the memory or overflow the buffers to see if the audit program can detect the error and correct it.

   (e) Process errors. Insert a fault/error such as sending to the wrong address, deadlocks, live locks, process looping, process hung, or using too much resources to see if the audit program can detect it.

   (f) Message errors. Insert a fault/error such as lost message, corrupted message, misordered messages, duplicated messages or timeout waiting for message to see if the audit program can detect it.

   (g) Alarms. For each alarm situation, create a fault to activate the alarm to see if proper alarm level is activated and reported. Also observe if the alarm is reset after the problem has been resolved.

   (h) Network related errors. Insert an error to simulate network anomalies, such as network congestion (traffic overload), link oscillation, and routing error to see if the audit program can detect it.

13.7 APPLICATION AND RESULTS

The SFIT methodology proposed in this chapter has been applied to more than ten telecommunications systems, including end-office circuit switches, common channel signaling systems, signal transfer points, broadband Asynchronous Transfer Mode (ATM) systems, SONET-based Add-Drop Multiplexers (ADMs), and digital cross-connect systems. The total number lines of code for the system tested ranges from 500,000 to more than 5 millions. So far, most of the tests following SFIT methodology were conducted by Bellcore technical analysis organization and network element software system suppliers. Bellcore has been performing SFIT as an agent to the telephone companies and is independent of the development organization of the network element suppliers. Since individual software systems and their developing environments vary from one to another, the preparation of software faults, actual insertion of software faults, and the results are different.

When supplier's development/testing/quality assurance organizations have good cooperation with the organization conducting SFIT, we have experienced a 2 to 10% of hit ratio (percentage of problem identified with respect to the total number of tests). This 2 to 10% of hit ratio includes both design/implementation deficiencies and actual software bugs in the program. Some examples of common software problems are:

- Incorrect condition check — This includes missing a condition check before processing information, incorrect boundary condition check (e.g., checked value being off by one), and incorrect semantics condition check (e.g., checking predicates contain incorrect value or variable).
- Use of incorrect data value — This is the result of using incorrect data value. For example, instead of using variables that will change values under different situations, the programmer hardcodes the actual number, thus provides inflexibility of the program. Another example is to access a variable with a wrong variable name which is similar to the intended variable.
- Missing or incorrect signal data — This type of fault is due to sending the incorrect signals to other software components or sending a correct signal but with incorrect data value.
- Incorrect set or reset of variables — For example, data is assigned with the incorrect value (or sometimes variable). Uninitialized variables or pointers are another examples.
- Incorrect branching — This type of fault is common in software system with "spaghetti code". In the program with many GOTO statements, it is very easy to branch into an incorrect function or subroutine. Incorrect branching often occurs in a IF-THEN-ELSE statement, where the programmer mistakenly reverse the THEN and ELSE condition.
- Missing or extra code — This is caused by some missing statements or some extraneous code. For example, missing an EXIT statement in a loop, or missing an instruction to reset the memory buffer.
- Incorrect execution order — The order of execution determines the sequence of actions in the software. When the order of execution is reversed, adverse condition can happen.

With software fault insertion testing, passing the test cases only means that the system reacts to the inserted fault as designed. It does not mean that the design is correct or sufficient. Our experience has shown that in many cases, the system reacts to the inserted faults as expected, however, can be improved if more fault tolerance is considered in the design. The following are some examples of design deficiencies found during SFIT:

- Lack of software audits. Software audits are used to detect and correct inconsistencies in the program and data. In many cases, we have found that consistencies checking of program and data are not adequate. Also, software audits should be run periodically (if not run continuously) with priorities assigned so it would not detract the service quality. However, these objectives were often ignored by some design.
- Inadequate system recovery. The current practice for many telecommunications system in reaction to software errors is to take a system-wide restart to clear all variables and counters. During this period, customers suffer loosing connection or no dial-tone. Depending on the severity and frequency of errors, different level of recovery actions should be provided

to minimize service impacts to customers. Also the time for recovery actions needs to be minimized. With many SFIT test cases, we are able to identify areas for service improvement if more levels of system recovery are available.

- Recovery action too drastic. This is related to the previous design deficiency. In many cases during SFIT, the result from a simple mistake (such as one subscriber line interface is hung) caused the system to restart, affecting thousands of subscribers. The system's reaction to this type of fault — taking a system restart — may resolve the problem, but it reveals a design deficiency with respect to minimizing service impacts to customers. Therefore, how to confine the problem to a smaller area and recover from it locally becomes an area for further investigation.
- Lack of system recovery escalation mechanism. When a local-level action to a software problem can not resolve the situation (such as clearing the hanging subscriber line interface in the previous example), a typical telecommunications system is to escalate the problem into a higher level. This is called recovery escalation. We have found that in many test cases there does not exist any guideline as to when to escalate the problem to a higher level. In other cases, we observed there are different recovery escalation mechanisms in a system, but are not followed consistently.

13.8 CONCLUSIONS

The telecommunications network and service providers have been demanding quality and reliability of software delivered to them from the telecommunications systems suppliers. As an agent to the regional telephone companies, Bellcore in conjunction with suppliers has been using SFIT to analyze and test circuit switches, common channel signaling systems, signal transfer points, broadband systems, add-drop multiplexers and digital cross-connect systems since 1992. Through putting SFIT into practice, SFIT has evolved to be an effective method to validate and improve the system's fault handling capabilities for telecommunications systems.

The important benefits resulting from SFIT include:

- Improvement in network/system robustness: This is achieved through more systematic analysis and testing, enhanced system recovery mechanisms, more software audit functions for the critical operations, and enhanced built-in exception handling routines.
- Improvement in network/system operations: This is achieved through operation guidelines or tools that help operators to recover from failures based on the rules, event patterns, and correlation derived from the analysis of observed behaviors in SFIT and field data.

Some SFIT experiences based on practices are summarized below:

- The software architecture analysis is an important first step before conducting SFIT. Through the analysis of the service manager and fault manager of the target system, one can identify the software components that are important for the testing.
- In order for a customer or any independent third party to test the software through SFIT, planning has to occur well ahead of the actual testing. For example, one must collect information with regard to the service manager and fault manager modules, negotiate with the supplier for expert support to create software patches, and schedule lab. time for the testing.
- The most effective way to improve system robustness is that telecommunications system suppliers make SFIT a standard part of their software development process.

- Participation from the supplier's software experts is extremely important for SFIT. Software patches need to be prepared before the test. Expert support should also be available to cooperatively develop detailed test cases and interpret the actual system behavior.
- Tools need to be developed or refined to make SFIT more efficient and automatic. Software development environment to support design for testability and observability can make SFIT more cost effective.
- Many design deficiencies in fault tolerance in various products have been found through SFIT, such as lack of software audits, inadequate recovery, and lack of recovery escalation mechanisms. These design deficiencies should be used as input to further enhance the fault tolerance requirements in the telecommunications community.
- SFIT helps identify the role of the various fault tolerance mechanisms systematically with respect to fault, error, and failure types. This information can be used to simplify and improve the design and implementation of the fault tolerance mechanisms.

ACKNOWLEDGEMENTS

We would like to acknowledge Dr. Chi-Ming Chen of Bellcore for his joint work related to this chapter. The summer job performed by Mr. Tsanchi Li of Purdue University also provided valuable input to this chapter.

REFERENCES

[Arl90]   J. Arlat, M. Aguera, L. Amat, Y. Crouzet, J.-C. Fabre, J.-C. Laprie, E. Martins and D. Powell. Fault injection for dependability validation — a methodology and some applications. *IEEE Transactions on Software Engineering*, 16(2):166–182, 1990.

[Arl92]   J. Arlat. Fault injection for the experimental validation of fault-tolerant systems. In *Proc. Workshop Fault-Tolerant Systems*, pages 33–40, Kyoto, 1992.

[Avi87]   A. Avižienis and D. Ball. On the achievement of a highly dependable and fault-tolerant air traffic control system. *IEEE Computer*, 20(20):84–90, February 1988.

[Avr92]   D. Avresky, J. Arlat, J.-C. Laprie and Y. Crouzet. Fault injection for the formal testing of fault tolerance. In *Proc. 22nd International Symposium on Fault-Tolerant Computing (FTCS-22)*, pages 345–354, Boston, 1992.

[BCR90]   TR-TSY-000929. *Reliability and Quality Measurements for Telecommunications Systems (RQMS)*, Issue 1, June 1990.

[BCR91]   TR-TSY-000474. *OTGR Section4: Network Maintenance: Network Element (A Module of OTGR, FR-NWT-000439*, Issue 3, November 1898, plus Revision 2, July 1991, and Bulletin 1, November 1991.

[BCR92]   SR-NWT-002419. *Software Architecture Review Checklists*, December 1992.

[BCR93]   SR-NWT-002795, Bellcore Special Report. *Software Fault Insertion Testing Methodology*, December 1993.

[Coa93]   Brian A. Coan and Daniel Heyman. Reliable software and communication III: congestion control and network reliability. *IEEE Journal on Selected Areas in Communication*, December 1993.

[Chi89]   R. Chillarege and N. Bowen. Understanding large system failures — a fault injection experiment. In *Proc. 19th International Symposium on Fault-Tolerant Computing*, pages 356–363, 1989.

[Chi92]   R. Chillarege et. al. Orthogonal defect classification — a concept for in-process measurements. *IEEE Transactions on Software Engineering*, 18:830–838, November 1986.

[Dem88]   R. A. DeMillo, D. Guindi, W. McCracken, A. Offutt and K. King. Extended overview of the mothra software testing environment. *Second Workshop on Software Testing, Verification and*

Analysis, pages 142–151, 1988.

[Dil91] T. Dilenno, D. Yaskin and J. Barton. Fault tolerance testing in the advanced automation system. In *Proc. 21th International Symposium on Fault-Tolerant Computing*, pages 18–25, 1991.

[Ech92] K. Echtle and M. Leu. The EFA fault injector for fault-tolerant distributed system testing. In *Proc. Workshop on Fault Tolerant Parallel and Distributed Systems*, pages 28–35, Amherst, 1992.

[Eri93] R. L. Erickson, N. D. Griffeth, M. Y. Lai and S. Y. Wang. Software architecture review for telecommunications software improvement. *IEEE International Conference on Communications (ICC'93)*, pages 616–620, May 1993.

[Hor92] Marc W. Hornbeek and Robert M. Caza. An integrated design and test strategy for large switching systems. *International Switching Symposium*, pages 444–448, 1992.

[Hor74] J. J. Horning, et. al. *A program structure for error detection and recovery*, pages 171–187 in *Lecture Notes in Computer Science 16*. Springer-Verlat, Berlin, 1974.

[Iye93] R. K. Iyer and D. Tang. Experimental Analysis of Computer System Dependability Technical Report CRHC-93-15, University of Illinois at Urbana-Champaign, 1993.

[Kan92] G. A. Kanawati, N. A. Kanawati and J. A. Abraham. FERRARI: a tool for the validation of system dependability properties. In *Proc. 22nd International Symposium on Fault-Tolerant Computing (FTCS-22)*, pages 336–244, Boston, 1992.

[Kao93] Wei-Lun Kao, Ravishankar K. Iyer and Dong Tang. FINE: a fault injection and monitoring environment for tracing the UNIX system behavior under faults. *IEEE Transactions on Software Engineering*, 19(11), November 1993.

[Lai92] M. Lai, C. Chen, C. Hood and D. Saxena. Using software fault insertion to improve CCS network operation. *GLOBECOM'92*, pages 1723–1728, December 1992.

[Lev91] N. G. Leveson and S. S. Cha. Safety verification of ADA programs using software fault tree. *IEEE Software*, 8(4):48–59, July 1991.

[Li94] T. Li, C. M. Chen, R. Horgan, M. Lai, and S. Y. Wang. A software fault insertion testing methodology for improving the robustness of telecommunication systems. In *Proc. ICC 94*, May 1994.

[Lap92] J.-C. Laprie, editor, *Dependability: Basic Concepts and Terminology, Dependable Computing and Fault Tolerance*, Springer-Verlag, Vienna, Austria, 1992.

[NRC93] Network Reliability Council. *Network Reliability: A Report to the Nation*, June 1993.

[Ros93] H. Rosenberg and K. Shin. Software fault injection and its application in distributed systems. In *Proc. 23rd International Symposium on Fault-Tolerant Computing*, pages 208–217, 1993.

[Seg88] Z. Segal, et. al. FIAT — fault injection based automated testing environment. In *Proc. 18th International Symposium on Fault-Tolerant Computing*, pages 102–107, 1988.

[You93] C. R. Yount. *The Automatic Generation of Instruction-Level Error Manifestation of Hardware Faults: A New Fault Injection Model*. PhD dissertation, Carnegie-Mellon University, 1993.

Index

5ESS system recovery software 296–298, 300

Acceptance tests 201
Action-level fault tolerance 191
Ada 211
Application layer software fault tolerance 229–245
Architectural issues 47–76
Architectures tolerating a single fault 65–67
Architectures tolerating two consecutive faults 67–71
AT&T 229, 234–235, 242
ATM 329
Atomic actions 4

C & D protocol 30
C++ 16–17
Checkpointing 167–185
equidistant 173–176
in modular programs 176–180
random 180–183
Common-mode failures 48
Community error recovery 27–28
Computer security 41
Consensus recovery block (CRB) 9, 10
CORAL 8
Correlated software failures 257
CRB
see Consensus recovery block
CREATE 99

Decider failure probability 134–135
DEDIX 32
Default exception handling 99–103
DELTA-A 11
Dependability modeling 109–136
Design & coding phase 36
Design diversity 26, 47–76

Design hole conjecture 287–289
Design notation 15
Designing dependable systems 303–310
Distributed recovery block scheme (DRB) 189–207
design parameters 198
recursive shadowing 192–198
with parallel processing multi-computer testbeds 202–204
with LAN based DCSs 204–205
Distributed recovery block system (DRB) 111, 115–119, 128–132
Diverse software 220
Domain analysis 304
DRB
see Distributed recovery block scheme/system
Error distributions 255–256
ESPRIT 11, 18, 76
Evaluation & acceptance phase 37
Exception handling 81–105
in hierarchical modular programs 94–104
in hierarchies of data abstractions 103
Execution time modeling 167–185
Experimental data analysis 119–124, 126–128

Failure dependency 214–218
Failure domain 93
Failures 153
Fault categorization 320
Fault diversity research 211–213
Fault manager in SIFT 319–320
Fault span in experiments 212
Fault tolerance capability 316
Fault tolerant systems dependencies 140

Fault-tolerant software models   26–28,
    38–39, 144–152
Faulty value output   196
File replication technology   240–242
Forward error recovery mechanism   6, 13

Generalized stochastic Petri nets (GSPNs)
    inhibitor arcs   142–143
Generic forward recovery   191

Hardware fault tolerance techniques   190
Hardware-and-software fault tolerant
    architecture
    dependability analysis   71–76
Harware-and-software fault tolerant
    architectures   62–76
Hardware error confinement areas
    see HECAs
HECAs   65–73, 111
HERMES   76
Hierarchical program structure   95–96

IBM/MVS system   250–251, 253–254,
    258–259, 264–266, 270
Idealized fault-tolerant components   2
Inconsistency closures   97–98
Information smuggling   14–15
Integration faults   191
IRIX   241
ISDN   325

Libft   236–240
Library of C functions   236–240
Linguistic support   15
Log managers   98
Long-running programs   167

Markov modeling processes   109–110,
    114–115
MASCOT   39
Measurement-based analysis   249–274
Models
    high level   266–270
    low level   270
Models of fault-tolerant software   109–136
Modula 2   211
Multilayer diversity   40
Multiple processor halts   261
MVS   232, 247–248

N self-checking programming
    (NSCP)   50–75, 111, 119, 128–136,
    140, 156
    models   147–152
N-version programming (NVP)   23–25,

30–31, 111, 115–119, 128–132
    models   146–147
    operational environment   124–125
    practical application   221
N-version programming research   210–218
N-version software (NVS)   26–28
    design paradigm   33–34
NCCP/2/1 architecture   68
Network Execution Platforms   306–308
NSCP
    see N self-checking programming
NSCP/1/1 architecture   66–67
NVP
    see N-version programming
NVP/1/1 architecture   67
NVP/2/2 architecture   69
NVS
    see N-version software
NVX   24, 28–29

Omission failure   196
Operating systems
    software fault tolerance   247–310
Operational error distribution   125–126
Operational phase   38

Pair of self-checking processing nodes
    (PSP)   192
Parameter estimation   124, 126–128
Pascal   8
Performance measures   162
Primary-shadow pair   192
Process control deficiencies   286–287
Process pairs
    evaluation   259–260
Program design   81–105
    failures   89–94
    semantics   83–89
Program execution without
    checkpointing   171–173
Programming pyramids   307
PSP
    see Pair of self-checking processing
    nodes

Quantitative system-level analysis   128–132

RB/1/1 architecture   65–66, 71, 73
RB/2/1 architecture   68
Real-time computer system DRB
    scheme   189–207
Recovery blocks   4–7
    conversation   11–15
    distributed execution   9
    extensions   9–11

Recovery blocks *contd*
    models 145–146
    nested 5
Recovery block mechanism 102
Recovery caches 5, 27, 98
Recovery distributions 258
Recovery routines
    evaluation 259, 264–266
Recovery software methodologies 309
    recursive shadowing 192–198
Reflection 16–17
Reliability
    measures 159
    models 115–119
REPL 240–242
    research 211–213
Retry blocks 10
Reusable software components 230–242
Reward analysis 268

Safety measures 160
Safety models 115–119
SECAs 68–70, 73, 111
Self-configuring optional programming 10
Sensitivity analysis 132–134
SESAME 101
SFIT
    see Software Fault Insertion Testing
Simplex units 26
Software Assembly Environment 308
Software dependability
    improvements 281–299
Software diversity 35, 209–226
Software error clustering 287
Software error confinement areas
    see SECAs
Software fault insertion 317
Software Fault Insertion Testing
    (SFIT) 315–332
    methodology 322–324
    test plans 326–329
Software fault tolerance 232–233
    cost analysis 59–62

dependability analysis 51–59
    measurement 260
Software requirement phase 35
Software reuse 304
Software specification phase 36
SPN
    see Stochastic Petri nets
Stochastic Petri nets (SPNs) 141
SRN
    see Stochastic reward nets
Stochastic reward nets (SRNs) 139–164
    dependencies 152
SUN 241
System functional decomposition 294–295
System partitioning 291–292
System structuring 2–4

Tandem/GUARDIAN fault tolerant
    system 250, 259–260, 263, 266–270
Telecommunication service dependability
    cost effectiveness 277–310
Termination mechanism 82–83
    test plans 326–329
Testing metrics 298–299
Testing phase 37
Tolerance of software faults 81–105

UNIX 229, 238, 240–243
Untampered test metrics 290–294

Variants 140
VAX/VMS distributed systems 251,
    254–259, 266
VAXcluster 267–268
Virtual DRB stations (VDRB) 199
VDRB
    see Virtual DRB

Watchd 235–236
Watchdog component 235–236
    with LAN based DCSs 204–205
    with parallel processing multi-computer
        testbeds 202–204

User Interface Software

Edited by
Len Bass
Carnegie Mellon University, USA
and
Prasun Dewan
Purdue University, USA

A good user interface can be a large determining factor in the success of any software system. Designers and developers need to ensure they use the best and most up-to-date technology available. The technology is developing very fast and in several directions.

With this in mind, *Trends in Software* commissioned Len Bass and Prasun Dewan to put together, in one volume, papers written expressly for those at the sharp end of software design and development who must implement the new technology almost as it still evolves.

Current new interface design technology and techniques are described; problems of implementation and evaluation are addressed; implications for the future are discussed.

There is particular coverage of the new technology and techniques needed for: multi-media, multi-user, animation-based, and direct-manipulation user interfaces, plus those needed to support virtual reality and advanced software development environments.

User Interface Software provides an accessible and authoritative overview of current new techniques and what they mean for the practising developer and programmer.

Trends in Software is a major new series to partner *Software Practice and Experience.*

ISBN 0 471 937843

JOHN WILEY & SONS
Chichester · New York · Brisbane · Toronto · Singapore